Wet Behind One Ear

Billie McDonald Foster

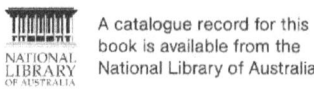

A catalogue record for this book is available from the National Library of Australia

Copyright © 2019 Billie McDonald Foster

All rights reserved.

ISBN: 1-87-692220-6
ISBN-13: 978-1-87-692220-7

Linellen Press
265 Boomerang Road
Oldbury, Western Australia
www.linellenpress.com.au

Dedication

They say memories are for the elderly and dying
who have nowhere else to go.
These, then, are mine, for you, my family.

This book is also dedicated to
Charles Henry (Paddy) Spence
who made my life worthwhile.

Contents

Dedication iii
Contents v
Acknowledgments vii
East Taieri 1935 - 1945 1
Otakia 1945 – 1953 48
Dunedin 1953 112
Oamaru 1953 - 1955 123
Australia 1955 – 1957 170
England 1957 - 1961 231
New Zealand Again 297
Australia Again 376
England Again 458
New Zealand Again 484
Epilogue 509
About the Author 514

Acknowledgments

To my Darling Paddy for giving me a name for my book.

Also to Author Teena Raffa-Mulligan for putting me in touch with Helen Iles of Linellen Press.

East Taieri 1935 - 1945

I was born at Mosgiel, a small town on the Taieri Plains, south of Dunedin, New Zealand, on the 10th February 1935. My father was David Donaldson, my mother Rebecca, nee Callaghan. At the time we were living at our ten-acre property a mile or so south of East Taieri on the main road south. I was the last of the four children born to my parents, all under five at the time of my arrival. My sister Lorna was born in 1930, Colin thirteen months later in 1931, my other sister Alma in 1933 on the 11th February and I, just two years later on the 10th February, so we almost shared a birthday.

Big families were the norm in those days, no condoms or contraceptive pills, family planning hadn't been heard of, besides no-one talked about things like that. It just wasn't "nice".

My father was the youngest of seventeen children born to William (Manny) Donaldson, who had emigrated from Scotland not long after the first settlers, and Eliza, (nee Mercer). Poor Eliza, she died in Chalet Hospital, Dunedin, at the age of forty-nine, with cancer of the uterus. She is buried in the Andersons Bay Cemetery, Dunedin. When she died my father was just four years old.

Some of the Donaldson family
The young carried child in the back row is David Donaldson

My mother was one of the oldest in a family of twelve. I believe her family was quite well to do, as her father, my grandfather, who came from Donegal in Ireland, was a builder. I never got to know the Callaghan family well but Lorna remembers their big house. I was never to know any of my grandparents.

David and Rebecca Donaldson's wedding

In March 1936 when I was just thirteen-months-old, tragedy struck our little family, our mother, at the age of twenty-six, died after a long illness. They called it yellow fever, which I now believe was Hepatitis. Her absence left no sudden hole in my existence that I can remember. There has however always been a feeling of something missing all my life.

My first memory is one of the Presbyterian Orphanage at Andersons Bay when I pooed my pants. I remember sitting on the floor alone in this big room playing with my toys when suddenly I just had to GO. I ran to the door but it was shut; it was one of those big colonial doors with the high door handle. I jumped and jumped trying to reach it. I called, shouted and banged, but no-one came. My cries turned to sobs and then it was too late. It went everywhere, down my legs and onto the floor and I cried as if my heart would break. I felt sure I would be punished. But then Ga-Ga came and she wasn't angry at all, just led me along the long corridor to the bathroom, cleaned me up and put me in fresh clothes. Ga-Ga was Miss McGregor, the lady in charge of our "house". My other siblings hated and feared her but I was the youngest and her special baby. I can remember only kindness. I remember also waking up in my bed in her room and her saying for me to come and get in with her. I leaned over the bed and looked underneath, it was dark under there.

"I can't."

"Why not?"

"There's bogies under the bed," I told her.

I remember sitting in her bed early morning while she tried to sleep and looking at her lips and the thick coat of sticky white stuff around them and thinking she must be a very old lady. Now, of course, I realise she was probably only in her twenties.

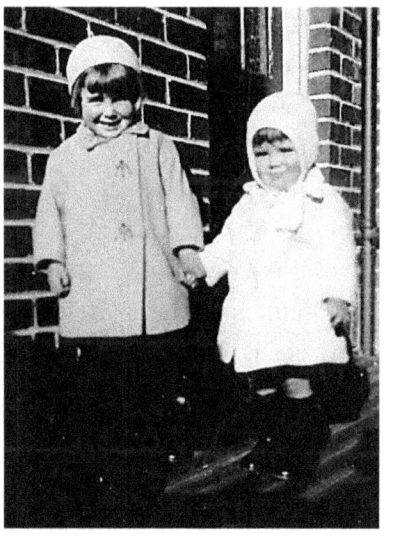

Alma and Gwen (now Billie) at orphanage

The orphanage had a holiday home up in central Otago at Middlemarch. There were no refrigerators in those days; most people had a meat "safe' with four walls of fly-wire that they kept out under the trees. It was so hot in Middlemarch that our food "safe' was a square hole cut in the ground and lined with a damp sack. This was covered with a wooden lid and another wet sack was placed over the top. I recall being taken out by one of the carers, to fetch the butter for lunchtime sandwiches.

My father had a Model T Ford with a soft top and he sometimes bought his new girlfriend up to see us on a Sunday, to take us all out for a ride. I remember just one snippet of me sitting in the front seat with them and everyone laughing at me. I thought it was great; even then I liked to be the centre of attention. In later years my step-mother often told the story about how they had come to pick us up and they had sent me out in a hat several sizes too big. When I turned my head, the hat stayed still while my head turned inside it.

My very last memory must have been just before we left the orphanage. My father had given me a tricycle; it was red with the front forks in the shape of white wings facing upwards. The night had been wet and there had been a frost, and the worms had come out of the lawn and onto the paving bricks where they had frozen. Edwin, my little blond-haired friend and I sat on our trikes discussing them and running our front wheels over the poor dead things.

I was to find out much later that our father hadn't wanted to send us to an orphanage. When our mother died, he tried to keep us at home, but it proved not to be possible. Apart from the farm he also ran a small droving business he had started during the depression. During the week the farmers around the Taieri Plain would ring to tell him which cattle they wanted driving to the Burnside stockyards, thus - the day before the sale he would leave in the early hours on his horse to collect them. He had several small holding places around the plain so he could bring them from different directions and when he had them all together, he would set off towards home where they would be camped overnight in our camp paddock.

The next morning before daylight he would be on the road with them again to drive them over Saddle Hill to the saleyards at Burnside. There Dad would wait all day to see if there were any cattle for the return journey; sometimes arriving at dusk with a sizable mob to once again spend the night in the camp paddock. The next morning, he would be on the road again to deliver the stock to their new owners. He was away from the farm three days a week and this had to be accomplished after he had milked up to ten cows by hand night and morning.

I learned later that several families wanted to adopt me; two families wanted Alma and one wanted Colin. At six years of age, nobody wanted little Lorna and she was probably the one hurt most by the loss of our mother. Our father refused to let us go, saying that we all had to stay together.

At first, he tried to manage with housekeepers who came in during the day. We heard later of two, one was an alcoholic and if Dad wasn't home by four o'clock, she would just down tools and leave. The other just decided one day that four kids were just too much to handle and she just walked out without notice. He came home that night to find us alone.

In those days sugar was bought in twenty-five-pound hessian sacks. It seems I had got onto the kitchen cupboard and pulled the sack over, and there was sugar all over the kitchen floor. Poor Lorna was sweeping it up, dust and all, and returning it to the bag. It was the final straw. We were packed off to the Presbyterian Orphanage at Andersons Bay in Dunedin, where we stayed for the next three and a half years.

Strangely I don't remember returning home – that part is a complete blank. Perhaps the trauma of leaving Ga-Ga, the only mother I could remember, was too much. I do have a memory of Dad bathing us three girls in the bath altogether, I was shy but he was happy and laughing and making a big fuss of us. Maybe that was our first night back.

Our father had married Elizabeth (Lylie) Thompson, a shop-girl from Arthur Barnett Department Store, the one who had laughed at my hat. They had met at the Otago Hunt Club where they both liked to ride, but a less unlikely farmer's wife you couldn't hope to meet. "Mum," as we were instructed to call her, at age thirty-one had been left on the proverbial shelf. I expect a man with four children was better than none. And Dad didn't just gain a wife, he gained a mother-in-law as well, who, until the day she died never had a good word to say of him.

I vaguely remember him building "Grandma's" cottage, which he put in the back garden. It had two rooms, a bedroom, a lounge with a brick fireplace, and a scullery-kitchen lean-to. The outer covering was the asbestos sheeting much used at the time. "Mum" also had a sister called Francis, that they both called Bubs. She had married Stewart Thomson, a stock and station agent, and was the much more outgoing of the two, not nearly as straight-laced and prudish as "Mother" – she also had very good fashion sense and a real sense of fun.

Our house was a little back from the road behind a thick macrocarpa hedge which went along in front of the orchard to the yard gate. An archway was cut through it onto a path that led straight to the front door, along the front and around the side. The dry toilet was on that side of the house covered in a flowering Clematis creeper, the hole in the wide wooden plank inside worn smooth and shiny from countless bottoms. A tall soft asparagus fern grew beside the chimneystack. Follow the path around and come to the back door. The outbuildings, which housed the wash house with copper boiler, wooden tubs, and the wood and coal shed, were separated from the house by another archway. This path led along past the orchard to a hen shed and the big farmyard. There was another hen shed at the end of the cow byre on the other side of the yard.

The orchard had a good variety of fruit that helped us greatly through the war years. Those I remember were two big cooking apple trees – I think they were called Bramley's – how sad we can't get them today – several plums, big purple ones, small red ones and a delicious greengage. There was also a small tree with bright red and very sweet eating apples that we liked to take to school. Unfortunately, the codling moth liked them as well and it was a little disconcerting to bite off a chunk and see a white grub waving its head at you, even worse when you actually bit through the thing. Most times we managed to eat around the intruder. In between the rows of trees Dad planted the vegetable garden. We also had a big cherry plum tree out the back of the house which kept us in cherry plum jam the year-round.

There were lots of animals, including six working dogs. Roy, big, black and hairy had a lovely nature. He was Dad's heading dog, keeping his place at the head of the herd to ensure they didn't get too strung out. Dad put reflectors on his collar so he wouldn't get run over on dark winter mornings as he took the mob over the hill to Burnside. Then there was Sweep, short-haired and black and tan. He was a good guard dog. If anyone tried to enter our gate Sweep would be there to meet them with a snarl. If they walked down the road to the farm gate Sweep would follow inside the hedge and meet them there as well. Then there was little Fly, our breeding bitch, short-haired, black and tan and very timid. We lost the poor wee girl one year when the river was in flood. Dad had been called out at 4 am by someone knocking on his bedroom window.

"Davie, can you come and help shift the cattle. The river is rising," so off he went on horseback with all the dogs. On the way home mid-morning he reached a bridge and was almost cut off on the other side by water. Spurring the horse, he rode into the water with the dogs swimming behind, he was halfway across when he looked back and saw Fly standing on the bridge. We heard him telling Mum that the water was already up to the horse's belly and rising so fast he couldn't go back.

"If I had remembered that she was afraid of water I would have put her on the saddle.' We found her body two weeks later caught high in the branches of the hawthorn hedge beside the road.

There was a big brindle dog that must have been sold not long after we got home, and Chance who was born about the same time. He was big, black, and hairy and mean, but never to us. Then there was Jack, a long-haired, friendly black and white huntaway, whose untimely death I was to learn all about many years later. It seems that Dad, who had a violent temper, had thrashed him to death one day on the road for some small misdemeanour. I am glad I was in my forties when I learned that. How strange that a man who most people thought highly of, who would give anyone his shirt, could do such awful things. Step-mum too had added to the dogs by bringing with her a purebred Pomeranian called Pixy, and a little brown Pomeranian crossbreed called Middy.

There were always a few horses: our father's stock horse called Monty, Mum's riding mare, Peggy, and when she was put to stud, we acquired Alannah. She liked nothing better than to stand in the pond on a hot day and belt the water with a front hoof until she was soaked and covered in mud. Old Blackie, the draught horse, stayed a few years until he developed arthritis in his back legs and Dad decided he was not fit for hard work. Over the next few years, we accumulated cats, hens, roosters, ducks, a pet black swan, a pet wild duck, and pet wild rabbits. It was against the law to keep wild rabbits as the country was infested with them, but if we dug out a nest and found a lovely little black one, we just had to keep it.

So, life began again for us. The older ones rode off to East Taieri school on their bikes; I followed a few months later riding on my brother's crossbar. We were always well dressed: gym frocks and long black stockings in the winter; pretty dresses in the summer. One year, Mum learned how to make dirndls and she ran us up several in bright floral prints. These were made from two straight lengths of material, a square neck cut out, puff sleeves added and then shirring elastic was loaded into the bottom bobbin of the sewing machine and sewn many times around at the waist and again at the bottom of the sleeves. We always had good shoes and always wore a big ribbon in our hair, which was cut straight around just below the ears. The hairdresser used to shave our necks up to the hairline, how I hated that bristly neck. Sometimes "Mum" would trim our necks at home with the hand clippers and we would be yelping as a hair got caught and pulled.

I didn't like riding on Colin's crossbar – he was a real boy, always doing mad things with the bike while I held on for dear life, yelling with fright. One night coming home he did something really silly. There was another drover on the Taieri called Doug Lindsay. He didn't work every week like Dad but came through with a mob at odd times. That night we caught up with him at the top of the small hill just south of East Taieri, (I used to think that hill was a mountain) when he was driving a herd of skittery black, poll cattle. Instead of riding quietly down the side of the herd, Colin said, "Right here we go," and took off. We belted down the hill at a rate of knots, weaving in and out of the frightened cattle now racing every which way to avoid this strange contraption in their midst. We had almost reached the small bridge over a culvert when it happened – we came too close to a frightened steer racing ahead of us and it lashed out with both back legs catching me a smashing blow to the side of the jaw. Next thing we had crashed into the bridge uprights all in a heap while a steer behind us with nowhere to go leaped over us. Mr Lindsay came riding down through the herd, asking, "Is she alright?" Then he gave Colin a mild telling off for being so stupid.

It was a miracle my jaw hadn't been broken, as it was, I had an enormous bruise and several bad grazes for quite some time. Colin, needless to say, had his hide lathered by Dad and told to take more care in future.

Because my class finished school earlier than the older children, I had either to wait around to ride home on Colin's crossbar or walk the two miles home. Dad caught me up sometimes when he was coming back from Burnside without any cattle; he would lean down and swing me up onto the front of the saddle and we would ride home together. I wished he could do that every day.

Not long after the kick in the face episode, I was deemed old enough to have my own bike. How proud I was, my very own bike. But first I had to learn to ride.

World War II was now in its second year and army vehicles passed our gate occasionally, sometimes in great convoys. Very few people had cars and those who did used them sparingly because of the petrol rationing.

"DON'T GO ON THE ROAD," warned my father. "Stay in the yard." So, for a week or so I rode around and around the big yard in front of the barn-cum-milking shed.

One day, sick of being restricted and seeing that no one was looking I slipped out the gate and wobbled north along the road. When I reached the next farm, I decided I had better turn back before I was missed. So I hopped off my bike and started to make a U-turn. There was the most God-awful scream of brakes and a huge army truck skidded to a stop not three feet from me and my bike. I looked up at the cab window and saw two white young faces staring down at me. I was terribly embarrassed and I ran to the other side of the road, jumped on my bike and rode home. I will never know to this day why I didn't hear the truck coming, but as I sit here writing I still see those faces. I hope those two young lads came home from the war unscathed. Needless to say, I told nobody about my close call, and I didn't go back on the road until given permission to do so.

To understand the Taieri Plains you have to envisage a giant basin, the sides of the basin being hills that enclose seventeen thousand acres of rich volcanic farmland, with the Taieri River, meandering its way through. Above our farm stood Saddle Hill, named by Captain James Cook as he made his way by ship up the coast. And that's exactly what it looked like, a giant saddle with the pommel facing south. The foothills sloped away from the pommel to stretch the length of the plain and follow the coast to the mouth of the Taieri River. On the other side, the Maungatuas, 2,997 feet high or thereabouts, its steep slopes clothed in Manuka – a kind of tea tree – the lower slopes covered with gorse.

Years later I discovered a book written by an early settler minister who wrote about his life in New Zealand after he went back to England. He described the plains as a giant swamp clothed with thick tall native flax bushes, the first early settlers had to get the local Maori to guild them safely through.

Being on a farm we didn't have any close neighbours. Going south on our side was a paddock belonging to the Kirk family then a gravel road that went down to Owhiro railway siding, then private golf links and no houses until the outskirts of Allenton, the next village south. Going a few hundred yards north on our side, we came to a nice cottage on another ten acres. At first it was owned by an elderly couple, who sold out during the war to two men, Michael and John. I think they had just retired and I realise now they were probably gay. Michael, tall and solid with a round smiling face, was the more outgoing of the two; John was smaller and quieter but just as friendly. They proved to be good neighbours. It was to these two that Dad gave Blackie, our draft horse when he could no longer do hard work. They were thrilled with the gift and looked after him well in return for the small jobs he could do.

Over from them, coming south, lived Bill and Jean Blair. Bill was our coalman. They had a nice brick house at the top of a long drive; his parents, from whom he'd inherited the business, lived in another brick house also on the farm. South again and almost opposite us was an old wooden cottage, the *two-eyes-and-a-nose* type. I never did know who owned it, but it was rented from time to time by various people. During the war, a woman with about six children moved in – her husband was away at the war. The family didn't have much money but the children were always kept immaculate. They didn't have proper shoes, just gym shoes, which were given a new coat of white every night. I see them now going off to school in their pretty, homemade floral dresses and sparkling "gymies'. I think they stayed just one summer. Going south again, just past us on the other side, lived the Allen's in a very pretty, two-storey house. I didn't find out until many years later that there was no flooring in the upper storey; I expect it was pulled out because it had been attacked with borer and not replaced for lack of money. Mrs Allen was the most appalling snob, all the locals called her "The Duchess', her long-suffering husband, Jack, was just an ordinary working man. They had sons, John, the eldest, and Ron, I think it was. John was my age and I used to go over to play, that is until I was banned for swearing. Being a sharp little madam, I had very quickly picked up my father's drover vocabulary and the wonderful 'bloody' word has stayed with me for a lifetime. South again a few hundred yards and we come to another early settler's two-storey house made from grey granite stone, tall and square. It too was on about ten acres of the foothills and the old lady who resided there was Miss McMillan. The house had a large overgrown garden with plum, pear and apple trees growing over the front boundary. Cherry trees shaded the side door, which was covered with a wide veranda.

A little further along the road, lived the Stevensons, with children Drew, Trevor, Helen, and little Janice. They had a nice big brick house up on the hill, and the boys rode their ponies at the agricultural shows. They used to accompany us on the way to school; we had a cooee call that told us if they were in front or behind us on the road.

I look back on my childhood at East Taieri as the most idyllic a child could have. My siblings and I were free to roam the land, wander neighbouring properties and climb high into the foothills of Saddle Hill. Up there we fished the mountain streams for the freshwater lobsters, or Kuru as the Maori call them, not to eat, just for fun. We would take a ripe yellow berry from a shrub we called Bulli-bull, tie it to a long string then tie the string to a stick. The berry was then lowered into the water a little in front of the lobster and it would come over and grab it in its pinchers. A quick jerk on the string and the lobster would sail over our heads onto the grass. One day we caught a lot and instead of throwing them back we stacked them into a few old tins we found lying about and carted them home, tipping them all out on the lawn at the back door. One of the dogs jumped in the air when he came to investigate and got his nose nipped.

Unfortunately, Mum had visitors who thought it was very funny but Mum was furious and demanded that we take them all down to the creek at the bottom of our property. Lorna and I picked them up gingerly, put them in a big enamel basin and set off to the creek. There she was, holding the basin in front of her with some trepidation, as our captives were trying to climb out. It was all too tempting. I snuck up behind her and gave the basin an almighty kick from below. Lobsters went everywhere … in her hair, down the neck of her dress, and while she screamed and jumped around like a frog on a hot plate I rolled around screeching with laughter. It was a naughty and cruel thing to do. We did eventually get the poor things to the creek but it was running too swiftly for them and they probably died anyway. Little did we know but those small lobsters made really good eating when dropped into boiling water.

One day when we were roaming the foothills, we did something that could have been disastrous. I would hate to give the impression that we were naughty children or even little vandals, we weren't. Most of the trouble we found ourselves in was the result of innocent curiosity.

Up behind Bill Blair's (the coalman's place), near the top of his farm, was a small coal mine. In the early days of the war, the father of my friend Elinor Johnson used to work there alone as a miner. I would often meet him going home on his pushbike, looking as black as the fire back when I was coming from school. When Mr Johnson joined the forces, the walk-in mine was shut, the big wooden doors across the mouth of the tunnel closed and locked. There were rail lines running down the hill to Bill Blair's back yard and on the lines at the top sat a big, very heavy steel coal truck. This truck, when the mine was being worked, was let down the hill on a steel rope and winched up again when empty. For some reason the rope had been disconnected and the truck just sat there with chocks under the wheels. Colin said we should see if we could push it, so we took the chocks out, let off the brakes, and with us all pushing we got it slowly moving. Suddenly it was too late to stop it. Over the brow of the hill it went and started hurtling down at an incredible speed while we watched in horror. We waited just long enough to see it hit the bollards behind the house with a huge bang and upend itself before we took to our heels to hide in the nearest trees. I don't know if Mr Blair knew it was us, but he must have had his suspicions, certainly "The Parents' got to hear of it and questions were asked. I have often thought about what could have happened had the bollards given way: their house could have been badly damaged.

The golf links was another place we would explore, and I came to know every inch of that place. In those days the club-house had a dry toilet, as did everyone else. It was out the back in a small grove of pine trees. One day Dad was driving our draught horse Blackie down the Owhiro Road with us all in the dray behind when Colin whispered as we passed the club-house: "Me and Tommy pushed the dunny over and it rolled down into the creek."

He hadn't counted on Dad's good hearing. He pulled back on the reins to stop Blackie, swung around in his seat and roared, "You did what?"

Silence.

"Right! I am going to take you to Mr Kirkland and you can tell him what you have done."

I don't think he ever carried out his threat. Actually, I think he thought it was quite funny, though he would never have let on.

During the war, Colin set rabbit traps on the golf course. I often went with him to see what he had caught. Sometimes we got a hedgehog, which was sad, sometimes a ferret, and once someone's cat, but mostly we got rabbits. Colin would skin them and stretch the skins over a bent wire to dry and sell later. The meat made a useful addition to our wartime diet.

We were on rations during the war; each family member was issued with a ration book. I can't remember the amounts of each item but I know we had two ounces of butter each per week.

Out in our dairy we put the milk through the big separator to get the cream. The separator fascinated me no end – you filled the big vat at the top with milk, turned the handle then cream came out one funnel and the skim milk the other. The big handle was hard to turn at first but once it got going it seemed to flow. Sometimes when our own butter supply was low, Grandma would filch some cream (highly illegal of course) and make some homemade butter. I would be allowed to turn the handle of the churn until I got fed up. We couldn't drink the buttermilk because it was too salty so instead, we used it for cooking. When the butter came out of the churn Grandma used wooden butter pats with a pattern on to shape it into squares or roll it into tiny balls so we could have one pat for each slice of bread. I never liked the homemade butter as it had a tainted taste.

Many years later I came to realise Dad did a lot of bartering to get paid for his droving services. We once got a whole side of bacon; someone must have killed and cured a pig. It used to hang in the cool room at the side of the house and Mum would cut thick slices off for breakfast. Sometimes we went out Sunday driving and Dad would leave us sitting in the car while he went to someone's house. Often after these visits, things would turn up at home with no explanation.

Once we called at the Wheeler house – they had a big family, about eleven, I think. Mum always said they were rough but then to my snobbish step-mum most big families were "Rough'. Well, there we were sitting in the car waiting. All the kids must have been banished to the front room while the Dads did business because lots of giggling heads kept popping up from under the window sill. We watched while the giggles progressed to face pulling and upside-down legs in the window until finally Mum said, "My God, they've set fire to the curtains," and sure enough flames were leaping toward the ceiling. The curtains were pulled down and the flames disappeared. After that the nonsense stopped – they probably realised they had gone too far. After all it was an old wooden house and the results could have been tragic.

A week or so after this visit a large wooden dining table, the type that would cost a fortune today, and all the chairs were delivered to our farm. The lot had been painted with mid-blue kalsomine paint, the type that washes off. Our father set us to scrubbing it all back to bare wood. On tipping up a chair to wash underneath I found the entire under edge of the chairs coated with layers of hardened chewing gum, and was horrified. In our family chewing gum was considered disgusting and an absolute no-no. When I pointed it out to Dad he laughed and said the Wheeler kids probably came to the table chewing gum and just stuck it under the chair so they could eat. That's how I found out where it all came from.

I met most of the Wheeler family many years later at a school jubilee. They were nice people, a close family still full of fun and mischief.

There was one shadow over my years at the East Taieri farm and that was the health of our sister Alma. While in the orphanage she had become epileptic. I learned many years later from Lorna that it was the result of a fall from a top bunk onto a concrete floor at the holiday home in Middlemarch. She was knocked unconscious at the time and they didn't call a doctor. Alma had an addiction to climbing anything climbable, and it was to become a real problem. We were all charged with her care. "Look after Alma," we would be told as we set off somewhere to explore. She was a lovely natured kid, a mad Aquarian like me, and was my closest friend and playmate. She loved to talk to people. As she got worse, she had long periods away from school when she would wander off to talk to the golfers along the road and collect golf balls that had been hit into the rough outside the fence and on to the road. Eventually she had a large basketful she had collected. If she was there when the ball came out on the road, she would help the player to find it and this way she made many friends we didn't even know she had. Not something that could ever happen in today's immoral world.

One sunny day when the clover was long and full of flowers, we were playing down at the bottom of our paddocks when I stood on a bee with my bare foot. (We loved to run barefooted.) I was stung and it was her turn to look after me; she put me on her back and carried me all the way home for Mum to scrape out the sting.

We quite often got a warning when she was going to have a fit. She would say, "I've got a headache," and seconds later she would drop to the floor or start spinning around and around. One day she gave us a bad fright when she did this on the side path before crashing down and hitting her head on the top of the bricks edging the garden. She had a big dent and a cut on her left eyebrow. Another day when we were at school Mum let her go off to pick mushrooms; she came home later with a basketful of broken bits saying that she'd had a turn and when she came to she couldn't find her little knife. She had collected up the broken mushrooms and come home most upset about the loss of the knife. It wasn't all doom and gloom though: she was always happy and rarely complained. We always had lots of laughs.

Once she found an abandoned duck's nest down by the creek. Ducks often nested too close to the water so the nest would become flooded after heavy rain. Alma picked up the hem of her frock to make a holder and collected all the eggs to bring home. Unfortunately, on the way back she had a turn and all the eggs were broken. More unfortunately, the eggs were extremely rotten. When she arrived home we had four visitors who had come out from town – all ex-workmates of our new mother and no doubt she was trying to impress them with her new country life. They were sitting in the lounge enjoying afternoon tea from Mum's beautiful china when the door opened and in came this little girl covered from head to toe with the foulest smelling muck you could ever imagine.

Have you ever smelt rotten eggs? Within minutes the stench had pervaded the entire house.

Alma was hospitalised twice for investigations. She told me they had stuck red hot needles into her head and I wonder now if they gave her electric shock treatment. Whatever it was, it was to no avail and her fits became worse and more frequent over the next two years.

At school we always had end of year concerts. I made my debut as an entertainer at the age of six singing *Ten Green Bottles* while ten of my classmates, clad in green crepe paper with brown tops, stood on a wooden form behind me and crashed backwards onto a mattress one by one, until there were no green bottles hanging on the wall. That year, Alma, who of course was two years ahead of me, also had to sing. Her song was about a little girl lost in the fog for which she had just one prop, our dog Pixie. Everything went fine at the daylight rehearsal. Wee Pixie trotted around on her lead just as intended. Unfortunately it was not "all right on the night'. Pixie trotted on, took one look at the audience, got stage fright, and sat her bottom firmly down on the stage. Poor Alma! She walked twice around the stage singing, "Me and my dog are lost in the fog, won't some kind gentleman please see us home," with Pixie skidding around behind her on her bottom. Of course, it brought the house down.

Being home on her own so often Alma devised some games of her own. One of her favourite things was to cut a long swishy stick from a poplar tree and pull all the leaves off. She then used this to go around all the outbuildings collecting spider webs and spiders until she had a ball on the end. She loved to chase us with this. Another use she had for her swishy stick was to lob windfalls or potatoes, which she would poke onto the end of her stick, put it back over her shoulder and then bring in forward as hard as she could ... like casting a fishing fly. It was amazing how far the missile would go.

One day, Dad was bending down digging potatoes between the trees in the orchard when Alma decided to lob a few. She pushed one onto the end of her stick and swung it back over her shoulder (unfortunately, a bit too hard) it flew off and hit Dad on the backside. He jumped a foot in the air and turned to see where it had come from. Alma, realising what she'd done, took off with Dad after her. Now Dad was never good at running, and seeing him trying to run in his gumboots was a sight to behold, his knees almost to his chin. We all had a good laugh.

Alma was a strange child in a lot of ways. Living on a farm we were all reasonably fearless but we knew how far to go. With Alma it was different, she had no such qualms, and she could do things that would get the rest of us into serious trouble. Over by the camp paddock gate were two big poplar trees, one on either side of the gate. Like a lot of the poplar trees in Otago they had probably been early settler fence posts that had sprouted. One of the trees had a hole in the trunk that was home to a hive of bees. Alma got a stick and started poking bits of honeycomb out.

"No, Alma, don't. Please, Alma, come away. You will get stung." She took no notice just went on eating bits of honey. The bees ignored her, but they went for me standing about twenty feet away. I took to my heels and ran. Another time she and I went with Mum to have afternoon tea with the Croziers. They had a smallholding and kept about six hives. Sometime during the afternoon Mrs Crozier looked out the window and said, "Oh my God, she's lifted the lid off the hive." Alma stood there calmly looking at the bees and didn't get one sting.

When Dad bought his horse Monty, he had a dreadful habit of taking off at a canter as soon as a foot hit the stirrup. Dad said he'd been trained to do that, something to do with barrel racing. Dad never did manage to stop him from moving forward, but at least he got it down to a fast walk. We were forbidden to ride him.

Monty was a light bay colour, at least 16.2 hands high and fine-boned. I suspect he was part thoroughbred. One day Dad left him saddled in the yard and went back into the house to get something. When he came back Alma was riding Monty around the yard. Dad was shocked – he couldn't understand why the horse had stood still and let Alma climb aboard, with the help of the fence rails, of course. He never did it for anyone else.

During the summer holidays, we sometimes went to stay with Frances and Stewart in central Otago. At one time they rented an old schoolhouse at Sutton, which couldn't have had the electric power connected as I particularly remember the kerosene lamps. One night we were eating pudding, (the word *dessert* had not yet entered our vocabulary,) when Colin pointed at the lamp with his spoon. The spoon had a bit of red jelly on the end and it touched the glass funnel of the lamp and cracked it. Frances was most upset as the glass was hard to replace. We loved our holidays in Sutton where we were free to explore and wander. I still think of Sutton as a magical place, like a moonscape with huge rock formation everywhere, some long and skinny, standing up like sentinels, keeping watch. Sometimes the farmers used these as fence posts. The terrain was covered in a very fine, red-topped grass, about a foot high. I loved to lie on my back and watch the breeze make tiny waves in the seed heads, for miles and miles. High in the blue sky above me the skylarks would hover and sing, so wonderfully beautiful, and peaceful.

On the day we were to go home Alma was running around the house saying, "I can't find my belt." She had this dress that was made from a silky kind of material, a tiny red check with a white peter pan collar and the same coloured belt was missing. We hunted everywhere to no avail until Frances hustled us out to the gate saying we were going to miss the bus. There were two enormous trees at the gate, Norfolk Island Pines, I think. Anyway, they were the type that looked like round ladders, so easy to climb as the branches are bare and spaced just right. As kids will, we started to say goodbye to things out loud – goodbye house – goodbye creek – goodbye trees. As he said it Colin looked up to the top.

"There's Alma's belt!' he exclaimed.

We all looked skywards, and sure enough, there it was, flying like a flag from the very top twig of this high tree. We were all stunned, and poor Frances went quite white.

"You didn't climb up there …"

"Gosh," said Alma, "I forgot I'd put it there."

She gave me a dreadful fright another time: she and I had wandered down to the gravel road that followed the train line below the farm. Between the road and the creek was a small triangle where a few trees grew. One of the trees had been blown over in a recent storm and wedged in the fork of its neighbor. It had no branches on the stem and wasn't very wide but it was like a red rag to a bull to my sister. She started shinnying up it like a monkey. No amount of pleading on my part was going to stop her and she made it to the fork of the tree at least twenty feet above the ground.

I was absolutely terrified. Not Alma! Oh no, she sat there saying how great it was up there and how much she could see. Eventually she decided to come down but looked a bit worried.

"I can't get down," she announced.

I felt sick. I didn't know what to do. If she fell I would be blamed, I just knew it. Then she saw a car coming – it was Baldy McLean and his taxi from Mosgiel. Everyone called him Baldy McLean because of his round shiny head. He was jovial with a big smiling face, and we knew him quite well.

"It's Mr McLean! Go and stop him!' she commanded, but I was too shy to do that, and then he was gone, and I cursed myself for not having the courage.

Eventually, she plucked up the courage to back down the trunk, inch by inch. I stood with my heart in my mouth until her feet hit the ground.

"Don't you ever do that again," I scolded.

"Don't tell on me, pleeease … you won't tell on me?" and of course I never did.

When we first came home from the orphanage, we had a black

wood stove cooker, as did most people. It had a water chamber at the side and a brass tap in the front so we always had hot water. *Daddy's* chair, a big seagrass affair, sat to the side of it and it was there he read his paper when he came in at night, his woollen sock-clad feet on the shelf in front of the oven. The stove was polished weekly with zebra black until it was black and shiny. One night before Dad came in, we were all having a scrap about who could sit in *"Daddy's* chair. We all piled onto the chair, me on top until someone gave me a shove and I put my right-hand flat on top of the hot stove to save myself.

The palm of my hand was quite badly burned. Now, we all know that a burn should be put in cold water for ten minutes, but my stepmum with her old wive's tales insisted on holding my hand in front of the fire to, and I quote, "draw out the burn.' Needless to say I screamed the roof off. Next day the entire palm was covered with a blister about one inch deep.

Our Uncle Neil, the closest of our father's brothers, came to visit. We all loved our Uncle Neil; he seemed to be the one who cared for us most. I showed him my hand and he told Mum that a pin should be put in the blister to release the fluid and it should be bandaged. Strangely, it healed without a scar.

One night, Colin wanted to play a trick on Dad. He had some horse chestnuts and said if we put them in the firebox they would go off with a bang. When we heard Dad coming two chestnuts were placed in the flames. Dad settled down with his paper while we waited and waited. Just as Dad was dozing off there was a big bang; the steel door of the firebox flew open and hot coals spewed all over the hearth mat. He leaped out of his chair and frantically threw the coals onto the hearth.

"What the bloody hell was that?"

Then he saw us all giggling, but trying to keep straight faces, and demanded to know what we had put in the fire. Colin explained, and he gave us all a mild telling off and settled down once again to read. But we all knew there was another to come. Minutes passed. We thought nothing was going to happen, when bang, not so loud this time, but again the firebox flew open and Dad leaped from his chair.

"How many more did you put in?" he demanded. Luckily, he wasn't angry and we all had a good laugh.

Not long after this Dad had an electric stove put in. Mum was very proud of this newfangled gadget, and the old black stove was taken out and replaced with a fireplace with a "wet back' to heat the water. The old stove was put out at the side of the yard for us to play with. What fun Alma and I had; we spent many hours happily making mud pies and "baking' them in our oven.

When the rainwater ran down from the hills it caused erosion, burrowing underground to make long under burrow tunnels that ran below ground to pop out again further down. The water brought with it a lot of clay that collected in the culverts going under the main road. We collected tin's full of this and fashioned cakes, plates, and buns before leaving them to dry in the sun. One of the culverts had dark grey clay so our artworks had different colours. Many years were to go by before I worked in clay again as I trained to be a sculptress.

Before our step-mum married our father, she had plenty of time to collect her "Glory Box'. The fact that she had worked in Arthur Barnett's Department Store must have helped. She brought to the family many nice things including a full set of silver, bone-handled cutlery, nice dinner sets, crystal, and linen. So it was that our table was always set nicely, crystal or cut glass jam dishes with jam spoons, butter dishes with butter knives; we had to use the utensil provided to transfer what we wanted to the side of our plate and God help anyone who used their own knife to take some butter or jam. It usually meant a swift crack over the knuckles with the side of Dad's knife. The table was always covered with a nice cloth, and all talking at the table, except "please pass the jam' etc. was strictly forbidden. (Little girls should be seen and not heard.) Small wonder then that we often got the giggles. Mum often recounted the story of how, one night, Alma started giggling about something.

"Leave the table," said our father. That got me going.

"Leave the table."

Then it was Lorna's turn. "Leave the table," then Colin, "You too, get." By this time Mum was doing her best to keep a straight face so she had to leave as well and pretend to be doing something so we couldn't see her laughing. Dad was left alone, sitting at the head of the table while we spluttered ourselves silly all around the kitchen. Eventually he started laughing as well and ordered us all back to the table, "And behave yourselves!"

Lorna never accepted our step-mother and used to get very angry when "Mum' would say, "Your mother had nothing."

When we were in the orphanage, which I imagine our Dad had to pay for, he rented our house out fully furnished. He fenced a small triangle off on the other side of the camp paddock and bought two army huts. One he used for sleeping and the other had a small wood stove for cooking. He planted a little plantation of radiata pine around them and they quickly grew tall and hid the huts.

One day, when we were playing under the floor of the shed by the house, we found the remains of quite a lot of pretty plates that had been thrown there. Lorna said they must have been our own Mother's plates and she *did* have some nice things – so there! – before other people broke them.

Being on the main road south, we occasionally had some strange visitors. In the early war years, there were still a few old swag men around – we called them *swaggers*. If I saw one when I was coming home from school I would hide under a culvert until he had passed. I can laugh about it now because they must have known full-well I was there. Sometimes one would call in and ask for work or for an odd job and, if Dad was home, he wouldn't see them go hungry and they could sleep one night in the barn.

At that time there was an old salesman called Mr Glass. He travelled the road with a skinny black horse pulling a tall, square, canvas-covered wagon with his name and trade written on it. I expect in England they would call him a tinker. He never came to our house trying to sell; I expect we were too near Mosgiel. I do remember vividly the night, on his way back to Dunedin, he pulled into our yard, unharnessed his horse, watered it at the trough, then put it in the stable with a large bucket of our oats to eat. When Dad went out to see what was going on he was about to cook his dinner and settle down for the night.

Now our Dad had the vilest temper and he just blew it! He told Mr Glass that if he'd had the decency to ask then he would have been welcomed to stay, as it was, he could harness up his "blankety-blank' horse and get the "blankety-hell' out of it. We saw no more of Mr Glass.

One of my favourite visitors was an old swagger called Sam McCready. If ever there was a disreputable, grubby, smelly, mischievous, likable leprechaun, it was him. He always had a big smile and a twinkle in his eye. What teeth he had left were rotten and black, in fact, he was just about all we were told never to be. He didn't call very often as he roamed far and wide doing odd jobs and telling his suitably embellished, I am sure, stories to anyone who cared to listen. Our father found him most amusing and was very tolerant of him but he shocked Mum and Grandma to the core.

One day he arrived late in the afternoon and stayed yarning with Dad out in the yard until teatime. In New Zealand, the evening meal is always called tea, even if it is the main meal of the day. Anyway, Dad asked Sam to stay for tea and came in to tell Mum – she was horrified.

"Oh my God, what did you invite him for?"

Anyway, an extra place was set for Mr McCready (we children had to call all adults Mr or Mrs) and he was sitting right in front of *me*. His table manners were atrocious! My siblings and I watched aghast as he reached across the table with his own knife, which he had licked, to get a large knob of butter then he talked with his mouth full as he regaled us with all the stories of his time on the road.

I remember one story he told that night about a lady from one of the high-country sheep stations who had given him the job of weeding the vegetable patch. "Huge weeds they were, never seen the likes of, roots went down to China. I had just got them all out and into a big pile when she rushed down the path and screamed, "Oh my God, you've pulled out all my sparra grass' (Asparagus)." He laughed uproariously, and reached with his knife to get some jam, then seeing the spoon he used it to put a large dollop on his bread then licked the spoon both sides before putting it in his mouth and sucking it to make sure he had it all. He then returned the spoon to the bowl.

"Mmm, nice homemade jam that."

No one touched that dish of jam for the rest of the meal, and it was tipped out after he'd gone.

"After all," said Mum, "you don't know what we might catch."

I was always an inquisitive child. Let me be aware of every single moment, none to escape, so that whatever the years may bring I will remember. Every insect, flower, and all things intrigued me. I became a proper little know it all. In fact, had I not been so pitifully shy I may have been downright precocious.

Out in the raceway between our paddocks I discovered a minute yellow and pale blue viola. The entire plant stood no more than six centimetres high, with the tiny face of the flower about a centimetre. Whenever it would appear in the spring I would hunker down and stare at it in awe. I believe this was the beginning of my love for all things small. Over the years I have often thought about that tiny plant, but I have never seen it again. Does it survive today on that farm? Or it is just another species lost forever?

I was forever asking questions. Our father was quite a good bush carpenter and I would often come upon him building something.

"What are you making, Dad?"

"A wigwam for a goose's bridle."

"Oh, Dad, it's not … what is it?"

"I told you, a wigwam for a goose's bridle. Here, skinny (his pet name for me), grab a hold of this for me while I nail it." Or, "Sit your weight on this while I saw it."

At the outbreak of the war, Dad, who was then thirty-seven years old, joined the home guard. As a farmer he would have been exempt from active service, also we had already lost one parent. We all remember that first night he came home in his uniform and greatcoat carrying a 303 rifle – with one bullet. The one bullet amused Colin no end. Dad parked the rifle in the foyer and we were given a stern warning not to touch. After that he would disappear off into the night at least once a week.

As the war dragged on there were rumours that a Japanese submarine had been spotted off Brighton and things started to get serious at school.

Our teachers at East Taieri were Mr Borrie, the headmaster, who taught the upper classes, and Miss Hoffman who taught the primers and up to standard two. I thought Miss Hoffman was old until I looked at school photos years later. She was a good teacher and kind, even if she did wash my mouth out with red Life Buoy soap for swearing.

Mr Borrie declared we should all start training to be soldiers. I can't imagine how long he thought the war would go on for when even the older boys couldn't join up for six years. So, there we were each morning lined up in a long crocodile in twos while he marched us around and around on the wet grass. Quick march, left-right, left-right, left-wheel, right-wheel, eyes right! Abouuuuut Face! he would shout. One morning my special friend, Frances, and I, were at the tail end while all the big girls and boys were up the front. "About turn,' he shouted, and there we were, two little dots, at the front of the column. It was all too much. We got the giggles and laughed and spluttered all around the playing field. We all went home at night with very wet shoes and Mum said if I came home with them wet again, I would get the strap. When I told her that we were marched through wet grass and puddles and Colin "stuck up' for me I was let off.

We also had to learn to play dead. If an enemy plane came over, we were to drop flat down on the ground and lie very still. He took to coming out in the middle of playtime, giving a shrill blast on his whistle and we all had to drop flat. Poor Ivan Hammer had carroty red hair and Mr Borrie said there wouldn't be much good him trying to hide with his hair like a beacon. At sewing classes, we all had to make a small felt purse with a long cord to go over the shoulder. We had to wear the purse at all times. In it we had a cork, (to chew on if there was bombing) and cotton wool to plug our ears with. One day we were told that we were to have the half-day off but first we would all be given special places to hide in the event of an attack. We were told that groups who lived near each other would be kept together and it had been worked out how we could get home the quickest way, avoiding the roads where possible.

The Stevenson kids – Drew, Trevor, and Helen – and we Donaldson's, who all came the biggest distance, were to hide over the road under a big pointed conifer tree just inside the church driveway and behind the wall. The other kids were scattered around everywhere. After we had hidden for quite a while, amid much whispering and laughing Mr Borrie came around blowing his whistle, the signal for us to set off for home as fast as our legs could carry us. Our group had to go through the cemetery and out the other side, over several paddocks until we hit the road north of East Taieri, and then follow the road to our homes. We were to hide if we saw or heard anything coming.

Poor Mr.Borrie … I expect he was trying to do his bit for the war effort.

I was always quite bright at school. Miss Hoffman told me I was to jump a primer class as I was so far ahead. Out in the grounds, I quickly gained the reputation for being a daredevil. Kids were forever daring me to do mad things and I could never resist the challenge. On one occasion' Miss Watt (all ladies were Miss to us) came to start planning our school concert. She came every year about three months before break up, and during afternoon playtime she was in the classroom talking to Miss Hoffman. Some of us were over near the school boundary by the big macrocarpa hedge where grew some enormous fungus puffballs. When they are young the flesh inside is white and I am told, edible, but later the inside turns to brown dust spores.

"Bet you're not game to throw one of those at the teacher," came the challenge.

"Bet I am so." I selected the biggest one I could find, about the size of a basketball, and ran off with half my school mates behind me. Up the passage I crept; the door was ajar. Misses Hoffman and Watt were at the other end of the room with their backs towards me. I lobbed the puffball, waited just long enough to see it burst into hundreds of pieces then took off. We all stood around outside waiting for something to happen. After what seemed like an age, Miss Hoffman appeared (I suspect they had been having a good laugh).

"Who threw that puffball?" she said, trying to look severe. The kids looked at me.

"I did," I squeaked.

"Well, young lady, you can just come in and sweep it all up."

I was given a dustpan and brush and had to crawl around on my hands and knees, it was everywhere. When I happened to look up both ladies were trying to keep straight faces.

Things were not always good at school. With the classes ranging from primer one to standard six, the age group was from five years old to twelve or thirteen. Some of the big boys were bullies and we littlies tried to keep out of their way. At East Taieri, by the general store, lived a big family who I will call the Cooks. They were known to be rough and wild. The oldest boy had a really cruel streak, and would take baby birds from their nests and poke his thumb nail through their protruding, featherless bellies, making their guts squirt everywhere – that was just one of the things he loved doing to harmless animals.

He did it right in front of me once and it splashed onto my face and dress. I hated him. In class I sat beside the youngest brother Edwin in one of those old-fashioned double desks. He was a nice quiet wee boy, with light red hair, so I forgave him the fact that he wet his pants and always smelt of pee.

Beside the Cook's lived the Miller family. I think they owned the store, while another Miller family – Joy, Beris and a brother – lived a few doors down Riccarton Road. They were a nice and well brought up family.

I have no idea how or why the feud started but the East Taieri mob decided to block the road so we – the Donaldson's and the Stevenson's – couldn't get home. This didn't affect Edwin and me as we got out of school earlier.

Now both parents of our group had strict rules and we were expected to be home at a certain time otherwise questions were asked. There were two ways of our getting to school; one was to ride to East Taieri, turn left down Riccarton Road, then right along the bottom road. Or, we could go straight on to Mosgiel Junction and turn left at Cemetery Road. The first blockade happened on Cemetery Road so the next night our lot went home via the bottom road. Not to be outdone the East Taieri lot split into two halves – they outnumbered us three to one – and blockaded both roads.

Before many days had passed, tempers flared, and things got nasty. Alma was knocked off her bike into the ditch and that alarmed the parents. Strangely enough in those days, teachers were supposed to be Gods, and few parents ever complained. If we came home saying we had got the strap, they would say we must have deserved it. So, nothing was said to Mr Borrie, although I heard Dad saying there was no discipline in the school.

One night, when it was wet and windy, Colin had been kept in for some misdemeanour, so was late leaving school. Lorna arrived home unscathed but Colin didn't arrive until 7 pm. He said he'd been set upon on the bottom road and had come to lying in a ditch with his bike on top of him. He was sporting a large bump on his head and had obviously been knocked unconscious.

That was the last straw for The Parents. The next day Lorna, Colin, and Alma were enrolled at Mosgiel District High school, another two miles away. Mosgiel taught all classes from the primers to school leavers.

They considered the extra two miles would be too much for me, especially as I would have to ride through the Mosgiel traffic. So I stayed on at East Taieri.

A few days later the big Cook boy caught me alone in the schoolyard at playtime. He didn't say a word, just stood a few yards away glaring at me with a sneering face. He stared and stared. I felt like a mesmerised rabbit. I tried to run toward the school but he cut me off so I turned and bolted into the girls' lavatories, petrified. I kept peeking out hoping he'd gone away, but each time I looked he made sure I saw him lurking in the shrubs. Eventually the bell went for us to return to lessons but by this time I truly felt he would be brazen enough to ignore the bell and grab me on the way out. I stayed put until someone came looking for me. When I entered the school corridor, I was met by Mr Borrie, who wanted to know who had upset me, and why I was hiding in the lavatory. I burst into tears and blurted out the whole story.

Furious, he said, "Why wasn't I told?"

He must have realised by that time why my siblings had been removed from the school. There was hell to pay: everyone concerned was questioned; the "nice' family Miller admitted they'd been bullied into joining the gang, and the ringleaders were soundly punished. They were told never to threaten me again and I was told that if I had any more trouble I was to come and tell one of the teachers. Apart from a snide remark at the end of that day I had no more trouble. I finished out my school year at East Taieri and was enrolled at Mosgiel to start the next year.

A strange thing happened when the New Year started at Mosgiel High School ... the rule was that the children went back to the classroom they had been in the previous year. I was directed to the standard two-room where I found myself in a class of about thirty, instead of the usual six I was used to. We were told we were to collect our things and move up to the next classroom, which was for standard three, but before we could do so, a harassed teacher put her head in the door and said I should be back in the standard one classroom. I was duly moved back and then up again into standard two. That's how I came to spend a second year in the same class. I was too shy to keep telling them they had made a mistake and my parents, who should have intervened, didn't. After the end of year exams, I was top of the class, with five Excellents and two Very Goods. I was also one year behind which was ultimately to make a big difference to my life.

We had all adjusted to the eight miles of bike riding a day and the much larger school, but I wish I could say that my year at Mosgiel was incident-free. It wasn't.

The usual teacher had gone to join the armed forces and during that year we had about five teachers, most of whom were inexperienced students. The headmaster, Mr Kane, (the kids called him Paddy Kane,) had a son in the army, tall and handsome in his army uniform, and even he came to teach us when he was on leave. We loved him; he was a great teacher with a wonderful sense of humour.

One of the student teachers we had seemed to take an instant dislike to me. I never knew why. I'd always had a good rapport with my teachers. The girls called her Miss La-Dee-Da as she was flashily dressed and used far too much makeup. She obviously couldn't cope and was forever shouting at someone, usually me, as I was forever getting blamed for something I truly hadn't done. Her favourite form of punishment was to rap you over the knuckles with her ruler.

One day we were told that the British Prime Minister, Winston Churchill, was going to give a speech and there was to be *no talking*. Halfway through his speech, Marjorie, across the aisle, whispered something to me, which I ignored. When she did it again, I hissed "Don't Talk!' Unfortunately, Miss La-Dee-Da saw me, and when the radio was turned off, I was hauled out and given a vicious belting over the same knuckles that had been attacked the day before. Had I been Marjorie, I would have said, "Sorry, Miss, it was my fault. She was telling me not to talk,'" because I was always honourable and owned up to my mistakes, but few children were like me. When I got home that night the backs of my hands were red and badly swollen. All Mum said was, "It must have served you right." I was very angry and I thought the world unjust. Had this sort of thing ever happened to my children I would have gone down to the school so fast you wouldn't have seen me for dust. I did get the last laugh, however. When I was hauled out the next day to get my daily beating for some trumped-up misdemeanour, she grabbed my hand to belt it, then stopped. "How did you get that swelling?"

I looked her straight in the eye, and said coldly, "You belted me with your ruler.'

She looked quite frightened and went red in the face, then said something about letting me off this time and go back to your seat. She stopped picking on me after this and very soon after she left, much to the relief of the entire class.

The war was still on at this time so riding to and from school could be quite entertaining. One day, Dawn, Olive (who I found out years later were my cousins but nobody had bothered to tell me) and I saw a long crocodile of soldiers marching towards us. We jumped off our bikes and hid in a shallow ditch beside the road. They all laughed as they passed and called out:

"We can see you."

"Like your pretty dress."

"Can I borrow your bike?"

We felt silly, but were too shy to get up until they were well passed.

Pilots were being trained in Tiger Moth planes based at the Taieri airport. Along the bottom road, we would watch all twelve planes as they set out each day to do their stunts over the plains. Sometimes we would hop off our bikes and watch while they looped the loop, spun round and round like a corkscrew while tumbling earthwards, flew upside down or engaged in mock battles. I used to think I would like to do that. Little did I know that I would get my wish some fifty years later high over the beach at Surfers Paradise.

One of the things the pilots loved to do was called hedge-hopping. They would fly low over the fields hopping over any tall hawthorn hedge they encountered. Dad came home one day in high dungeon. "Little sod, I didn't even hear him coming ... jumped right over the hedge beside the road ... good mind to report him to his Commanding Officer," he blustered. It seems that Dad had almost been thrown from his horse and the cattle had stampeded – he was not at all impressed.

Both of our pets, Donald, the duck, and Pee Wee, the swan, came to live with us on wild and windy days. Donald arrived in Colin's sou'-wester coat pocket, having been found abandoned and alone by the roadside. *He* was a little ball of fluff and we all took care of him in a box by the fire. It soon became apparent, when he grew feathers that *he* was a *she*, but Donald she was and Donald she stayed. When she became old enough to fly, the butcher, Mr Ralston, who came with his van every week, said he would cut the tip off one wing so she couldn't fly away. This was common practice in those days but I am sure it would be frowned on now.

So it was that poor Donald was grounded for life, not that she seemed to mind. She just trotted along behind us all around the farm. Every year in the spring she would disappear for a few weeks, only coming back night and morning to eat. We knew she had a nest somewhere but she was the master – or I should say mistress – of cunning. If we tried to follow her, she would sidle off in the opposite direction; no matter how uninterested we would try to appear she would outfox us.

One year, when Alma was at home sick – she was beginning to spend more time at home than at school – she determined she would find the nest. And find it she did, about half a mile away from the house under the hawthorn hedge.

Every year Mum put a dozen fertile Khaki Campbell duck eggs under a clucky black Orpington hen, and, feeling sorry for Donald sitting yet again on a clutch of infertile eggs, she gave Alma a fertile one from the hen's clutch to exchange with one of Donald's. I will never forget the night she came home to introduce her baby … she stood quacking at the door until someone opened it then stood there bobbing her head up and down. "Look at my baby. Aren't I clever?"

The hen had also hatched her brood, and on the first day they were let outside the ducklings rushed straight into a rainwater puddle. Poor Mother hen was very confused. She Puck-Puck-Pucked and ran around and around the puddle telling them to get out of there.

After a few days of having to put baby food out for both the hen's brood and some for Donald's one, Mum decided it would be better to put the one duckling in with the hen's lot in the shed. She should have known better, Donald walked around the shed calling, and eventually got her baby back, although we never worked out how. There just didn't seem to be a hole anywhere that it could squeeze through.

Seems to me there must have been quite a few confused animals on our farm – ducks who thought their mothers were hens, and hens that thought they had hatched some strange looking chickens.

As I have said, Pee Wee also came to us after a big storm. Mr Allan had found him in his side paddock, seemingly unable to fly and very tame. He brought him over and asked Dad if we would have him. "Mrs Allan doesn't want it around the place."

Dad said that he could join the menagerie. He was quite young (almost an ugly duckling) and just like the ugly duckling story, he grew into a beautiful swan. Big and black, with red bill and feet. He was very tame and very quickly told the dogs who was boss. We called him Pee Wee because that was the funny noise he made. Leave a door open and Pee Wee would come waddling into the house, on the scrounge for a titbit.

One day when we had "townie' visitors being entertained in the lounge, the front door was open. Pee Wee wandered down the passage to say hello. The visitors were most impressed, that is until he squirted out a great runny poo onto the floor and was hustled outside.

About a year after he arrived, Pee Wee laid a big egg, so just like Donald, *he* became she. Poor Pee Wee came to a sad end. Colin had been instructed to dig a hole and bury the guts of the rabbits he had skinned, but one night he just scraped a small hole and covered them with earth. Pee Wee was found in the morning choked, with about a yard of gut down her throat and the rest hanging out. Colin was, for a time, about as popular as a stink bomb at a wedding service.

Miss McMillan, the elderly lady from the two-storey house down the road, was the source of one of the strangest stories I have ever come across. She came to our house every Thursday night for a roast meal. On another night she went to Jean and Bill Blair. This was her neighbourly way of making sure she had two good meals a week.

She was a very severe lady, tall and thin, and clad in black. I see her now riding by on the old "sit up and beg' bike, or was it a broomstick? To me she was a colourless, grumpy lady, who never seemed to smile, and was totally devoid of character. She had a reputation for being mean. Every day, usually Colin or Lorna would deliver our day-old paper to her, and sometimes she would give them something for their trouble, a piece of fruit or a biscuit. One day she gave Lorna a piece of fruitcake, but it had mould on it so Lorna threw it into the road verge. Unfortunately, when the old lady came down for dinner, she saw the cake and arrived in high dungeon.

"Why has Lorna thrown away a perfectly good piece of cake?" she wanted to know. I am not sure how they got out of that one, but, as Mum said later, "I can understand you throwing the cake away, but did you have to leave it where she could see it?"

Miss McMillan milked a few scrawny Friesian cows by hand, and one night when Dad was riding home on his horse, he saw her lying face down in the mud of the cow yard. She was unconscious, so he carried her inside and called the doctor, who admitted her to hospital. We took the cows down to our place to milk in our shed where we now had new milking machines, and later the cows were sold, as the old lady was never fit enough to do the milking again. Miss McMillan had had a stroke, but before long she was back home again trying to be independent. It soon became quite apparent that she should not be left on her own. Mum began the twice-daily walks up to see her. On one occasion, she arrived to find a whole pound of butter had been put up on the rack above the wood stove to soften. It had melted and was running down onto the stove where it had caught alight and the kitchen was full of smoke. Miss McMillan was just sitting staring at the fire. Now our step-mum was never the bravest of people and the old lady began to freak her out. Bill Blair came to help, but he was at work all day, so he and Mum would go together each evening to see that the old lady had eaten and was ready for bed. They could never understand her absolute refusal to let them help her up the stairs.

One night, when they had made the fire safe, and Miss McMillan had promised to go to bed as soon as they left; Mum and Mr Blair went out and waited on the veranda where they could see her through the window. They waited and waited and she just sat there. Suddenly Mr Blair lost his patience and went back in yelling, "If you don't get up to your bed this minute, I will bloody well pick you up and carry you there!"

The old lady was shocked into moving and they waited until she was up the stairs before going home.

At last, a government agency became involved. "We have located relatives," they told Mum, "and they will come and look after her."

"Thank goodness," said Mum.

A young couple arrived when Mum was there so she left with a sigh of relief.

I was playing out on the road that evening when this small car pulled up and asked to see Mum, so I went to get her. "We're leaving now; we'll leave her to you," they said with big smiles, and before Mum could answer, they drove away. The car was packed to the roof with sheets, blankets and any other loot that had taken their fancy. We never saw them again and everything was back to normal.

Mum looked after the old lady for three months, and then one day in the mid-afternoon, before we returned from school, she began to make her way up the hill towards Miss McMillan's house. About halfway there she began to hear a strange noise, which seemed to be coming from the house. She went a little closer and becoming very frightened, turned, and ran all the way home. Bill Blair was home and together they drove to the house.

The noise, a high-pitched squealing, reached a crescendo as they opened the door. The downstairs was empty, but climbing the stairs they found the reason the old lady would never let them upstairs. *Rats, dozens of them, pets for a lonely old lady.* She was dead, and the rats were sad. They jumped through a manhole from the attic above, onto her bed, out the bedroom door, up the attic stairway and down through the manhole again, all the time squealing and squealing. They were saying goodbye to their friend.

Miss McMillan didn't own the house, as we children all thought. I was to find out later that she'd been the "housekeeper' to one of two brothers who had pre-deceased her, and she'd been left the right to live there until her death.

A relative of the brothers was found. Harry Bain from Mosgiel Junction, who I believe was also a relative of ours on our mother's side, was installed by the public trust to catalogue all the contents for auction. We went to visit often. Colin and I explored the house from top to bottom – the rats were gone – and we climbed into the attic. It was completely empty, except for a large fruit cake sitting on the floor with just a couple of small nibbles in it.

The pantry had tins of things like dates, raisins, sultanas and many things that hadn't been available for years because of rationing. She must have stockpiled them before the war. Here was everyone worrying about her not eating and she had more food stashed away than anyone.

Harry Bain asked Mum to take anything she wanted in return for all her work, but she was too embarrassed to ask for anything good and came away with a small pottery ashtray.

Auction day was exciting. It seemed half the populace of the plains turned up. There were some wonderful things on offer: big fluted misty pink Venetian glass ornaments, an old cylinder gramophone in working order, and other wonderful antiques all went for a song. Someone bought a nice round table with a central leg and four feet. We all climbed on the thing to get a better view and all was well until a classmate jumped down leaving all the weight on one side. *Crack*. We were dumped into the crowd when one of the feet broke off – the table was full of borer. We thought it prudent to become invisible.

Frank Dickson from Allenton bought a chamber pot with flowers on and then put it upside-down, on his head to make everyone laugh. Mr Dickson was always full of fun. He had a big family of eight girls but really wanted a boy, so they decided to have one more try. He got his son, but when the baby was six months old Mrs Dickson got cancer and died.

One morning a drama was to unfold right outside our gateway. It was quite hard for anyone driving a car towards Dunedin to see as the morning sun came up over the horizon. Mr. Allan used to ride his pushbike to work every morning and as he passed our gate he was hit from behind by a Rover car being driven by a young lady who didn't have a driver's licence. Mum phoned for the ambulance and rushed out to help. Mr Allen was quite badly injured, and we children caught a fleeting look before being told to get off to school and stop staring. He was unconscious and covered with blood, the sandwiches for his lunch scattered over the road. All Mum could talk about afterward was how awful it was that Roy (our dog) wandered around eating Mr Allan's lunch while the poor man lay there. Sometime later he got quite a big payout and it was the talk of the Taieri how Mrs Allen did a lot of redecorating, sent a lounge suite to get recovered then before it could be unloaded sent it back to be done again because she didn't like the colour.

In 1943 we had an addition to the family: our step-brother was born at Nurse Gibson maternity home in Mosgiel. Mum told me many years later that he was "an accident' as she was already thirty-five years old. They called him Malcolm Mawson, after Sir Douglas Mawson who Grandma said was a relation. We were told we could visit her on the way home from school and see the baby. Wanting to give Mum a present, I used a flat kitchen knife to raid my money box and managed to prise out a whole five shillings. But what to buy? I had never been shopping before. My school friend and I found a dairy and I found I could get a small chocolate bar for one shilling. So I bought *five* of them. Mum asked where I had got the money so I told her, and she said she didn't know I had that much in there.

I adored my little brother and was tickled pink to have him home and watch him being fed. The subject of the money for the chocolates came up again. Mum agreed with her mother that I couldn't possibly have had all that money in my money box and Grandma said I had stolen it out of her handbag. Nothing I could say would change their minds and I was deeply hurt. My joy and act of kindness had turned to ashes.

As Malcolm grew up, he became my little shadow; he was a cute kid, but utterly spoilt. Mum had most of his clothes made, there not being a lot of children's clothes on the market at that time He was a proper little Lord Fauntleroy, all dressed up to the nines. He had piles of toys, all the things we'd never had, and was to grow up expecting everything for nothing.

Alma, Gwen (Billie), Colin, Lorna

Each year Dad would shut off one of the paddocks to let it grow into hay, so at the weekend and half the summer holidays, we would be instructed to take the cows out to feed on the side of the road. We would let them graze their way to the golf course, down Owhiro Road, and spend the rest of the day on the grass road that ran alongside the railway line. This way Dad could keep ten cows and two horses on ten acres. There was a fairly deep creek draining from the golf course and going under the road, black and white striped Perch swam languidly underneath, but try as we might, we never did succeed in catching one with our pin on the end of a string.

One hot, humid, summer's day, Colin and I wandered off barefooted, down the road towards Allanton for no particular reason. I wore my favourite sleeveless, linen dress, the cream-coloured top hanging straight down to the hips, the big pleats completing it a light tan. A real 1920's design and how I loved that little dress. We had just passed the Stevenson's place when an amazing summer storm arrived – lightning, thunder, and torrential rain. There was nowhere to shelter save for a small willow tree on the other side of the ditch, so under there we went. Within minutes we were soaked and the rain showed no sign of stopping. The nearest house was an old two-storey wooden house where the three Miss Stevensons lived. It was the old original early settler home before their brother (father of our friends) had built the new brick one on the hill for his wife and family.

"We have to go for shelter," Colin said and grabbing my hand we raced across and down the road, up the drive and banged on the door.

The two elder Miss Stevensons were at home. "Oh, my goodness, look at you, come in, come in, you will have to dodge the buckets, the roof is leaking." It certainly was. They had buckets, pots and basins everywhere with leaks making big plopping noises as the drips landed. We were ushered into a room with a roaring wood fire, towels were produced and we were towelled down. We had never met them before but they seemed to know who we were, and they were two of the nicest old ladies I have ever met. How they laughed about what we could wear.

"We can't send you home in wet clothes and we have no children's clothes."

An assortment of clothes was produced and eventually I was kitted out in a singlet, shortened at the top with safety pins, an enormous pair of bloomers, safety-pinned at the waist, a blouse and a jacket coat which came down to my ankles. Colin had similar attire without the bloomers; he was given a towel to wrap around his waist and secured with a pin. We were not exactly happy with the spectacle we presented but being well brought up children we would not have dared argue with an adult. Eventually the rain stopped and, fortified with cups of cocoa, we were sent on our way, slinking along the road verge ready to make a dive for cover should a car appear. Luckily none did, but the luck ran out when we got home. We had just got in the back door when Mum came out of the lounge and burst out laughing. We were dragged in to be shown to her visitors and everyone had a good laugh, except us.

While we lived at East Taieri we went to the Presbyterian Church opposite the school every Sunday. At first, we had a really nice minister, good looking, smiling and outgoing. He came to our house to baptise my siblings and I. We had to go to him one by one, where he dribbled water onto our heads; he said his words and the parents said theirs. When it came to my turn, I was so embarrassed I tried to dart away after the water bit but he grabbed my arm and pulled me back – I wanted to crawl into a hole and die.

At church, all the young ones sat up the front for the first part of the service while he included us in his talks, after that we went out the back to Sunday School. Here we learnt all about Jesus being born in a stable, how he walked on water, changed water into wine and even fed thousands with three loaves and a few fish. It all sounded a little fishy to me, and I gave it a good deal of thought. I guess I was born a sceptic, and I remember thinking I had never heard such a load of rubbish in my life.

Soon we were to lose our minister when he went off to be an army chaplain; he was replaced with a man as dull as ditch water. He had black hair, a face like a long drink of water, gloomy and white. His sermons were just as gloomy. I don't think I ever saw that man smile. His name was Horace someone or other, so the older boys quickly labelled him Horace Horse-face and soon the inside cover of almost every hymn book had a caricature of him with Horace Horse-Face written underneath. I thought it was funny at the time, but now that I am old I realise how hurt the man must have been. Children can be so cruel.

We gave the nice Mrs Miller a lift home from church one day. I sat with her in the back and couldn't take my eyes off her. The poor woman had a nervous affliction: every time she breathed in, she flared her nostrils alarmingly, like a horse that had just run the Grand National.

Sometimes if we were good and didn't have school in the morning we would be allowed to stay up and listen to the nine o'clock news from London. This was a nightly ritual and you could have heard a pin drop as we waited. It used to start with Big Ben striking nine, then "This is the nine o'clock news". The broadcast was full of static and weee-wooo noises. I used to think these noises came straight from the battle field, and conjured visions up in my mind's eye of bullets flying, and shells exploding.

This and the papers were how we kept up with the war news. Every week the Auckland Weekly, a journal with a deep pink cover and a lot of photographs in the middle, printed the photos and names of soldiers fallen in battle.

For three consecutive years during the war our mare Peggy was put to stud with a stallion called Sir Galahad, at Wingatui, with sad results. The first year the foal met with an accident that I can't remember the details of. The next year Peggy was being led home along the road home with foal at foot when a car passed. The foal took fright and darted out under its wheels and was killed instantly. This was a terrible blow and Dad was visibly upset: I expect the stud fees had been expensive. But Peggy was quickly collected by another farmer who took her away to suckle a foal whose mother had died giving birth. The third year it looked as though we had finally got lucky – she had a filly we called Kenwin, and she and her Mum had the run of two paddocks. The foal, as foals are wont to do, used to race through the gate between the two paddocks and back again as fast as her part-thoroughbred legs would take her.

We had Taranaki gates on the farm, these are made from four strands of barbed wire, attached firmly to one gate post then nailed to, and held apart, with four or five stout stakes, usually straight lengths of Manuka. To shut the gate you hooked the end stake into a loop of wire on the bottom of the other gate post, threaded another short and thinner stake, attached to the post with twisted plain wire, through the top of the gate and pulled it right around until was lying flat along the top wire and held with another small loop. This strained the gate tight and it became part of the fence.

October 25th 1944 started out like any other day. Lorna and Colin were roused early to help Dad with the milking; Alma, who had been sick with a cold for a week was sleeping out in Grandma's cottage where Grandma could mind her; I got up and did my usual chores. I washed, dressed in my school clothes, made my bed neatly and emptied my chamber pot – we used to call them our *jerries*, goodness knows why, but our brother called his *the gozunder*. After that I did my usual "push your breakfast around the plate and pretend to be eating it' routine while Mum nagged that I would be late for school. Lorna and I set off on our bikes while Colin, who was late doing his chores, said he would catch us up. He never did.

Dad went out to see the foal and found her lying flat on the ground in a pool of blood.

She had a jagged tear running from between her ears and down almost to the tip of her nose. It was obvious that she'd tried to run through the gate full belt before it was quite light and smacked hard into the Taranaki gate.

He went in to tell Mum that disaster had struck yet again, and she and Grandma went out with him to the paddock. When Grandma returned to her cottage, she found Alma dead.

Mid-morning at school the door of my classroom opened and Headmaster Paddy Kane stood there, asking if I could please be sent out? My sister Lorna was with him in the corridor. He took us both back to his office and sat us in front of his desk. He had some sad news for us, he said. We had lost Alma.

The next few days are somewhat of a blur. We are riding our bikes towards home. I ask Lorna, "Do you think perhaps she isn't dead. He said she was lost …"

Lorna said she didn't know, that we will have to wait until we got home. I don't remember getting home. I was crying and needed somewhere to hide. I left the house by the front door and went around the side. Grandma is standing by the washhouse crying. She sees me.

"It's all your fault," she said. "She would have still been alive if you hadn't brought that cold home."

Horrified, I turned and ran, broke the outside green cover of the macrocarpa hedge and climbed inside. It was safe and sheltered in there, and I climbed up on a branch and curled up.

The next day the coffin came home. The place was full of visitors, who brought flowers and said kind words. Mrs Sutton, the wife of Colin's bagpipe teacher, walked all the way from East Taieri bringing a bunch of flowers cut from her garden. It was worth more than all the others. The coffin was open but I kept out of the way.

On the day of the funeral, Mum called me to the room where Alma was lying. Did I want to see Alma before they closed the coffin? I said no. *Why did I say that? Yes! Yes! I want to see her.* But I said nothing, kept hanging on to the door frame as the coffin lid was closed. Later, when the room was quiet, I slipped in and said my quiet goodbyes. The coffin lid had a thick white enamel plate on it – on it was her name and date – the lettering yellow or gold – how pretty it was. We children were taken to Bill Blair's while the funeral took place. Jean, his wife, stayed with us. Bill came in in his best black suit; asked Jean to inspect his ears to see if he had washed out all the coal dust. He had. I thought it funny. We asked if we could watch the funeral go by and she said yes. Their house was on a rise a little way off the road. The funeral cortege was coming – we counted the cars – nineteen – and were amazed. We had never seen so many together and there was petrol rationing.

I really missed my sister, her passing left a big hole in my life, but I was to see her just one more time.

About six weeks after her death I had an awful nightmare. I still see it now, legs without bodies, a parade of them walking past my face. I woke up absolutely petrified. Dad arrived almost at once to get Lorna up to milk the cows. She got dressed while I told her all about it. I asked her to leave the light on when she left and she did, then Dad came along and turned it off, saying we couldn't waste power. I curled up in my bed and cried.

Lorna and I slept in single beds, one on each side of a casement window. When I opened my eyes, Alma was there. I could see her quite plainly: she was facing the window and her head was turned towards me. The very early morning light was just beginning. Her lips were closed but she was smiling down at me. She had on her favourite dress with the white Peter Pan colour, the one whose belt she'd left at the top of the tree. I forgot she was dead, and just poured out my troubles:

"I had this awful dream, and Dad won't let me have the light on," etc. then I felt very peaceful. I must have dozed off, and when I looked again it was still not light but Alma was gone.

I believe her spirit stayed around for several months after she died, as several times I heard her calling me. That summer I was sitting on my knees in the orchard, on a spread-out blanket in the long grass and was playing with some toys when I quite distinctly heard her calling me: "Gwennie." Startled, I turned around to see where she was, but of course there was no-one. It is interesting that she showed herself to no-one else, but then as far as I know, I am the only member of the family who is a little bit psychic.

Colin told me many years later that he'd still been home when Alma was found dead. Dad had left with the herd, and he'd been sent to catch him up.

He was already a mile south when he'd reached him. "I just said "Alma's dead' and he said "put the dogs out to turn the cattle and put them in Doug Murray's paddock', then he'd turned the horse and galloped home." Colin also told me that Alma had choked on her tongue, something we'd not been told.

There were lots of things never mentioned in our family, our mother was just one. It was as though she had never existed. "Grandmother' was the only one I ever heard speak of her and that was when she was telling me spiteful things about our father. Maybe they thought that by being silent they would cause us less hurt, who knows? I do know that, as I grew older, I became increasingly angry and more resentful. I read a book with a Rebecca in it and thought what a strange English name – it wasn't until I was fourteen that Frances told me our mother's name was Rebecca and that they had called her *Beccy*.

Our father was a strange and taciturn man, quite happy in his own company, a typical Capricorn. Oddly he could be quite amusing in company and was an amazing mimic. But none of us can remember him showing us any sort of affection and we wouldn't have dared to ask a question about a forbidden subject.

Not long after Alma's death Dad announced that he had bought another farm at Otakia, we would be moving further down the plain. He said the house was a dreadful mess, old Ma Morrison and her son had lived there and the son had kicked some of the door panels out when he was drunk. The place was actually a Shand lease, 144 acres, a piece of it on each side of Centre Road. The Shand brothers owned large tracks of the plain and many farms were leaseholds. When a farm changed hands only the improvements were sold, that is house, barn, byre, fences, and these were all in bad condition so I expect Dad got the lot for a song.

Dad was very well known on the plain – everyone knew Davey Donaldson and surprisingly he was well liked. Mrs Morrison had probably told him she was desperate to sell.

Dad moved all the four-legged stock south and stayed down there a month or so to clean up before we moved in. Meanwhile Grandma made arrangements to have her cottage jacked up and put on a truck to be moved while we all got busy packing.

A Mr McClellan bought our place at East Taieri and was to live there many years until his death.

When Dad came home that last weekend to help with the shift, I heard him telling Mum the most awful story that was to give me the horrors for years to come.

Seems there was a wood stove at the new house and in the evening after milking he would open the oven door to let the heat out into the room. In the morning he would shut the oven door and light the stove, banking it up with coal before going out to milk the cows. One morning he came in and smelt meat cooking, he opened the oven door and found a half-grown kitten, nicely cooked on the oven tray. He said it must have climbed in there to keep warm sometime during the night, and it made him sick to think about what he'd done.

That then was my farewell to East Taieri.

Apart from the death of Alma I don't remember being unhappy there, but sorrow lies deep like the winter snows.

Otakia 1945 – 1953

The old wooden house at Otakia faced west towards Centre Road; it was the usual two eyes and a nose variety, the nose being the front door in the middle with a casement window either side. The door led into a central hallway that had two reasonably sized bedrooms either side with built-in wardrobes at both sides of a fireplace in each room. The fireplaces fascinated me: they were completely made from iron; their deep fireboxes had a trap door above so you could shut off the chimney. Not too many years later, when people started to restore old homes, these fireplaces became very expensive and hard to come by. Some of the models had coloured tiles on each side but ours had tiles under the firebox only and on the hearth.

Past the bedrooms, the hall door opened into a room that stretched from a metre past the left of the door to the south wall with another casement window. To the left of the door, on the north wall of this room were two small rooms and directly opposite the hallway a half glass door led out into the back yard. Dad said it used to be the front door.

"Old Ma Morrison used to sit here with the hall door open and she could see what was going on down at the road."

On the back wall stood the aforementioned wood stove and to its right, another door led into the scullery where Dad installed a new kitchen sink and an electric stove. The wash house was behind this again with its big brass copper and concrete twin tubs. The house had no bathroom so Dad built a stand for the tin bath at the end of the wash house. On bath night the copper was lit to heat the water, which was then ladled into the bath.

The house stood a little way in from Centre Road; the drive crossed over Duck Creek a few metres inside the gate and bumped its way up along the front of the house and around the south side where stood the outbuildings, comprising garage, workshop with the big open woodshed behind.

If you stepped out the scullery door a path led up to the outdoor lavatory and behind that stood the henhouses facing north.

A lifetime before, the house had been surrounded on three and a half sides by a macrocarpa hedge, the trees from it on the south side were now massively tall and hanging over the drive, those going north from the hen sheds and along the north side and halfway along the front were now just a row of tall white stumps. It was out beyond the stumps facing the hen sheds that Grandma's cottage found its new home and Dad built a six-foot high wire netting fence around it for her garden. There were no fences around the house at all and Lorna and I were often shocked to see a cow looking in our bedroom window, especially if it had a white face and it was the middle of the night. The window had no curtains or blinds, nor did it ever have them. After all, our parents argued, who was there to see? It looked out onto a paddock. How I came to hate that window.

As to the allocation of the bedrooms, Lorna and I had one, Mum and Dad had one front room and Malcolm the other and the room opposite us was the "guest room'. This was of course quite ridiculous, just pandering to Mum's snobbery as we can remember it being used just twice in all the years we were there. There it was, all decked out with a pink satin bedspread and matching pillows, while poor Colin had to sleep in one of Dad's army huts that had been brought from East Taieri. It had been put out in the garden beyond the two big pear trees and it was freezing out there in the winter. We used to heat bricks in the oven, wrap them in newspaper and a towel to put in his bed to warm it up. He had a heap of heavy patchwork quilts on his bed made from pieces of woollen clothing.

Thank goodness it wasn't too long before Dad fenced the garden in with wire netting. We planted a quick-growing hedge along the north side, and a wooden fence was eventually installed along the front and south side leading up to the house. I recall this well, as I was given the job of painting it all with old engine oil, both sides – it seemed to take forever.

About fifty metres behind the house was a big flood bank that protected us from the Taieri River just beyond. I didn't know it then, but the river was to become my refuge and escape in the boring years ahead.

With so much to do when we first moved in, everyone was put to work. After doing my house chores, I had to feed the hens and ducks every morning and night. In the morning they got mash, which meant mixing the pollard and bran up in the required proportions, stirring in hot water, and putting it in their feed bins. Sometimes I would boil up all the potato peelings and vegetable scraps and add it to their mash. At night they got wheat. I collected the eggs the ducks laid first thing in the morning. They couldn't be let out too early or they would toddle off to the river and drop their eggs in the water. The hens laid sometime during the day and could be relied on to come back inside to lay in the nest boxes. I raked over the deep litter in the sheds and once a week scraped down the dropping board under the hens' perches. This was a job I loathed and sometimes left it for weeks until I got told off and I couldn't put it off any longer. Dad had installed the dropping boards to keep the floor clean, I would scrape the manure into buckets then cart it to the compost heap.

One of the first jobs that had to be done was the building of a new cow byre, the old one up near the house being totally inefficient. The new one was built to the latest design down near the road and opposite our forty-four acres on the other side of the road. It is still there today, and still in use seventy years later. It featured a walk-through design, and when the cow was finished milking we simply pushed the door open with a long pole attached to the door, and out she walked.

Before too long all the fences were repaired or replaced and the paddocks acquired names. The acres over the road were divided into four squares and called the bottom paddocks, the dry cows were usually housed there over winter. One bull paddock was beside the cow byre, the other one beside the drive and near the house. The front paddock was in front and up the side of the house, the bridge paddock went up into the corner beside the old wooden bridge over the river. In front of that was the Manse paddock, so-called because nestled in the corner was our small Presbyterian church and beautiful two-storey manse. No chance of getting out of going to church now, mores the pity. All we had to do was walk over and climb through the fence. There were also several small paddocks mostly near the house

Because the wind from the south could be vicious Dad planted windbreaks of fast-growing Radiata pine and fenced them in to stop the cattle smashing them down. It became my job in the summer to cut all the long grass from around the small trees until they grew high enough to survive. Later the tops were cut off each year to keep them low.

After a big storm uprooted two big macrocarpas not far from the house Dad had the contractors in to take the side off those that hung over the drive. If one of them had fallen it would have smashed the house. He then strung three strands of wire the length of the row of trees and threaded Manuka brush through them, pushing it up tight to make a wonderful windbreak for the house.

At first, Colin and Lorna helped with the milking, and then Colin was sent to boarding school, the Otago Boys High, where he frittered his time away for two years. The boarding hostel was run by Aunty Frank (Frances) my step grandmother's sister.

I then had to take my turn in the byre with Lorna. I delighted in teasing my sister, squirting milk at her from a cow's teat when she walked by or turning the hose on her; she would belt me and I would yell and then Dad would shout at me.

Over the road from our drive gate lived the Taylor's, a family with eleven children; Mum said they were rough. Some of the clan had already left home and were living on other farms. I thought it very odd that some of the grandchildren were older than their aunties. Mr Taylor always kept Mrs Taylor very short of money and she had a dreadful struggle to make ends meet. Of the children still at home there was

Rita, a lovely girl who I was to meet again several years later and who became a lifelong friend; Ronny, a quiet and shy lad who was Lorna's age; Betty, who was my age; Murray, an outrageous child who once cut the leg off a rooster with the axe and watched it trying to run around the yard. Beverley was the youngest and forever a lovely person.

They had a pet magpie that had its wing clipped so it couldn't fly. It was called Maggie, (of course) and for some reason it hated Beverley. Maggie would always fly at her and peck her feet. Maggie was under their car when I saw the family going to leave one day, and as they climbed into the car Maggie rushed out and attacked Beverley's legs. She could even tell whose feet they were. No one ever worked out why she attacked Beverley, as she had never been cruel to her. Luckily, Maggie took a liking to me.

Just inside our road gate Dad had a crisscross pile of split blue gum posts, and every afternoon Maggie would make the trip over the road to sit there and welcome me home from school. As I reached our gate and put my arm through to release the chain, she would say, "allo."

How I loved that little bird. I always stopped to talk to her. "Hello, Maggie, how are you today?"

Maggie had also acquired other phrases, one of which was, "Get and get the cows,"– that was Mrs Taylor shouting at Murray, we said. It was rare for me to see a car on my way home from school but one day a car sped past me outside our cow byre. I was angry as I was showered in stones and dust. When I reached our drive gate I found Maggie lying in the middle of the road, dead. She'd been coming over to welcome me home when the speeding car had struck her. I picked her up and burst into tears. Poor faithful little Maggie had given her life for me.

We always kept a small mob of sheep that Dad called killers. About once a fortnight he would bring them into the sheep yard, under two big willow trees beside the flood bank at the back of the house. The next morning he would select one and kill it for the table. After cutting its throat he would attach the hind legs to a meat hook and pull it up on the pulley to punch off the skin. This he would hang to dry on the fence before gutting the carcass, covering it with cheesecloth, and pulling it high into the tree above the flies. The meat would hang there for a day to set. It was then bought down, sawed down the middle and carried into the scullery to be cut into useable pieces. Neck chops, forequarter, chops and back legs. He would save the liver as well, unless it had tiny hydatids cysts on it, in which case it would be boiled up for the dogs or buried with the rest of the guts. The meat was stored in our meat safe out behind the shed, under the trees where the cool southerly breeze blew through it. Surprisingly it kept well out there. We ate meat three or four times a day. Liver or chops for breakfast, roast or boiled mutton cooked with carrots and onions for lunch, and cold meat for tea. I never liked liver the way Mum cooked it. She would put it in the pan before we even left the cowshed and it was like trying to eat a thick piece of shoe leather. It was years before a London butcher told me, "Skin it, slice crossways very thin and fry quickly on each side." Now I like to soak it in milk and toss it in seasoned flour.

When we left our cowshed after milking we would walk along the road to our drive gate and in doing so would have to walk past the Taylor's cowshed. Lorna and Ronnie grew to an age where they were very conscious of each other and Ronny would be watching as we went by. This was a situation just made for me.

"Oooh, look, Ronny's watching you."

"Shut up," she would say, staring straight ahead. Then I would run ahead of her, just out of striking distance, bend my legs and stick my bottom out as far as I could and walk along in front. Poor Lorna used to be so embarrassed.

"Just wait till I get you," she would snarl through closed teeth.

Lorna told me many years later that Dad told her that if she had anything to do with Ronny Taylor he would kill her. I often wondered if it was Dad's serious lack of education and restricted vocabulary that made him say some of the dreadful things he said.

When the first summer holidays came to an end I was packed off to the Momona School. No more nice tar sealed roads for me, just four miles of rough, corrugated, gravel road. I am not sure what was the worst, the corrugations or after the grader had been and spread several inches of loose gravel over the road. This was to be my route for five days a week for the next five years, through frosty mornings, to howling southerly headwinds on the way home, although, a few times when the weather got really wild Dad would bring the car to pick me up. I was given a strict time to be home by 4 pm never mind the weather. Our teacher throughout the war years was a Miss (Mrs) Sproule; she drove a little car down from Mosgiel each day. In the schoolhouse next door lived Mrs Jenkins and her infant son. She was the wife of the incumbent teacher, her husband Ray, having gone off to the war. Miss Sproule was a mild-mannered, competent teacher. She always wore a light-coloured tweed suit to work, and long white bloomers almost to her knees. We all knew because there was no front to her desk, and you could almost see what she had for breakfast. The boys thought it was a huge joke, and she never seemed to catch on.

I was surprised to find that the games we played at Momona were the same as the games at Mosgiel and East Taieri schools, and I was to find later they were also international, many going back to early England.

We would join a line holding hands, the first in line leaning her arm on the school wall, then thread the line through each space until everyone had crossed arms and faced the other way, all the time singing,' *The good ship sailed through the alley alley oo, the alley alley oo, the alley alley oo, the good ship sailed through the alley alley oo on the nineteenth of December.*'

Then there was *What's the Time, Mr Wolf?*, *Hide and Seek*, *Hopscotch*, *Oranges and Lemons*, skipping and many more. I was very proud that I was the only one who could skip Double Dutch (using two ropes) until I taught some of my friends to master it.

On the farm, Dad was endeavouring to start a milking Shorthorn stud and to that end began to buy up a few pedigrees. The first acquisition was a cow called Hurricane, a very nice cow with beautiful conformation – straight back, long body – but she had a small udder and didn't give a lot of milk. He bought a bull, whose name I don't remember, then another cow called Remu, who was dark red and solid – she cost a whole £100. We got one heifer calf from her, and then sadly she died after dropping her next calf, a very big roan male. We had her in the small paddock between the back of the house and the flood bank and it took forever for her to calve, then she just lay down and wouldn't eat or drink. I bought handfuls of lush grass to her nose, talked to her and pleaded, but to no avail. She appeared to be quite well, the vet thought she might have milk fever, but after a few days she died. We worried about the calf. He was languid and slow, so we took milk from other newly calved cows and handfed him and eventually he rallied. We called him Douglas and he ended up being very cheeky and needing a firm hand. We never did succeed in having a full shorthorn herd, not like our neighbours, the Bryant's, who had a magnificent herd of Friesians. Our herd was made up of Jerseys, flighty Ayrshires, Friesians, (low butterfat but plenty of volume) Shorthorns and goodness knows what else.

At East Taieri, Colin had learned to play the bagpipes and in the early days at Otakia he was still playing. He joined the Taieri pipe band for a while and had a magnificent kilt in the McPherson tartan. They competed one year in the massed bands at Carisbrook but were not placed anywhere. He normally practiced his playing on the chanter out in his hut. One delightful summer evening, not long after we took over the farm, he decided to play his bagpipes out the front of the house. What followed remains to this day one of the funniest things I have ever seen. Cows love music; they let their milk down more quickly if there is music in the cowshed. My father once drew my attention to an old jersey cow rocking back and forward to the beat of a good tune – but I don't think they had ever heard the bagpipes. So there they all were, out in the paddock in front of the house grazing quietly after milking when Colin started to play. I saw the nearest cow jerk her head up and look; then she stuck her tail straight up in the air and started racing around in circles. It wasn't long before her frivolity had infected the entire herd of about seventy cows; they all followed suit and rushed madly around, tails in the air with the fluffy bits on the bottom waving like flags. I rushed inside to tell everyone and they all came to look. How we laughed. I kept thinking they were going to collide with one another, but they didn't. Dad was heard to say, "If they carry on like that much longer there will be no milk in the morning."

Over the years I stayed at Otakia we acquired a few horses. In the early days on the farm, we would ride the mare Peggy, as she was never put to stud again by us. On one memorable occasion I rode her bareback at a canter up the drive at the side of the house. I had completely forgotten that our clothesline, a piece of number eight fencing wire, held up with a prop, went from a pole at the back of the house to the shed. The wire caught me right across the throat and dragged me off her back to land with a thump on the ground behind her. Apart from a sore throat, I was unharmed. It was a mistake I was never to make again.

Dad, who was a real wheeler-dealer – I expect that's where I get it from – would go to the yearly horse sale at Allanton and usually come back with something. Once he bought a beautiful horse gig with brass lamps. He spent time restoring it, painting it grey and black. It was in the barn for some time before he sold it at a good profit. The first horse to arrive was our draught horse, Baldy. He was the workhorse, a big placid bay with four white feet. He developed "greasy heels' and would stand out under the trees near the house stamping his back feet so hard the ground shook. He did all the farm work until we got the tractor. Next came a little brown pony for Lorna which came to a very sad end. One morning early, she was found to be standing between the drive and the bull paddock fence with a big slash about five inches long at the top of her back leg. It was about two inches deep, and the vet said it was too deep to stitch. He left Lorna some solution to paint on twice a day. We were at a loss to know how it had happened. Dad said she must have been standing with her back end against the fence and been gored by one of the bulls. But even this seemed unlikely; their horns didn't seem sharp enough. Poor wee pony, she was so sore she refused to move, and pull as we might she wouldn't budge. Nor would she lie down, until many days later she went to sleep standing and fell, breaking a front leg. The vet said she would have to be shot, so Mr Bryant came with his 303, and she was dragged away with the tractor to be buried while Lorna and I hid away and cried.

The next horse to arrive was a big horse of unknown history. Someone said he looked like the horse that had won the open jumps at the Taieri show one year. Looking back now I think he must have been a thoroughbred hurdler, and what fun we had with him. He was an unusual dark red colour and no paddock could contain him. We named him Red Racer.

Just after we got him Dad was bringing in the cows when the horse got the bit between his teeth and bolted off down the road. Now Dad was a good horseman but Red Racer took him all the way to Henley before he could pull him up and turn for home.

Red Racer calmly jumped out of everywhere we put him, so Dad, being fed up with his nonsense, put him in the bull paddock near the house. It was surrounded with a high, seven-wire fence. "Just let him jump out of there," he said.

Oh dear, famous last words. One day we saw him walk over to the fence to measure the height, just like a showjumper, then he turned and trotted back to the other side of the narrow strip. With a flying run he flew over the seven wires with a foot to spare, across the front paddock, hopped over into the manse paddock, across that, over the fence onto Otakia Road, over the fence into Bryant's, and so on. Dad found him later quietly grazing two miles away in a paddock at Henley. I think he was missing the excitement of the race track.

Strangely enough, I was the only one who could catch him; he wouldn't have a bar of anyone who ran after him. I think he must have been badly beaten by someone before we got him. The trick was to walk quietly around the paddock behind him, however big it was, (and did that cheese me off) and whenever you got near to him to stop and talk quietly. Then I would approach him one step at a time, still talking quietly. No use holding the bridle behind your back, I kept it in full view. By the time I was right in front of him he would be shaking like a leaf. I would put my hand up slowly and touch him and every nerve in his body would jump. I jumped myself the first time he did this, after all, he was much bigger than I. But I kept my cool, scratched him behind his ear and quietly slipped the reins around his neck before getting the bit in his mouth.

One night after milking I was riding him around the yard at the back of the cow byre to turn the cows back into McLeod's paddock when Dad yelled, "Keep a firm hold of that horse or he will bolt on you."

"Oh Dad, he won't," I said, and he never did. I think he knew that I would never do him any harm. Dad eventually sold him, at a profit no doubt, because Dad was like that.

The next horse to arrive was Jean. Dad rode her home from the sale one day before milking. I was about seventeen at the time and working out by the barn.

"Oh, my God," I exclaimed, "she's ugly!"

"Well just for that you can't ride her," he said.

But ride her I did. The best little horse I've ever had. She was a pony size, about 13.3 hands and built like a half draught horse – big feet, feathery fetlocks. Her tail, which should have been long, had been chewed by calves. (I never could understand why calves liked chewing horsetails.) She was bay coloured – black mane and tail, and black hairy feet. Years later, when I knew much more about ponies I realised she was the epitome of a Dales pony. She was strong, with incredible stamina, but free of movement and not only light-footed but sure-footed as well. I could ride her down into a borrow pit, across and up the other side, then up and over the flood bank at a canter without her breaking stride. By nature she was gentle and placid and was to prove it one night shortly after we got her when I made a bad mistake. I had ridden her home from the cowshed after milking and went to dismount in front of the barn. I had been taught to take both feet out of the stirrups and jump down, but this night I took my right leg out, swung it over her back and stepped down, only to find my left foot, clad in a gumboot, firmly wedged in the other stirrup. I knew I was in big trouble – had she bolted I could have been killed or at least seriously hurt.

"Good girl, Jean. Stand now, Jean," I murmured quietly as I struggled and pulled. After what seemed like half a lifetime but was probably half a minute, my foot came free. She hadn't moved a muscle. I gave her a rub down and an extra dipper of oats that night, just for being good.

For about a month I had another pony. Isobel and Eric Bryant, the nice Brethren folk from next door had bought a white pony for their three small children. They couldn't have made a worse choice. He was a proper little monster, as cunning as a cartload of monkeys. Apparently, he'd been dumping the kids off at every opportunity. Now my father was never one for handing out praise – I usually heard it second hand, and when I did, I collected the words of praise like precious gems. When I heard him say to Mum, "I told him to send it over here for a month and let Skinny lick it into shape."

I was both proud and perplexed: proud that he had the confidence in me, and perplexed because I didn't believe I could do any such thing. Well, the little beast arrived. Dad told me I should ride him every day between milking and not to let him get away with anything. The very first time I mounted him he told me who was boss within one minute. Just about twenty yards from the house there was a small borrow pit that we used for dumping household rubbish; tins, bottles, and such. I had no sooner sat in the saddle before he set off at the gallop and straight through the rubbish hole which I fell off into with a thump.

Right, you little shit" I thought, *from now on it's war.*

I caught him again and remounted. The pony's worst vice was pig rooting. Just when he thought you were relaxed, he would stamp both front feet suddenly into the ground and throw his head down at the same time. This was a carefully calculated move to throw the rider over his head. He almost unsaddled me the first time, it happened so quickly. However, I managed to scramble back into the saddle. Apart from a verbal telling off, I did nothing about it. For the next two days I tried to teach him obedience. Walk, trot, canter and stand, but no ride was complete without him trying to dislodge me at least twice. On the fourth day before saddling him, I went over to the river and cut a soft springy willow branch and stripped it of leaves, then saddled up and walked him down the front paddock, keeping a very firm hold on the reins with my left hand, but fairly loose on his bit. We had almost reached Duck Creek before he figured I had been lulled into a sense of security. Then bang, down he went. But I had been waiting. I let out a yell, jerked back violently on the reins and at the same time brought the switch down as hard as I could on his rump three times. He got the shock of his life; bucked and bounced around a bit.

"Stand!" I roared, and when he didn't he got another whack. "Stand!" He did. "Now walk!" A very shocked and subdued pony spent the next hour doing just what he was told and never again did he try to dump anyone. I don't believe in cruelty to animals, but many times a short sharp lesson is needed to stop dangerous behaviour.

After a month he went home. I had completed my task and hoped I had made Dad proud.

Baldy, the draught horse, was pensioned off when we got the small Ford/Ferguson tractor. He was asked to work, just once more, when, during a very wet winter, even the tractor got stuck in the deep black mud of the gateways. We hitched him up to the sled, much to his disgust, to feed the hay, turnips, and greens out to the cows.

Baldy and Peggy spent their last days at the farm on the skinny paddock that comprised the flood bank to the river and up to the bridge. Baldy was given to a new young farmer at Henley who was pleased to have him because he couldn't afford a tractor. Peggy developed a huge swamp cancer on her fetlock, a massive lump of proud flesh about half the size of a football, which didn't seem to worry her. I was later to learn that these growths are common amongst the horses on the cattle stations of northern Western Australia, where they wade in water a lot during the wet season. A man from central Otago rang to ask Dad if he would sell Peggy, he said he would like to get one more foal from her. Dad told him he could have her for the price of the vet removing the growth on her leg. They took her out under the trees, anaesthetised her onto a big groundsheet and performed the operation. Peggy went to her new home. The last we heard was that she'd had, not one, but four more foals.

I should explain the aforementioned *Borrow pits*. When the flood bank was built to protect the main portion of the Taieri plains from flooding, the draglines gauged out large shovels of earth to make it. They left behind large pits, some deep, some shallow, some long, some short. In McLeod's paddock the pits were long and shallow, say eight to ten feet deep, and on the farm side of the bank. The one nearest the house was deeper and had water in it most of the year. A cow got bogged in it one year and we had to pull her out with the tractor by tying a rope around her horns. I felt sick, thinking at any moment the poor beast's head would come flying off but it didn't, and with us all pushing we eventually got her unstuck.

The borrow pits on the south side of the house were all on the river-side of the bank; here the bank was further from the river. We had a small long paddock there, from the barn to the bridge. The pit nearest the barn, and by the row of old macrocarpa trees, was round and about twenty feet deep. It had water in it all year round and was quite dangerous – no way could we have pulled a cow out of there. The rest were long and shallow and made wonderful paddling pools with grassy bottoms after heavy rain, and soon had trillions of tadpoles. I have visited the same paddock after fifty years, and all the pits are gone.

The war ended in 1945 and the incumbent teacher, Mr Jenkins, came home later that year or early the next. He was a strange man, tall with dark, thickly greased hair combed back over his head. I think he had trouble settling down after the war; certainly things were not at all well in his household. I would never say he was not a good teacher, in a lot of ways he was, but he had the most violent temper. He would scream and yell, go puce in the face and his hair would fall down over his face in greasy coils. It was all very frightening. Once he threw a wooden-backed, board duster, and caught Russell Gulliver my classmate on the forehead. Certainly he wouldn't have been tolerated in today's world, and rightly so. However he did recognise in me a talent for the arts and encouraged it. He liked to hear me sing, and when Mrs Blair came to train us for the school concert he was amazed that I knew all the words of the Scottish songs. I loved to sing! I was a tiny girl with a very big voice, and knew the words to all the popular songs. He also taught us elocution, which I took very seriously and which was to hold me in good stead for the future. He was also keen that we should know about nature. We were given chores to do in the school gardens like weeding and planting out flowers. Perhaps this is where I developed my love of gardens and all things beautiful. We had to learn all the names of the trees in the schoolyard. There was a Rowan, with white flowers followed by red berries, a sycamore, which the boys made propellers from by sticking the seeds on pins. There was also a tall English Yew and I loved to suck the flesh from the berries. In the corner by the pedestrian gate, there was the beautiful wattle, *Acacia Dealbata*. It had a big spread of silver-grey leaves and brilliant yellow blossoms. The masses of tiny pompoms fascinated and amazed me. There were more – too many to list.

My best friend at school was Isabel Bissett. I called her Issie. I spoke about her so much at home they began to tease me: "And how was Issie today," or "And what did Issie say about that." Poor Issie, little did I know what the future was to bring.

My other friends were Dawn Gulliver, daughter of the manager of the cheese factory near the school, and Rhonda McDonald, whose father had a dairy farm that I passed on my way to school. Issie was a tall, gentle girl and solid like her mother – I think it was the attraction of opposites that made us close friends. Dawn was lively and full of fun, whereas Rhonda was thin, white-faced and always a good girl. She had developed hydatids when she was younger, caught from her pet spaniel dog, and had lost part of a lung. Hydatids, which was quite a scourge in New Zealand for many years, is a disease passed from sheep to dog, to humans.

Anyway, it was under the shade of the Acacia one summer's day that Issie told the three of us all about menstrual periods. "Do you know what happens to you when are fifteen? You start bleeding once a month." She went on to tell us how her sister screamed with pain all the previous night while her mother ran back and forth with hot water bottles. It was all quite frightening stuff. I remembered seeing Lorna washing a bucket of bloody rags and when she tried to hide them I said, "You don't need to hide them. I know they are covered with blood."

Later Mum said to me, "Don't you dare to make remarks about Lorna's clothes." Here again she missed a heaven-sent opportunity to tell me the facts of life.

I must admit that I never heard Mum and Dad fighting, but they must have done because one day Mum took Malcolm and went back to Dunedin. Dad seemed to take it well and allotted us all our tasks. Colin was to prepare the vegetables, Lorna was to cook the dinner, and I was to make the pudding. That was unfortunate because the only thing I could make was semolina. My first attempt was just plain and simple, but later I found some bottles of food colouring and used these to add the artistic touch. The next day I used yellow colouring, the next day pink. That looked very pretty, so I got a bit bolder and the next day it was a light blue. This got a few funny looks but as nobody complained I produced a dark red the next day. Now there was no stopping me, and I produced four plates of luminous green.

"I think that is enough," said Dad. The next day he sent Colin into town to ask Mum to come home and, thank goodness, she did. After all, I had run out of colours, and I might have had to learn to cook something else.

In March 1946, when I was eleven, we were all practicing for the school sports. Mr Jenkins had us out every day running, passing batons for the relay, doing the hop, step and jump, broad jump and high jump. For the first time since the war, we were to compete against all the Taieri schools. It was to become a yearly event, and for it to be fair for everyone, we were to be marked on the number of pupils at each school. Mr Jenkins was very keen that we should win.

I was in my element: I planned on being a great runner. One lunchtime I suggested that we bring the high backed form from beside the school wall out on to the lawn to use for our high jump practice.

Everyone agreed and the boys lugged it out past the flower beds. It looked quite scary at first as it was all of three feet high, but I flew over in my first attempt. Round and round we went. Little did I know, as my feet left the ground the next time that in an instant my life would be destroyed forever and become a lifetime struggle. I cleared the top rail, hit the ground, and my leg collapsed under me. I tried to stand but fell again. I was in no pain, and nothing seemed to be broken, but my right leg just wouldn't work.

One of the boys ran to get Mr Jenkins and he picked me up and carried me over to the schoolhouse, and put me on the sofa. He then rang old Dr Shaw, our doctor in Mosgiel. Mrs Jenkins had left him, so I was alone in the house while he went back to the classroom, and was asleep when Dr Shaw arrived. He examined me but could find nothing wrong, so he picked me up, carried me to his car, and took me home.

"Bed rest," he said. "I can't find anything wrong, but let her up as soon as she can take the weight."

A month went by, but one Sunday just after we had all sat down to eat our dinner in the middle of the day, Dr Shaw arrived.

"I've just come to see how Gwen is getting on," he said. "Come out from behind the table and let me see you walk."

By this time I had developed a bad limp. He looked very concerned. "It shouldn't have taken all this time," he said. "I want you to take her into Dunedin Hospital for x-rays."

A day later I went with Mum on the bus to Dunedin and was admitted, after x-rays, to Dunedin Public Hospital. No disrespect to Dr Shaw, I had a very rare complaint. I had a slipped epiphysis in the neck of my femur. The epiphyseal cartilage is responsible for the growth of long bones in your body; they produce new cartilage cells at the top end and ossify, (that is, turn to bone) at the bottom end against the shaft of the bone, thus your bone grows until about the age of twenty-one when the whole bone becomes solid. A slipped epiphysis usually happens only to pubescent girls.

One of the orthopaedic surgeons at Dunedin Hospital in 1946 was Mr White, a brilliant but outrageously eccentric man.

Mum said, "I always said I wouldn't let him operate on a cat of mine," when she knew who was to be my doctor. She made an appointment to see him, "And all he would say," she recounted, "was "trust me woman, trust me woman.'"

The first day in the ward Mr White came to see me with his retinue of about twelve student followers. I was lying in bed watching each student as he quizzed them about what was wrong with me. He had them all examine me. It was all very embarrassing as I had no knickers on and was sprouting new pubic hair. There was a student who looked part Chinese and had big horn-rimmed glasses. For some reason I gave him the name "Polly.' Mr White, called Effie White behind his back by everyone, asked me to describe how I had jumped over the form. *Well how the hell did I know how I had jumped over the form?* I thought.

He pointed to Polly. "You," he said, "get that stool and jump over it."

The poor boy obeyed, running up and down the ward jumping over the stool, first landing on one foot and then the other. I felt quite sorry for him. Eventually, to put him out of his misery I said that "yes, that must have been the way I landed." They were then commanded to ask me any questions and gathered around the bed, then each was invited to give a diagnosis. Nobody attempted to do this except "Polly' who was now standing on my left-hand side.

"I think it's a slipped epiphysis," he said.

Effie was ecstatic. He rushed around the bed, scattering students in his wake and pumped Polly's hand enthusiastically. I began to wonder if in fact I had been admitted to a lunatic asylum.

They decided to try and put the cartilage back into place without invasive surgery, so off to theatre I went. I had bad dreams about that anaesthetic for many months to come. I was floating in a black sea of nothingness, and far away one tiny star called, "Quuu, Quuu". I was very frightened. An even bigger fright awaited me when I came to. I was in plaster from just under my small developing boobs, down to and enclosing my right foot. I had just one leg that I could bend at the knee, and then only if I could get on my side, and had my arms free.

Worse still, they had put the plaster on when I had been breathing shallowly, and when I tried to take a normal breath, my chest hit the plaster and bounced straight back.

I panicked. "I can't breathe, I can't breathe."

Eventually, they gave me something to quieten me down and I went to sleep again. When I awoke, the plaster had been cut at the top, each side, to relieve the pressure.

Next day I was sent for x-rays. The news was not good: the operation hadn't worked. The cartilage had adhered somewhere it shouldn't have in the month before me getting to hospital. Invasive surgery was now the only option.

When next time I became aware, my bed was just inside the door of Victoria Ward. The plaster was the same, but this time it was not so tight. It also had a huge patch of blood across the front – not a wholesome sight when you don't feel very well. After three days it was starting to smell badly, so back to theatre I went again where they put me under again to change the plaster, and no doubt dress the wound. I don't remember much of the next few days, except that, with the weight of the plaster cast and the hard horsehair mattress, I developed a bad bedsore. They turned me on my face to relieve the pressure.

It was awful. There was a pillow under my head and the heavy plaster was weighing me down. My neck became very sore and I turned it this way and that, crying with frustration. I was caste like a sheep, unable to turn over. They allowed me just one hour a day on my back. That hour seemed like minutes, the rest of the hours like days. When that healed up, I developed a temperature of 104 degrees. The wound was infected. For days I boiled inside the thick plaster lined with flock, the stuff they put in ordinary mattresses. One day a piece of gauze worked its way out the top. I pulled it all out and found a line of bright green goo on it. The junior nurse I handed it to was very insecure and was going to throw it away but I had the sense to tell her to show it to Sister.

Eventually, I came right and got bored and cheeky. Dear Uncle Neil came to see me several times bringing me good things. One day he arrived with a precious gift: a kaleidoscope, a tube I could look into with lots of coloured pieces in the end. When I turned the end it made wonderful patterns. I couldn't have had anything better. At Easter he arrived with a big Easter egg – I felt like a princess as I'd never had a big Easter egg before. Mum came to visit a lot at first, but Dad came just once, and as I got better Mum came less often. In these days of fast cars the miles would be nothing, but back then it meant a whole day away from home and several changes on the bus.

Effie White came to visit me several times a week and frightened the hell out of me. "Give me a kiss," he would demand.

"No, go away." I'd pull the sheet over my face.

"Well, just for that I will take you to theatre and get all the kisses I want."

Oh God, would he really do that, I was never quite sure.

Another day he arrived, walking quietly into the ward; Sister and all the nurses disappeared like magic. He walked past my bed saying nothing. All the children watched, now quite used to his antics. He went around the ward collecting all the cloth dolls from the children's beds, even some from the toy box. (Ragdolls were all that was allowed because they could be put in the autoclave and sterilised). He piled them all on the centre table. Then, picking one up in his right hand and pointing at me with his left, he proceeded to throw every doll at me. I grabbed the ones that landed on my bed and shoved them under my bed cradle. When he ran out of ammunition, he ran, full belt, out of the ward – he'd not spoken one word. When he had gone the Sister and nurses reappeared shaking their heads as they collected up all the dolls to redistribute them, but they would never have dared to say anything derogatory about a specialist.

Sometimes the nurses from the autoclave room came to give us some occupational therapy. They demonstrated to the older children, and to those who were recovering but still bed-bound, how to roll swabs. It was a boring job but we rolled a few dozen each day. One day, when it was quiet one of the boys suggested we try to stick some on the very high ceiling. We got one of the walking kids to soak some swabs in the ink on Sister's desk that sat at the top of the long ward. We got them to hit the ceiling, but they wouldn't stick.

"Why don't we dip them in milk," I said, indicating the glass of milk on my locker. So we did, and they stuck. We thought it hilariously funny. Nobody, but nobody gave the game away. It was several days later that Sister came in and looked up; obviously someone had tipped her off.

"What have you been up to?" she said, trying not to laugh. She fetched a chair and a long window mop and had the devil's own job trying to dislodge them.

A few years later when I visited Malcolm who was in the same ward with a broken arm, I looked up and there they were, blue and red splotches.

"See those," I whispered. "I put those there."

I was shifted down to Jubilee Ward below Victoria Ward. There was an ancient lift between the wards, the only one I have seen of its kind. The orderly would push one's bed in, shut the cage doors, and then pull on a rope that went through the corner of the lift. If he had a very big load on he would have to pull very hard before the lift started to move and trundle up or down. Ever the sticky beak, I asked how the lift worked and was told it worked by water pressure.

By this time I had learned to stand up in my plaster cast. Whenever no one was looking I would use my free leg to push myself up so that I was standing, leaning against the bed head. Then giving a triumphant yell I would push off and land flat on my back with a thump. I managed to crack two plasters in the weeks to come and was forever being scolded because they had to be changed. But what else could a girl do when she is bored stiff.

I had become very good friends with another girl my age, Fay Farmer. Fay had been admitted months previously with appendicitis but had contracted rheumatic fever, which had damaged her heart. She was on complete bed rest but was not averse to sneaking out of bed when no one was looking. Fay's mother was a lovely lady who came to talk to me when I had no visitors. Fay was shifted down to Jubilee at the same time as me and our beds were next to each other.

One of the patients was a little boy who had been seriously burnt. Several people in white coats came each afternoon to soak him in a salt bath. Whenever he saw them walk into the ward he would start to scream and his screams echoed out of the bathroom all the time he was having treatment. It was really upsetting for all the other children.

At one stage I had in the bed next to me, the most beautiful little girl. She was about six months old and had lovely black hair. She seemed to sit quietly in her cot most days and I don't think I ever heard her cry. They said she had been born with cancer and would eventually die, which made me very sad.

The hit song of the day was, "You are my sunshine, my only sunshine, you make me happy when skies are grey.' We all knew how to sing it and sometimes we had a little sing-song. My favourite nurse also sang a little ditty that was popular. She was a tall, rather solid girl with light red hair. She seemed to be older and more self-assured than most of the other nurses who kept to a strict protocol. She used to make us laugh. Every afternoon when she came on duty she would come swaggering down the long ward singing:

"Chicory Chick, cherar cherar,
checkaterony in a bananaca bollocka wollica,
can't you see – chichory chick chick is me.
Every time you're sick and tired of just the same old thing,
Doing just the same old thing all day,
Just be like the chicken who found else to do,
Open up your mouth and start to say
Chickory chick and so on...

She certainly brightened up our days.

My parents had been told that I would be in plaster from three to six months, so it was with some surprise that I was taken to the plaster room about six weeks after the operation to get my plaster off and hear

Effie White say, "Get her back to the ward and get her up and home out of it." His registrar gave him a startled look but accompanied me back to the ward to impart the instructions to Sister. She, in turn, gave the registrar a startled look.

"Get her up? Get her home?"

"That's what he said."

Effie White had decided to use me as a guinea pig. It was, and wasn't, to work.

But the staff had something better to do than worry about me. The first two jet planes in the New Zealand air force were doing a flypast over Dunedin that day. We could hear them coming. Everyone – staff and mobile patients – rushed out to the balcony to watch.

"Come on," said Fay. "You are allowed to walk now." She walked unsteadily to my bed.

"I can't. I'm frightened." I'd been sitting on the edge of the bed looking at my skinny, scaly, hairy leg trying to get the knee to bend.

"I'll help you," she said. She got on my bad side, put her arm around my waist and together we hobbled out.

What a sight it all was. The planes flew over several times, and they were past us before their sound caught up with them. One came so low past our balcony that we could see the pilot. Then they were gone. Only then were we noticed and bundled back to bed.

In the coming weeks, I had physiotherapy every day. At first I was taken by wheelchair to the hot pool, not the one they have now but a much smaller, above-ground one. One day Effie's young intern came to see me at my bed. We chatted a while and then he said, "Of course, you realise that you will never walk properly again, don't you?"

I was stunned; couldn't say anything. He said goodbye and left. For a long time, I lay on the bed wallowing in self-pity. I had always assumed that I would be normal again like kids were when they had broken legs. Why hadn't someone warned me? I shed a few silent tears hiding under the sheet, and then I got angry. How dare that man tell me that? *Well, I'd show them.* Telling me I couldn't do something was like a red rag to a bull.

After a week or so I was allowed to walk to the Physio pool but was so stiff when I came out of the water I had to be wheeled back. I stopped mucking about and making mischief and did my exercises. Life had suddenly taken on a whole new challenge.

I had never had the opportunity to learnt to swim, and one day the Physio said, "Look, it's easy, just push off, kick your feet and reach out for the wall. I promise I'll catch you."

I finally plucked up courage. I didn't reach the wall, and she didn't catch me, well not until I had breathed in a mouthful of hot water. I was fifty-two before I found the courage to go to a swim coach and learn, and although I can swim well now, I have never felt comfortable out of my depth.

Suddenly, it was time to go home.

My parents had planned a surprise. The lounge-cum-dining room had been redecorated in the fashion of the day – new brown linoleum and patterned wallpaper with a brown background. It was all very modern but made the room even darker.

A few weeks later I was reading the newspaper, and there it was in the death notices: my lovely little friend who'd been so full of life and vitality, Faye Farmer, was dead.

"I was hoping you wouldn't see that," said Mum.

Over the next few weeks, I grew stronger; made several visits to see mad old Effie which always involved hours of waiting. He said I had the best movement of any other case that had come out of Dunedin Hospital, and indeed I had. My right leg was about half an inch shorter than the left one and arrangements were made for me to have my shoes built up at the special hospital department. What a joke that was! Nobody took into account that on the farm I spent most of the day in gumboots. My built-up shoes were worn only on my infrequent visits to town, or to church.

It wasn't easy to walk up straight. I tried hard, by pulling bottom in and shoulders back and then trying to walk like that. It was so tiring. Mum was forever patting me on the bottom. "Walk straight," she would say, while Dad threatened jokingly to get a board, strap it to my back then lash my shoulders back to it.

It was months later that I was pronounced fit to return to school. The whole schoolyard stopped to look as I arrived. I was very self-conscious and balanced on one bike peddle as I pushed with the other foot across the grounds. All Mr Jenkins could say was, "Don't ride in the school ground." He told me later that I had been away too long to catch up. I would have to return to standard three again to finish out the year.

Another school year was lost.

Before long, things were almost back to normal: I played tennis, softball, cricket, (which I hated) and kicked the rugby ball with the boys. I even trained for and competed in the school sports and did well. However, I still had my stoop and limp. That year thanks to a concerted effort by all the kids and Mr Jenkins training we won the competition. Every day he had us out running around and around. One lap fast, the next slow, it certainly produced results.

Back home I was still being mollycoddled. My parents and I had been told that if I was ever to damage my hip again it would be unrepairable. Mum and Dad kept the damper on all the things I did. I wasn't allowed to ride for about four years, thus Dad's concern when I rode the rebel, Red Racer. By the time I was fourteen my stoop had become quite pronounced. We were walking through the Exchange in Dunedin one day when Mum said, "You see that lady over there?" She indicated an old lady walking on the other side of the street who was bent over from the hips. "Well, you walk just like her."

"I don't, do I?"

"Yes, I'm sorry but you do."

That worried me a lot; I must have looked like a freak. Not long after this, my leg started to ache badly. When Effie White had operated he had cut so many nerves with the huge slash he made that my leg had been frozen to the knee ever since. I could have stuck a pin in and not felt it. Moreover I had a scar so wide and hideous that every doctor I have ever had since has remarked about it.

About this time there seemed to a return of some feeling in my leg.

I eventually became distraught with the pain and told Mum and Dad that something had to be done. Effie White had now retired and the new orthopod was a Mr Allen Aldred, a lovely man and quite handsome.

"Look, Gwen," he said, "I can operate and take away all the pain but you are going to lose all the wonderful movement you have in that leg. Did you know that you have the best movement of any slipped epiphysis patient I have ever seen? I'll give your Mum a prescription for some pain killers and I want you to bear it for just a little longer because I feel the pain will eventually go away."

What else could I do but agree. He went on to say that he wanted me to come back to physio for three months to teach me to walk straight again. So, that's how it was: the pain eventually went and after toing and froing twice a week, a trip that used up most of the day, I was almost back to normal. I was never to lose my slight limp. Sometimes people who have known me for years will say, "Have you hurt your foot?"

I look at them and laugh, "I always limp," and they are so embarrassed. However I have never got over my tendency to stoop, and the more tired I get, the more I bend over.

Colin came home from boarding school where he had been time-wasting and spent maybe a year at home. He helped with the milking and did some of the tractor work. Dad put in at least one paddock of new grass each year, and a field of Chowmolia and Swede turnips to see the cows through winter. By this time we had the Ferguson tractor. It had hydraulics at the back to which you could attach a plough, scuffler or hay mower. The paddocks were ploughed, then scuffled, then harrowed. We had a big set of harrows that for some reason had prongs both sides so one had to be careful not to run over them. The tractor had a ratchet throttle and you controlled the speed by how far you pulled the handle down. If it had one fault it was the ease that you could pull the gear stick back to neutral and accidentally put it into reverse gear. Both Colin and Lorna did this, one puncturing one tyre, the other puncturing both. When it became my job to do the tractor work I was careful not to make the same mistake.

Colin got a job on the rabbit board at Kurow and left home. Lorna had left school by this time and worked at home all day. I helped with the milking each morning then ran back home for a quick wash, had breakfast, and set off to ride the four miles to school. My wash was just a lazy lick and a promise and it wasn't until Rhonda told me that I smelt of cows that I started washing properly. Being such a dreamer I was often late for school, and in my final year Mr Jenkins told me that if I was late again I would get the strap, and after he kept his promise by giving me two cuts of the best, I tried to be there on time.

Mr Jenkins now had charge of his son, Craig. It was said that Mrs Jenkins had developed Tuberculosis, though this may not have been true. It was certainly true that he transferred his violence from the mother to the son. It was quite appalling and very distressing for the rest of us to hear him beating the child in the back room while we were out for playtime. Goodness knows what small misdemeanour the child had committed. Nothing, but nothing, could have warranted those thrashings. Rhonda and I once stood below the high windows of the back room and listened in horror as he ranted and raved and lashed out with the heavy leather strap while Craig sobbed and screamed.

The Jenkins left later to go to Christchurch and I heard that Craig had left home as soon as he was old enough. Everyone knew about this man's violence, but nobody did a thing about it.

It must have been about 1948 that New Zealand had a poliomyelitis epidemic. Some people ended up in grotesque iron lungs because they were unable to breathe by themselves. Others, less affected, were crippled for life. The government closed all the schools and put us all on correspondence. It must have been a massive task, but somehow the lessons arrived each week by mail and were posted back. Crowds, we were told, must be avoided at all costs, and I think the picture theatres were closed. Out on the farm we were fairly safe, and it was three months before the schools were opened again.

At home, Lorna was paid a pittance of a wage and her board. She had to pay for her clothes and anything else she wanted out of this. She was a hard worker, much better than I, the dreamer. She was not allowed to go out at night, not like the daughters of other farmers. In fact Dad had made it quite clear that neither of his girls would be allowed to leave home until we were twenty-one.

Many years later, at a school jubilee, Lorna and I were talking to a lady I could barely remember, who said, "You know, everyone on the Taieri Plains felt sorry for you girls being shut up there on that farm and not allowed out. Everyone used to try and think up ways to get you away from the place." That remark explained a lot.

Looking back now, I wonder if our father was trying to protect us from all the bad things that could happen to us – things they hadn't told us about or was it just a desire for cheap labour. I know that the accountant must have declared that we were both being paid a good wage, because twice when I collected letters from the box at the gate I found a letter addressed to me and in it a cheque for £25 from the Inland Revenue.

"Oh," said Mum when she saw that I had opened it. "That's your father's money, not yours."

Small wonder that the accountant got a goose each year for Christmas and another for New Year. It fell to me to pluck four geese each year which really took the shine off Christmas for me.

Lorna decided to take a dressmaking course in Dunedin during the day so she could make her own clothes. She was taught to use fancy rulers to draught clothes and became an extremely good seamstress.

She was still at home when we started taking our cattle to the agricultural shows about 1948. We went to the Taieri show at Outram, down to Milton, and Balclutha and to the big winter show at Dunedin a few months later. We had a very impressive line-up. There was the big bull, a cheeky yearling bull, Hurricane the cow, and four yearling heifers.

At the Milton show one year I was a bit late bringing my heifer into the judging ring. The steward looked at me, "Here's another Donaldson," he said. "See one, see the lot."

The line up of our cattle at the Taieri Show

It was true that the entire Donaldson clan had an uncanny likeness. Our Uncle Jack, who bred Red Poll cattle at Balclutha, was sometimes called upon to judge them at the Taieri show. Mum sent me to tell him and Dad that our picnic lunch was ready at the car. I found them walking together and looked from one to the other. They were so alike I wasn't sure which one was my father until I remembered that Dad was the one with the moustache.

Step-grandmother, Lorna, Gwen, Alma, and Step-mother

One year we scooped the pool at the Taieri show. Hurricane was first in her class, also Best of All Breeds, which I didn't think she should have won. The heifers were placed first, second and third, and the bulls both first in their class. I loved the shows, being a big show-off myself. I particularly loved participating in the Grand Parade at the end of the day.

Dad would always lead the big bull, and, after Lorna left home I advanced to the small bull, with all our helpers tagging along behind with the females.

It was hard work. We had to get up to milk about 4 am; get the stock loaded and away; rush back for breakfast and then off in the car to the show grounds. The animals had to be groomed and their white patches and tails washed in Sunlight soap. We would put covers on them until they paraded for judging, and tie the ends of their tails up with a tape to the cover clip so that they couldn't soil them with manure.

Dad was invited to the Presentation dance to receive the trophy for the most points in the show, or it may have been the most points in the cattle section. Lorna asked if she could go and was given permission. The next day she said she had never been so embarrassed. Dad had been asked to make a speech and he got up and said, "If I'd knowed I had to make a speech I wouldn't have <u>came.</u>" Poor Dad, his grammar always left a lot to be desired.

That year, we also cleaned up everything at the Dunedin winter show. It was a very wet and miserable day, and much to my disappointment Dad decided we would not march in the Grand Parade. He sent me to collect up all the ribbons from our stalls, which were inside out of the rain, thank goodness, before the cattle were loaded and sent home. Not wanting to miss the parade I ran out on to the bank to watch, carrying this great armful of ribbons, red, blue and yellow fluttering in the wind. Suddenly a lady's voice said, "Goodness me, did you win all those?" I turned and saw this really high-class looking elderly couple, and was so shy I just said "Yes."

Later I realised I should have explained that we had quite a few cattle competing, but I really wasn't any good with strangers.

Being so much farther from town we rarely had visitors, so my siblings and I never got used to mixing with strangers, but there were some memorable occasions. The most frequent visitor, of course, was the stock and station agent from Wright Stevenson and Co. As soon as his car pulled into the yard any dog that was off would surround it and he would sit tight until someone came to rescue him. Our dogs had a bad reputation. Mum once asked one of the neighbours why she never popped over and she said she was afraid of our dogs, and I can't say I blamed her. The dogs were mostly tied up between each milking, but as Roy and Sweep grew old they were left to roam free.

One day some of Mum's old workmates came out to see her. One of these was a lady who had moved to Sydney, Australia some years before and was now the chief buyer for Myers fashion house. I can see her now in her smart, pale-green, fine wool suit and green court shoes with stacked leather heels. I told myself that one day, I would have some shoes with heels like that.

Another visitor, a Mr Cook, arrived unexpectedly one day. He had come to fish for trout in the river. It should be explained that, even though my father paid £100 a year for the lease of the strip of land between the flood bank and the river, everyone could walk on the "Queens Chain.' This was a law passed in the days of the early settlers, which allowed every citizen the right to walk, picnic, fish and play, on the twenty-two feet – one chain – each side of a river or along the coast, unlike England where the wealthy owned the river and the fishing and people were prosecuted for poaching if caught.

Mr Cook popped over the flood bank one day and asked if he could dig for some worms for bait. He was a gregarious man with a real gift of the gab, and my parents were soon under his spell. I wasn't so sure, so stood back and watched. Before long he was coming every weekend and getting cups of tea and the trimmings. Then he asked if he could bring his wife and the parents said, "Come for tea." He did, bringing not only his wife but their two boys as well. One was my age, the other a bit younger. Mrs Cook was a tiny fluffy lady, always trying to please, and the boys were polite and well brought up. Needless to say, all the good china came out and, after dessert, tea was served in the very best china cups.

There was a step down into the scullery from where we ate and Mrs Cook insisted on helping to clear the table. Down the step she tumbled, two good cups and saucers crashing on to the painted concrete floor. The poor woman was so embarrassed.

"Oh, my goodness I am so sorry," and on and on. I could only see the funny side of the performance and almost had apoplexy trying not to laugh. I mimicked her for weeks after and Mum would laughingly say, "Stop it, you're awful."

I believe that by the next year the relationship with the Cooks was wearing a little thin. After all, they were on a good thing, tea and cakes, milk and fresh vegies to take home. But the final straw came one lovely spring day when Mr Cook arrived with the two boys. They suggested we played cricket on the small flat patch just the other side of the flood bank from the house. I didn't like cricket because the ball was too hard but agreed to play. I took first bat and was bowled out first ball.

"That's not fair, I wasn't ready," I said and refused to be out.

"Right, boys," said Mr Cook, "let's throw her in the borrow pit."

Now we'd had quite a bit of rain, and the grassy bottomed pit beside where we were playing was about three feet deep in water. Before I could escape I was grabbed.

"Grab hold of a leg each, boys," and, with Mr Cook holding me under the arms, they began to swing me back and forward. I was terribly embarrassed: I'd never been manhandled before. Besides, I had on a skirt with big pleats, and the boys could see my knickers.

"One, two, three," they chanted, swinging me back and forward.

Just then Mum appeared up over the flood bank, her face like thunder. "Get back over here this minute," she shouted and disappeared again.

I was plonked on the grass and scrambled to my feet.

"What did we do wrong?" Mr Cook asked, looking very worried.

I shrugged. Apart from feeling a fool, I knew it was just a bit of family fun. I copped it well and truly.

"It's filthy to play around with men," she said. "From now on you will stay over this side of the bank."

It was all a mystery to me and I felt resentful that once again I was being blamed for something that was not of my choosing. The Cook's didn't come again after that.

Another night, we again had a visit from some of Mum's old friends, one of whom had returned to Dunedin on holiday. Eager to impress, our big table was carefully laid with a spotless white cloth. All the best dishes got an airing and a large leg of home-killed lamb was roasted. Vegetable tureens were filled with fresh garden peas, roast parsnips, potatoes, and pumpkin. The two larger, quite jovial, ladies sat on one side, and the thinner one on the other.

Now we had at the farm quite a menagerie of cats, most of which stayed outside. No cat was ever allowed to jump on the benches or thieve, in fact, any cat that thieved was always got rid of. So what happened next came as a surprise to us all. Mum was sitting at one end of the large table, a black cat unnoticed near her feet. Dad was at the other end carving the roast. One large lady was just remarking how great the food looked when onto the table sprang the cat. Everybody yelled, the cat took fright and hurtled the full length of the table putting one back leg into the peas as it passed. Of course, the tureens had sloped bottoms so its foot slipped sideways sending a great shower of peas all over the table and the two large ladies. There was a small stunned silence. Mum's face was a sight to behold. Poor Mum, here she had been putting on all her usual airs and graces and the ruddy cat had to go and ruin it.

The guests took it in good part, but I can't remember what happened to the peas. What I do know is that I have screeched with laughter ever since whenever I think of that night. I would have given anything to hear the conversation in the car on their way home.

We had never really kept in touch with my real mother's family. When we were at East Taieri, Uncle Lionel dropped in sometimes, a bit tiddly more often than not after a few drinks, but he was nice. He would sit me on his knee while the adults talked. As for the rest of Mum's family, I had rarely seen them, so it was with some surprise that someone rang and asked if several uncles and their wives could come to visit.

Dad decided that we would have an eeling party. Sometimes the river would be devoid of eels, other years they all came back. This was one of those years.

A week before the visit Dad collected up the guts of the sheep he had killed for the table and strung them under one of the willows that had fallen into the river. The eels came from everywhere. On the river bank we built a large bonfire, not only so we could see, but because eels are attracted to light. Dad had a gaff – a very large fish hook – fastened to the end of a wooden handle, and he stood on a small muddy ledge by the water. Time after time eels came close to peer at the light and were gaffed and hauled out. The eels were the big silver-bellied kind and quite good eating, but I didn't like them because of all the small bones. Dad was to meet his match that night when he gaffed the biggest eel I have ever seen. He managed to get it several feet up in the air prior to swinging it up on to the bank, but because the shelf where he was standing was by then wet and slippery he lost his footing and the eel escaped. Needless to say, it became the old "one that got away story" and no one believed him until I backed him up. I learned many years later that these enormous eels are in fact, sterile males.

We had a group of visitors another afternoon, though because of what happened I can't remember who they were. It was the day I got my first period. I had just turned fifteen. I had gone to the bedroom and discovered the blood and was shocked, and didn't know what to do. It wasn't a subject that had ever been discussed. Eventually, I plucked up courage to stick my head in the sitting room door and ask Mum if I could see her a minute. She came into the hallway and I held out the offending knickers.

"Oh," she said. "I will get you some clothes." And that was it, bottom line.

I hated having periods, not just then but forevermore, all because nobody had the guts to explain to me that it was a natural body function and no big deal.

The next day, Lorna and I left with Grandma, and Lorna's friend Gwenda Spencer, for a bus trip around the South Island. Grandma often went to bat for us against our parents, but how she managed to convince them that we should <u>both</u> go on holiday with her was a mystery.

The trip was great! We went north to Christchurch, on to Picton where we stayed a few days in the Anakiwa Guest house out in Queen Charlotte Sound. This was later to become an outward bound school and later again a guest house once more. From there we went to Nelson and down the west coast. The bus kept boiling on the way through the pass and we had to fill the radiator with water collected from the creeks in our hot water bottles. I have photographs from that time – I look like a gauche kid of twelve in a cut down floral dress, socks on under my sandals, and hair cut straight round beneath my ears and held back with a clip. But the trip was memorable for something else: I fell in love for the first time. His name was Norman, the bus driver, and I thought he was wonderful.

When we returned home I was sad at the thought that I might never see him again, and also my pet rabbit was gone. They told me the poor thing was starving and had to be destroyed; they said I hadn't been feeding it enough. So I had lost the two things I loved most and cried for weeks, not only for the loss but for the fact that I had been unwittingly cruel to my pet.

I was to have two more holidays before I left the farm, thanks, I found out later, to the connivance of some of the other Taieri families. The Bryant's, further down the plain, had an adopted daughter called Jocelyn whom I barely knew. Her parents asked if I could accompany her to a Bible class camp for two whole weeks at Queenstown. We were to camp in the classrooms of a school and bed down on mattresses made from sacking filled with straw. It was mid-summer and wonderful. We spent the morning doing bible studies and the afternoon playing. We went on a boat trip to another bay where wild gooseberries grew in profusion and stuffed ourselves with the ripe red berries, sunbathed and explored. There was a trip on the old steamboat, the *Earnslaw*, (still going strong today after sixty-plus years.) It took us up to Deer Stalker Bay in the morning and picked us up again at night on its way home. That day we walked nine miles to the Greenstone Falls and back, mostly through magnificent beech forests where the fallen leaves made a soft carpet. Almost every day we swam in the freezing water of Lake Wakitipu under the ragged peaks of the Remarkables and watched the tiny teal ducks diving in the crystal clear water.

Unfortunately, I had developed a very bad cold and it was my own fault. "Don't," Dad had said, "hang out of the windows of the train … there is no quicker way to get a cold." But of course I did – I was wild and free.

The camp was run by Deaconesses of the church, all good sorts who could take a joke, thank goodness because they had to contend with apple pied beds or a hedgehog in the bed. We would hear the laughter coming from their room but never a word was said. They had employed two non-religious ladies in their twenty's, one a cook, the other a swimmer to make sure none of us drowned. They were not paid, just got a free holiday. All in all they were a great group.

There always has to be one amongst a crowd that is an absolute pillock, so of course, we had one. She was a tall awkward girl with little personality. French berets were in fashion and everyone had to wear a hat to church. She wore hers with the sides standing up so it looked like a flat-topped muffin on top of her head. The girls teased her unmercifully; they would pinch her bottom from behind, or flick her hat so it fell over her eyes. Anything to get a reaction and that got us all laughing. Instead of taking it in good part she would spin round and say, "Orr, stop it," and get really mad. The more she reacted, the more they teased.

Came the morning when we all marched into church. The leaders sat in the front pew and we girls in pews in an alcove that faced out into the body of the church. The awkward girl, *Crazy Hat*, was in the pew in front of me, and two girls to the left. I had become very friendly with a girl called Margaret Ryder from Dunedin, who was sitting on my left. The sermon was boring so the girl sitting behind Crazy Hat decided to liven up the proceedings, and reaching forward she gave the hat a flick so that it fell off completely. "Orr, stop it," hissed Crazy Hat, spinning around and glaring. The sermon groaned on, and then Margaret poked her in the bottom. "Orr, stop it," and we got a repeat performance.

This went on for some minutes until it became serious naughty and we were all in fits of silent laughter. I pulled my hat pin out and whispered to Margaret, "Stick this into her." After all, up to now I'd had no part of the proceedings so I might as well get in on the act. Margaret nearly choked as she pushed my hand away. By now we were passed the point of no return. My imagination got the better of me. I sat there conjuring up visions of the girl leaping out of her seat and yelling, "Bloody stop it," in the middle of the sermon. Margaret and I were almost apoplectic. I tried stuffing a handkerchief and then a glove into my mouth to stop the noise, only to have it come snorting out my nose. This just made the rest of the culprits laugh all the more. Eventually the head Deaconess turned her head ever so slightly in our direction to let us know she knew what was going on, but not one word was mentioned about our behaviour.

Our ribs were sore for days after that, but there is nothing better than a good giggle, especially if it happens to be in church.

The other holiday I had came from a request from the Allen family at the north of the plain. I didn't know them but Dad did.

"Could Gwen please come to stay a week and accompany Grace to the country girl's week in Dunedin?" the Allens said to Dad.

It was agreed I could go, but first I needed a new coat. Several were sent out on "apro.' from Arthur Barnett's, and luckily for me Aunty Frances was with us at the time. She talked Mum into letting me have the most beautiful creamy white soft wool coat, with slim sleeves and double wings going out backwards from the elbow, instead of the ghastly green tweed thing that Mum wanted. I felt like a million dollars.

I stayed with the Allens for the week and Grace and I travelled each day into Dunedin. We visited factories, took a tour of St Paul's Cathedral, the Anglican church above the Octagon where we were allowed to climb the circular staircase to the top of the spire and look out over the town. Out on the front steps we had our photo taken for the Otago Daily Times. Of course, there had to be at least one dork amongst us, another one who wore her beret like a muffin, and I laugh now when I see the photo.

One night when we returned home Mrs Allen had cooked tripe and onions for tea. She asked me if I liked tripe and onions and I said, "Ahh, well … I'll try it."

Mum was an awful cook: she used to cook tripe for us at East Taieri and we could never eat it. Unlike the tripe you get in England, which is really well cooked and can be eaten cold, the tripe in New Zealand was bought almost raw. Mum would never cook it long enough, and on one occasion when we were all still young she made it for our tea. When my siblings and I tried to swallow the long slimy pieces, they just came straight back up. There was an awful row at the table that night. She told us that if we didn't eat it we would get it again for breakfast, and sure enough, there it was on the table. That morning we all went to school hungry. By night time she must have realised the futility of the whole exercise, and we were never served it again. I told Mrs Allen this and she said, "Oh, but you will like mine," and I did. She taught me there and then how to cook it, and I have enjoyed tripe and onions ever since.

Someone gave us a Harmonium organ; at least I think that was what it was called. It had lots of stops that you could pull out or push in and two big peddles in front of your seat that you used to pump air with your feet. It was decided I should learn music so off I went on my bike every Saturday afternoon down to Miss Sinclair's at Henley. I did learn to read music but very slowly, and of course I didn't practice nearly enough so was never a good player. The organ spoiled me for playing a piano where you strike the keys with jerky movements, whereas on the organ your fingers glide from one key to the next without a gap.

Lorna was going on for twenty years of age before she plucked up the courage to ask if she could leave the farm. She had seen an advertisement in the Otago Daily Times asking for experienced sewers with accommodation provided. Reluctantly, the parents said she could go, and so I became the sole sibling to work on the farm. The accommodation provided for her was in a hostel for immigrant girls from England where she made a few friends. She asked Dad if I could come in and stay for a few days and it was agreed.

The hostel was out at the beginning of the Otago Peninsular where my grandfather had farmed and where he was the last owner of the Highcliff Hotel. The Peninsular is between the sea on one side and the long harbour on the other. As Lorna was at work all day I was free to roam, and wandered down to an inlet one day and was amazed to find dozens of large octopi dead on the edge of the water. I had never seen an octopus close up and was completely enthralled; I went around poking them with my foot. They were so fresh I couldn't believe they were dead, and expected at any minute to be grabbed by a tentacle.

Another day I borrowed Lorna's bike and went further down the Peninsular. I visited Larnach Castle, which was run down and neglected. The fish pond was green with algae. The front door was open but I didn't have the courage to go inside, thinking maybe I wouldn't have the money if I had to pay. But one thing was decided that day ... one day, I would own Larnach Castle and restore it to its former glory.

Anzac Day was celebrated while I was there and I wanted to see the dawn service. Lorna said I could borrow her bike so I set off in the dark to ride to the cenotaph. Another experience chalked up for me.

While going out with the English girls, Lorna met Jack. He was a fitter and turner from Lancashire, England. She bought him home to visit. The parents were not impressed – to a couple of red neck country bumpkins he was just a Pom, to be avoided at all costs. In order to get money for them to marry, Jack changed his job and trained as a diamond driller to work at the Roxburgh hydro dam which was then under construction. He made great money and bought himself a motorbike to get back to Dunedin on his days off. He'd been working there for some time when he developed a bad skin rash from the grease used on the drills. Lorna asked if he could stay at the farm until he was better as he had no digs in Dunedin.

So Jack came to stay, and it was a disaster. From day one he was not accepted, his accent was wrong, his yellow ointment stained the sheets, he was useless around the farm, he would go and sit on the toilet for long periods when there was work to do. He couldn't do right for doing wrong, and both Colin, who was at home at the time, and Dad, made fun of him. With his squeaky little voice, pointy face and reddish hair, he definitely wasn't my type either, but I felt genuinely sorry for him. He was a city lad, way out of his depth. Eventually, he went back to work, and he and Lorna came the odd time to stay the weekend because Lorna was still living in the hostel.

One weekend, when they were home, Lorna asked Dad if I could come with her and Jack to the dance at Momona Hall. Momona was so well known for its dances that a busload would come out from Dunedin. Much to our surprise Dad said I could go. Lorna gave me a tight-fitting pink polo necked skivvy and a black skirt to wear, I had never worn anything so revealing. It soon became apparent that I had caught the attention of many young men in the hall, much to my consternation, and I didn't lack for dances. I had several dances with Stewart Crozier, whom we both knew, but not well. He asked if he could take me home and I said he would have to ask Lorna.

She said, "Yes, if you take her straight home."

He tried to talk to me on the way home, but I was way out of my comfort zone and said very little. He parked at the top of our drive, put his arm around me and kissed me full on the lips.

"I've got to go," I said and, opening the door, jumped out and ran all the way to the safety of the house like a frightened fawn. He must have thought I was mad. My first kiss and it had frightened me silly, so ill at ease was I with the opposite sex.

Arriving home one day, I rode around the side of the house to put my bike in the shed, and what I saw shocked me to the core. Lorna was backing around the yard with Dad following, lashing out at her with the heavy leather strap. I was absolutely horrified. She was twenty-one years old. I hid in the shed not daring to go out. Eventually, the voices stopped and after a while Lorna and Jack came out, climbed on his motorbike and rode away. It was many years before I was to see her again.

It transpired that she had told Dad that they were going to get married and he said, "If you marry that Pommie bastard you won't get me paying for the wedding."

Lorna then reminded him that he'd been claiming for years for wages that he hadn't paid her and that's when he laid into her with the strap. About two weeks later a solicitor's letter arrived telling Dad that he owed Lorna £365 in back wages and unless he paid up the matter would be taken to court. He had no option but to pay. Lorna requested that the things she had saved for her "Glory box' be packed and forwarded to her. Mum asked me to help with the job. She took out a crystal jam dish on a stem.

"I don't think we will send this," she said. "Why don't you keep it?"

"No," I almost screamed. "I don't want it."

I hated her at that moment and couldn't believe her dishonesty. She had never liked Lorna and had even treated her cruelly at times. If it hadn't been for Lorna's hard work on the farm Mum may not have had the money to spoil her son, our half-brother, so outrageously.

After Lorna left, life became a lot harder for me: up at 5 am and off to the cowshed, driving the tractor, chopping thistles or numerous jobs during the day before setting off, dogs in tow, to get the cows in for the evening milking. Milking took two to three hours, depending on the time of the year and the number of cows in milk. Afterward, we had to flush out the milk lines, clean the teat cups, pick up any manure from the concrete yards and hose the whole place down. Only then could we wend our weary way home for tea, after which I helped with the washing up. I was never allowed to sit idle at night. Mum kept a flour bag of Dad's woollen socks that needed mending, and when there were no socks to do, I did embroidery. I still have some of the pieces today.

When we went to Otakia, the minister was a Mr Pullman. He was a young man who had been brought up on a farm in the North Island. He would surprise all the mill workers or haymakers by coming to lend a hand. He was quite capable and earned every ones' respect. The men also apologised when they let slip a naughty word.

Mrs Pullman was tall and pretty. She wore no makeup and her long hair was plaited and curled around her head, just like all the Brethren ladies that lived around us. When he left after about two years to go on with his theology studies at Dunedin University a Mr Neville arrived from the North Island to take his place. The Nevilles had five children and the big manse was soon filled with chaos. Mr Neville had a big square Buick car with a long back seat and dicky seats that pulled up from the floor. It must have been made for the well-to-do, as the back could be shut off from the front by a wind-up window. Mr Neville's duties included not just taking the church service at our church but the churches at Berwick, Henley, and Allenton as well. He used to boast that he could fit fourteen kids into the car, and he decided to round all the teenagers up and take them to Bible class, either at the Manse or in one of the other district churches. I was no keener on religion at this time than before, but it was a way to escape the house and mix with people my own age. He also organised Bible class socials where we played games and danced. Some people were a bit concerned that we were allowed to dance as they thought it not fitting, but that was where I learned ballroom dancing and we all enjoyed the evenings. Sometimes on the way home we would wind up the window and laugh and joke in the back. David, the Neville's oldest boy was very handsome and he knew it. He was the same age as myself and rather too good with his hands for my liking. The oldest girl, Anthea, was really nice and could play the organ and sing, as could their mother. One night on the way home we thought we had wound up the window, but when we were nearly home I noticed that the window was about two inches down. Mr Neville would have been able to hear us. David had told a couple of almost smutty jokes so I expect he got a flea in his ear that night. I swear it wasn't me, sitting in the dicky seat, who wound the window down again.

On social nights, which were held every few months, Mr Neville would round us up, one group after another and deposit us at Momona Hall. Mum and Dad were never really happy about me going to the socials and I was given a strict time to be home: 11 pm and no later. One night David Neville asked his father if he could take the Allenton girls home while the rest of us cleaned up the hall and locked up. He was given permission and we expected him back in about twenty minutes. We finished cleaning up, locked up and went out to wait, and wait, and wait. We must have stood out in the frost for about an hour and it was 12.30 when I eventually arrived home. I knew when I was walking up the long drive to the house that I was in serious trouble, but was unprepared for the accusations. Where had I been? Who had I been with? What had we been doing?

I was furious. I wanted to ask Mum if she thought I'd been in the ditch with some boy. I tried to explain but she didn't want to know, and I felt she would rather think the worst of me. She kept on the next day until I finally exploded and eventually answered back:

"Well if you don't believe me, there's the phone ... ring Mr Neville and ask him," I yelled. Of course she didn't; she didn't want to let go of what she had in her dirty mind.

Dad, with help from Lorna and I, had built a big Dutch barn to keep the hay in. It was just a roof on long stilts. I was twelve years old and Malcolm, a little lad of two, were standing holding hands while we watched the haymakers load the hay bales from the lorry on to the new-fangled escalator that carried the bales up to be stacked. Colin came and told me that Mum wanted to see me, so I went back to the house.

"Colin says you are hanging around men. How dare you hang around men? It's filthy to hang around men."

I didn't have a clue what she was talking about.

Our brother Colin was a little tell-tale, always running with tales. He never said, as most kids will, "I am going to tell on you,' he just did it.

Another time Dad had given me a job to do out in the garden but the tool I was using was broken. When Colin asked what I was doing, I told him, "It's no good, this thing is up the shoot." Everybody at school said that when things were broken. Later Mum said, "Colin tells me you have been saying rude things."

"What did I say?"

"You said "up the shoot' and that is disgusting."

I stared at her open-mouthed; I didn't know what she was talking about that time either.

All our lives we had been taught to dig out rabbit holes – rabbits were a dreadful scourge. It is said that a rabbit could eat as much in a day as a sheep. We could always tell when a nest had babies, as mother rabbit would cover the hole carefully with soil. One day we found a nest near the gorse hedge by the bridge. The dogs set to work to dig it out. It contained six fluffy bundles, which we put into a sack, maybe it was because they were so cute that we didn't kill them straight away. While we were filling in the hole again I stepped back and accidentally stood on the bag. Appalling screams issued from under my foot. Colin brought out the tiny bundle, bleeding from the mouth and quickly dispatched it. I had broken its jaw. This episode has been another cross for me to bear because the screams of that tiny creature have echoed down the years.

We had two bad floods while I was at Otakia. All my siblings were at home when the first one came. It doesn't have to rain hard on the Taieri to get a flood. The river begins its journey away up at Middlemarch in the hills. A lot of rain up in the hills sends the water roaring down the Taieri gorge where it spreads across all unprotected parts of the plain. The river in flood was an awesome sight, a massive sheet of clay-coloured water from the top of the flood bank fifty yards behind our house to the far eastern hills. It was a fascinating and sad sight as great trees, dead cows and sheep swirled passed. A few days before the flood we, and the dogs had dug out a very deep rabbit hole on the riverside of the flood bank, fortunately near the top. Dad found the hole as the water reached it and had to hastily sandbag it.

"Little buggers," he told Mum. "They could have breached the flood bank."

We were given a serious lecture. It was a sad flood also in the fact that we lost our precious pet duck, Donald. It was also duck shooting time as I recall and although we usually kept Donald at home in these times, she managed to trot off with the other ducks to the river. Maybe she ended up on someone's table or just got washed too far away to get back. The second flood came when six-year-old Malcolm and I were the only ones left at home. The river had long since become my refuge and where I spent my idle hours and I knew every inch of it. As the flood waned it became a new and exciting place to explore. Near the bridge, part of the riverbank became an island, where water ran into one of the long borrow pits and out the other end. I waded over in my gumboots. Wow! My very own island, even if it did look a little forlorn and grubby.

In my last year at school, Mr. Jenkins referred to me as the head girl. Certainly I was two years older than anyone else. The last winter Mum had made me a full circle tweed skirt and I had a brown jersey to match. My boobs were still very small. One day I decided to augment them with a couple of rolled up handkerchiefs, but later that day, after a game of tennis, I looked down and saw that I four boobs, two of them in very strange places.

That year, standards five and six – five pupils in all – were given the task of painting a big mural about the logging industry in Canada. This was part of our Social Studies, previously called geography and history. I was given the job of painting the people as I could draw reasonably well in those days and we were allowed a couple of hours one afternoon in the backroom to paint. Now the back room, the old second classroom, was also used as a storeroom for all the bits and pieces and stored there were a pile of small sandbags for teaching weights. They ranged in size from ounce bags to pound bags. So, there we were all working diligently when someone made a funny crack about one of the others and the latter playfully picked up sandbag and threw it. The next thing sandbags were flying everywhere until the pound bag landed in the big basin of grey water in which we had been washing brushes. Russell picked it up by the corner and it hung there dripping while we all laughed. Then we discovered that two of the other ones had burst. We knew we were in trouble. The damage was discovered several days later. The three from standard five had gone off to Mosgiel School to do woodwork and cooking classes and Russell wasn't at school. That left just me to face the music. Mr Jenkins' face was like thunder when we came in from lunch.

"Who," he demanded, "was responsible for the damage to the weight bags in the next room?"

"It was us," I said and owned up to our silly pranks.

"Who's us?" he stormed. For the next few minutes we were subject to his usual performance; we watched his face grow puce, his greasy hair fall over his face and saliva spew from his mouth. How dare I behave like that! I was the head girl! I was supposed to be setting an example to the younger children! (That was a laugh; the only thing I had ever taught them was to stand up for what was right and not bow down to people who were away out of line.)

"Get out here and be taught a lesson and the others will get their punishment when they get back tonight."

I received two vicious cuts on each hand. I hope it taught the younger children one thing and it's this: it isn't always smart to be so honest. I lingered awhile that night before going home and when I saw the bus arrive bringing the others back I met them at the gate.

"Don't come in for God's sake. Go straight home."

They did, and the next morning all had been forgotten.

The end of the year arrived at last, and it was exam time. Both Russell and I, the only two in form two, almost failed our arithmetic exam. I got the highest marks in the school for arts and had ten more points overall than Russell. Mr Jenkins had once told Russell and I, "If you don't understand anything, come up to the desk and I will explain."

Great, we thought, but we were to find that when we did as he advised, he still lost his temper. The school had had a Dux system for many years, and the names of the Duxes were painted in gold on the big board on the school wall. In my mind, I could already see my name there and I was proud. *What a joke!* My father had never approved of Mr Jenkins, whereas Mr Gulliver, Russell's father, was a drinking mate of Mr Jenkins and lived just over the road. For the next week, when I arrived at school, I found Russell beside Mr Jenkins desk being tutored in arithmetic. When I came in he said, "You can go now, Russell." Maybe he thought I didn't know what he was up to. Anyway, at the end of the week we were set another arithmetic exam, which I thought was highly illegal, and Russell got one more problem right than I and received ten more marks.

The school concert arrived and I was on and off the stage all night. Mrs Blair had wanted me to sing a song and had suggested her favourite. So I sang *April Showers*, a song that didn't really, and still doesn't, suit my voice. The first line of the verse is "Life is not a pathway strewn with flowers.' And, oh, how true that turned out to be. Then it came time for Mr McDonald, Rhonda's father, and the chairman of the school committee, to announce the Dux.

"It was very close," he said. It was Russell Gulliver. Mr Jenkins then spoke, telling the audience he didn't believe in Duxes and that he would like to award a prize to the child in the school who deserved it most. We were all sitting in the front row and everyone expected me to be called up. But no, it was Rhonda McDonald. I felt quite humiliated, not only had I been cheated out of the Dux, I was also made to look foolish by this degrading man. I didn't envy Rhonda her prize. She deserved it as she never made waves, did nothing wrong and was, and always has been, a thoroughly nice person. When she came back to sit beside me she apologised. She too had thought that I was to get the prize. But it was I who had stood beneath his window at playtime and roared with laughter after being belted with the strap. I often wondered if my father's opinion of him had influenced his behaviour towards me. Or was it just that he never got the better of me? He also knew I had his measure, and he didn't like it.

On the way home from the hall that night Dad and Mum discussed the evening in the front seat as though I wasn't there. They had a few nasty things to say about Mr Jenkins. "She carried the concert on her back," said Dad. "And then he has to humiliate her – everyone thought she was going to get that prize."

I had always thought I would go on to high school. I asked Dad if I could go to Colombo College, the private school in Dunedin and he just grunted. When he and Mum told me I would not even be allowed to go to Mosgiel District High each day, I was thunderstruck. It had never occurred to me that I wouldn't go on to high school and on to University.

As it was Dad became quite ill over Christmas. For weeks he walked around as white as a ghost and could barely get through milking, so I resigned myself to being a full-time cowgirl, and so began the loneliest years of my life.

Dad and I got on reasonably well in the cowshed; we rarely spoke except to make the occasional remark, just worked our way up and down the shed. We pulled down on the teat cups to extract the last, and richest, of the milk, changed the cups from one cow to the other, let the finished cow out and put another in her place. Chain up, leg rope on, teats washed, and she was ready for the next change over. It all flowed smoothly.

The one thing that really horrified me was Dad's appalling cruelty. He had no patience. If a new young cow didn't want to go into a bale he would grab her tail and twist it until I was sure it would break, and sometimes he would kick the cows viciously in the stomach. Every time he put on one of his tantrums he upset all the cows in the shed. Some of them would manure in the bales, and then we would have mess to clean up. It was all so counter-productive. I used to try to get in first to feed the young calves from a bucket. When they are born their natural instinct is to put their heads up to feed. We would let them suck our fingers then push their heads into the bucket of milk. It usually took about three days for them to get the message and they would drink from the bucket without help. One year we got a small black and white calf which was a slow learner. He looked fine, but I think he must have been a difficult birth. He didn't seem to be as bright as the others. On one occasion Dad came out to *help*, as there were too many for me to handle. He got the slow learner, and try as he might the calf would not drink with its head down. Eventually it butted the bucket, knocking it over and spilling all the milk. Dad snatched up the heavy galvanized bucket and smashed the calf around the head with it. Then he kicked and kicked it until I thought he would kill it. I wanted to scream "Stop it, stop it!" and to smash *him* around the head, but I didn't dare. I just cried inside.

The bobby calf truck came once a week to take the calves to the abattoirs where they were killed for veal. Some of the calves might be seven days old when they left by which time I had got quite attached to them. The truck drivers could be heartless beasts as well. We were paid by weight for the calves and first they would be roughly slung into a sling to record the weight, then literally thrown into the back of the truck I wanted to scream at them too, "You don't need to be so rough," but was too shy. I sometimes wonder, if all the things I wanted to say then and didn't, have made me the outspoken and forthright person I am today.

Very few visitors came to the cowshed. The Cook boys came once and I had to keep a straight face when the eldest one pointed to the small false teats on the back of the cows' udder and said, "Those are the ones the cream comes from."

Another night we had a man who came to the shed and stopped for tea later. He didn't come right in, just watched from the side, so I did not speak to him.

I had gone out into the bull paddock to see if the trough was full and the biggest bull, a hefty dark red fellow, started putting on his "I'm the boss here act." He lowered his head, started pawing the ground and bellowing. Now, it's always a good thing to get in first with a bull. I ran at him shouting, "Get out of it," and gave him a poke in the nose with my boot. He turned tail and ran off. I didn't realise that I had an audience. Over the tea table the man said to me, "Aren't you frightened of those bulls?"

"Her? Frightened?" guffawed my father. "She doesn't know the meaning of the word."

Did my father just pay me a compliment? It was true: I wasn't the least bit frightened of bulls. Dad was always saying, "You should take a stick into that paddock with you – one day they will turn on you and then you'll be in trouble." Certainly he would never go in there without a big stick.

But Dad was wrong about me not knowing the meaning of fear – he didn't know it, but I was very much afraid of the dark. How I hated the uncurtained window in my bedroom. I always felt that maybe someone was out there in the cow paddock watching me, even though I knew that nobody in their right mind would walk around in a cow paddock at that hour of night – for one thing you would probably tread in something nasty. And that old coat, hanging on the back of my bedroom door … why did it always turn into someone sinister, just standing quietly watching me?

It was all so silly. But fear has a way of dispelling any common sense. It was many years after I left home that I finally conquered that fear.

We had another visitor to the cowshed one night that we had cause to remember. He was selling insurance and was dressed in a pale grey suit that looked new, and a smart shirt and tie. After Dad told him he wasn't interested, he bravely came right into the shed and prattled on and on while we worked quietly up and down the bales.

He was standing mid-way down the shed, about six feet behind a young heifer. Now cows can get very nervous about strangers in the shed, especially when they keep talking, and she lifted her tail to defecate. It was spring and the cows were a bit skittery with the new grass. Unfortunately, she coughed, and manure flew straight out behind her catching the pesky salesman full-on, great four-inch splats of runny manure all down the front of that lovely suit.

"Oh my God, look at my suit," he cried.

Dad tried not to laugh, but I just lost it. I sat on the stool between the top bales, rested my head on a cow's belly and had a good laugh. Why is it that we always laugh at other people's misfortune?

Dad helped him wash the goo off with a rag before the man took himself off home. We didn't tell him that his suit, tie, and shirt were probably ruined, but we were willing to bet that never again did he try to sell insurance in a busy milking shed

My favourite time in the shed was early morning in the summer, when the sun peeked over the eastern hills, and the first beams hit the tops of the Maungatua's on the western side of the plains. As the sun rose higher the brilliant light pierced the deep dark gullies of the mountain and showed up every nook and cranny and small streams. I would lean my arms on the top rail of the yard and watch in fascination until Dad yelled at me to get back to work. When the sun was finally up, the gullies darkened again and hid their secrets once more.

When Grandma first shifted to Otakia with us she took a great pride in her garden. Behind her six-foot-high fence, she planted lots of annuals and her garden was a picture. As years went by she lost interest and the place became untidy. The doctor advised her to take up smoking for her nerves, (can you believe that?) but she took pains to hide the packet very quickly when I came in. I don't think she ever became a serious smoker.

She had a canary, and one day when she was in our place talking to Mum, she asked me to run out to her cottage to get something for her. As I went in her gate I noticed an owl. This owl had been a nuisance as it had been swooping down and carrying off our baby ducklings. We had lost two before we caught the culprit in the act and the ducklings were shut away out of reach. Now, here it was, sitting on the tall bleached white tree stumps, eying the canary in his cage inside the window. I ran around the path, threw open the door and the canary fell off its perch and had a fit. Looking out the window I saw the owl still there watching and guessed that by me flying in the door while the canary was mesmerized with the owl, I had given it such a fright that it went into shock. I grabbed what Grandma wanted and went back to tell them what had happened, but nothing would convince her that I hadn't let a cat in to attack her bird. She gave the bird a drop of brandy and it seemed okay, but the next day it died.

Once again I was being accused of being a liar and I wasn't happy.

Grandma was a very ignorant lady full of old wives tales that scared me at times. Once, when I had my period I got thoroughly soaked while working out in the paddock. She told me in no uncertain terms that I would be in big trouble. "I knew a girl," she said, "who got wet when she had her period, and her periods stopped and she got consumption and died."

If all her prophesies had come true I wouldn't be here today.

After *I* had killed her canary she got a dog, a purebred Pekinese she called Bowsie. Colin used to say he looked as though he had been hit on the nose with a cricket bat. For a while she took good care of him, but later he was locked up with her all day and never got out. On the rare occasions I visited home after I'd left the farm, I would run out to see Grandma, and Bowsie would go ballistic. He would jump right up to chest height and slide his sharp unclipped claws down my front and shred my nylons. I was not impressed. When no one was in our house, Grandma would take the opportunity to go in and phone the neighbours and talk for long periods. Word came back that she had some harsh things to say about her daughter. This was very unfair because Mum did try to do the best by the bitter old lady.

Occasionally Grandma would take herself off to town. She was always nicely dressed, black dress, coat, hat, gloves, and lace-up shoes with Cuban heels. Looking back I now realise what a lonely life she must have had, but it was of her own making. She could have taken herself back to town and lived on her Widows Pension, but then, she wouldn't have got free meat, vegetables and rent.

She could have taken Bowsie for walks along the river bank or anywhere on our large acreage, but she chose not to. Grandma once told me that it was because of Mum and her sister Francis that she had lost her rented home in Kaikorai Valley, Dunedin because the girls wouldn't pay the rent. When I told Mum this many years later she became angry.

"Do you know," she said, "… after Dad died at Wakari Hospital of T.B. she wouldn't go out to work – she thought she was too much of a lady. Bubs (Frances) and I had to pay all the bills. She sold the house at Maori Hill because we couldn't pay the mortgage and rented the place in Kaikorai Valley where we could have our horses. When Bubs got married I was left alone to pay everything."

Grandma formed the habit of coming into the house every afternoon and sitting on the chair in the scullery when we were working there. She became very absent-minded. I would be standing washing the dishes and she would ask a question which I would answer, then a few minutes later she would ask the same thing. When she asked a third time I would snap, "I just told you that, twice."

Off she would go to Mum and say I had been rude to her. I was always being told by Mum, "Don't you be rude to my mother."

I always thought of Grandma as old, but she was only in her mid-fifties.

Our little half-brother Malcolm looked like an angelical child when he was very young, however, he got up to some awful mischief, and I bore the brunt of his misbehavior as I had to pick up the pieces. He seemed to take delight in dropping animals down holes. I heard the plaintive yowls of a kitten one day and traced it to the long drop lavatory. Looking down the hole I saw the poor wee thing literally floating on the top of the stinking morass. It kept pulling a leg out and trying to climb out. I raced inside to get Mum.

"Oh, whatever shall we do?" she wailed, never being the most practical person. I suggested that perhaps I could reach it if she held firmly to my legs. It was agreed, so, taking a big breath, I slipped through the hole – that will give you an idea of how thin I was – with Mum hanging on to my ankles. Luckily the lavatory pit was filled to within a few feet from the top and by reaching as far as I could, I managed to grasp the kitten by the scruff of the neck. Unfortunately I had to take a breath and it almost made me puke.

"I've got it. Pull me out, pull me out!" I yelled.

Getting back out was a darn sight harder than getting in. What would have happened if Mum had dropped me doesn't bear thinking about. We hosed the kitten down and bathed it in warm soapy water. Not long after, the hole was covered in, and a new very deep one dug behind the hen shed, and the "dunny' perched above it. Dad expected it to last so long that he laid another concrete path up to it.

When we went to Otakia, Dad put in an underground concrete tank, just as he had at East Taieri. It had a concrete top that served as a tank stand and an entry hole with a wooden lid. This tank, which took the overflow from the rainwater tanks, held two thousand gallons. On hot summer's days it was the only place we could get cold water from, in the absence of fridges. When the mill men came, or the haymakers, the lid would be opened to get out a big jug of water for the lunch table. On one occasion someone hadn't put the lid back on and it wasn't replaced until nightfall. A few weeks later when the lid was again removed we found one of our khaki Campbell ducks dead, a floating carcass of feathers, bones, and maggots. Darling Malcolm said he thought it had wanted a swim so he dropped it in, but it could have been him who fell in and drowned.

We used the pump to empty all the water out, and I was given the job of sweeping up the egg she had laid, the dead maggots and debris, scrubbing all the walls with disinfectant, flushing it all out again and removing the water. It took me days, and for the rest of the summer, we had to go on water rations. The horrible death of that poor duck haunted me for years after – if only it had quacked to let us know it was there.

When I was thirteen years old I knew where babies came from but it had never occurred to me how they got started. Needless to say then that it came as an appalling shock when the penny finally dropped.

Dad suffered badly from indigestion and one night during milking he asked me to run back to the house and get him some antacid. He had put a cow into the bull paddock to be served and as I took the shortcut over to the house I had to pass by them. The terrible awful truth hit me like a sledgehammer, so much so that I faltered in my step. I had seen animals copulating all my life and never realised the significance of it. How could I have been so blind? It was obscene, disgusting, and vile; I wanted to vomit. Never, never, in all my life, would I ever let a man touch me, I promised myself.

Somehow I made it back to the house for his antacid, but was so quiet on my return that he asked me if I was alright.

When I was about sixteen, Dad employed an older man to prune the sides off the few big macrocarpa trees just inside the gate at the top of the drive. I had never met him before, didn't even know where he came from, but they must have trusted him as I was given the job of taking his morning and afternoon tea out, and the billy of tea at lunchtime. He must have been there for a few weeks as there were no chainsaws in those days and he cut each branch by hand, trimming and stacking them for Dad, who would later cut them up for firewood with the circular saw that was run with a pulley from the tractor. For some reason I was perfectly at ease with him, not shy like I was with most strangers. He was nicest, kindliest, older person I had ever met. He was the first person ever to speak to me as an adult, and for once Mum didn't come out and shout at me to come away as though he was some leper.

While I waited to take the tea things back, we talked of many things, all sorts of interesting subjects. He was like the grandfather I had never had, as apart from my step-grandmother, who left a lot to be desired, I had never known a grandparent. He must have seen a gauche, lonely, teenager in search of knowledge and he talked to me as a teacher. He taught me a trick one day, which I vowed I would never forget, but eventually did. He gathered up the small tree cones and made a square, nine cones each side. He then gave me three more and said, "Add those three so that you still have nine down each side." Of course I couldn't, so he showed me how, and I laughed because it worked. I was sad when his job was done and he went away because I had to go back to being the lonely girl who nobody had a sensible conversation with.

One day Mum and I went to a church garden party that was held at a home in the foothills of the Maungatua's. A husband and wife lived there with the wife's sister. They explained that the wife worked inside and the sister did the garden. They had diverted a mountain stream so it ran through the garden. I especially loved the big Gunnerer, with its big rhubarb like stems that grew on the banks of the stream. It was a place of incredible beauty and instilled in me a love of gardens.

When electric fences were invented, the work on the farm became easier. No longer did we have to pull swede turnips and cut Choumolia every day to feed out to the cows that were milking over winter. All we had to do was run a strip of electric fence across a sliver of the paddock and let them help themselves. When the first strip was eaten bare, the wire would be moved to expose a new strip. When we first got the fence Dad was trying it out in the scullery as I walked through.

"Here, Skinny," he said, "grab a hold of this."

I took hold of the wire and he attached the other clip to the battery. I leaped across the room and was so angry that I swore at him. He just laughed. But I had learned a healthy respect for electric fences from day one.

Dad did all the ploughing on the farm, and at least one paddock a year was renewed, either with new grass or another crop. After the ploughing I did most of the scuffling, and then the harrowing, then I would ride on the back of the seed drill to make sure the hoppers didn't run out of seed. I used to sing at the top of my voice when I worked alone on the tractor. I could sing country and western and yodel with the best of them. I knew all the songs, such as, *When the Rain Tumbles Down in July*, *Mother, Pal and Sweetheart*, *The Overlander Trail*, *The Shearers' Jamboree*, *There's a Bridle Hanging on the Wall*, and *Old Shep*. I'd have a good cry when I sang that, it was such a sad song. It's true what they say, Country and Western songs are indeed "white man's blues.' I used to love the hours alone on the tractor, just because I could sing. I thought the noise of the tractor would cover the sound of my voice, but Leonard Miller from the farm next door shattered all that.

As we walked back from bible class one night he said, "You like to sing, don't you? Oh yes, we hear you singing on the tractor, Gwen."

I wished he had never said that, because I could never sing aloud on the tractor after that in case someone was listening.

When I was seventeen, Mum, Dad, and Malcolm went for a holiday to the North Island. They had been once before a few years earlier and Dad had put the big single front seat of the Vauxille on hinges, so it could be folded back and they could sleep in the car. This time they were to stay in hotels. It was winter so we had only thirty cows in milk. Dad arranged for one of the Horne boys, from a Henley Brethren family, to come and help me. I think his name was Brian. He was nice and had a horde of sisters. Dad couldn't have chosen better. Brian came in the morning to help with the milking, stayed the day to work on the farm, do the evening milking with me, and stay for tea before going home. I was to do the cooking.

Oh, horrors! I didn't have a clue how to cook. Whenever I had asked Mum if I could help she would say, "I am much better without you; you will just be in the way."

Luckily, when we came in the first night, Grandma had made a beautiful meal for us; I could have kissed her, because Grandma, unlike her daughter, was a really good cook. She had moved into the house – *as a chaperone?* – and continued to cook for us for the fortnight Mum and Dad were away. I was ill at ease with this new young man for the first few days, as I was with most strangers, but we worked well together and I became more relaxed as the days went by.

He said to me one night, "Your father must be making a mint with all this milk."

In the summer we were paid by butterfat content as the milk went to the cheese factory, but in winter we reverted to gallon rates as we went on to town supply. Most farmers milked only in the summer and their cows were always dry in winter. We always had a few cows to milk on gallon rates during the winter, giving the farm an income all year round.

One night I went out to feed the heifer calves we were keeping for future milkers. They were in McLeod's paddock and all I had to do was pour their milk into the trough for them to drink. Unfortunately, Douglas, our spoilt bull, now two years old, was also in the same paddock. He decided, the big sook, that he wanted a drink of milk as well, so he and I had a big fight. While the calves were drinking he tried to muscle in, so I grabbed his head, gave him a smack, and turned him around, not once, but several times while the calves were drinking. When I turned around to go back to the shed I realised I was being watched.

"My God," Brian said, "I was watching you. You wouldn't get any of my sisters going anywhere near a bull."

I gave him some cheek one night in the shed and he grabbed hold of me and said he was going to throw me in the water trough. He was obviously used to wrestling with his sisters and I was acutely embarrassed. Sensing my discomfort, he let me go.

One morning, after milking and breakfast, I grabbed the hedge clippers and started to cut the hedge that bordered one side of the garden. Brian came to me and asked what I wanted him to do. I must have given him a funny look. "Your father told me to ask you what you wanted done," he said.

"My father said that?" I asked in surprise. I was on Cloud Nine at the thought of my father putting me in charge.

"Right," I said, handing him the clippers, "you can cut the hedge for me."

When the end of the week approached he asked me if we had to cut Choumolia and pull swedes to feed to the cows on Sunday. He must have been worrying about going to church. "No," I told him. "We cut a double load on Saturday, and dropped the second load out in the next paddock. Close the gate, and open it again after the Sunday morning milking so the cows can eat what we have left out for them. That way we can have the day off, apart from the morning and evening milking."

I did play hooky once while they were away – I didn't ask, just told Grandma, I was going to the Henley Hall to play table tennis. The Neville kids from the Manse, Anthea and David and a boy who was staying with them, and I were all going down on our bikes. I found a pair of blue air force trousers – Dad used to buy job lots from the end of war auctions – and put them on. They were several sizes too big, so

I pulled them in with a belt. Heaven knows what I must have looked like, but I thought I was the bee's knees. Grandma was horrified because she knew I wasn't allowed to wear unladylike trousers, but I wasn't listening. One thing she did insist was that I had to be home at 10.30, no later.

We enjoyed the evening, but it started to get late and I started to nag. Finally, I got them moving homewards. The hall was on the main south road so we decided to go back up the smooth tar seal way, and cut across instead of taking the gravel road we had come by. Anthea and her friend were riding together, talking, talking, until eventually they decided to get off and walk. David and I rode on and had to keep stopping for them to catch up. We had almost reached our Otakia turnoff when he suddenly realised we were too far ahead, and that he would have to go back and get them. I said I was already very late and would have to go on.

Suddenly, I was alone, and it was dark and spooky. I rode as fast as I could, without any bike lights, just the glow of a half-moon, down the narrow gravel road to the Otakia railway siding, across the rail lines and into a dark and scary bit. From there the road went in a half-circle to the right, a thicket of dense willows on the left, where I imagined all sorts to be lurking, and a paddock on the right, with a field full of scatty white-faced steers. The road ended at the old wooden bridge, long since decommissioned, at the edge of our property. I was petrified, the white faces of the steers raced to gawp at me over the fence before rushing off to come back for another look further down. I stuck to the right-hand side in case someone should leap out of the darkness.

It was a relief to reach the bridge, but the danger had not yet passed. When it was first closed, posts had been put at both ends to block it, but people had removed them and carried on using the bridge. The planks had then been removed from both ends and just a narrow walkway left for pedestrians to cross. Months later some idiot had cut a hole, about two feet square in the decking, probably to fish through, and a little later another was cut further along on the other side. That meant that to negotiate the bridge safely, one had to cross from one side to the other. Luckily I knew every inch of that bridge, but when the moon went behind a cloud my confidence waned. I counted the steps, then tap-tapped with my foot to feel the holes. I was desperately afraid of the river because I couldn't swim, so falling through a hole into the middle of it was not something I wanted to contemplate. I made it to the other side and was almost on home soil.

Would I go the long way down to the Manse, along Centre Road and up the drive, or along the flood bank and in the back way? I opted for the flood bank, lifted my bike over the fence, climbed through, walked along the top of the bank to the next fence, and over that. I snuck passed the dog kennels. They must have known it was me because they didn't make a squeak. Quietly I put my bike in the shed. With a bit of luck I could get tucked up in bed without Grandma finding out I had come in at nearly midnight.

Wrong! When I quietly opened the sitting-room door, there sat Grandma in her nightdress on a hard-backed chair, glaring at me. She just got up, said, "Humph," and stormed off to bed.

When the parents arrived home, I expected to get a haranguing as I knew Grandma would tell them everything, but nobody said a word. Maybe they thought that as everything was just as it should be that I had done a good job and it was best not to mention the misdemeanours.

There was just one mishap that I felt very guilty about. High up on the wall, in the porch, just outside the scullery door, we had two budgies in a wooden cage. Mum was the only one who ever dealt with them. Neither Grandma, nor I, had thought about them, and poor Billy, the male, was dead. I felt very sad about that, and due to our neglect, he had probably starved to save his mate. I had wanted everything to be right, and I had blown it. I wrapped him up, put him in a shoebox, and buried him under one of the big trees. I shed a tear and told him I was so, so sorry.

The only trips I ever made to town were to get my teeth attended to by the dentist. I would walk along the flood bank, over the old bridge and around to the main road to catch the bus. I went to a Mr

Cartwright in upper Moray Place. He was quite elderly and had been Mum's dentist. He said my teeth were very soft, that once the enamel had a hole in it, the tooth just fell to bits as they were like chalk inside. Being brought up on soft rainwater without the addition of fluoride had caused the problem. Every molar had an amalgam filling, put there by the school dentist.

Came the day I needed a tooth out, he pulled and pulled but it just wouldn't come. Eventually, he told me he would have to take me to see Dr Dodd, the Dean of the dental school who was a specialist. He then rang my parents and said he would bring me home, as I would miss the bus.

Dr Dodd x-rayed the offending tooth, cut it in half and removed it piece by piece. That was to be the beginning of another lifelong problem. When we got home, Mum gave Mr Cartwright a big jar of cream for his trouble.

When there was nothing to do between milkings, I would escape to the river. Sometimes I would race along, leaping over the fallen trees or jumping up on them and down the other side, always being sure to land on my good leg. I became very surefooted. Sometimes I would hunt for clams or just wander. One day I saw an eel lying under a fallen log in a small shallow inlet at the river's edge. I wondered why it didn't swim away and thought it might be sick. I found a long stick and poked it and it moved a little. Out of the corner of my eye, I saw a black streak, and another smaller eel flew straight out of the water and barked right in my face. I dropped the stick and almost fell into the water with fright. Somebody had told me that eels could bark and I hadn't believed them, now I had living proof. The smaller eel put itself between me and its mate and turned to face me, almost daring me to make another move.

One day I found a tree that had long ago been undermined by a flood and fallen over. It had three long straight branches, one just above the other and a little apart, going out over the water. By running along the bottom one I could sit on the middle one and lean on the top one, just like a church pew. Below my branch, a shoal of black and white striped Perch swam languidly around and around. It was magic. This became my special tree that nobody knew about and I was to spend many hours there over the next two years, dreaming about the time I would become a film star and all the lovely clothes I would buy. No more smelly overalls, or cotton dresses worn with ghastly thick lisle stockings, or long elastic-legged bloomers that I had to wear now. I would have a big box of nylons and pretty picture hats and high heeled shoes.

The river was tidal at the back of our house, even all those miles from the river mouth. When the tide came in, the river rose as the water banked up and it would flow again quite strongly when the tide turned. If I just sat and looked at the flowing water I would go sailing away in the other direction, free as a bird. It was often Mum's raucous voice that disturbed my reverie: something I hadn't done, or time to go to work again. If she came over the flood bank I would sit very still and wait until she went back fuming, then I would run back to terra firm, sprint along the river, so as not to give away my position, before popping over the bank. Once she was so wild she picked up a big willow stick and gave my legs a belting. I had bruises for weeks after.

On one occasion we missed a cow at milking. Dad, who had noticed her non-appearance, set out later to find her. The poor, silly cow had walked down a little slope to get a drink at the river and found she couldn't walk out. The fact that she could have backed out was neither here nor there because cows just don't think like that. She was dead, still standing upright, wedged between the clay bank and a tree, her head resting on a fallen branch. When the river rose during the night she would have been belly deep in water so she must have died from hypothermia. It is always sad to lose valuable stock and made worse by the fact that she was a Friesian and a good milker. Worse still, she died quite close to my tree so that was out of bounds for some time. The flies came, eels came to feed, and a year later all that was left was a pile of bones, a bit of skin, and a sad memory.

The winters could be extremely harsh on the Taieri. Around the full moon, we often got hoar frosts when the fog froze on everything.

When the sun came up in the morning the place was like a fairyland, a beautiful white picture with millions of sparkling diamonds. Even the big spider webs, unseen by day, now added to the magic. I quickly learned not to pick up anything steel after having a bar stick to my skin and take it off. A young neighbour, who kept bees with his father, recorded the daily temperatures. One night he recorded 16 degrees below zero. At least we had wonderful sunny days after a frost before it started to get cold again about 3 pm.

The days could be worse when it was wet and cold. Feeding out from the back of the trailer when the rain turned to sleet cut little slashes in my face and froze my ungloved hands. When I got back inside and put my hands in warm water to thaw them the pain was excruciating. Lorna and I never had gloves, even on the coldest day, nor were we given any hand lotion. Every winter my hands were rough and cracked: I still have the scars today, and have had ugly old hands all my life.

My siblings and I often fed the stock on our own. We were all dab hands at backing the tractor and trailer up to the stack to load up with hay. We would drive to where the feed was to go, point the tractor in the right direction, jump off the seat, run along the tow bar and climb onto the trailer, letting the tractor drive itself. Then it was just a matter of cutting the strings and feeding out the slabs, all the time watching. When it looked as though we were about to run into a fence or topple into Duck Creek, we would run back along the tow bar, jump onto the seat and turn up the paddock again. New Zealand had a fairly high incidence of children being killed when driving tractors. Later, a law was passed making it unlawful for children under twelve to drive tractors.

I was an avid reader. I read everything I could lay my hands on. The school committee had always given me a book at year's end, and Mum and Dad gave me a book for my birthday and Christmas. I had the complete set of the *Anne of Green Gables* books, by L.M. Montgomery. Sometimes, if I had something good to read, I would hide under the bedclothes with a torch and read after lights out, because I couldn't put it down, and of course I devoured the daily paper after my parents had finished with it.

Halfway through my eighteenth year, I saw an advertisement for nurses to train as midwives at Dunedin's Queen Mary Hospital. I asked if I could reply and was surprised to hear that I could. I had to go early for an interview so Mum suggested I ask Aunty Kate if I could stay the night with her at Green Island. Aunty Kate was my favourite aunt. She was the only Catholic in the family and always went to mass. Her son, Geordie, used to tease her: "Been down on your old marrow bones again today, have you?"

She said she would love to have me, so I caught the bus from her place, had an interview with the matron and was accepted. However, because of my age, I couldn't start training for another six months.

Aunty Kate had pretty rag mats on her floors and she taught me how to make them by cutting strips and sewing them on by machine. Thank you, Aunty Kate, I have made many since when times were tough.

About two months later I saw an ad for Nurse Aids at Braemar Hospital in Dunedin. Bed and board found, it said. I knew the only way I would get away was to get a job with accommodation so I mentioned it to Mum. It was almost as though they'd been waiting for me to make a move.

"Why not ring and ask for an appointment," she said.

A few days later I went to meet the Matron and got the job. Within a week I was packed and away. I couldn't believe my luck.

Whoopee, free at last!

Dunedin 1953

Braemar Private Hospital had been converted from someone's Victorian-style, two-storey home. It was in lower George Street, one of Dunedin main streets, and owned by general surgeon, Mr Vicky Pearce, and orthopaedic surgeon, Mr Waldron Fitzgerald. Mr Fitzgerald had borrowed me once when I was in hospital when he was lecturing in a huge theatre. Unlike Effie White, he was a real gentleman; he held my nightgown to cover me while he pulled it up to show my style of plaster.

The matron of Braemar at the time was (Miss) Prudence Borlace, or Pru behind her back. She had been the Charge Nurse of Men's Medical at Dunedin Hospital for many years and was filling in for the real matron, the lovable Sister Kinnimont, who was away for an extended holiday around Europe. Several other specialists operated on their private patients there as well, so the place was almost always full.

Our accommodation, an ugly two-storey wooden house one street over and two blocks further north, was owned by a member of the Dunedin city council. He was a greasy little man, who came to inspect from time to time – well, that was his excuse – we thought he just came to leer at us. The best part about the house was that it was just a stone's throw from the back gate of the Dunedin Botanic gardens. A minute down the road, over the bridge across the Leith stream, and one was in the rose garden. I was to spend many happy days off exploring the gardens and the hothouses in the months to come.

The top floor of our house was occupied by three older girls who were dental nurses or secretaries and looked down their noses at us. We were a bit in awe of them when we met them occasionally as they came in the front door and crossed the foyer to their stairs.

There were initially six of us downstairs, mostly country girls like myself. Marion came from a sheep station up central, Yvette came from Palmerston, June, my roommate was a townie from Auckland city. Two other girls, who moved on soon after I arrived, shared the back room. June and I had the front room – it was big with a fireplace on one side and the beds on the other. It had once been divided in half with a curtain but only the curtain wire was left. We used each end of it to hang our clothes on.

June was a small dark, rather sullen girl. She told me off for throwing an apple core on to the hearth and leaving it. "It's been there four days, disgraceful, and I will not tolerate it."

She was quite right. I would never have dared to do that at home and I was ashamed. I picked it up and stopped my "just-left-home' rebellion after that. Marion was fun, but Yvette was even funnier. She was tall with carroty red hair, white skin and freckles, and almost white eyebrows. She also had a way of turning almost everything into a farce. We became the best of friends.

There was always one girl on night duty, the rest on morning or afternoon. When the night girl wasn't sleeping we played our wind-up gramophone, we had about three records, which we never tired of playing. But when June broke up with her boyfriend, she bought the record *Seven Lonely Nights Makes One Lonely Week'* and played it almost continually, until someone told her if she played it again they were going to break the thing over her head. I still remember every word of that song after fifty-four long years.

Poor June. A few weeks later she left and went back to Auckland. And then we were three. Other records we had were Debbie Reynolds and Marlene Dietrich singing *Too Old to Cut the Mustard*, which still makes me laugh, (but I have never heard it since), and a hit tune called, *It's in the Book*. This was a double-sided record, top of the hit parade for weeks, and so-o-o funny. It was a send-up of a church service. Side One was a sermon on *Mary Had a Little Lamb*.

"Now turn the record over and we will sing hymn number? MMMMM" – he hums a note for the organist. "Thank you kindly

Connelly."

"Mrs O'Malley/ down in the valley/ suffered from ulcers/ I understand/ she swallowed a cake /of Grandma's Lysol/ now she's got the cleanest ulcers in the land.' Chorus- So let us sing/ of Grandma's Lysol," etc.

"Little Herman/ and Brother Sherman/ had an aversion/ to washing their ears/ Grandma washed them/ with the Lysol/ and they haven't heard a word in years," and the chorus again.

It was such a catchy tune, we loved it and sang along at the top of our voices. Quite suddenly the radio stations stopped playing it, never to be mentioned again. As chance had it, a friend of one of our girls got to see through radio station 4ZB's record library and asked what all the records were that had a skull and crossbones sticker on them. She was told that the Catholic and Presbyterian churches paid millions of pounds out each year to ban certain records they didn't approve of. One of the records was *It's in the Book*. I was screaming livid.

Just before I left home our church had been scrounging for money. They wanted to raise £60,000 to train more preachers, and now I hear they were forking out millions to ban records. I felt the church should have been able to rise above a funny joke, and as far as I was concerned it was the final nail in the coffin of religion.

Our duties at the hospital were 7 am to 3 pm – 3 pm to 11pm and 11 pm to 7 am. With my fear of the dark I found it frightening walking the streets alone between 10.30 pm and 11 pm, and developed a real paranoia about anyone walking behind me. It wasn't so bad coming home at 11, as there were usually two of us. There was supposed to be two on mornings, two on afternoons and one on nights; however we found that being on a shift for just two weeks and then having to change to another was very disruptive and tiring.

Before June left we had a run-in with the girl upstairs. No matter how quiet we tried to be when we got up for morning duty, the girl above would knock on the ceiling. One morning when we had been whispering as we got dressed she knocked again. I'd had enough; she had been doing it all week. I had noticed when shifting the coat hangers on the coiled steel curtain wire that they made the most wonderful noise.

"I'll fix her," I yelled. I leaped on the end of the bed, grabbed a hand full of coat hangers and began rubbing them back and forth on the wire. The noise was truly amazing, better than I could have hoped for. A great cacophony of reverberating sound filled the room and bounced off the walls. June, who rarely smiled, collapsed on her bed with silent laughter. Miss Smart Arse upstairs never banged on the ceiling again.

The food for the off duty girls in the flat came from the hospital – we carted it back when we came off duty, and great food it was. If we didn't want to cook, we could go back to the hospital to eat. The hospital cook was in her mid-twenties and a fabulous cook. At work, we all ate around a long table and could order anything on the menu. I was introduced to sweetbreads, for light diet, and properly cooked Tamarillo (Mum cooked them in their skins, which made them very bitter,) and many things I'd never tasted before. Everyone smoked at the table after meals and on the first night, one of the girls offered me a cigarette. There were a few smirks around the table as I tried to smoke it, but smoking was the excepted thing so I felt I had to join in.

My first days on the wards in the company of Yvette were a trauma. I was still terribly shy and taking urinal bottles and pans to patients made me embarrassed. We had a dear wee patient I will call Miss Morgan. She'd been the Head Mistress of a well-known girl's high school, and Yvette had been her student before going on to Colombo College. Miss Morgan had cancer of the bowel and had no control of the foul-smelling faeces that flooded her bed several times a day. It was our job to clean her up and the poor dear kept saying how sorry she was that we had to do that. She also had a bedsore that worried me, given my own experience of bedsores I knew how painful it must be.

"Shouldn't we put some ointment on it?"

Yvette said that you should never put ointment on broken skin as it softened it and made it worse. Cleaning up Miss Morgan shook me to the core, I seriously contemplated writing home saying I wasn't cut out to be a nurse. But weeks passed and I became desensitised, as all nurses do. Miss Morgan died while I was on my day off and her place was taken by a lady I will call Mrs Fraser. She was just in her thirties and also had cancer. After surgery she had a drain in her side and was forever pulling it out. Her condition made her labour intensive so I spent a lot of time trying to make her comfortable. She died while on my duty, my very first death. I was so sad.

Many, many years later, Braemar Hospital became a restaurant. The room where Mrs Fraser died was the main dining area. I couldn't bring myself to dine there; felt I would be haunted by the spectre of Mrs Fraser there before me dying in her bed.

I had another embarrassing episode in the first weeks. We were all having tea (dinner) in the dining room. Yvette and I had agreed to answer bells alternatively. That afternoon we had admitted an eighty-three-year-old man who had never been in hospital before. We had already delivered his meal to him upstairs when the bell rang.

"I want," he said, "to make water."

I hoofed off to get a urinal bottle and delivered it, covered in a cloth, to his bedside locker. "I'll just put it there," I said.

He gave me a funny look, and I knew he didn't understand, but I wasn't about to hang around and explain how to use it and almost flew out of the room. The bell rang again a few minutes later. Yvette went to answer it and came back laughing. "He thought you had bought him water for his tea," she said.

All the Sisters on the staff were great, except one, an English immigrant. Everyone called her "a crawler'. It was obvious to everyone, even to the young nurse aids, that Pru was way out of her comfort zone as a matron. She was always hassled and nervous. The English Sister lived in, the garages behind the hospital having been turned into several rooms, and she quickly ingratiated herself with Pru. Together they would spend hours talking in Pru's office, while the other people on duty did her work in the wards. Nobody, but nobody liked her.

My leg was standing up quite well to all the racing up and down stairs, but it ached very badly one day as it was prone to do every now and then. Pru asked Allen Aldred, who had a patient there at the time if he would see me. He was happy to oblige and I reminded him that I had already been his patient. He gave me the day off and told me to rest. He had caught Yvette whistling that morning and asked her if she'd had birdseed for breakfast. The specialists were far more relaxed with the staff at Braemar than they dared to be with the nurses at the public hospital, so we could always have a laugh with them.

Unfortunately, while I was there I also got a cold while I was on night duty, which went to my chest. Pru arranged for me to see a chest specialist in rooms just up the street. He said it was just congestion and gave me a script for pills. However he told me he was worried about my husky voice (a real singer's voice) and arranged for me to see a Dr Butcher at Dunedin Hospital. Well, he certainly lived up to his name. Dunedin Hospital specialists had a reputation of behaving like little gods and this one was no exception. "Why was I crying?" he yelled. I wanted to say because your bloody steel spatula has slipped off my tongue you stupid bastard, and is now digging a hole in my gums. But I couldn't, he had a hold of my tongue with a cloth and had it pulled down to my belly button. He told me he couldn't find anything wrong with my throat. Did I sing?

"Yes."

"Well that's it then – you've been singing too many Johnny Ray songs. Come back and see me in a week."

Not bloody likely.

Marion was the next to leave; she had other plans, so now we were two. Marion had moved into the front room after June had left, and I shared the other front room with Yvette. We had a habit of dancing around in the evenings in our underwear and doing gymnastics accompanied with gales of laughter. The pull-down blind was all tatty and broken at the bottom and the lady from next door came to warn us that she had seen a man watching us several times from the street. We had to pin a towel to the blind.

On the day Marion left she decided to spring clean her room. When the man arrived to collect her trunk, she was on her hands and knees polishing her way out of her room and out into the hallway. I had a white face pack on, and it had just started to crack when he came to the front door. I decided, ever the show-off, to make an entrance. It was worth it. I'll never forget the look on his face.

As Yvette said afterward, amid shrieks of laughter, "He must have thought he'd come to a tenth-rate boarding house. There was Marion with her bum stuck out into the passage, flinging dusters over her shoulder, (she wasn't) and you walk out looking like something out of a horror film."

I got to one dance while I was at Braemar. Every Saturday night they had a dance at the Dunedin town hall. I had met a very handsome boy who looked Italian, and he asked to take me. I had only one good dress: Mum had had a piece of beautiful floral organza which I had admired, and she said she would get a girl at Momona to make a dress for me. She put cream-coloured taffeta under it, which was just right, but unfortunately, it also got puff sleeves, so far out of fashion. Off I went to this dance, and there were all the city girls dressed in the latest fashion, so self-assured, and there was I, in a dress too long, with stupid puff sleeves. I felt like a country bumpkin fool, which of course I was. I decided to do something about my clothes. I bought a Harris Tweed coat from a secondhand shop. It was far too big around the middle for me, but I solved that by wrapping it over and putting a belt around it.

"My God, what do you look like?" said Mum, when I went home to visit, but I thought I was just the bee's knees. The people of Dunedin didn't bat an eyelid, so used were they to the hordes of university students that flooded Dunedin every year.

Yvette, when I told her I was going on to be a maternity nurse, said, "Why don't you come with me to train as a general nurse at Oamaru."

I had never had a good friend like her and didn't want to lose her. I applied to Oamaru and was told that, as I hadn't gone to high school, I would have to get a report card from my last year at primary. I wrote to the new teacher at Momona. He wrote back saying there was no record of me having been at the school, but he had done a report card for me anyway. My God, what a chance he took. I was able to thank him many years later.

The report wasn't quite as good as the one I'd got, but he had Excellents in all the right places. I was accepted, but then, staff of any kind were hard to get in the 1950s: the hospitals were desperate.

One evening at Braemar, when we were all at the dinner table, the Matron received a phone call. She came back in and announced that the call had come from Wellington where she'd been advertising for staff.

She told us that Australian nurses, four trained and one nurse aid had just arrived for a working holiday. "I said I would take them all."

There was a moment's silence around the table while we digested that little bombshell; it was nurse aids that were needed, not trained staff. I let them in the front door at tea time two days later.

"We thought we were coming to a huge hospital," said one, as well they might. They were a noisy brash mob, so unlike our slim and ladylike crew. They were all in their forties or fifties except for the nurse aid who was about thirty-five. They were all overweight but not obese and had flat nasally accents. I thought the nurse aid was almost common. They had been promised accommodation and our flat was the only place they could go. They moved in, took over the place, and Yvette and I might just as well not have been there.

Yvette was the next to leave, so I was left alone. Her Mum and Dad wanted her to have a holiday before she started training. I spent a weekend with them up at Palmerston and we went for a picnic up to Trotters Gorge. Her Mum was a talented and artistic person, and they had a lovely home with wonderful marble sculptures.

After Yvette left, I was put on night shift. The nurse aid, and one Sister had the room behind mine, the door to their bedroom just through the wall from the head of my bed. The nurse aid would leave her room, talking at the top of her raucous voice, and slam the door. None of them gave a moment's thought that I was trying to sleep, and would clump around all day in their sensible shoes.

After a few days, I was desperately short of sleep. My alarm would wake me at 6 pm – it was already dark – and the flat would be quiet.

I'll just lie here a little while and then I'll get up, I'd tell myself, but I would doze off again and it was sometimes nearly midnight when I awoke. I would dress quickly and run through the silent streets, pour out my woes to the night Sister knowing that she would never expose me. But I hadn't reckoned on our Pommie crawler. She was a night person; always stayed up late, and one night near the end of my fortnightly stint, there she was when I came rushing in late. The next morning she went straight to Pru and reported me.

To make matters worse I had two small deep burns on my thigh made by my hot water bottle. I'd been so exhausted I didn't even know I was being burnt. I still have the scars today. Pru left a message that she wanted to see in the morning before I went home.

Why was I so often late? she wanted to know. But I'd had enough; I didn't even want to discuss it.

"I'm leaving," I told her.

She was horrified. "Why? Why do you want to leave? I need you here."

But I was past it. I didn't have the confidence, the education or the words to explain. I was tired. I just wanted out. I finished my last week on day shift, rang home and said I was coming back, and left.

When I was still on the farm, Mum, Dad and I had had a rare night out at the Momona Hall: we went to see a variety concert produced by Peter Dawson, the morning radio announcer at 4ZB. I'd never seen a show and lapped up every minute. They had a young female impersonator – a bit rich for country folk – comedy acts and singers. But the one that took my heart was a pretty Samoan hula dancing girl in a hula skirt made from many layers of shimmering red cellophane paper. Her act was the most magical thing I'd ever seen and vowed that somehow I would learn to do the hula.

My first week working at Braemar, I started to make inquiries. In no time I was directed to a Charlie Murray, a full-blood Samoan, who had a restaurant in George Street.

I went to see him and we talked in the kitchen while he casually flicked oysters from a large bowl of batter into hot fat. He told me the girl I had seen was his sister. He agreed to give me at least one lesson a week; gave me his address and we made a date. After introducing me to his wife, he began my first lesson by sitting me in their lounge alone, to let me absorb the sounds of Polynesian music. Each week after that, we arranged a time to suit both our shifts and I had one or two lessons a week. Every time I mentioned money he would say, "Let's leave it a while until I see how you get on."

When I knew I was leaving I went to see him in the restaurant kitchen. "Charlie," I said, "I'm leaving. I have to pay you." I knew I owed him more than two week's wages.

"No," he said, "I don't want any money. You are so good, and you have been a real pleasure to teach."

Dear Charlie Murray, you would never know what a gift you had given me.

It was good to be home. I had just one month to go before going to Oamaru to start my training. Mum was pleased. She'd had to help with the milking when I left, but here I was again, decked out in overalls and gumboots, and strangely enough, I was being treated like an adult for the first time.

I went to a dance at Henley during that month and ran into Issie, my best friend from Momona School, and her boyfriend Joe. We stopped to talk at the edge of the dance floor. What a lovely couple they were; everyone expected them to marry. It was many years before I saw her again and by then she was completely different. When Issie left school at the age of fifteen she got a job as assistant cook at the White House Hotel at Henley. It was an old wooden place, very pretty, on the main road south, by the river. Soon she was working overtime and getting £12 a week. This was a huge wage for a fifteen-year-old girl. Her early goal was to become second cook and she worked towards that end. She and Joe went out for eight years. He kept asking her to set a date but she kept saying she hadn't saved enough. Finally we heard that he'd given her an ultimatum – marry me next year or our relationship is off. She didn't and they broke up and he was never to marry.

I don't remember how old she was when her father died at their Momona farm. He was burning off the haystack bottom, and it wasn't known if he died and fell into the flames, or fell into the flames and died. On the day of his funeral, Issie was missing. When asked why she hadn't come to his funeral she said that she couldn't afford to take the day off. It was then the family knew that she had a serious problem.

She spent the next few years at a private mental hospital, a beautiful place with majestic trees in the foothills above Dunedin. The weekly fees were enormous and must have come from Issie's bank account. Later she was transferred to Cherry Farm, the public mental hospital at Palmerston where she, at last, seemed to improve. Eventually she was discharged and lived out the rest of her short life with her brother Robbie at the family farm. It was about 1968 when I last saw her. I had flown down from the North Island to go to a school jubilee, and she was not long out of hospital. She had the vague look that some mental patients get, her hair was cut in the trademark fashion of the hospital, that is, straight around the bottom. We waved and smiled across the crowd but, to my everlasting shame, I didn't go to speak to her, I just didn't know what to say. Her life was such a waste of a very beautiful person. I hope we meet again in the afterlife so I can make amends.

Janet Frame, the famed New Zealand writer, spent time in Cherry Farm at the same time as Issie, and in one of her short stories she talks about the lady whose only ambition was to be second cook.

The month at home was soon up – it was time for me to leave again. I'd been given a list of things I had to take, x many knickers, petticoats, nightwear, white nurse's shoes, a bathing suit and a watch with a second hand on it, to list a few. It was like going off to boarding school, which I suppose it was.

Going down to meet the bus, I sat on the back of the trailer with my tin trunk, and said goodbye to the farm for the last time.

Oamaru 1953 - 1955

Oamaru is a pretty little town on the coast, about 114 kilometres north of Dunedin. It is surrounded by hills, and on top of the steepest one stood the hospital. The early city fathers no doubt had placed it there to keep infection away from the town. It was a wise choice as it had sweeping views of the town below, the coastline, small harbour and the breakwater. The original hospital, just two large rooms with a smaller room in between, was on a small corridor to the right as you entered the front door. This was now the Children's Ward. Further along the corridor were the next two wards to be built, Fraser Ward, men's medical below, and Hall ward, women's medical above. Then, the original hospital kitchen, now abandoned. Two more modern wards came next: Murray, men's surgical, and Forrester Ward, woman's surgical above that. All the auxiliary departments, x-ray, operating theatres, biology laboratories, physio, kitchens and staff dining room were on the left side of the corridor. Out the back door, up some concrete steps on to the next plateau stood the Nurses' Home. It was shaped like a capital E, with the middle bar missing, because that was our basketball and tennis court, but from the bottom bar of the E, out towards the hospital was the original Nurses' Home, now the Sisters' wing. Also in the spacious grounds was a biggish maternity annex, a tuberculosis annex, an infectious diseases annex (not used since the polio epidemic) and the morgue.

When Yvette and I arrived we were given a double room in the Sisters' wing as rooms in the Nurses' Home were in very short supply. The other four girls in our class had rooms of their own. All nurses had to live in, even the Sisters. It's hard to believe, that if a girl got married she was sacked. The only Sister who lived out was Sister Pope, the Nurses' Home Sister because she had to look after her elderly mother.

The first few days were quite frightening as we had to endure the yells every few minutes of a demented old lady in Forrester Ward, which was the closest to our room.

The day after we arrived, we were fitted out with our new uniforms. Whites to be worn in the wards and on special occasions, and greys to be wore out of the wards. We had veils that had to be worn a special way and white shoes; they provided us with ugly white Lyle stockings. It wasn't long before I started folding my veil in a much more attractive fashion, more like a Sisters' veil, which I starched stiffly using boiled up cornflour. Strangely enough I was never pulled up for this. We also opted for white nylon stockings as soon as we could afford them out of our meagre wages.

We spend the first six weeks in the lecture room doing preliminary, (prelim. for short) where we learned the history of nursing, nursing technique, and spent a few days in the biology department, where we learned just how many germs could be found on our "clean' hands, in our mouths, in fact almost any place. We learned also how to identify germs by their shapes. I loved biology and thought I would have become a biologist had I known such a job existed.

We were especially warned how easy it was to get into trouble with false teeth: one nurse working in women's medical had collected them all up one morning and taken them to the sluice room to clean. When she had finished she didn't know which teeth belonged to whom; it took some time to sort them all out and they had to be cleaned repeatedly after patients tried them for size. Another girl thought it would be a good idea to sterilise them so she gathered them up and boiled them. Alas, they came out all twisted and melted and it cost the hospital board a large sum of money to get them all replaced. Unfortunately for me, throwing them down the sluice was not mentioned.

Sister Smith was the nursing technique Sister. She would take us around the wards, teach us how to make beds, how to change the pillowcases, and how to point the wheels on the beds all the same way for ward inspection. Then there was how not to shake the blankets to avoid spreading infection; how to stand when someone our senior, even by three month, walked into a room; how to, and how not to, lift patients, and no end of other how not to's. Came the day we had to learn how to give a bed bath, and she couldn't have chosen a worse patient to demonstrate on. She chose Mrs Lobb – "Lobby' to every member of staff. Poor Lobby had been admitted several years previous with a stroke and had since wizened up to a tiny distorted creature with one knee bent almost up to her chin, and the other halfway. One arm was also bent completely, the other arm, which was incredibly strong, she would use to fling around your neck so tightly she would pull your veil off and almost choke you. This was accompanied by a very loud oooooooooo! – the only thing she could say. She had fallen out of bed at some time and was still very frightened. To greenhorns like us it was all very disturbing. I doubt if I was the only one who wrote home that night to say it was all too much. I was positively shaken, but the letter was never posted.

Failing the exams at the end of the six weeks meant you were out. Luckily none of us did.

The nurses' dining room on the first floor was another place to become used to. It was a large square room with another small square servery just inside the door that attached to the kitchens below. The new recruits sat just inside the door in front of the serving hatch, while everyone moved up one. You could tell a nurse's seniority by where they sat as none of us, apart from registered nurses, wore any identification. The tables went up one sidewall, and along the top, with the long Sisters' and Matrons' table right in the middle. The Matron sat at the top end against the wall, from where she could survey the room. The main meal was in the middle of the day and it was to the first sitting that Matron came. At this meal we all went and sat at our tables until Matron came breezing in and we all stood up and remained standing until she had seated herself. At all other meals we could dash in the door, collect our meal from the serving hatch, and take it to our table.

The menu was fairly predictable: like most institutions, in those days we always had bread pudding on Mondays, there being no preservative in bread, or fridges and freezers. This also meant that most of our food was fresh, and we were lucky because the gardeners kept a large vegetable garden in the grounds.

Over the next months, I learned to eat vegetables in new exciting ways, like baby beetroot, cooked whole and served hot, and broad beans, young and fresh-cooked in the pods.

After we passed our preliminary exams and set to work in the wards, Yvette and I were given separate rooms near each other on the top floor. Each week all nurses had a study day where we spent the day at lectures, and we had one day off, thus we worked a six-day week. We spent some evenings and spare time swatting for our weekly test, but Friday had late shopping nights and Saturday had the dance at the Scottish Hall. However, as we were on alternate morning and evening duties, getting out happened only once every two weeks.

Yvette and I were lucky, for the first sixteen months of our training we were almost always on the same duty. Yvette liked to lie in bed in the mornings whenever she could, but I would be up early and go to her room, collect her tray with the teapot and jug and head off to the kitchenette at the end of the corridor to get our tea and make breakfast. Each floor had a kitchenette stocked with bread, butter, jam, marmite, cheese, and honey. This was mainly for the use of the girls who were on afternoon shift so they didn't miss breakfast, and of course anyone who wanted a cuppa or snack. When the small Kakanui tomatoes came into season we would buy some and have them sliced on toast. Tomatoes on toast is still my favourite breakfast. Yvette took it as her right that I should be the lackey. I even mended her clothes and made a dress for her as she hadn't a clue. She was blessed with a mother who had done everything for her.

All the wards had an established routine. When reporting for duty at 6 am, we first had to sign in, then read the night report from the night nurse. Then hand basins and tooth mugs were handed out to the bed patients and the walking patients helped to the bathroom. When washing was finished, bowls were returned to the sluice room to be emptied and stacked for cleaning later. 7 am – breakfast, Sister served; everyone handed out trays, patients hand-fed where necessary, trays collected and returned to the ward kitchen for the nurse aid to wash. She also was responsible for handing out the fresh water jugs and orange juice, but otherwise had no patient contact.

The next job for Sister and the senior was the pill round, while the divide, if we were lucky enough to have one, and the junior began getting patients up and out to the lounge where possible. Beds were made and changed. Heaven help anyone if Sister Smith came into the ward and found us walking down the ward with an armful of dirty linen because we had omitted to take the dirty linen trolley with us. Next, the cleaning: we all, from senior to junior, did that. First damp tea leaves – saved by the nurse aid in the ward kitchen in a large fruit can with holes punched in the bottom – were sprinkled over the floors, and the floors swept. Then armed with cloths wrung out in disinfectant, we dusted every bed, locker and window sill until not one speck of dust remained. The divide nurse, or if no divide, the junior, then cleaned all the specials, where hand basins were added to the list. After that the senior did the dressings, the junior – or "grub' as she was known – answered the bells, and dished out pans.

Lunch followed the same routine as breakfast, then patients were prepared for visitors. Visiting hour was between 1 pm and 2 pm and strictly adhered to. The ward doors would be closed while we scurried around putting lockers straight, lined up all the bed wheels to face inwards, straightened bedding and ascertained that the under-bed stools were all in the exact position When the ward looked regimented and perfect, and only then, would the doors be opened to let in the visitors. Two only to a bed.

During visiting, the junior attacked the sluice room, cleaning all the pans and utensils with *Clever Mary*, cleaning the sluice and washing the floor before drying everything and stacking it away. The senior attached to the duty kitchen did much the same, but she had to sterilise everything and wipe down the stainless steel benches with mentholated spirits. These duties had to be done even on days when the workload had been heinous – it was not unusual to do an hour of unpaid overtime.

Afternoon shift was much quieter. Apart from leaving your duty areas clean and tidy, there was no cleaning to do, just one meal, dressings, pans and settling patients for the night. The divide nurse, on the second half of her shift, was responsible for giving any enemas that were needed, but these were mostly in the surgical wards when a patient was going to surgery the next day. She also did the "prepping' of surgery patients for the morning. This meant shaving all body hair for many inches around the operation site and painting with whatever colour the operating surgeon had a passion for. Some liked mercurochrome (bright scarlet), others Gentian violet, (dark purple), or sulphanilamide, (yellow).

The night shift girl had to more or less manage the ward on her own. Her main duty was bed bathing all the really sick patients in the specials, starting the first one at 3 am. And she was responsible for cleaning out the storeroom where all the shelves were stacked with large bottles of potions, sterile packs and all the serious things the ward needed. The ward doors were opened at 5 am when she started the rounds to poke thermometers into the mouths of sleepy people, check their pulses and write up their charts. A last-minute wipe down of the benches and it was off to have breakfast with the rest of the night staff, regardless of rank, all at one table.

My first ward was Children's Ward. Mothers were not permitted to stay with their children, so it could be very noisy at times. Trying to feed food into the mouth of a screaming toddler was frustrating. I would get quite worried when I couldn't get a child to eat, but Sister said not to worry that they would eat when they were hungry, and she was right. We stayed on a ward for two months at a time, alternating between morning and afternoon shifts.

The next two months for both Yvette and I was as juniors on night shift, and didn't we have some fun. There was one nurse on each ward at night, and Yvette had to help the two girls on the surgical side and I had the two medical wards. The nurses on Children's Ward and the T.B annex had no help apart from the night Sister when she was needed. Our other duty was to cook the meal in the big hospital kitchen for all the night staff. If they didn't have cast-iron stomachs before we were inflicted on them they must have developed them as neither of us could cook. At least I had a few clues, having on one occasion cooked for fourteen mill men, but Yvette had none. There was hilarity in the kitchen most nights.

There was a potato peeler in the kitchen, a big drum with very abrasive inner walls. All one had to do was pour the potatoes in the top, turn on the tap and set it spinning. To get them out one held a bucket under the door of the drum while it was still turning and they came flying out. One night Yvette opened the door without a bucket underneath and the spuds spewed out at a thousand miles an hour and skidded across the tiled floor. We had to crawl around on all fours, laughing ourselves silly, to retrieve them from all their hiding places.

After we'd taken all the meals out and they'd been eaten, we collected the dishes and washed up in Hall Ward kitchen. Then it was back to work running between wards to help with the bed baths in the "Specials' and answering the bells.

Early morning, when the ward was awakened at 5 am, saw us handing out bedpans and urinal bottles. Most patients were kept on bed rest, two weeks about average after an operation, and a large percentage of the patients in the medical ward were not mobile. How different from today when you are up and moving the day after most ops.

By this time we were beginning to become more adventurous and ventured out to the dance on Saturday night. I became friendly with a guy who I allowed to walk me home. He wanted Yvette to chum up with his mate, but she wasn't having a bar of it, saying she was frightened. It took me weeks to talk her into it, and then we all walked home together. Little did I know that once she started she would become a horror! I can't even remember who these nice lads were. Anyway it died a natural death after a month or so.

One lad who was very much attracted to me was called John Hore and he was a damn pest. For one thing, he was an appalling dancer: he had no rhythm and stomped all over my toes. He'd been set up in a rotary hoe business by his Mum but he definitely wasn't the full quid. We all tried to avoid him; insults bounced off him like a rubber ball, and the problem was, that once you had refused to dance with him you couldn't accept anyone else. One night he dived in front of me and said he was going to stand there until I said I would dance with him. Another night when he managed to snaffle the last dance, much to my fury, he asked if he could drive me home. As I was on my own I said he could, and as soon as we got to the Nurses' Home I jumped out, but he was too quick for me and grabbed my arm.

"Oh, Gwen, I love you so much. Will you marry me?"

I was appalled and shouted, "Don't be so bloody silly!"'

Quite apart from the fact that he was "odd', just imagine being a Mrs Hore. Can you picture the scene in an auction house, you have successfully bid for something and they ask for your name.

"Whore," you reply. Dear God, the whole place would be apoplectic.

There were no serious boyfriends for a while, but we got to know lots of lads at the dances and never lacked for partners.

Our leisure hours were strictly controlled by the hospital – we all had to be back in by 10 pm. If we wanted to go to a dance we had to sign the book and ask for dance leave, then we had to be in by midnight. Before leaving the Nurses' Home we would check the book to see if leave had been granted, then sign ourselves in when we arrived back. We even had to fill in the time. It wasn't smart to cheat because when coming in the front door we could be seen from the hospital.

Hall Ward again, women's medical, the least popular ward in the hospital, as old ladies can be more grumpy than old men. My senior nurse was Shirley Ireland, daughter of the people who owned the big local flour mill. Many of the nurses found her very intimidating as she was always immaculate, her hair tied back in a big bun, a style I was soon to emulate, and she looked quite severe. But we got on like a house on fire, she and I always together in our drama club plays.

We admitted a lady who'd had a stroke and, try as we might, nobody could get her to rally – she just seemed to give up. One morning we found her in a very wet bed and it had gone right into the mattress. We decided to change her from one bed to another. Unfortunately the other bed was higher as it had an innerspring mattress. Shirley lifted her top half and I lifted her feet, but she sagged in the middle and no way could we lift her bottom high enough. Moreover the bed started rolling down the ward with us trailing behind it. We both got the giggles and had to put her down onto the cold floor. Shirley rang the night Sister who came, picked her top half up no trouble at all and popped her on the bed. The patient herself deteriorated quickly and developed a bedsore which eventually rotted away until it was the size of a dinner plate. It was dreadful to behold: there was a big dead flap of skin around it and we had to pack eusol lint in under it to slough away the dead tissue. Sometimes we couldn't always find the lint it was packed so deeply.

We also had a lot of long term, senile, bed-ridden patients, including Lobby, because there was nowhere else to send them. This made for a morbid workplace, but thankfully some of the speaking patients made life easier.

There was a Mrs Patton who had a large space allotted to her out on the balcony. The poor lady was crippled with rheumatoid arthritis and had very twisted arms and legs. Her entire body was covered with severe eczema caused by a violent reaction to gold injections she'd had years previously for her condition. Everyone's first reaction was to pick the bedclothes up with thumb and forefinger but of course we had to resist doing that. Flaking skin spread for yards around her bed – it got into everything. The only thing she washed was her face and hands, the rest of her body had to be scraped with a knife every day and have a thick coating of Vaseline applied. She had a bad habit of leaving her false teeth in the tooth mug and one day I collected her hand basin and mug and emptied her teeth down the sluice. I had to put my hand down to retrieve them. I didn't dare tell her what I'd done or what indeed her teeth had shared the sluice with. The poor lady had become addicted to pethidine and every day at 4 pm she would be sitting on the bell to get her fix. We became quite friendly over time and we corresponded for some time after I left.

My confidence and mischievous personality were beginning to emerge, thank goodness. It saved my sanity, and I got up to all sorts of tricks to amuse the patients.

Quite a few of the old girls each morning were put into large wide armchairs on casters and wheeled out to the sunny balcony at the end of the ward. This gave us time to change and remake their beds. One of my other favourite tricks was to get them into the chair, say "Right, here we go," and I would bend right down, hands on the wide chair arms, and go screaming down the ward. This never failed to get squeals from the chair occupant and lots of smiles from the others, but the old dears loved every minute of it. Dear Sister Pinkerton, a little blonde, was in charge of the ward, a real sweety, (we called her Pinkie) and she didn't once tell me off. Maybe she realised I was bringing a spark of joy to their sad lives.

However, my little prank backfired on me one morning. By this time I had learned the nurse's trick of rolling my stockings down to below my knees. That way we didn't need to wear suspender belts (or *easies* as the elasticised girdles of the day were called). The trick was to roll the stocking down, hook a finger into the top, twirl it around a couple of times to tighten it, then tuck it under another roll. This way they stayed up all day under your knees.

So there I was screaming down the ward, bum in the air, when unbeknown to me, in walked the Matron, the Medical Superintendent, and Sister to do a ward round.

As the Matron said later: "What a sight! If you must roll your stockings down, please do not bend down in front of the Medical Superintendent. All we could see was six inches of bare leg and a mile of frilly petticoat."

I couldn't believe I had got off so lightly.

I had joined the nurse's drama group. Each year a nurse's drama competition was held with all the South Island nursing groups competing. There was much prestige in winning the trophy. We practiced every Wednesday in the old infectious diseases building where the evil-looking iron lung stood in the corner to remind us of the past.

I auditioned and was given the part of an eighty-three-year-old woman. Nineteen, and I had to be eighty-three? It was a period play, our costumes borrowed from the local Oamaru drama society. My dress was black with had a row of tiny covered buttons from the neck to below the waist that made it hard to get into. I soon learned to walk with a stick, like an old shaky lady – after all, hadn't I spent months working with them. I hated the dialogue of the play – so stilted and old fashioned – but no doubt written in a way to suit the period. I don't think any of us felt comfortable in our roles.

To get my hair grey they used white poster paint, which went stiff and flaky when completely dry, but it looked good from a distance.

Our first performance was at the Oamaru Opera House, one of those magical old theatres with the best seats upstairs. The place filled me with awe. We were competing for the British Drama League prize, which we also did each year.

I have never been so nervous. I had heard of knocking knees but thought it was an exaggeration. It is not. When the curtain came up I was sitting in a chair and my knees were shaking so badly I thought they would never stop. My mind was a blank, but then I heard my cue and the words came flowing back. Somehow we got through the play, but it came as no surprise that we were not among the prize winners.

The stage manager of the Opera House was a short little man who dressed in a dinner suit and bow tie, the tails of his jacket coat almost reaching the floor. Judy Mirfin, one of our cast and always a wag, said he reminded her of a little bantam cock, and she couldn't have been more right. He was to provide us, quite unwittingly, with a few laughs over the next two years.

Eric was the lighting man at the theatre and was known to like a drink or two. One night he arrived late and a bit the worst for wear. He climbed the ladder to the lighting box in the wings and began setting the lights for the first scene. Somehow he couldn't get it right, lights were going off and on, first this then that. The bantam cock stood in the wings on the other side of the stage gesticulating wildly. Finally with just a few seconds until curtain up time he could stand it no longer. Completely forgetting that he was standing forward of the curtain, he stormed across the stage pointing and roared, "Put that bloody spot on!"

I maintained that it must be the first time in the history of the Oamaru Opera House that the house was brought down before the curtain went up.

The Nurses Drama Festival was held that year at Dunedin, so on the night, we trundled south in a big bus with our director, (one of the nursing sisters) and our supporters.

I had let Mum and Dad know that we would be there and asked them to come to see me and truly thought they would come. After the show, which went quite well, I looked for them but found they were not there. I felt let down and bitterly disappointed. If I remember rightly it was Invercargill who won the Honours that year and there was supper and tea for everyone in the Nurses' Home afterward. I felt a bit of a clown with my white poster paint hair, now flaking badly, and on the way home I fell into an exhausted sleep and left white muck on the condensation of the window where my head rested.

Just a short time before this there'd been a gigantic scandal at Dunedin Hospital. A young lady doctor had shot dead her ex-lover, another young doctor, at the Doctors' quarters attached to the hospital. It seems he was a real cad; had promised to marry her; got her pregnant; forced her to have an abortion and then dropped her. Needless to say, the girl was bitter when he started parading other girls right under her nose and she took a violent revenge. One of the girls, a pretty blonde, who got caught up in the mess, was in the cast of the Dunedin play and was pointed out to me that night.

After Hall Ward I was sent back to Children's Ward for the next two months, then on for a two-month stint in Forrester Ward, women's surgical. Two patients from that ward will live forever in my memory.

The first was a lady who had a Scottish name so I will call her Mrs McLean.

Forrester was one of the newer wards so it was comprised of four specials in the corridor by the duty kitchen and office. And inside the ward door were two two-bed wards and four four-bed wards each side of the centre aisle. It was in one of the two-bed wards that Mrs McLean lived on her own.

She was a lovely lady in her forties, who always had a smile. As she was ambulatory and could do for herself I didn't have a lot to do with her. All nurses on the wards were supposed to read the patient notes so that we knew what was wrong with them, but the junior very rarely had the time. I was embarrassed because when Mrs McLean spoke to me I could understand very little of what she said. Her records told me she had inoperable cancer of the tongue.

When I next worked Forrester, (a week on relief many months later), she was much worse: her neck and face were swollen, and she was unable to eat and being fed with a tube. Another eight months later, now a senior nurse, and working divide on Forrester, I found Mrs McLean in a special, being kept alive with a drip in her arm. Her tongue was black and protruded down onto her chest, and the stench was gut-retching. Every breath was a gasp as this monstrous growth threatened to choke her. We placed bowls of deodorant all along the passage both sides, but the smell was so bad it was still noticeable to anyone walking along the main corridor past the end of the ward. I remember it was Christmas, but on the ward we had little to cheer about. Being an extreme case she was being cared for by the senior, the Sister, and the doctors and that was all I could be thankful for. After weeks of her being in that state, I was passing her door one morning when Dr Robinson went in, took one look, turned to come out and said curtly, "Take the drip off." Twenty minutes later the poor little lady was dead.

The hypothetic oath says: "Where there is life there is hope," but that is a blatant lie. What a load of bollocks! No miracle was going to heal her tongue and put it back the way it was. She should never have been put on a drip, but in the "50s patients had to be kept alive until it was no longer possible to do so. It was far and away the most abhorrent thing I have ever seen and I have been in favour of euthanasia ever since, or at least giving patients the wherewithal to end their lives when they want to call it a day.

The second memory was of a young lady in her early twenties, whose husband was serving in the army in Korea.

We arrived one morning for our study day and our tutor said there was something rare in the operating theatre that she wanted us to see. The young pregnant lady was admitted during the night with a ruptured uterus; they had been unable to save neither the baby, nor her uterus, and it was this that we went to see. It was an interesting sight, lying as it was in a bowl of water. The walls were all very thick except for one place. Down where it joined the cervix it was paper-thin with a large six-inch tear in it. It seems that she'd been warned not to get pregnant but had decided to risk it with near-fatal results.

As I was the divide on Forrester I was in charge of cleaning the specials. She was very ill and had become severely depressed, rarely spoke, never smiled, yet every morning I tried to cheer her up. Her husband who was in the army was brought home from Korea but that didn't help.

One morning when I breezed in to clean the hand basin I cracked a joke, and behind me, I heard her laugh. Amazed, I spun around.

"You laughed ... I finally got you to laugh."

Every day after that she improved a little more until eventually we were talking like old friends. I've often wondered what life had in store for that girl, but I will never know.

That Christmas was a bleak one for me, both in the ward and out. A lot of the girls were on holiday, Yvette included and there is nothing lonelier than a Nurses' Home when your friends are away.

"You should have joined our glee club?" one girl said. "You can come tonight … we are putting on a concert in the nurses' sitting room for the Matron and Medical Superintendent."

"I can play the spoons," I offered and raced off to the kitchen to borrow some. What a great night. I knew all the songs and played the spoons so hard I ended up with a bruised thigh.

For many months I had had a boyfriend called John Macaw. It was never a grand passion but we both loved to dance. He was very tall and well-built and there wasn't a dance that we missed whenever I was off duty. We could get around the floor in a quick step faster than anyone, truly dancing as one. One night he told me his father had bought a transport business down at Palmerston and they were all moving down there to work. He was to stay there for the rest of his life. I missed him badly. I hadn't danced with anyone else in all those months we'd been together, and have never danced properly with anyone else from that day to this.

Billie and Dance Partner at the Territorial Ball

One day I was called to the phone. It was John – he was coming up to Oamaru to the open-air dance down at the beach and would I come. *Would I!*

We met down the bottom of the drive; it was great to see my good friend again and we had a fabulous night.

"I see you and John are back together again," people remarked. Oh, if only that were true.

Next, I did a stint in men's surgical and met the nicest patient I've ever had and high on my list of the most beautiful people. His name was Charlie Murray and he worked at a big home for retarded children near Kurow.

He'd been admitted because he was having a problem with his right arm which was defying diagnosis. Charlie, who was in his early fifties, had dark wavy hair and a handsome face that always had a smile. He was in a four-bed ward with three other ambulatory men. In the afternoon they would lie on top of their beds in their sock feet and I would come in and pounce on the nearest foot to tickle. It got that all feet shot off the bed when I walked in which made me laugh. Other afternoons I would come on duty and walk down the ward singing, as my lovely nurse from Children's Ward had:

"Chicory chick, chara chara checkatarony" etc. and I would hear, "Oh God! Look out, here she comes."

Charlie had a beautiful baritone voice and he would sing a song I'd never heard but have loved ever since.

> *Oh I love to hear the choir*
> *In the chapel in the moonlight*
> *As they sing oh promise me*
> *Forever be mine.*

I don't know where it was that we met the boys from Kakanui, a small village down the coast because none of them danced. But there they were – Jack, whose surname I have forgotten, Les Dalgety and

Fred Stewartson. They were to come and go in our lives for quite a while, and I have to say we had more fun with them than anyone else. I think it may have been a nurse aid called Audrey who introduced us as it was she, Yvette and I who went out with them.

Jack, the quieter one of the three, was a labourer and drove one of those coupe cars with the long sloping back and a single three-seater seat in the front. Les was the clown, given to making outrageous comments and telling near the mark jokes, yet beneath the happy-go-lucky veneer lay a very kind and caring person. He didn't have a car because as he said he liked to have a drink and I am not going to be caught for drunken driving. Fred, at twenty-three, was the oldest; had a round face, black wavy hair, was well dressed and the most mature. He was my favourite. I always felt more comfortable with older men with whom I could have a sensible conversation. He had his own floor sanding business, drove a big black car and had masses of friends on whose welcoming doorsteps we would all arrive unannounced, with a couple of dozen beers and party until long after we were due home.

It wasn't safe to go up the road to the hospital late at night, and even more stupid to go in the front door as both could be seen from the hospital. Up behind the hospital, running down over the paddocks, was the clay Burma Road, and it was from here we would climb over the gate and sprint down the hill to climb the fire escape if you lived upstairs or in the back door if we were down.

I didn't drink when I went out with John, but started after going out with these three – always very cautiously I should add, as I loathed not to be in control. Sadly it wasn't the same for Yvette; she could be very funny when she was drunk, and so the boys encouraged her. I had a habit of speaking out without thinking first, and there was never a party when she didn't find a time to say drunkenly, "Donaldson, every time you open your bloody big mouth you put your bloody big foot in it."

Everyone thought she was very funny so she milked it for all it was worth.

I didn't find it funny later when I was trying to drag her up the fire escape while she made enough noise to arouse half of Oamaru. How we were never caught still remains a mystery.

On one memorable occasion, it was very frosty, and when the frost got on the steel fire escape it rang loudly when knocked. I had got her, giggling, laughing, and singing, all the way over the lawn to the bottom of the steps.

"Take your shoes off," I ordered, knowing that the flat clodhoppers she wore would make a racket. I pulled them off, thrust them at her, put my arm around her and started helping her up. We made it to the top but as I reached out to pull the fire door open, she dropped a shoe. It bounced, ping, ping, ping ping, all the way to the bottom.

"Oh my God!"

"Bloody bastard shoe," she slurred.

I flew down the steps, snatched up the shoe, raced up again, shoved it at her, opened the door and pushed her in.

"Now shut up or you'll get us both sacked."

I shut the door, flew down the steps, in the back door, over the corridor into my room, flung off my coat and jumped into bed fully clothed. She must have got her shoes on again because I heard her clomping progress all along the top corridor. "Bloody bastard shoe, bloody bastard shoe."

If the night Sister had come to check on me, I would have been slowly breathing, sound asleep and perfectly innocent. In the morning I read Yvette the riot act. Not that it did any good.

The strange thing about those three boys is that they rarely made a date to take us out – they would just bowl up to the front door in one of the cars and ask for us. Fred did ask me to go out not long after we met but he drove down to the breakwater where a lot of courting couples went. There was no one else around and I was scared stiff, after all, I hardly knew this man.

"Fred, I don't like it here. Please take me home."

He tried to reassure me but I wasn't having any of it.

"I'm going to walk then," I said, jumping out of the car and taking off.

After a while he started the car and came after me, driving alongside. "Come on, Gwen, get in the car, I'll take you home. I am not going to hurt you."

"No, I'll walk."

After pleading with me again he drove off. He was a bit frosty when we met the three on the street on next late shopping night, but he soon thawed out. At least he had learned that I was not one of *those* girls.

One lovely Saturday afternoon when we were swatting like good girls, Les and Jack arrived at the door saying, "Let's go for a drive." We drove down to the beach and sat awhile. When Les found out we both had Sunday off he suggested we go pig hunting, and we said, "Why not."

"There's a place I know where we can stay the night, and we'll come back tomorrow."

We knew full well we would be in big trouble if our beds were found empty, but what the hell: you are only young once. Les drove back to his place at Kakanui, packed sleeping bags, cooking things, tea, eggs, bacon, bread, sausages, potatoes and rifles, and off we went. We travelled south to Maheno and turned inland towards the hills, eventually pulling off the clay road and travelling over dry grass paddocks until at last, we came to a shepherd's hut built of stone slabs. On the big stone lintel over the door were carved the words: THE DOGS DEN.

It was like another world, so fresh and clean and far from the maddening crowd.

We unpacked while Les lit the little open fire to boil the billy. Billy tea, none better, then after a lecture from Les how not to handle rifles we set off. Not a pig was to be seen, nor a sheep, just a few rabbits, (a bit small for a 303) and a hovering hawk.

Back at The Dogs Den we did a bit of target practice. Uncle Neil had taught me how to use a .22, but Les said the 303 had a kick like a mule and showed me how to press both hands in towards one another and pull the gun tight into my shoulder.

"I'll shoot at that rock on the brow of the hill," I said.

"No, Donny, (he always called me Donny) you won't. Never, never, shoot at anything on the brow of a hill. No matter how isolated you think you are you never know if some joker is going to pop his head over the top of that hill just as you squeeze the trigger. Now you wouldn't want to blow someone's brains out, would you?"

Well I must admit there had been times when I was tempted, but I could see what he meant.

When we got sick of target practice it was almost dusk so we set about gathering more firewood while Les cooked the sausages and potatoes for dinner, followed by another billy of tea. Afterward we sat in the firelight and talked, laughed and joked, before piling into our separate bunks and sleeping like logs. In the morning the sun was long up before I woke, the boys had breakfast on the go and the delicious smell of fried bacon, eggs and the rest of last night's potatoes filled the little cabin. Yvette and I made our ablutions over at the nearby creek running with crystal clear water and went back to full plates. Later, after packing the car, we went off for another walk before heading back to town, and we drove back through Oamaru with open windows singing, *We're just back from away out yonder, tell us where the good times are.*

I didn't want to go back to the Nurses' Home and break the spell. I felt we'd been away for a week and it had been a great break. There had been no shenanigans and no drink, just three good friends together.

There hadn't been a room round done while we were away so we got off scot-free, but we were back with noses to the grindstone.

Another Sunday when Les and Jack called, just Audrey the nurse aid, and I were free. Oamaru in the 1950s was a dry area so to get an alcoholic drink one had to go to one of the pubs dotted around the border. Les suggested a trip up to McCrea's Flat, an old gold mining area in central Otago. As we had never been there, we readily agreed.

McCrae's was lovely. There was a little stone pub and behind it big areas now filled with water, which had been dug out in the search for gold. Many years later this was to again become an open cut gold mine where much more gold was brought from the ground. But then it was just the sleepy remains of the old gold rush.

I was never a beer drinker nor was Audrey so after a while we grew bored with the boys rabbiting on with other patrons and decided to explore the ancient cemetery up on the hill. We climbed the hill and over the five-barred gate into this spooky little place. For some reason the place gave off awful vibes, sending shivers up my spine. Elderly pine trees with long low branches reached well into the cemetery and threw dark shadows. We had been reading tombstones awhile when in a dark corner I saw a headstone with her surname on it.

"Look," I said, "there's your grave."

"I don't know what you are laughing about," she said. "There you are right beside me."

She was right. There we were, Morris and Donaldson, side by side. We turned as one and ran, flew over the gate in one jump and down the hill.

It was late afternoon when we finally prised the boys from the pub and set off home, or so we thought. But it wasn't to be. Back on the main road and about to pass the Shag Point turn off, one of them said something about a party at so-and-so's bach at Shag Point so let's go in. I could have killed them, it had been a long day.

The said *bach*, or *crib* as beach cottages are sometimes called, was almost at the end of the spit, clinging to the clifftop above the beach. We reached it down a narrow drive and Jack turned the coupe in the big front yard, pointing it back the way we had come. There were already a few people there, then who should turn up but Fred and Yvette making our little group complete.

Later three young lads (who probably weren't old enough to drink legally) arrived and parked at the end of the drive. I didn't like them, in fact felt less than comfortable with most of the people there – they were all a bit uncouth for me, so I kept nagging to go home. Much later, Jack, who was usually very placid, became really angry and accused the three of stealing several big bottles of beer from the car boot. They were found later when someone shifted a car and broke the bottles under a wheel where they'd hidden them. That did it! Jack declared he was leaving and stormed out.

"Wait for me," I said, racing after him with Audrey hot on my heels.

We dived into the car and Jack gunned the motor. It was as we left the yard that I realised there was not enough room between the boys' car in the drive and the edge of the cliff.

"No, Jack," both Audrey and I screamed, but he didn't listen. With the engine roaring he drove straight for the space and gave me one of the biggest frights of my life. How we made it past I will never know. Yvette told me next morning that she'd called out to say she was coming too, grabbed her jacket and bag and rushed out only to see what was happening.

"I thought there was no way the car would get past. I envisioned you all lying dead on the rocks and me having to explain what we were doing out at Shag Point at two o'clock in the morning. Worse still, why did we have a young nurse aid with us?"

We didn't see the three from Kakanui for a time after that which was just as well because we needed to study hard for our first state exams.

During that first summer, I saved enough to buy a lady's sports bike. This let me ride off in my shorts and roman sandals to explore pastures new. My favourite ride was down to the breakwater around the harbour where I would leave the bike and walk along the cliff path to the tiny coves. One magical place could be reached only at low tide when the water was about ankle deep. I would wade out to a rocky protruding point and there, under the overhang, was a myriad of tiny shells of all shapes and colours. One day I spent too long there and was almost cut off by the tide, and had to wade waist-deep to safety.

Audrey asked one day if I would like to ride up to Waitaki River to see her family. It was a lot further than I would normally go but the day was lovely so we set off with a few of her male and female friends. The trip was to tell me a lot about Audrey and explain her problems.

Along the south bank of the river were a lot of old public works huts that had housed the workers when the bridge had being built. Audrey's Mum lived there in two of the huts with about six children, the youngest about five.

She was surprised to see us and had to think what she could give us for lunch. Eventually, she decided on mock whitebait, grated cheese and potatoes in a batter and fried as fritters. The table was duly set, no cloth, just a plate of sliced bread, pepper and salt and a butter dish that held the remains of a pound of butter and looked as though it had been rolling around the floor. When someone said, "Would you like some butter," I took one look and declined. It was covered with grubby finger marks, dirt, and hairs. I was quite appalled at the way they had to live and the grubby unkempt children, although the kids seemed happy enough, if not a little wild.

Audrey had never discussed her home life with anyone, but she confided to me as we biked home that her father had abandoned them, his whereabouts unknown. She told me that most of her wage went to help her mother.

For months there had been whispers about Audrey stealing clothes from the drying room in the basement, which I had refused to believe. Unfortunately, I soon found to my sorrow that it was true.

The hospital was always short of rooms for nurses, given that everyone had to live in. Sometime during the summer the stocking room at the end of the corridor, next door to the room Audrey shared with three more nurse aids, was converted into a bedroom. And guess who the room was given to? How I loved that room. They had put in a bed, wardrobe and dressing table, but the best thing was the big half-round corner window and the fabulous view of the harbour and the breakwater with the waves crashing over it. I could sit up in bed in the mornings and be at peace with the world.

"How did you get such a big gorgeous room?" all my visitors used to ask.

The only downside was the lack of a key to lock the door – the one that fitted was the master key and I couldn't have that. Sister Pate promised that she would get the carpenter to fit a lock, but she never did.

On the list of the things to bring had been a bathing suit, and Mum was appalled that I had spent a whole £4.5 shillings on a really upmarket one. Thinking back today I'm not surprised, as this was about two week's pay. However, I got my money's worth as I used them for many years.

One day I wanted to go for a swim and my togs were nowhere to be found. I was told that so-and-so had borrowed them. I was furious and went to her room.

"Oh," she said, "I hung them on the line."

They had been hanging on the line, right side out, for two weeks in the blazing sun.

I spoke to Sister again about the key but it fell on deaf ears.

Later I was to go on holiday and when I came back, the expensive, soft kid gloves that Mum and Dad had bought me were missing, as were some nylon stockings and miscellaneous other small items.

Weeks later I was talking to Audrey in her room when she opened her bedside locker and there were my gloves for everyone to see. She shut the drawer quickly and I pretended not to notice. I asked Sister Pate for another room and was given the afore-mentioned room just opposite the downstairs back door.

As for the girl who borrowed my swimsuit, well she'd left, and as I sit here writing I have to wonder if she was pregnant. That girl had the most remarkable eyes I have ever seen; they were yellow with brown spots, and she just loved the boys. Several nurses had complained that she'd pinched their boyfriend. One minute she was there and then she was gone, and no one knew why.

It was about this time I found myself back in men's medical, on divide duties. The Sister was a tall buxom blonde with big breasts held high with an uplift bra. She had a reputation of being hard on junior nurses. The junior on this occasion was a woman of about forty-five years who had decided she would like to become a nurse. This was her first ward after coming out of preliminary so I hadn't met her. She seemed to me to be hardworking but, as my duties were entirely different to hers, she and I didn't really get to work together. At the time we had an infectious patient in the ward and it was my duty to look after him. His bed was just inside the door and heavily screened off. Every time I visited him I had to don a mask, gloves, and a large coverall. Everything that came out from behind the screen had to be disinfected before being disposed of. I received not one complaint from our haughty Sister, in fact she barely recognised my existence.

Sadly things were to change. We arrived on the ward one morning to find no junior nurse. Thinking that she'd overslept, someone was sent to find her. Disaster! Her bed was empty, so was her room – somehow she'd managed to pack up and depart without anyone knowing. We all felt sorry as we knew how hard the bitter old maid had been on her, but I was sorrier for myself because I was relegated to junior for the last month. Imagine my disbelief when she started picking on *me*.

She didn't find me such a pushover though. I was just two months from being a senior nurse so dared to answer back. Something she did NOT like.

She had this habit of tearing a strip off me then marching up the ward with head held high and her veil seeming to float out behind her. I used to think she looked like a sailing ship under full sail. She didn't seem to notice that the men's faces showed what they thought, but she did notice when the patients in front of her were trying not to laugh as I took the mickey and sailed up the ward behind her. She would spin around and glare at me, but I had been watching her carefully and by the time she got round there I was, just strolling up the ward all sweetness and light.

Of course, she got the last laugh. The two old medical wards had ancient dishes and pans made of enamel, while the two newer surgical wards had nice stainless steel. The last thing the junior did before going off morning duty was to scrub every bit of enamel, pans, tooth bowls, kidney dishes and sterilise them. After being cleaned for many years with abrasive *Clever Mary* the enamel didn't have one bit of shine left. Worse still they were covered with black marks where they had been stacked inside one another. Sister declared that they were filthy and ordered me to do the lot again. An hour and a half later they still looked the same but I was allowed to go off duty a very tired girl.

At the end of each two month period, the ward Sister wrote a ward report on each nurse. Mine read: *Nurse needs supervising in all her duties.* I could scarcely believe my eyes. I kept my temper and picked up the pen to sign and suddenly she was shocked. I am sure she realised she had gone too far, especially after the junior walking out without notice.

"Oh, nurse," she simpered, "you don't need to sign it you know."

"That's all right, Sister," I said with the sweetest smile, "I've never had a bad report, so one from you isn't going to make much difference," and I turned and walked out leaving her open-mouthed.

A short time later she got herself a boyfriend and they started showing up at the dances. He was a good foot shorter than her and as Judy Mervin said at breakfast, "He seems to dance around on her bosom."

Seems he was a farmer from up Kurau way, and some months later they married and she was gone. I hope she was happy.

It was Christmas. For weeks we'd been putting up the decorations to make the wards look bright and happy. We had a lovely dinner with roast turkey and all the trimmings, and afterward I put Yvette in a wheelchair and rushed her along the top corridor. Unfortunately coming out of one of the wards I almost collided with Matron. I thought, *oh Lord, now I am for it*, but she just smiled and walked on. Amazing what a bit of Christmas cheer can do.

The night before all the nurses who were not on duty had donned their white uniforms and red capes to parade around the entire hospital, holding candles and singing carols. I saw our Medical Superintendent Dr Bevan-Brown tucked in an alcove to watch us go by. I felt so sad for the lonely old man, who was supposed to have retired years previously but stayed on. We were his only family. I always flew to his defense when the girls said he used to say hello to empty beds every morning when he did the ward round with Matron, that is until I saw him do it myself.

He was the one responsible for giving us our inoculations against disease. There we would be, all lined up, and he would always tell his funny story. It went like this. There was this doctor giving a showgirl her inoculation ...

"You can't stick that in my arm, it will leave a mark."

"Well I'll put it in your leg."

"No, you can't put it anywhere on my body. I am a dancer."

"Okay then, stick out your tongue."

Dear Dr Bevan-Brown ... it was a few more years until he eventually went, letting Dr Trotter at last take over as surgical superintendent.

Suddenly it was almost time to sit our junior state exams. For six weeks we were to sit in the lecture room every day and review everything we'd learned. After rushing around in the wards and now sitting still most of the day, we had all piled on weight. I went up to ten stone, the heaviest I have ever been.

Our wonderful tutor was Sister Ellis who we all had great respect for.

Eventually, the dreaded day arrived and we all presented ourselves in our white uniforms at the dining room for breakfast, not that I felt the least like eating.

Just inside the door was the notice board where we also collected our mail. There were fourteen girls sitting the exam and thirteen girls got telegrams wishing them luck. Once again my parents had showed how unworldly they were, but if I'd still had my own mother I almost surely would have had a telegram as well.

One of the minor tutor Sisters supervised the exam and told us later that when she opened the paper her heart sank into her boots – it was by far the worst exam paper she'd ever seen. We had been warned to expect a question on the heart and it was there so I tackled that question first drawing a careful diagram. I left the ones I was unsure of till last. I managed to finish the paper before time was up. Now all we could do was wait. Afterward, we sat for photos and I ordered one of our little class.

The day we passed our State Exams

It was holiday time. Yvette and I wanted to do different things so we went our separate ways.

A girl in our class, who I will call Beatrice, was a strange girl, who had been adopted by older and very Victorian parents. She was tall with a round, slightly coloured face devoid of makeup, and a head of curly greasy hair full of dandruff. The poor girl was totally without personality. Worse still, she had an appalling dose of thrush and smelt really badly. Nylon knickers that you could wash and dry overnight had come onto the market, and one doctor noted that they were the worst thing ever invented for women because they didn't breathe thus making a haven for thrush. Of course, it wasn't the *done* thing to comment on these things, but an older girl in our class did eventually approach the tutor with our concerns, but even she declined to broach the subject.

Beatrice wanted to go on a cycling holiday and when asked if anyone would come with her I volunteered. We planned to go by train with our bikes in the guards van as far as Blenheim in the north, ride to Picton, over to Nelson, down the west coast and back to Christchurch via the Lewis Pass, where Beatrice was to meet her mother for the final week. First I spent a week at home. My visits to home were rare as I needed two days to get home and back. That meant a sleep day after coming off night duty then a day off.

Just after I had left home Dad had employed a share milker to look after the top farm and then moved to the small fifty-acre farm at Henley. They had bought a big wooden house and had it moved there, and this was the first time I was to see it. It was lovely with a new bathroom and kitchen. I spent a few days helping to rake up the couch grass Dad had scuffled out with the tractor and was burning it in heaps. We had to be careful of the fires as the land was peaty. Dad had had draining ditches dug, and with new grass sown it soon turned into a productive little place. I also enjoyed a day on the tractor harrowing one of the peaty fields and learned just how deceptive peat soil can be. When I drove a wheel through a small, innocent-looking puddle, the tractor tipped sideways and sank right down to the axle. I had to walk back to the barn for a rope and tie it to the harrows one end, then on to the tractor. That way I could drive out and not leave the harrows behind. I learned another lesson when I stopped at the creek to get a drink and found the water draining from peat is almost pure acid.

I told them that I needed to get a pair of walking shoes before going on holiday so Dad told Mum to go with me to town and buy some. We got a pair of brown leather brogues which cost Dad over two weeks of my pay.

Back to the Nurses' Home we delivered our bikes to the station and ordered a taxi to take us to the station. Denise who lived north of Timaru was coming with us.

Beatrice's brother had loaned us panniers, mine were big floppy ones that hung over the carrier and Beatrice had two neat ones that strapped to the carrier.

We excitedly loaded our gear into the taxi at 7.15 pm and we were away.

"You girls aren't going to catch the express, are you?" asked the driver when we were almost there. We said we were.

"But you have missed it. I just dropped someone off there before picking you up. It left at 7.15."

Oh no! What were we to do?

"We might catch the train at Waitaki if I hurray," he said.

"Right, let's do it." Why not, we had our holiday pay.

The Waitaki Bridge at that time was a dual train and road bridge. There was a keeper who rode a bike back and forth opening and shutting the gates at either end. The train beat us to it, the gate was shut. Eventually, we saw the bike light coming.

"Quickly, quickly," we urged. The driver asked the gatekeeper to ring ahead and tell the driver that three nurses were chasing the train and would he please wait for us. We rushed on but lady luck was still against us. A detour sign! The main road was closed, we had to go all the way into Waimati and out again to the main road. Unbelievable! Well, they say that everything comes in threes and so it was, the car developed a knock, obviously the big end was gone. We went slower and slower. Waimati at last, the driver found a phone and ordered another taxi that took what seemed like hours to arrive. Moreover, the driver was in a bad mood and refused to hurry; he drove slowly all the way to Timaru.

Oh, miracle of miracles! The big steam train was there. We threw some money at the driver and ran. Four men were on the platform and a cry went up.

"Here they are," and everyone cheered.

"We heard there were some nurses chasing the train … we have been here over three-quarters of an hour," one said. While nurses were held in high esteem in those days, I still find it hard to believe that an express was held up for us.

The road from Blenheim was hilly and we had to hop off our bikes and push so many times. It had become obvious that we were carrying too much luggage, but luck was with us, a farmer with a flat top truck stopped and took us almost to Picton. We found a divine camping ground up a wooded valley, and were allocated an old army hut with a small wood-burning stove to cook on. Picton, at the head of the Marlborough Sounds is a heavenly place so we stayed two days, doing the mail run around the sounds by launch one day and walking up to the reservoir through a beautiful wooded valley the next. It was on the way down that we ran into strife. I suggested a short cut over a field with a horse in it. Having always got on well with horses I was a little surprised when this one took exception to our being there. It came screaming up and started rearing and snoring aggressively. We stood our ground at first, but when it rushed off rearing and kicking we took to our heels and ran, just making it through the barbed wire fence as it arrived back threatening to stamp us into the ground. Despite some small rips in our clothes and scratches from the barbed wire we'd gotten off lightly.

The road from Picton to Havelock winds in and out the inlets of the Sound, up and down steep little gullies. It was a nightmare. Moreover, the road was gravel that had just been graded and some of the stones were the size of tennis balls. We walked and pushed and puffed, stopping at night in some secluded spot to cook a meal on our small stove then climb, exhausted, into our sleeping bags. We decided not to take the main hilly route into Nelson but go instead via Lake Rotoroa, a small very pretty lake surrounded by bush. The last downhill run into the village was a delight after a very hot day on gravel roads. We camped by the lake among the trees and swam in the lake to cool our sunburnt arms. The only things to destroy the peace were the large bush flies which buzzed us until nightfall. I had packed one of my most precious possessions, a soft, polo-necked, red jersey. Unfortunately the fish we had for dinner had also shared the pack for a brief time. In the morning I found the flies had laid eggs all through my jersey and I was beside myself with rage. I had to sit for ages picking out these maggots-to-be.

We made it to Nelson at last and camped at the park at Tahuna beach, again in an old army hut with bunks and stove. Two day later we were on our way to Motuaka, Kaiteriteri, and Golden Bay, so-called for the wonderful yellow sand, then on towards Takaka. Looking at a map now I can't imagine what possessed us to go that way as we would have to come all the way back to get down the west coast, moreover it is nine miles up and nine miles down to Takaka. As we plodded upwards a public works truck stopped to give us a lift – what a relief – and the young driver said we could stay the night at their camp. All the wives had moved on to the next site and there was just a skeleton staff left, so there were plenty of empty huts, he told us.

They gave us a hut well away from the ones occupied by the men and told us to come to the dining room for dinner at six. There were about eight men already eating when we arrived.

"Help yourselves," they said, waving at the big wood stove.

There was a big pot of potatoes and a stew with lots of vegetables. We filled our plates, more than a little embarrassed as they all watched. Beatrice guffawed and sniggered, so it was left to me to make conversation. They were all very nice guys, friendly but not too friendly, and after pudding and a cuppa, we left to shower before turning in for the night.

Beatrice washed her nylon knickers and hung them over the rafters in our hut. Within minutes their stink had pervaded the place and I blew a fuse. After bottling it up for so long I went up like a volcano and said some awful things. *I* wasn't going to sleep in there with her stink. The girls are fed up with you stinking out the lecture room. God knows what the men in the ward must think of her, and why the bloody hell didn't she go and get something done about it? And another thing, why can't you talk to men in a civilized manner instead of behaving like a dawk, because *I* found her embarrassing.

I felt a bit ashamed afterward about my outburst because I knew why she hadn't done anything about it: she was too damned shy and awkward to pluck up the courage.

We had a long talk that night after I had thrown the offending knickers out the door. She told me of her strict and prudish mother who she couldn't talk to … well, I related to that. She told me that when she was fifteen and walking home from school a man had jumped out of the bushes and raped her and that was why she was ill at ease with men. When she told her mother she was told she shouldn't talk about those things and not to tell anyone as she probably encouraged him. Poor Beatrice.

Rest stop on the bike holiday

I told her to get rid of the nylon knickers as they were the problem, (they didn't have cotton gussets in those days) and made her promise to go and see one of the nursing staff when she got back. I promised never to divulge anything that she'd told me, and I never did.

The next day we set out for Takaka, not that there was much to see when we got there, so we stayed the night in a bed and breakfast and set off back. So there we were struggling up the hill again when who should stop but the lad who'd picked us up on the way up the other side. He took us all the way to Nelson.

I think our next stop was Pelorus Bridge, a beautiful place in the National park. The campsite was deserted and the grass was long and the rain meant we had to encase our sleeping bags in oilskin covers. They sweated inside and in the morning our bags were wet anyway.

I had a habit of yelling daft things at Beatrice when I got bored. She would be riding in front of me and I would yell something like:

"Lookout, Beatrice, your back wheel is going round."

Well, there we were, screaming down a long hill on the way from Murchison to Inangahua when I noticed that one half of the back fork of her bike was broken clean through and the wheel was wobbling precariously.

"Beatrice, lookout, your back fork is broken."

"Oh, shut up. I'm fed up with you being silly," she growled over her shoulder.

I felt like the little boy in Aesop's fables who kept crying wolf, so when there really was a wolf nobody came to his aid.

"It's true, honestly I'm not fooling this time."

She still didn't believe me and I thought at any moment she would have the most awful crash. Finally, (she said it was the look on my face,) she pulled up. There was nothing else for it but to walk the last few miles into the village.

It was Friday night, and the only person who did welding had shut up shop and gone home and wouldn't be back till Monday. They told us that a bus would be through in the morning that would take us back to Christchurch. Over the campfire, we talked. If we waited until Monday we would never make it back in time for Beatrice to meet her mother. She seemed quite afraid of her.

"She'll be wild," she said. "I'll never hear the end of it."

So the bus it was. Unfortunately, we had to sit in the back and I had to ask the driver to stop and then to sit on the step the rest of the way to Springs Junction where I fetched the sickness pills from my panniers.

After a few days at home, it was back to work. I'd told Dad about the mad horse and he said it would have been a stallion and we could have been killed.

About six weeks after our exams I was walking along the top corridor of the Nurses' Home when I passed Sister Pate.

"Hello, Sister."

"Hello, nurse," then realising who I was, "Oh, you are through."

I swung around. "Pardon?"

"You are through; you are all through," she said.

"Oh, my God, oh my God! Can I wake Yvette and tell her?"

She said I could so I rushed into her room and bounced on the bed.

That evening we went into the senior nurses' sitting room, just because we could. We found out later we were the only class in New

Zealand to get a 100% pass. We all thought we were terribly smart, but pride comes before a fall … isn't that what they say?

For the next six months, we would be working for our junior medicine exams. I did two months in the T.B. annex, the same in Children's Ward as the divide, and the next two as senior nurse on night shift in Fraser Ward, men's medical yet again!

The T.B annex was a breeze: with just eight patients it was like a holiday camp. There can be nothing worse than having a combination of tuberculosis, where one has to eat lots of healthy food, and diabetes where you can't eat much carbohydrate, but we had one such man. He was as thin as a rake and didn't want to eat even after I had prepared his carefully balanced diet. In those days we worked on a line diet, that is, one ounce of potato might be ten red lines and one ounce of greens might be ten green lines, and he was allowed so many red and so many green lines each meal to balance his insulin injections. Of course if he didn't eat it he could go into insulin shock and if I got the balance wrong there was the risk of diabetic coma. How I hated doing those meals.

With so little to do, we had extra jobs outside the ward. One of these was to clean out the mortuary next door. I was over there sweeping when just out of curiosity I opened one of the fridge doors and there to my surprise was a body. I hadn't heard of a death in the wards so it must had been a D.O.A. (dead on arrival.) I lifted the sheet and found it was an old man, the heavy sheet had flattened his beaky roman nose so I worked it back in to shape again, it felt like cold, soft putty. Another day when I went over, a doctor had done a post mortem and this time I was shocked. The cadaver was naked and had been cut from under the chin to the bottom of the pelvis and then stitched up roughly with course hay bale twine. It all seemed very disrespectful to me. I thought at least he could have been covered with a sheet.

Children's Ward again, where once a week I filled in for the afternoon senior when she had her day off. For some reason the ward seemed to fill up when I did that shift.

"Who's afternoon senior today?" asked one of the morning staff before going off duty.

"I am," I replied.

She moaned, "Oh God, the ward will be full in the morning," and it was: a boy with nephritis, a child with burns, a tiny starving baby who weighed less at three months than he did at birth, and a boy with the artery cut in his wrist were just some of the patients that arrived. I never got less than two, but more often it was three or four, no wonder they called me the Jonah of Children's Ward.

The mother who had the starving baby didn't seem to think she had done anything wrong and I found it hard to be civil to her. To make matters worse the tiny boy had thrush in his mouth caused by his older siblings putting their dirty fingers in for him to suck. The afternoon supervisor sat in my office for hours trying to get some milk into the tiny mite with an eyedropper.

This baby got me into a spot of bother later. As divide nurse, it was my job to look after the babies in the nursery and for a few weeks we had nine, much more than usual. As well as feeding them I also had to make up their individual milk formulas, all different, as devised by the dieticians. This could take me up to two hours working in the big disused kitchen along the corridor. The tiny baby's milk was fortified with something I had to cook first, then wait until it cooled before adding it to the milk. One day I made the mixes in the wrong order and added the thick mix to the milk when it was still warm. When the night nurse went to heat the milk for the 2 am feed the mixture curdled, so the night Sister came and got me out of bed to make another lot. Just as well it wasn't one of the nights when I was out partying. By the time I had finished it was almost time for me to go on duty again.

Trying to look after nine babies on your own can be quite a handful. I never got away for my lunch on time – we had just half an hour and most days I rushed in really late, grabbed something, bolted it down, and then rushed over to the Nurses' Home for a smoke before rushing back. This involved two uniform changes so it was quite a feat.

The nine-year-old with the cut artery caused a little drama as well. I had applied a pressure bandage and left his bed in the corridor waiting for the doctor to come. The one on duty was the only married one of the three house surgeons we had, and he was popular with the girls because he was so nice to work with.

So there we were standing each side of the bed, I attached the belt of the sphygmomanometer (the blood pressure machine) to the top of his arm and pumped it up to cut off the blood supply while we unwound the bandage. Unfortunately, I neglected to keep the pressure up and as the bandage was released a huge spurt of blood flew upwards, up the front of my uniform, over my face, veil and on up the wall behind me. The doctor too had a liberal sprinkling.

"Pump, nurse, pump," he said.

I pumped, then goodness knows what the poor kid thought, but there we were, both sides of the bed, having a fit of the giggles.

Fraser Ward was a challenge. Not only was it the base for the night Sister so everyone would know where to find her, but the main telephone switchboard was directed to Fraser Ward as well. Most of the calls came from doctors attending accident scenes and doing callouts to homes from where hospitalisation was needed. I then had to ring the ambulance driver on roster and direct him to where an accident had occurred or to the home.

I can't remember the junior nurse who was supposed to be helping me on the ward, I can't even remember her being in the ward, although she must have been at times. All I know is that it was full-on for most of the night. Looking back now I think it was a tremendous challenge for a twenty-year-old girl.

We had admitted a very old man who lived as a hermit out on a sheep station out Kurow way. It was winter and we'd had a very cold, wet month. The station owner, worried about the old man, rode out to the old man's bivouac on the side of a hill and found him lying in his makeshift bed suffering from pneumonia. Several inches of water were running down the hill and through his shelter. He was absolutely filthy when he arrived, but after a bath and a scrape down his beard and hair came up snowy white. Apart from his habit of coughing up phlegm and spitting it on the floor, he wasn't a lot of trouble during the day, but oh dear, after dark!

His bed had been put just inside the door with another elderly gent, a Mr McLean in the next bed. One night I was sitting writing the report when a huge bellow came from the ward. I flew in and found Mr Simms using Mr McLean's bed as a urinal and Mr McLean shouting "Bugger off, you stupid, old bastard."

I spoke quite sharply to Mr Simms and he became aggressive so I had to backtrack quickly to quieten him down. By the time I had changed his wet pyjamas and got him back to bed, dragged the screens on wheels around Mr McLean's bed and changed that, half the ward was awake and bells were going off everywhere. These altercations between the two were almost a nightly occurrence. Such fun! One night the fun started a little early just as the afternoon senior was going off duty. I went to arbitrate.

"Just Mr Simms again," I told the night Sister.

"Mr Simms?" said the girl. "He is as good as gold and asleep most of the day."

"Ah," said Sister giving me a wink, "the fun just starts around here at 10 pm, doesn't it, nurse!"

Another night the ambulance arrived with a very agitated and rambling old man suffering from dementia. "Five c-cees of paraldehyde, nurse," the doctor said and disappeared. I drew the dose and shot it into a muscle. No effect. He went on talking gibberish, jumping out of bed and wandering off. Half an hour later, almost beside myself trying to cope with my normal work and putting him back to bed, I rang the doctor again.

"Give him another ten c-cees."

I did, and that still didn't work. Working in the treatment room I heard a big bang and rushed out; his bed was empty but the door to the first special was closed and should not have been. We always kept the special doors a little open and put a screen around the bed to keep the passage light off the patient. My slippery patient had wandered in, the screen had fallen on him, he had fallen on the door, and the door had banged shut. Now this man was not small – he was at least six-foot-three tall and solid. I put my shoulder to the door and pushed ... and pushed, eventually getting it open enough to squeeze through. Don't ask me how, but somehow, I managed to extricate his long legs from the screen and get him on his feet and out the door into bed. He seemed to settle, so I went back to work. Five minutes later I looked out the door and he was gone. I found him out in the main corridor trying to get into the empty lift well, thank goodness he couldn't open the door, but he had managed to divest himself of his pyjama pants and there he stood with his long willie hanging down. I couldn't help seeing the funny side of it, or perhaps it was just that if I hadn't laughed I would have cried. Yet again I rang around the wards to find the doctor, (no such things as tracers in my day) and eventually he arrived.

"Give him another fifteen c-cees, nurse. That should do the trick."

"Fifteen c-cees, Doctor," my voice squeaked. I had visions of giving him an overdose and killing him.

"Yes, nurse, fifteen c-cees."

Now paraldehyde has the vilest chemical smell. Almost immediately after administering it the smell erupts from the pores, so the poor man was already smelling like a poker devil. I asked the doctor to write up the dose and injected it. A few minutes later it was peace at last. I slunk into the office to write my report, but my head dropped onto the desk, fast asleep. When I awoke there was night Sister sound asleep in her favourite chair beside my desk. It was the first time I had seen her all night. I returned the favour and let her sleep.

We were now studying for junior medicine. Sadly our lovely Sister Ellis had moved to pastures new and we had a young tutor, who was always cracking jokes and acting daft, to replace her. She didn't command the respect that is essential between pupil and teacher. Also, after the triumph of our state exams, we let up on our swatting and spent more time partying. Fred seemed to have endless friends, all really nice people. We would just fetch up on someone's doorstep unannounced, with a couple of cartons of beer, and have a party.

The night before the junior medicine exam both Yvette and I were doing some last-minute cramming when who should arrive at the door but Les and Jack. We went down to see them in our grey uniforms and capes, me with slippers on.

"No way are we coming out … we have exams in the morning." They pleaded.

"Oh well, just for an hour then."

We piled into the car just as we were, which in itself was an offence, either full uniform or none at all was the rule, and off we went to park at the breakwater. With just two bottles of beer between the four of us we spent the next few hours sitting in the car telling yarns and acting daft. Time flies when you are having fun and suddenly it was 2 am. Jack drove us home and dropped us off at the bottom of the Burma Road. Down the hill we ran and went to take our usual route across the lawn to the side door, but hey, they were building an extension to the Nurses' Home and what had been the lawn was now a sea of mud.

"Now what do we do?" said Yvette.

There was a couple of sticks in the ground with a crossbar like rugby football posts ahead of us.

"Follow me," I said. I took a flying run and leaped the bar, my rubber slippers hit the mud and next thing I was lying flat on my side, my slippers, uniform and hair caked with thick black mud.

"Not bloody likely," and the bitch took off towards the trees behind the morgue and left me there. That was the last I saw of her until the morning.

I picked my way over the mud and in the side door, dropped my nice Bata slippers into the rubbish bin, stripped off my uniform – I would think how to explain that later – washed the mud from my hair and went to bed.

Exam day. The paper was awful and I had a job concentrating. My mind kept wandering and, realising that I was smiling, I looked up and saw our tutor looking at me with a puzzled look.

A week later we had our results.

"Your marks are so bad that I am not going to read them out or post them on the notice board," said Sister. "If you want to know what you got come to me one at a time and I will tell you."

That's what we did. We had all passed, but only just. I got fifty-eight out of 100 and Yvette got fifty-three. This was the first time I had ever beaten her, and I never let her forget it.

There was one lady called Hilda Shears who had joined our class when we were six months into our training. She'd been working at the old people's home in North Oamaru for about twenty years and, her Matron said, the only thing she couldn't do was sign a death certificate because she wasn't a registered nurse. Because of this she had been allowed six months off her general training. Hilda studied hard until all hours of the night. I would see her light on at 2 am when I crept in after a party. She always got good marks, but on the ward she was very slow. Nobody minded though because she was one of the nicest people you could ever meet. She went on to complete her training and returned to take over the Matronship of the Home that had been her life until she retired.

It was while I was working in Fraser that my step-grandmother had a stroke. When Mum and Dad had shifted to the new farm at Henley they had left her behind to annoy the married couple they employed on the other farm. For some reason, she wasn't hospitalised, but was shifted down to the new house for Mum to care for. After about a week Mum rang my Matron and asked if I could come down to help. So it was that I set off home after being on night shift.

Access to Dunedin from the north was still via the old Mount Cargill Road. Always being afraid of travel sickness, I sat in the front seat behind the driver with another driver sitting in the seat beside me. We chatted for a while then I must have dozed off. Now on the road over the mount there is one very sharp hairpin bend where I suddenly awoke and found I had been asleep for ages with my head on my companion's shoulder. I was so embarrassed and asked why didn't he wake me, but they both had big grins and agreed I must have needed my sleep.

In Dunedin, I changed busses for Henley. As I would be getting off on the main road at Henley about two miles from the house I had rung the next-door neighbours from Dunedin, (the phone not having been installed at the new house,) and had been told that grandma had died that morning. So I trudged on foot and soon after I turned into the road the farm was on. Two old arthritic dogs erupted through the hedge and wobbled to greet me, tails wagging madly. I found it hard to believe they had remembered me.

For weeks, while on the ward at night, I had been combing peroxide through my hair. It was now a pretty auburn. I was embarrassed as it was considered cheap and nasty to dye hair so I said I'd been combing stuff through for dandruff. Surprisingly everyone said how much it suited me with my dark eyebrows and eyelashes. I didn't have anything to wear for the funeral so Mum loaned me a smart woollen knit suit in pale green and everyone agreed it looked good with my new hair.

I arrived back at the Nurses' Home on a Wednesday evening when the rehearsals were held for the drama festival, so I wandered over after unpacking.

"Oh, you're home," they cried. "We kept a part for you."

I was surprised and pleased and learned that we were to do a drama called *Mr Hunter*. It was all about a man who gave a group of Shakespearean actresses the wrong advice about where to get off the train and they found themselves in a lonely, supposedly deserted country station. Of course Mr Hunter had seeded the place with things that reminded them of the actress who someone had pushed off a train to her death. Climax after climax peaked until the killer revealed herself and was shot by Mr Hunter who had been waiting. It was an absolutely brilliant drama and I loved playing the youngest actress, Paddy. Our wonderful producer was a short little guy who knew his job and it was a pleasure working with him. He always called us by our characters' names.

We won the Nurses' Drama Festival that year; had the audience eating out of our hands, and I experienced for the first time the amazing stillness of an audience who watched in rapt attention. But pride comes before a fall and we all learned a valuable lesson. Over the next few weeks, whenever we met in the kitchenette we would throw lines from the play at one another whenever they were appropriate, thinking we were so clever.

It was time to compete in the British Drama League competitions, and we were over-confident – no doubt about it, we were going to win. But it wasn't to be. Almost from the moment we started things began to go wrong, and none of us had the experience to get back on track. We allowed that first mistake to unnerve us, and the play unravelled from that moment. It was awful. Pamela, who played the oldest actress, was supposed to make this long speech while I was supposed to be lighting the fire. My cue from her was "Now in my young days' whereupon I would cut in and say sarcastically "Yes, dear, you travelled by pack pony and played in the market places.' And she would say "Very funny'. Imagine my horror when I heard my cue while I was still down on my knees – she had left out most of her long speech and I hadn't even put the kindling in the fireplace, never mind lit the match. I shot to my feet, dropped the matches, and almost shouted: "Yes, dear.'

What a disaster! I couldn't wait for the play to end. I remembered a children's book of long ago. "Pride comes before a fall when you are walking on a wall." I was never over-confident again, and know it is good to be nervous before a show: you give a much better performance.

After the junior medicine exam debacle, Yvette and I were never put on the same duty again, not ever, and there was no way it could have been an accident. No doubt our superiors had been made aware of our late nights. I was now at a loose end, and with no one to go out with I was very lonely. Strictly speaking, we were not allowed to go roller skating, or ride horses, or play hockey without permission, in case we injured ourselves. But I started skating and went every Wednesday night when I wasn't on duty. Once when I had a bad fall and badly bruised the bone in my elbow I just had to grin and bear it because I couldn't tell anyone.

One night I met a young trainee teacher called Doug, who was in his last year and already going out to schools to teach. He'd come down to Oamaru with a team from Christchurch, and asked me my name. I didn't want to give it in case he rang and asked for me. I was reading a book at the time called *The Fortunes of Billie* so I said my name was Billie. Doug and I started dating whenever he managed to get down. We were so intellectually suited. Sometimes we would sit on a shelf in the Begonia house at the lovely Oamaru public gardens, and there, amongst the brilliant colours of the flowers we would talk for hours and try to set the world to rights. When we parted after a night out we would have a snog at the door, but one night, when having a few drinks in a railway hut with friends, someone asked if we were engaged.

"Shall we? Will you marry me?" asked Doug.

"Well," I said, "why not?"

So there I was, engaged to be married. And from that day onwards, he kissed me with his hands behind his back. Just a chaste quick kiss on the lips.

"We are not going to have any of that before we are married," he declared.

As Judy Merfin said, "You know you are not going to give them anything, but you do like them to try."

He put me on a pedestal; I could do no wrong, and it made me so mad that I sometimes deliberately went out to shock him. He asked me to go up to Christchurch to meet his parents and I managed to get time off in a change of duties.

His parents, who lived in an old house with a big vegetable garden near Brighton, were very nice ordinary working folk. The next day, when I caught the bus home I took two gastric sedatives as I always suffered travel sickness. When we reached Timaru, and the bus stopped for half an hour for refreshments I felt quite odd. I seemed to be outside my body looking back at myself, but it didn't alarm me, even when three people came to ask me if I was okay. The last one was a young man. I told him I had just got off the bus and would go for a walk up the hill to stretch my legs, and he said he would walk with me. We sat on a seat overlooking the Fanny Bay beach and chatted until he said he had better walk me back to get the bus. As we came at last to the outskirts of Oamaru I felt deadly tired and had to really fight to stay awake, not wanting to be carried past my stop. When the time came to get off I alighted, still feeling very odd, and slowly made my way along the street then up the long climb to the Nurses' Home. The next morning when I awoke I felt fine but realised with horror that I'd had a drug overdose. I looked up my Materia Medica book and read: *in the result of an overdose the patient must not be allowed to go to sleep.*

Never again did I play around with drugs.

It soon became obvious that our "engagement' was not going to last. The distance between us was too great; I couldn't go out on my own nor could I go with another man friend. Doug had wanted me to transfer to Christchurch to finish my training but Dad said no. I was very lonely. If there is one thing a nurse, working under stress all day needs, it's to be able to get away and relax. I became very morose and down. Besides, I asked myself, "Did I really want to get married?" What had happened to all my dreams? Did I want to become an actress or a great country and western singer? The answers were no and yes.

I wrote to Doug to tell him and received an angry letter back, saying: "For the first time in my life I have managed to save some money. I have got £80 saved towards paying for the solitaire diamond you wanted, so thank you for that."

I had begun to have trouble with my back, just a dull ache whenever I was on my feet. I had a form that gave me the right to get my shoe built up at the workshop attached to Dunedin Hospital, but Dunedin was a long way away and none of my nursing shoes were ever built up when I needed it most.

I knocked around with Dave for a few months, one of the clan I had known for months. He was tall, over six foot, a bit of a dork and worked in the railway yards. Not exactly the marrying type, but he too wanted to get married. Poor Dave, he had no social graces, couldn't dance, and had no money but talked about an uncle who owned a building block we could probably get cheap. He drove a big square Buick car and sometimes on my day off we would drive out into the country with some of his male friends in tow.

One day he let me have a drive; it was the hardest car I have ever driven. The clutch was so tight I could hardly depress it, but eventually I got it into top gear. So there we were cruising along when we came to a water ford across the road, I didn't have time to change down so flew through in top gear. Water flew everywhere … in the open windows, and through the floor – we were soaked. The boys thought it a huge joke, just as well it was a hot summer day.

Dave often took me to see his mother who lived alone. She was a small dark woman with a very foreboding look, and the most bitter and twisted old shrew I have ever met. She didn't have a good word to say for anyone, especially men, because Dave's father had left her. She was, however, a fabulous cook and would put out lots of cakes which I would tuck into. We didn't get such luxuries at the hospital. When she thought we might be getting serious she warned me off.

"He's got nothing, you know, so don't think of getting married." She wasn't telling me anything – to me he was just a friend. We hadn't even kissed, but she didn't know that.

My back was beginning to be a problem and, being disillusioned with everything, I decided to leave. On examination, they couldn't find anything wrong and indeed it wasn't until fifty years later that I realised it was because I wasn't wearing a built-up shoe.

I had managed to save £50 out of my meagre wages, and it was enough to get me to Australia with some to spare. I would go there for a working holiday, join a country and western club and show the world I could sing.

It wasn't until my classmates went to study day while I had to work that I realised just what I had done, but the die was cast.

Mum and Dad were not happy about me going to Australia, but they didn't say I couldn't. I was to wish many times in the future they had stopped me. They both came to town with me to buy a suitcase. Mum chose a big one but Dad said I would not be able to carry it and paid for a smaller one for me.

So it was that one day he drove us to the Dunedin railway station to see us off. Mum was coming to Wellington with me.

Dad started to walk away when he had said goodbye, without even a hug or a kiss. The train began to move and as we passed Dad making his way along the platform I saw to my amazement that he had tears streaming down his face. I was stunned. All I could think was, "my father loves me, my father loves me.'

We took the ferry from Lyttleton to Wellington from where I was to leave on the *S.S. Monawai* for Sydney the next day. We had booked a cabin for the overnight trip across Cook Strait and an English steward showed us down to it. After we had thanked him I noticed he was waiting.

"Oh, here," I said, showing him our tickets. "Is this what you want?"

He looked at them briefly and left. It wasn't until months later that I realised he'd been waiting for a tip. I still had a lot to learn.

Australia 1955 – 1957

Mum stood on the wharf waving as the ship pulled away, the streamers of many colours that stretched from ship to shore tightening until they broke, severing the final link. I was suddenly tearful and rushed back inside to dry my eyes, almost colliding with another girl on the same mission. We had a bit of a laugh before going back out to wave a last goodbye. My new friend was Helen from Glasgow; she'd been in New Zealand for three years and was going back to see her family before marrying a butcher when she returned.

I was wandering around the ship taking it all in when I heard someone playing the piano in a small room and went to investigate. As I entered a man was coming out.

He stopped. "Oh, hello." He was immaculately dressed in a beautiful navy suit, shirt, and tie. I didn't much like the look of him. He was quite tall, swarthy looking with deep lines running down each side of his face, and black hair receding each side of his forehead. I said hello and went to join the girls singing around the piano. The player was Margo from Mildura. Paula, her friend, also from Mildura, and Blanch from Brisbane were the others. These girls, Helen and I were to form a happy band on the trip to Sydney.

And the man? Well if I could go back to the moment when I walked into that room I would turn and leave, as fast as my legs could carry me.

His name was Frank Naylor. He chummed up with all the girls on the trip over the Tasman and we soon became accustomed to his strong Yorkshire accent. He had a quick wit and was always amusing company, but strangely we never saw him in the dining room.

Sydney, new and exciting, and there we all were, Margo, Paula,

Blanch, Helen, myself, and Frank, seeing the sights of the town on a beautiful sunny day. All of us, except Frank, were to leave later in the day for other destinations. Helen was the first to go. We all traipsed down to the wharf to see her aboard the *S.S. Orion* bound for the U.K. I wonder if she ever went back to marry her butcher … and if she was happy.

Blanch was the next to go. It was getting dark when we took a taxi to the railway station, arriving just as the train was about to leave. She raced ahead while we snatched up her luggage and followed, the train pulling away as she leaped aboard, with Frank throwing her suitcase after her. We were still running beside the train.

"Billie," she yelled, "my handbag."

In all the excitement I'd forgotten it was under my arm, I flung it into the open doorway and it landed at her feet. It all seemed rather flat with Blanch gone. She was by far the most mature of us all and in N.Z. she had fallen for and had an affair with a married man. On the ship she'd been very subdued and sad. After realising the affair was going nowhere she had broken it off and was on her way home to lick her wounds. Margo and Paula left soon after to catch their transport back to Mildura, which left just Frank and I. I had planned to leave for Melbourne the same night.

Mum had asked me to go on to Melbourne, as I was less likely to get in trouble there. To her, Sydney was a big evil and wicked city. How naive and countrified we were.

"Why," said Frank, "don't you stop tonight and go tomorrow?"

"No, I should go tonight. I promised I wouldn't stay here."

"Well one night is not going to make any difference, and then you can travel in daylight."

Well, he did have a point, and we set out to look for lodgings.

"And we are getting single rooms," I told him bluntly.

It wasn't to be. At three places we had asked for single rooms and none were available. After coming out of the last place it was after 10 pm.

"Look," said Frank, "we will have to ask for a double room at the next place."

I looked doubtful

"Well we can hardly ask for single rooms then say we will have a double, now can we?"

So reluctantly I agreed. "But you have to stay on your own side of the bed, and *not touch me!*" He promised he would. It must have been almost an hour before we found another bed and breakfast, it was a big, grim-looking place, and we were given a room on the second floor, halfway along a long corridor. I'd been walking all day in high heels, my feet were killing me and I was exhausted. The window looked out onto another brick wall and there was a very big ledge outside the window. I stupidly made the remark that it was so big you could climb out and sit on it. Frank said he was going out for a while and after he left I wasted no time in finding the cavernous washroom and toilets at the end of the corridor before climbing into bed and falling asleep.

I have no idea what time it was when he got back, but I heard him sneak in, undress and slip into bed. I pretended to be asleep but noted that he stunk of beer. I felt him edge nearer, and nearer, and then his arm was around me and he was rubbing his swollen member into my back. I was still a virgin, but as a nurse I had seen plenty of penises to know what was going on and was petrified.

"Get away from me. You promised you wouldn't touch me," I snarled.

"Come on. I'm not going to hurt you."

We had a fierce argument. The window above the door was open into the corridor, as they were in the rest of the rooms, and I worried that we could be heard. Eventually, he agreed to move away and I lay quietly, tense and fearful, unable to go to sleep and thought about what I could do. Of course it didn't last. Soon he was back whispering sweet nothings. I spun around and gave him an almighty shove.

"Get off me. I am going to the toilet."

Bouncing out of bed I snatched up my dressing gown and stumbled along the corridor to the loos, where I locked myself into a cubical, pulled the seat cover down and sat shivering with fright and cold. No way was I going back to that room.

It must have been over half an hour later when I heard the door open, some other lady coming to spend a penny, I thought. Suddenly there was a huge crash on my door – he must have bent down and seen my feet through the space under it. A dishevelled head appeared above the partition, I leaped with fright. He was back.

"What the hell do you think you are playing at?" he roared. "Get out of there and come back to bed.' Then he stormed out, slamming the door loudly. I was mortified – there was nothing I hated more than creating a scene, and by now I was quite convinced that everyone in the place must be awake and listening. I sat for a few minutes more then decided to sneak back lest he came in yelling again. The door to our room opened without a sound, in the half-dark I noticed the quilt had fallen off the end of the bed. I crept my way towards it, lowered myself to the floor and as quietly as I could wrapped myself up and lay quietly. I had thought he was asleep, but no. After a while I heard him shuffling down the bed and then fingers touched me.

"Come on, Billie, you can't stay there. Come back to bed. I promise I won't touch you."

I thought about it for a while then got up and slipped into bed as far away from him as I could get. He kept his word and eventually I slept.

In the morning he apologised for his behavior; said that when he woke up and found I hadn't returned he panicked and thought I may have jumped off the roof, especially after the remark I'd made about sitting out on the ledge. Besides, he thought at my age I wouldn't be a virgin. *Damn cheek.*

It's funny how everything looks better in daylight. Even so I refused to go into the dining room for the breakfast we had paid for because everyone would know who we were. He tried to convince me otherwise but I wasn't having any of it. So back out into the street we went where he had to pay for breakfast.

We had a few more hours before I had to catch my train south and by the time he saw me off, we had reached a truce. He said he would write to me care of the General Post Office.

I sat up half the night looking out the carriage window anxious not to miss a thing, but eventually realised it was too dark and there was nothing much to see.

I had booked a bed at the Y.W.C.A. before leaving N.Z., sending a good deposit and that is where I took a taxi to on arrival in Melbourne. For the next few days I explored, at the same time looking for a job. I loved the place, a beautiful city, the streets laid out in squares, with wonderful shops and boutiques, so different from little Oamaru or Dunedin. There were trams, but mostly I walked. After a few days I saw a job advertised: someone wanted a children's nanny, live-in, just what I wanted. I rang the number and went for an interview at No. 3 Lemprier Avenue, St Kilda. The lady was called Mrs Rose and the house was beautiful. I was given the job, to move in the next day, and I was to have my own room and bathroom, luxury beyond anything I'd ever had.

When I went to pay my bill on leaving the Y.W.C.A I was horrified at the price, but being as green as grass I didn't question it, Many months later I realised I had already paid with my deposit almost as much as I owed and it hadn't been taken into consideration.

The Roses were a couple in their late twenties or early thirties. She was about five foot six in height with thick, black, shoulder-length hair, with a round suntanned face and body. She had white marks around her eyes where her sunglasses had kept the sun off.

"Had you been here a few weeks ago you would have come to Surfers Paradise on holiday with us," she told me.

He was about five foot nine, not handsome but with a young cheeky face and a ready smile.

The oldest child, Phillip, was four, and the youngest, whose name was Paul, I think, was two. Lovely kids, but very spoiled. I soon felt at home and one of the family. The wages were £6 a week and all found very good considering my last wages at Oamaru had been £4 something a fortnight. I was to have every Wednesday and Saturday afternoon off and all day Sunday. I had to get up each morning and give the children their breakfast after taking cups of tea to their parents in their bedroom. The two-year-old hadn't been potty trained which horrified me and it took me two months to achieve this. Mrs Rose bought a little toilet seat for him and I rushed him into the loo after breakfast until he eventually got the message.

The Roses were Jewish. I had never knowingly met Jewish people before and found their way of life interesting. Every Friday night Mr Rose and Phillip donned their little Jewish skull caps and we ate kosher foods. I helped Mrs Rose cook the meals. Mr Rose was a character: he took a delight in teasing me about my use of the Scottish word *wee* to describe something small. One night I really excelled myself. Mrs Rose and I were preparing dinner and I was peeling a carrot. I asked if that was big enough and she said it was a bit small. I replied, "Yes, it is a *wee* bit *wee*." I never lived it down.

"Would you like a weee bit of this, Billie? Or perhaps a weee bit of that," he would ask at the dinner table.

Mr Rose and his father were property developers, cutting up tracks of land for building blocks, putting in streets and naming them. One night he said they were ready to name the streets and he would name one after me. "But I can't call it Billie Street," he said. I told him my proper name was Gwendoline. "That will do," he said. "Gwendoline Street it is."

So somewhere in Melbourne there is a street named after me.

Amongst the Rose's friends were two couples who were about to leave for an extended holiday of Europe, and everyone, but everyone, had to give them a farewell party, thus they were rarely home in the evenings. It made a very long day for me. Mrs Rose said that as the wives were also company directors they could claim their travel expenses from their income tax.

It came the Roses turn to provide the party. I was to be teamed up with her unmarried cousin, a research doctor. He was very nice but after supper, he left early to tend to his rats and mice at the research centre.

Caterers had been brought in to provide the delicious food, and an enormous, metre long, ice cream cake in the shape of an ocean liner was ordered. It had all the right colours, and floated in a sea of azure blue. At the end of the night, after we'd all helped ourselves to bits of the ship it looked as if it had been torpedoed and started to sink very low into a strange coloured sea. After the food we adjourned indoors where the entertainment started. I did the hula, and funny jokes were told. I still remember one of them after all these years:

> *His daughter got pregnant and he asked her who the father was … and she said "I don't know," and he said, "What? I spent all this money on your education and bringing you up the right way, and you didn't have the manners to ask with whom am I having the pleasure?"*

One of the guests, who was into the new craze of barn dancing, had us all dancing to *Go Johnny Go Johnny Go*, over and over with much laughter until we finally got it right.

On my afternoons off, I shopped in Melbourne, getting used to its four climates in one day, the sudden downpours and then the brilliant sunshine and all the steam rising from the pavements. I bought myself some dresses, a sleeveless black one with tiny white pompoms at the sleeve line. It had a collar in one with the dress front that could be worn high, or folded over the cord that was attached behind and had tiny white pompoms on the ends. It was a pretty and versatile dress and I had it for many years. The other one was straight cut in bright yellow linen and had small diamante buckles on the pockets. I also bought a pair of black toreador pants and sent them back to Shirley Ireland at the Nurses' Home as requested. I hope she appreciated them as they cost me a whole week's wages.

Television was in its infancy and one of the big stores had this new invention on display. I stood with the crowd to watch this black and white grainy picture and was not at all impressed. How different it is today.

The Roses had a cleaner called Mrs Morris, a rough tough hard-faced old Aussie. She used to tell Mr Rose dirty jokes and all about the goings-on in the room next door to hers. She lived in a boarding house where the rooms had been divided with plywood and everything could be heard from next door. While Mr Rose laughed, it was all too much for me. I would get very embarrassed and take myself to the other end of the house. She was, however, a lonely and kind-hearted old lady, her truckie husband away driving goods around Australia for three months or more at a time.

She got away with murder in the house. I would hear her ticking Phillip off: "Get in here, young man," she would yell at the top of her voice, "and get this mess off the floor. How do you expect me to clean with these toys everywhere?"

Phillip didn't dare to argue, and it always gave me a giggle. Phillip was a spoiled young man. His father brought him home a toy every night and usually by the next night it would be broken.

One Sunday Mr Rose took the boys and me to the funfair and they wanted a ride on a small train. "Come on, Mum," said the attendant. "You jump in with the baby."

I was embarrassed and looked at the boss to see how he'd taken the remark, He was grinning from ear to ear, and seemed to like the idea of this young thing with the long ponytail being mistaken for his wife. As the weeks went by I began feeling depressed. I was home most nights, and they were out most nights. I read every book in their bookshelf, played all their records and learned to sing Ella Fitzgerald's *Body and Soul*. *My heart is sad and lonely, for you I sigh, for you dear only* – a beautiful song I still sing today.

I did get out one night. I made it to a pub where they had a talent contest and, under the name of Billie Lamont (*so exotic I thought*) I sang *Stupid Cupid*, but alas I forgot the words to the verse so sang the chorus twice. Never mind, I got second anyway.

Aware that I was getting fed up, Mrs Morris arranged to meet me in town on my day off. We had a drink, dinner and then went on to Luna Park. We had a fabulous night, I had never laughed so much in my life, and we went on the big dipper and did the lot. Last of all, we had our photo taken sitting on the moon, the first instant photo I'd ever seen. It showed up every line and made us both look years older.

I have the photo in my album to this day.

A letter from Frank arrived at the GPO. I wrote back giving him my new address and we arranged to meet in town. He said he had followed Margo and Paula to Mildura and scrounged a place to stay at Margo's, whose father had a vineyard and grew grapes to dry for sultanas.

One night, when the Roses were off to yet another party, they said to invite him to keep me company. He came, and I packed him off home on the tram long before they returned home. I don't know what he was doing during the day, he certainly wasn't working, and I met him once more in town before he took himself off to Adelaide. We had a heavy snogging session in his hotel room but once more I escaped with my virginity intact. Truthfully, I wasn't sorry to see him go.

The days at the Rose's dragged on, my life seeming to revolve around the children. I had no friends, and ladies didn't go into pubs on their own so all I could do on my day off was window-shop and be followed around by young men – the place was flooded with them, new Australians. I couldn't even stop to look in a shop window before one would pop up beside me.

"You come with me?" seemed to be about the only English they knew. I expect they were mostly nice guys, but *nice* girls didn't get picked up on the street. I would get fed up and go home early only to find the baby running around in stinking nappies and I would be obliged to change him. Mrs Rose really was the pits as a mother.

Eventually, I decided to move on and gave two weeks' notice. After all, I had come on a working holiday. I booked a ticket on the overnight train to Adelaide but, before I left, a telegram arrived from Frank. "When was I coming to Adelaide?"

I wrote back telling him the morning I would be arriving.

The carriage had three seats facing three seats and a nice Italian family sat opposite: Mamma, Papa, and a pretty teenage girl. They had no English but the girl and I tried to communicate. The heating was under the seat, and we both kicked off our high-heeled shoes and settled down to try and sleep. In the morning our feet were swollen up and we had a laugh trying to squeeze our shoes back on.

Adelaide at last. I piled out onto the platform and, carrying a suitcase, a tennis racquet, a guitar, a hula skirt made of clear tissue paper and a handbag, I struggled towards the exit intent on finding a taxi.

I hadn't expected to be met, but there he was, stepping out of the crowd. His first words didn't exactly please me. "What are you dragging that lot around for? Most of it has to go."

I felt like saying it was none of his business what I carried but refrained from saying so.

My first priority was to find somewhere to stay but he said he had booked us in for bed and breakfast at the *People's Palace*, the hotel run by the Salvation Army church. Whatever else it was, it was certainly no Palace, not in any sense of the word, but it was clean and cheap. A taxi took us there. I thought he had booked two rooms, but no, he had booked just one. I was furious but could hardly cause a scene at reception. But upstairs was a different matter. I started in as soon as the door was closed.

"How dare you assume ... who do think you are? ... If you think I am going to sleep with you!" etc.

"Agh, come on, Bill. I'm not going to hurt you, blah blah blah."

Mr Smooth, Mr Charming, on and on – he was good at that. In the end I thought, *Oh well, it had to happen sometime, I am twenty years old, might as well find out what this sex thing is all about.*

We spent the afternoon looking around Adelaide, the city of churches, a pretty place with the River Torrens running through it. By evening I was footsore and tired and, after the previous night sitting up in the train, all I wanted to do was to crash into bed and sleep. But it wasn't to be ... it was awful! If that was sex you could have it!

In the morning when I rose there was a bloodstain on the sheet. I freaked. Oh my god they will know what we were doing; I can't go down to breakfast. Frank said the housemaids would have seen it all before and no-one in the dining room would know who we were, but

I was having none of it. So once again we had to book out and found breakfast somewhere else.

My next priority was to find work. I scanned the paper and saw an ad for a semi-trained nurse to work in a maternity hospital, bed and board included. The semi-trained bit should have warned me they wanted everything for nothing but I rang for an appointment and was asked to come that afternoon. She gave me the suburb, Norwood I think, and how to get there. Firstly I went into Foy's, a big apartment store, to spend a penny. Because it was always catching on things, I took off the big jade ring Mum had given me, and put it on the top of the toilet roll holder, then walked out without it.

The district seemed quite old. I walked along the street following the house numbers and looking for something that looked like a hospital. I found the number. *This was a hospital?* I was shocked. It was an old house, the paint faded to that strange pinkie fawn that old paint gets, and the whole place looked unkempt. There was a veranda along the front, a window each side of the door, and beside the door the only clean thing about the place, a shiny brass plate that proudly proclaimed ... THE SO-AND-SO MATERNITY HOSPITAL.

I climbed the front steps and rang the bell. A large lady in uniform, the Matron, interviewed me and, finding me suitable, arranged for me to move in the next day. While I was talking to her I noticed the missing ring and hurried back to Foy's to see if it was still there. Remarkably it was. I called it my Lucky ring. The stone of that ring has been lost three times since – once on a dark wet night in the gravel car park of an ancient English pub – but it has always been found. I still have it today, fifty-five years later.

At the new job, my digs were an old army hut, one of three in the back yard. The inside was unpainted, the old black iron bed-frame bed had two mattresses, the old flock kind, both of which had numerous buttons missing so the flock had shifted into large lumps. I soon found that no matter which one was on top, and no matter how I tried to wrap myself around them, or furiously pound them, I could never avoid a bump or two. My nights were tortuous, my back a mess every morning. There was small set of drawers riddled with woodworm to put my clothes in and act as a bedside table.

The hospital had four rooms off the central passageway, two wards on one side and one on the other. The fourth room was the delivery room with kitchen and one old bathroom at the back. The rooms were gloomy and dark, the passageway and wards were covered in old brown linoleum, kept shiny but cracked in places. The nursery was at the back beside the kitchen.

The first morning on duty I met another elderly lady in mufti who introduced herself as the Matron. Seeing my confusion the nice English Sister I was sharing duty with explained that it was the hospital joke. The one in the uniform insisted she was the matron because she was the trained nurse, (albeit forty years before,) and the one without insisted she was the Matron because she owned the place. Neither one would give in. Good grief! I had moved into a lunatic asylum. It didn't take long to find out I was to be dog's body and do most of the work. Here's how it worked: I started work at 7 am. The night nurse had already taken the babies to their mothers to get the first feed of the day and returned them to the nursery. I started by delivering all the washbasins for the Mums to wash themselves and bedpans where needed, then clearing them away. Then I delivered all the breakfast trays and took them back to the kitchen. After that I started all the pelvic washes, this meant sitting each lady on a bedpan and flushing the pubic area down with a large jug of disinfectant, drying with a sterile towel and furnishing them with a new pad. When all that was finished I started delivering all the babies back to their mother for the 10 am feed. From ten until twelve I was off duty.

Twelve o'clock I start again and helped hand out all the dinner trays and returned them to the kitchen. All the time there are bells to answer, nursing jobs to do, babies to bath and change. My lunch hour was supposed to be between 1 pm. and half past. A joke: if a bell rang, I was supposed to answer it. The first time a bell rang when I was at lunch no-one around the table moved, nor did I until I found them all looking at me. Sometimes I would get several interruptions to a meal until my meal was cold and I was lucky if I'd had ten minutes, but I always had my half-hour meal time taken off. From 2 pm until 3 pm I had another hour off, then worked until 5.30, dinner for half an hour, still answering bells, then worked until 7.30 pm and was off for the night. At 6 pm I would start to take the babies out to the mothers. All had to be taken back to the nursery to be weighed to see if they'd drunk enough, if not they would have to go back until they had. I had one bad feeder who I had to take back several times, so sometimes I got away late. It took almost the whole day to do an eight-hour shift. It was downright exploitation, but I didn't have the guts to say so. However I rather liked my job, and I was certainly learning things.

The two other army huts in the back yard were the rooms of the night Sister and the young girl, Gladys, who worked in the kitchen. She also worked long hours and seemed almost simple. One evening, at the end of my day off I asked her to come for a walk with me. No sooner had we hit the footpath than a car screeched to a halt beside us, and four young men – new Australians – spoke to us from the open windows. Gladys turned and gave them a big smile.

"Don't, Gladys," I said, grabbing her arm. "If you smile at them you will just encourage them and we will never get rid of them."

She took my cue and looked straight ahead, and after a few minutes of curb crawling and being ignored they drove away. I asked her about herself and she told me that she was just fifteen and the hospital had acquired her from an orphanage. How much was she being paid, I asked and when she told me I was aghast. It was a pittance.

"Gladys, they are taking advantage of you! Why don't you complain?"

She said if she did they would tell the orphanage and she would get into trouble. We had a long talk as we walked the neighbourhood that night – she wasn't dumb, just a very naive young girl who nobody had ever told the facts of life or what went on in the big wide world. I can only hope that my words to her that night helped her along the pathway of life and helped her keep out of trouble. She was very keen to learn. I have often wondered what became of her.

Apart from the lumps in the mattress, the nights were not always peaceful. One night I awoke with a start as tremendous screams rent the air. My first reaction was one of fright as I couldn't think where I was. When I got my bearings I realised the screams were coming from the hospital. I went to the door and looked out, but nothing apart from the continuing screams seemed amiss. My watch said 1 am. I went back to bed and tried to sleep, but the screams went on intermittently until 5 am when I finally fell asleep. The night Sister banged on my door at 6.30 and I groped my sleepy way on to duty.

"What on earth was that screaming all about?"

"Oh, don't worry, dear, we admitted a Greek lady and all the Europeans seem to scream like that. You'll get used to it."

Well, I never did. I thought it damned undignified; the Australian ladies didn't scream like that.

While I was there, one of those things you can never forget happened. We admitted a young Australian girl, a slightly chubby twenty-three-year-old, who was in labour. Sister and I kept popping in to see how she was progressing. She was quiet and had a sweet smiling personality. When it looked as if the birth was imminent, her lady doctor, who'd already been warned, was notified, and she duly arrived. June (I will name her) was transferred to the delivery room, and I went on with my duties.

Shortly after, the door of the delivery room opened. "Nurse, come in quickly, we need you."

I went in and a bottle of ether was shoved in my hand. "You'll have to do the anaesthetic."

I gave them a wild look. I had never given an anaesthetic in my life! Wasn't it the job of an anaesthetist?

"Pour, Nurse. Pour."

June was already unconscious, a mask over her face. I poured, absolutely scared out of my wits. What if I gave her an overdose and killed her, but every time I stopped pouring I was told to keep going. The lady doctor was becoming very rattled and eventually sent someone to summon a male doctor from her clinic. He arrived in record time and measured June's pelvic bones with his knuckles.

"Didn't you examine her?" he snapped. He took up a pair of scissor and cut into her vaginal flesh. I cringed, but was to find out later that scissors were used instead of a scalpel because when stitched the ragged cut would heal better. Then the forceps were brought to bear. He slipped one side over the baby's head then the other, clicked them together and started to pull. June slipped right down the bed. Someone came to the head of the bed on the other side and together we pulled her back up.

"You two hold on to her while I pull," he barked. So with the bottle in my left hand and my right arm hooked through hers I kept pulling and intermittently pouring the ether, terrified now that she would come to and see what was going on. Three times more she got pulled down the bed and we hauled her back until finally, with a pull and a twist the baby came free and landed on the bed. It was a little boy. He had big red bruises on each side of his temple, and red marks down both side of his jaw. The baby was whisked away and I kept June anaesthetised until she'd been stitched, cleaned up and returned to the ward. I shook internally for the rest of the day and slept badly that night.

The next morning June was bright and smiling. When she said they were naming the baby David I told her that was my father's name. I longed to tell her what had happened in the delivery room but knew I could never do it. In the nursery, I watched David like a hawk. We didn't wrap our babies up like papooses as most hospitals do as it was hot and there was no air conditioning. We laid the babies on their backs and wrapped a small cotton sheet around them, tucked it firmly under the mattress but left their arms free. I felt her baby should be on bed rest but was told to deliver him to his mother to be fed, the same as the others.

On the second day, I noticed as I changed another baby David's little arms were shaking. I found the Matron, the one with the uniform, and told her. She followed me to the nursery, looked at the baby, said "Rubbish," and walked out. I wanted to howl with rage, but I was just the semi-trained nurse so what could I do. The next day I witnessed the tremor again and once again I was rubbished. I began wondering how I could get the doctor's phone number so I could find a phone box and report directly to him, but fate took a hand. The next day when I was attending to the nursery he had another fit, the Matron, the one with the uniform, just happened to be walking past the door. Forgetting protocol I shot out the door, grabbed her arm and literally propelled her into the room and said *"LOOK!"* She just said, "Oh ...yes," turned around and walked out saying over her shoulder, "I'll ring the doctor."

Ten minutes later I was told to put the baby on complete bed rest. How I would loved to have said, "He should have been on bed rest three days ago, you ignorant bitch!" She never discussed the subject again, not even to say sorry or that she'd been wrong. I was beginning to become seriously worried about the appalling inefficiencies in the place and didn't want to be around when they killed someone or there was an outbreak of infection. I have thought of David many times over the years, fearing greatly that he became a spastic because of the incompetence of a few people, and his little smiling mother would have had a lifetime cross to bear.

One night when I lay soaking in the bath the door flew open, a nurse I had never met came in carrying a big pan of water to heat on the gas ring that sat on a board over the end of the bath. She said she was sorry but an emergency delivery was on the way in.

As soon as she'd left I sprang out to dry and dress before someone else came barging in. It really was too much.

I hadn't had much contact with Frank. He rang me one day on the hospital phone and a very annoyed person came out to my hut to get me. We arranged to meet on my day off. He hadn't been working, just going to the races and frittering his time away, but now he had a job as a welder up at Leigh Creek in the South Australian outback. He wanted me to come with him. I wasn't sure. It didn't seem right to leave a job after just three weeks, but then … It wasn't as if I had good working conditions or a decent place to sleep, and why I thought should I care about people who didn't care for others. And hadn't I come to Australia to work my way around? I said I would go. Frank insisted that I get rid of some of my gear.

"Can you play this guitar?"

"Well, not very well," I replied.

"Well it's got to go."

I was upset about that. I still hadn't given up the idea of joining a country and western club and learning to play properly, but I could see his reasoning. My hula skirt went next, my tennis racket and a pair of shoes that had given me a blister.

"If you can't wear them, dump them," was Frank's motto. With the heat of Australia my feet had swollen slightly, but little did I think we would leave a trail of shoes wherever we went around Australia.

We travelled to Leigh Creek by train. I remember passing through Port Augusta, and Port Pirie – in one of those places, there was a drunk lying in almost every doorway. One night, when we'd been walking in Melbourne, we saw a man lying in a doorway and I went to help. Frank dragged me away. "Leave him, he's drunk." I was truly shocked at the drunkenness of Australia in the 1950's. Never had I seen drunk people lying in doorways in New Zealand.

Leigh Creek was, and still is, a coal-mining town owned by the South Australian electrical trust. It was a nice little place with all the mine houses, much alike, lined up in streets. There was a big bar with outside seats for entertainment, two long Nissan huts where the single men were housed, the Works offices, and a big canteen where all the meals were served. We presented ourselves at the Works office where Frank was expected, but they were a little nonplussed to see me. What to do with a single girl looking for a job? They had never struck that situation before. Eventually it was decided I could replace the Hungarian lady who worked in the laundry and was on holiday for a month. Would I mind? Not at all.

First of all, we had to be settled into accommodation and we were handed over to a nice guy called Bluey.

"Why do they call you Bluey?" I asked.

"Because I've got red hair," he laughed.

Well, of course, silly me, why didn't I think of that.

Frank was put in a room in the Nissan hut, but Bluey wasn't quite sure what to do with me. "I'll ask Jean if she will board you," he said. It turned out that Jean was the office tea lady and she said she would, but I was not to tell a soul. Taking boarders was forbidden under company laws. Jean was about the skinniest woman I'd ever seen: she had pernicious anaemia. There were two children, a sullen little girl of twelve and a boy of eight. I never did find out what happened to the father. I was to pay twelve shillings a week board and that suited me fine.

Frank

One of the first things I noticed about Leigh Creek was the Willy-Willies – miniature tornadoes that swept across the open spaces – whirling round and round, large at the bottom and thin at the top. They sucked up sand, rubbish, and dust, twisting here and there. Sometimes I would see one coming and try to outrun it, but the damn things seemed to follow me. I would just have to stand still while it swirled around me, coating my sweating skin with a liberal layer of red dust. I got caught almost every day as I walked back from work at the laundry.

Work started at 5 am and finished at 1.30, thus avoiding the heat of the day. From 12 to 12.30 we had lunch, the other two ladies at home, and me with the bosses in the canteen. I was very shy the first day, but the men were never less than gentlemen. One saw me eyeing his glass of iced coffee the first day and said, "Help yourself. There's iced tea as well in the fridge." Iced tea and coffee were new to me and very welcomed in the heat.

The laundry was very hot with very large circular washers. The laundry all came from the single men – sheets, towels, and all their private clothes. The irons we used were huge, weighing 7 pounds, and my arm ached for the first few days. My two companions were pleased to have a replacement for the holiday-maker as it made less work for them, and they took me under their wings to teach me the ropes. First I had to learn to iron and fold a shirt their way, shirts being a good 50 percent of the washing. I still iron them the same way today.

One of my companions was German and the other Polish but they both spoke German. I asked them to teach me a bit and I still remember the phrases. One day a week they would go to the men's quarters to collect the washing bags from the long Nissan corridor, to be returned later in the week, all clean and pressed. I was not allowed to do this duty as I was a single girl. I thought I would hate the work but when I got used to it, I loved it. It was the only job I'd had where I didn't have any responsibility, and the feeling was great. Living with Jean was great as well. She'd been living a very lonely life, now I got her to come out with me to the canteen bar some nights, or Frank and a mate would come over and we would sit out on the lawn and watch the spectacular sunsets and brilliant spectacle of the lights, like a wildfire of many colours flashing across the sky. Never have I seen the likes since.

New Year's Eve arrived and we set out with a group of mates to drive down to the hotel at Copley in Wally's big grey car. Wally was a Norwegian, and there were three other "Poms", plus Frank, Jean and myself. Sadly we were just enjoying our first drink when the lady owner came in and said she'd been tipped off that the police were on the way to raid the place and we all had to leave. It seemed this was not unusual. I never did find out who it was that rang, maybe it was the police themselves to save themselves the trouble of booking us all. And I certainly didn't want to be fined for being in a pub after hours.

Back to Leigh Creek we went, but we drove past because by this time some bright spark had suggested we head north to get a drink at the pub at Lyndhurst. We got there very late, about 1 am, and banged on the door to get the landlord out of bed. He served in the bar in his pyjamas. The law in South Australia said that a publican could serve a drink to travellers if they are passing through, no matter what the time. I think the boys gave him some cock-and-bull story, he probably didn't believe a word of it, but away out there he wasn't going to turn away any custom.

After an hour or so in the bar Jean and I started pestering to go home – it had been fun but now it was time to be responsible. It took at least another hour to shift them and at last we set off.

Leading away from the Lyndhurst hotel were several sand tracks, that all looked the same. We all agreed that the one we took looked right. We drove and drove and drove. Nothing. Just desert sand and a few stumpy trees. It was still dark when the car seized up for want of oil and stopped. Not knowing what else to do we snatched an hour of uncomfortable sleep all packed in the car. I was the first to awake to a beautiful sunrise and peered ahead. Across the bright orange horizon the shapes of trees appeared black, and far off in the distance. On the left of the track there appeared to be a building.

I woke everyone up, not an easy task, and several of us set off to walk the next few miles. We had found Maree. You couldn't call it a town, or even a village; it was just, if I remember rightly, an outback pub that sold stores and petrol. The owner was a bit surly at being woken so early, but he sold us petrol in cans and the much-needed oil. Luckily the car had a crank handle, so after pouring in the oil, the engine, after much grunting and pulling, eventually turned over. We turned back and arrived back at the Lyndhurst pub at 10 am and all the guys decided they needed a drink despite loud protests from Jean and me. In despair we stood by the car and watched their backs disappear into the bar. But unbelievably luck was with us, for at that moment a taxi from Leigh Creek pulled into the park and deposited two passengers. We made a run for it and hitched a ride back.

Back at Jean's house a nasty surprise awaited us in the form of two very disapproving policemen, and the first degree started. Jean just had time to mutter in my ear, "If they ask, tell them you just pay six shillings a week rent or I will get into trouble." I was aghast, that was just half what I paid her, but what could I do?

Jean's twelve-year-old daughter had rung the police when she woke up and found her Mum missing. We were annoyed at the time but, in a town full of single men, what else could she do? I tried to explain that it was not our fault: it had not been our idea to go to Lyndhurst and we had got back as quickly as we could. Of course they did ask what I paid for rent so I told them six shillings.

"Why was I paying so small an amount?"

"Well," I said, feeling bad, "that's all she asked for." I went on to say that of course I did work around the house etc. etc. but I knew quite well they didn't believe me. I just hated telling lies.

By evening Frank had still not returned. We had been invited to a party at someone's house that night and still being furious at his irresponsibility I decided to go alone. About 10 pm he arrived with an Italian guy I'd not met before and he stunk to high heaven. Never had I smelt anything so awful. He said he'd been in the guy's room eating strong garlic sausage. I had never smelt garlic before – another lesson had been learned – and I told him to keep away from me until he smelt better. The next day I found out what they had been up to. They had stayed for hours at the Lyndhurst pub and left once more to come home and yet again they took the wrong track. It wasn't until they'd passed the same dead horse twice that they realised they'd been going round and round in circles. Arriving back at Lyndhurst again they stocked up on bottles and set out again and much later found themselves at Maree again. He said that along the way they had picked up an Aboriginal girl and the guys took turns to have sex with her on the soft top of the car right in front of the place where we'd bought oil and petrol in the early hours of the same morning. The landlord had come out and told them to get out or he was going to call the police. They headed back to Lyndhurst again and this time took the right track back to Leigh Creek. I was so disgusted I felt degraded even to have ever mixed with them and refused to be in their company again.

The "you-know-what" hit the fan that same day. I had to move out of Pru's house because me staying there was against company policy. The South Australian Electrical Trust must have decided I was doing a good job in the laundry for I was allotted a room in the single women's house.

My housemates were two middle-aged ladies – very standoffish new Australians – who worked as typists in the company office. I had very little to do with them. Sometimes Frank came to stay the night, not that I wanted him to – he would leave by the bedroom window early in the morning. It wasn't long before he was spotted and word got around. The month was nearly up at the laundry when I had a visit from the Personnel Officer. He said he would like me to take a job at the hospital where I was badly needed. I wasn't at all keen to go back to responsibilities and asked if I could stay where I was. But it wasn't to be, so I shifted from the single women's house to the Nurses' Home.

Sister Sullivan and I were the only full-time staff. There were two nurse aids – a mother and daughter – with no training at all, who could be called in when the place filled up. Our Nurses' Home was a new house – three bedrooms, lounge, kitchen, and bathroom – and we had it all to ourselves.

I soon found that I loved the job. There was no pressure, lots of laughs, and great meals cooked by a lovely German lady. She taught me to drink tea without milk, as it was much better as a thirst quencher in that torrid heat.

We never knew from day to day what was going to come to our door, unlike the training hospital where new patients weren't seen by us until they got to the ward. Here we took them straight off the street. I learned so many new things.

There was the van that brought a man with a broken leg in from the talc mine some distance out of town. Until then I didn't know that talc was a soft rock mined from the ground and ground into powder. Another day a jeep screeched to a stop at the door creating a big cloud of dust. "It's Jackie," said the man who rushed in. "He's ripped his thumb off."

Jackie turned out to be a small, very black Aboriginal, with a cheeky smile and large mischievous brown eyes. After we had called the doctor, cleaned and bound the wound we got the full story from his boss. He said they'd been out mustering cattle and he had been standing talking to a stock agent who was sitting in his vehicle. "Jackie rode up on his horse and I said 'Just keep going, Jackie, I won't be long,' but a moment later I realised he hadn't moved and when I looked around I saw blood running down the horse's front leg. I looked up and he was sitting there fiddling with his thumb. I said, 'What the hell have you done?' and he said, 'Look, boss, thumb come off, me can no put him on again.' Jackie had roped a steer and got his thumb trapped between the pommel of the saddle and the rope.

"How long will he be in hospital do you think?" he asked. "He's my head jackeroo ... can't think what we'll do without him."

There was no way the thumb could be saved, it was just hanging by a thread of skin, so while Sister helped the doctor in the theatre I kept things running in the wards.

Jackie turned out to be one of our most popular patients – he loved every day of his stay. When he'd recovered from the anaesthetic I marched him to the bathroom to have a bath; he was more than a little grubby and very dusty. I have never seen anyone enjoy a bath so much, and he thought it was wonderful. He only had a shower back on the run where he lived. I gave him the sponge in his one good hand while I washed his back before starting on his hair. It came up snowy white, and every day after that he insisted on having his bath. I would wash his back and leave him to do the rest; when I got back he would be using the sponge to soak his hair with water.

"Oh no, Jackie, you don't have to wash your hair every day," but he did it all the same. He was so childlike and happy I didn't have the heart to stop him.

I also met my first case of the delirium tremors, or D.T's. Coming onto afternoon duty one day, I started ward rounds. We had quite a few patients in and both nurse aids, Kathy and her mother had been called in. In the men's ward I found Kathy with about five patients.

"Shut the door quickly, nurse, or they will get me," demanded a middle-aged man in the far bed. I didn't know what he was on about but complied to keep the peace. Everyone was looking at me as if they knew something I didn't. He went on to tell me how management were out to get him. "Listen, listen, can't you hear them talking about me? They are out there waiting."

Not ever having seen a case of the D.T's I was very confused. Serves me right for not looking at all the new patients' case notes, I thought and hurried back to the office to do it. The man was a real trial with his continual demands for us to do this or that. We all found it quite hard not to argue with him – it would have been useless to do so anyway. It was several days before he dried out and was discharged.

Another unusual case I would never have seen in New Zealand was that of a kangaroo tick bite that had become infected. The unfortunate victim was a tall Aboriginal, who certainly didn't have the effervescent personality Jackie had had: he was quiet and surly. The bite was in the groove between two fingers and his hand was badly swollen. Twice a day he was to soak his hand in saltwater to try drain the pus and was told in no uncertain terms not to squeeze or press on his hand because to do so may spread the infection. He was like Jackie and the hair: he took no notice and whenever I went back to check on him he would be squeezing long, fat worm-like threads of yellow pus into the basin. It was about two weeks before the hand healed and he could go on his way. Apparently he was to take the train back to where he came from and was asked if he knew where the station was. He didn't, and as I was off duty and going that way they asked me to go with him and point him in the right direction, which I did. A day later Frank told me everyone was talking about me – I'd been seen walking down the road beside an *Aborigine*, how dare I do such a thing!

I was livid and really lost my temper. I am a Nurse, he was a patient and a human being, and if they didn't like me pointing out the station to him they could go to hell. I have never been a racist and people are people no matter what their colour.

One of the good things about the job was the pay. I couldn't believe my luck. Money was piling up like I couldn't believe. I was going to open a bank account but Frank was vehemently against it. "In a little town like this everyone will know your business; keep the so-and-so's guessing," he would say. He pulled up the corner of the linoleum on my bedroom floor and I hid my money there. Inside two months I had an incredible £80 saved there.

It was in Leigh Creek that I learned of his mania to be secretive and also his insane jealousy. He announced one day that an Italian fellow had told him I'd been out the night before with one of his mates. Was it true? I replied coldly that he had been with me until 2 am and I was on duty again at 6 am, and when the hell did he think I had time to sleep?

One of the things Frank carped on about was the stupidity of the foreman on the job. They were constructing a tall crusher plant and, for the sake of safety, the men wanted to put the floors in as they built upwards. The foreman insisted that they go on last. So it was no real surprise when one morning the baby-faced foreman and a manager came rushing in with the foreman clutching the top of his head and panicking because he was all-over blood. Scalp wounds do bleed copiously as they are under pressure and it can be very frightening to the uninitiated. It appeared that a large bolt had been dropped from a height onto his head, and it didn't take much intelligence to work out that it had probably been deliberate. Nor would it have surprised me if it was Frank who'd done it. Anyway, after a couple of stitches and a clean-up, he was sent on his way. The floors of the crusher were put in forthwith.

Our nurses' aid Kathy and I had become good friends, but she was married to a crude Aussie. How she ever got together with him I could never understand, they were so unsuited, but the marriage was on its last gasp. One day we admitted a blond-haired, good-looking young Italian who'd been run over by a lorry. Had he not been on soft sand he would probably have been killed. Even so his injuries were dreadful to see. Two large tyre marks went across his midriff, his entire torso, back and front was blue and green – the worst bruising I had ever seen. Lucky for him his internal organs were just bruised and he was on bed rest for weeks. He was one of the nicest lads we'd ever met: well educated, polite and respectful. Kathy and I spoiled him and stopped by to talk and have a laugh with him whenever we could. Many months later, when I was no longer there, I heard they had married.

When we had just a few patients in the hospital Sister and I went on twenty-four hours off and twenty-four hours on. Somebody had to be there in case of an emergency, so we were there for help. Needless to say this swelled our wages dramatically as there were few nights when we didn't have to get up once or twice. One night when I was on, I admitted a lady in labour – no sleep for me that night – but after a few hours I called Sister as I didn't have the confidence to assist with the birth on my own. I needn't have bothered as her baby was not delivered until 7 am when Sister would have been on anyway. A week later I attended the doctor when he circumcised her baby boy. I couldn't believe that parents would put their child through this bizarre procedure, which was done without anaesthetic, and he screamed his head off. Did they think that the child had no feeling? and although it was another thing I had learned, it was not a practice that was done in

New Zealand unless some clinical condition warranted it.

We had been there a couple of months when the weather turned nasty. For a whole week it was extremely humid and everyone was snappy – it was like the lull before the storm. We had just one patient in the night it broke, and I was on duty alone. Never had I seen such rain. It was as though a huge tank was being poured on us from above. Massive claps of thunder fairly shook the hospital, and lightning turned the night into day. The power went off and the roof began to leak badly in the corridor where an extension had been added. I ran with steel buckets from the theatre but they were filled almost immediately. My only patient was in the ward furthest from the office so, taking my torch, I ducked under the waterfall and went to see if he was okay.

"Are you all right?" I don't know why I was whispering. He said he had been thinking of getting out of bed and coming to see if *I* was okay. I sat on his bed and we talked – he was a nice lad.

Then the bell rang at the main door and I went to unlock. It was the Personnel Officer who'd given me the job; come to see if we needed help. I let him in to see where the roof was leaking but assured him that everything was in hand. I didn't get any sleep that night, and it was a long time before the rain stopped and I could stop emptying buckets. Then there was the mess to mop up.

The next morning dawned bright and clear and everything was fresh and clean, even if the red mud did stick to the soles of my shoes and made me walk like a high stepping horse.

I had my twenty-first birthday while at Leigh Creek. When Sister found out she insisted I have a party. Kathy's Mum was to mind the hospital for the evening and I was to invite some friends. Mum and Dad wrote saying they couldn't think what to give me so they sent me Mum's blue opal ring. I thought that was nice.

On the morning of the party Sister came to me saying, "Oh, Billie, you will never guess what has happened: I asked the canteen to cook me a big fruit cake and you'll never guess what they have sent." She was quite upset. It seems that on the continent they don't have fruit cakes as we know them, so when she asked for a cake with fruit in it, that is exactly what she got. It was a large, long sponge with sliced tinned peaches in the middle and cream on top. I thought it was a huge joke and told her not to worry – it was nice of her to go to the bother.

The party went off well. Sister gave me a gold key with 21 on it and everyone bought presents. Kathy and her husband were there and he told a really smutty joke that silenced the room and she snarled, "Trust you!" I blew out my 21 candles and we all laughed about the cake, and eventually they all went home, except Frank – he went to sleep on the sofa, having had too much to drink.

Sister went back on duty, not being able to leave the night shift to untrained staff.

I awoke in my bedroom after two hours sleep to the sound of vomiting and went to investigate. It was Frank, and he had spewed all over the toilet, down the back wall, the floor, just everywhere. I was disgusted, somehow I had to clean it all up before Sister came off duty in the morning. I told him to get out and go home and set to cleaning up. The stench had me almost vomiting myself, but somehow I had it all clean and smelling of disinfectant before I went to relieve Sister at 7 am, to be on duty for the next twenty-four hours. I prayed I wouldn't be woken in the night.

For some reason things began to unravel – not with me, I had never been happier – but Frank became very dissatisfied. The 'Ities' were jealous, he said, because he had a girlfriend and they didn't. No one would talk to him; they all carried knives and he would get a knife in the back if he didn't leave. The complaints came thick and fast. I thought he was talking rubbish, but when we went over to the canteen, even I began to feel the atmosphere. We were ignored. I couldn't think what he had done to alienate them. On my own things were fine. He began pressuring me to leave but I didn't think it right, I had only been there three months and wanted to stay. He started the subtle pressure.

"You came with me and I think you should leave with me." "I feel responsible for you." On and on, never-ending. He had a very clever tongue, but then all con. men do. I argued with myself that I *had* come to Australia on a working holiday, and yes I did want to see more of the country, but …

Eventually, I gave in, I would go with him, and that was the biggest mistake I have made in my entire life!

Sister tried to talk me out of going. "He's no good, you know. He will get you into trouble and probably dump you."

But I wasn't listening. I worked my notice, said a tearful goodbye, and we caught the train to Port Augusta to catch the train that crossed the Nullarbor plains to Perth. It was a new train, German-built; all the windows were sealed because of the new-fangled air conditioning. The workers on the line had a habit of spreading along the line to receive the newspapers thrown to them by the passengers, but there was no way to get them out. I felt quite sad when I saw the puzzled looks on the men's faces when they received nothing.

There had been no cheap berths left so we'd had to buy a ticket for a twin-ette in the last carriage that had an observation platform looking back along the line. It was very expensive but worth it. At night our sofa was turned into beds, and we had the best of service. There wasn't a lot to see from the observation platform. Had it been wildflower season it would have been wonderful, but all we saw were thousands of rabbits dead and dying from the myxomatosis virus with its horrible cruelty, a few camels in the distance, and lots of small cairns of stones where I imagined some poor soul who'd been working on the railroad was buried.

Most, or all, of the staff in dining car, were what they now call 'gay'," my first ever experience of them. One had red hair with kiss curls – I'm sure he must have set it every night – and his mannerisms were hilarious. He had long fingers and would come poncing down the aisle with plates balanced on his fingertips. All four of us at a table would study the menu, then he would come, pick up the menu, and flick it in front of each face saying, "Orders please."

It was here that I learned that 'gays' were much attracted to Frank, and flirted with him outrageously.

After three days we reached the border of Western Australia and had to change trains. Stupidly, when the rail tracks were first put in, each state put in different gauge tracks, so we had to leave our luxury train and get into a much more decrepit carriage to finish our journey to Perth.

Perth was a beautiful place, but finding work was almost impossible. There were two labour exchanges, one for ladies, one for men, and the queues at each stretched out of the building and away down the street. Australia was bringing in thousands of immigrants – they became known as £10 poms – and they nominated which city they wanted to go to. Thus Perth was flooded with people looking for work and isolated there without the money to move away. Perth is so remote from all other places.

We had gone through a lot of the money we had earned in Leigh Creek when Frank applied for and gained, a job as a welder away up at Gwalia in the West Australian outback for the *Sons of Gwalia* gold mines. By some incredible fluke I saw an advert wanting a shop assistant at the general store in Gwalia, so I went to the head office in Perth and was signed on straight away.

To get to Gwalia we had to go back to the gold mining town of Kalgoorlie and from there take a small train called *the bud car* up to Leonora, the nearest town to Gwalia.

What an experience! The carriages of the little train all had separate rooms with their own toilet and washbasin attached and no communicating corridor. We rattled slowly along bouncing sometimes like a kangaroo as the rails were warped. At one stage we coasted to a stop and, looking out the window, found that we had become unhitched from the engine. It wasn't long before they noticed we were missing and reversed back to hitch us up again. In the early stages, we had in our cabin a lady who told us she came from a town called Menzies. I assumed by the way she was talking about it that it was some big town, but when she said "this is Menzies" I looked out the window and said "Where?" All I could see was a small railway siding and about two stone houses. It wasn't just the size of the town that surprised me … on the platform stood a group of Aboriginals and a few scruffy, skinny dogs. They were very dark and had few clothes on. A young mother, carrying a chubby baby about six months old, was naked from the waist up. She stood close to our window completely unashamed. They wanted a lift on the train but were not allowed to get into a carriage, instead they and their dogs all climbed aboard a cargo wagon carrying pit props for the mine. I thought it was disgraceful that they had to sit outside, but was yet to get used to the way Aboriginals were treated in Australia in the 1950's.

Accommodation was hard to get in Gwalia so we had to move into a room at the hotel. The whole town was a cultural shock with its quaint little shacks all set out in rows and their rows of lavatories in a row behind them. It was hard to take it all in.

I presented myself at the store and found that head office hadn't even bothered to tell them I was coming. They'd been hoping to fill the job locally. Nevertheless, I was welcomed, as the girl I was replacing was leaving to get married. She stayed just long enough to show me the ropes and from there I floundered on. One side of the shop was given over to groceries, my side sold material, shoes, boots, some jewellery and all the newspapers, which had to be ordered. One day a week I had to change sides to help the three men working there to fill the orders to be delivered to outlying areas. Each week big boxes were stacked with stores and loaded on the truck.

In the evenings Frank told me stories about the mine. It had the longest descent in the southern hemisphere as the shaft went down on a slope. The miners packed themselves into this long sleeve thing, sitting face to face with their knees bent. At one time several had been killed when the steel rope holding them broke and they went hurtling down. Life was cheap there: a miner was killed while we were there when a pit pony kicked him and his head hit the rock wall. They didn't bother to stop working, and that gave Frank some ammunition for his never-ending scathing comments.

During our stay in Gwalia, the Laverton races were run. For the locals it was the event of the year. I wore a summery dress I'd bought in Perth, the latest fashion with two bands of curtain wires fitted hoop wise on the inside of the skirt. It caused quite a stir amongst the ladies.

Most of the horses had been brought from miles away, not top class or able to win in the city, some locals hired them for the day and ran the horse in their name. The big event of the day for me was the race won by a most unlikely horse. The mare, owned by a tall attractive girl from one of the stations, had enormous feet – I suspect there had been a draught horse somewhere in its parentage. Everyone was grinning: fancy putting a station hack with feet like that up against real racehorses. The lady owner got the last laugh: the mare flew away in last few furlongs to win by about twenty yards and paid a small fortune.

There wasn't much to do when not working, so one Sunday we went for a walk and climbed to sit on the top of a hill near the mine. I will never forget the experience. You think places are quiet, but they are not, somewhere there is noise even though you are not aware of hearing it. On the top of that hill there was total, utter silence. The silence shouted at us. Many miles away a car was coming towards us, but the car was barely visible, just a big cloud of red dust left in its wake. I picked up a small stone and threw it. It bounced a couple of times and almost sounded like thunder. It was a really awesome experience.

We had been there a month, and all my pay was going to pay the hotel bill. Frank had alienated just about everyone with his caustic tongue so we decided to leave. He made the excuse that we couldn't find a house. So his bosses and mine tried to find us a one. We were shown an old shack with a clay floor; there were holes along the bottom of the walls where the timber had rotted away. I said no thanks. But the mine desperately needed a welder so they offered us the surveyor's house which was standing empty. As houses go it was great for the outback, but it was empty, the only things in it were an old iron, wood-burning stove and a claw-footed bath. We would have to bring furniture up from Kalgoorlie so it just wasn't feasible. Once more we were on the move.

I don't know why we thought Perth would be any different; the queues were just as long, and work just as hard to get.

We took a flat out at Scarborough Beach, a nice English couple having divided their house to make a flat. We went off to the supermarket to buy food, but I just looked around in awe.

"What do we get?" I asked. I didn't have a clue.

"Don't you know how to buy food?" he snapped, grabbing the basket. "You are twenty-one for God's sake."

"Well, no, I don't. I've never bought groceries in my life. Where I come from we pick up the phone and order them every week and they are delivered. We pay the bill at the end of the month." He gave me a scathing look and filled the basket.

Every morning we were up very early to get the paper and get away to try for anything likely. I met the same girls day after day all trying for the same job. It was useless. Who wanted a Kiwi girl on a working holiday? One morning there was an advert asking for attendants at the Graylands asylum, no experience necessary, board provided, start immediately.

"You'll walk into that job," Frank said.

I packed my suitcase and set off by train. Frank waited outside and I was shown into a room where about fifteen other ladies waited. I looked around at their faces, some were just out of school, so young and innocent. I thought, *they will never stick this job*. The wait went on and on, there was nothing to read and being someone who gets bored quickly I decided to go for a walk. I wandered down the corridor until it was blocked off from floor to ceiling by a large cage-like structure. Inside, two of the hardest faced nurses I have ever seen were talking. One had enough makeup on it could have been scraped off with a trowel. She turned to glare at me, her thick bright red lips pouted but didn't speak. I was shocked to the core, and thought, *my God, if that is what mental nursing does to you I want no part of it*. Turning on my heel I went back to the waiting room, picked up my suitcase and walked out.

Frank was sitting on the steps.

"Come on," I said. "I'm going," and stormed off towards the gate.

Back at the railway station, we had a terrific row. He wanted to know what the hell I was doing, I *had* to take the job, he said, we were almost out of money. I yelled back that no way was I going to work in a bloody place like that and turn into a hard ruthless bitch, and what's more he could go to hell. Eventually things quietened down, more people had arrived to catch the train and I wasn't going to make an exhibition of myself even if he was. Then he started his smarmy act trying to get around me, so I told him to save his breath. I was so incredibly angry.

"How much money do we have between us?" I asked. We worked it out to be about £38. "Right then," I said, "this is what we are going to do: we are going back to Adelaide on the cheapest tickets. That will leave us with a few pounds until we get jobs."

He started to argue.

"Suit yourself, but that's what I'm doing."

The train came and we didn't speak all the way back to town.

The trip back was not at all like the trip over, from the dearest to the cheapest makes quite a difference. I shared with three much older Aussie ladies, and we ate in the second class dining room. What a comedown! We arrived back in the city in the morning and the first priority was to find somewhere to rent. By 2 pm we'd still had no luck. By the time we reached the places advertised, someone else had got there first. Frank did something thoughtful, unusual for him.

"I think we'd better book you a room at the People's Palace," he said. "It doesn't matter about me, I can sleep at the railway station." So that is what we did. At about 5 that afternoon, we finally found digs, far from satisfactory but a roof over our heads anyway. Before retrieving our suitcases from the stored luggage and moving in we went back to the People's Palace to ask for our money back, about £3/50 I think. The young man at the desk was the usual strange kind that the Palace always employed and I explained that I had just booked the room because we thought we may not have anywhere to sleep, but now we had found digs and as we were very short of money, could I please have a refund.

"No," he said, "Our policy states we do not give refunds."

No matter how we tried to explain or plead the answer was still,

"No, come and see the manager in the morning."

I went up to get the small bag I had left in the room and as I arrived back in the foyer a young man was just leaving. "He has just told that fellow they had no rooms left," Frank said. "He could have had your room and they wouldn't have been out of pocket."

I was furious. The week's rent we had paid for our room was £3/8 shillings, and we had just £4 and a few pence left until we could get work.

I went the next morning to see the manager, first speaking to the man on the desk. He left the desk and, through the glass doors of the dining room, I watched him approach and speak to a skinny, peaked face man who was dining with two others. He came out and said, "The manager says there will be no refund."

How damned rude can you get! Little did they know that at that moment they had made an enemy for life. Later that day, still seething, I phoned and asked to speak to the manager, telling him I thought his refusal to come out to speak to me was the height of ignorance, and then I felt much better and got on with the task of looking for work.

Our digs were in a house owned by a Hungarian woman, a very cunning landlady, all six rooms were let separately to six couples. We all shared the one horrible kitchen with its one old, and very dirty gas stove and the one decrepit bathroom, so the place was more than a little crowded.

Our room was awful. Fully furnished meant an old set of drawers and an ancient iron bed. We were making love one night when the top of the bed crashed to the floor, the protruding piece of iron on the base that was supposed to fit into the bed head was missing – it had all been cobbled together with a piece of fencing wire. We thought the landlady would be mad but she just laughed and gave us another piece of wire and some pliers to wire it up again.

One of the things that struck me forcibly about Australia at the time was the really primitive plumbing compared with New Zealand. Nowhere in N.Z. would you see chip heaters in bathrooms to heat the water for a bath. You are supposed to burn wood kindling or even newspaper to heat the water in the jacket as it runs through. The one in our digs disgusted me beyond all comprehension. The first time I went to have a bath I found ours stuffed full of stinking sanitary towels, (fanny pads we called them) and there was no way they would burn. I had a cold wash instead.

Frank, being a welder, had no trouble getting a job, but I found myself, yet again, meeting the same girls every morning as we applied for the same jobs. Frank was on night shift and called at the newspaper office on his way home to pick up a paper as soon as they came off the press. I would sit up in bed at 5.30 am and go through all the Situations Vacant, before rushing out to apply for anything remotely suitable. It soon became obvious that I would have to rely on my nursing experience and within a week I had a job at an old people's rest home.

I have no idea whether Nursing Homes needed licences for their premises in 1954/55, if so, the ones I worked in should have been closed down, so appallingly were they run. This first one was owned by a talkative middle-aged lady, and apart from the cook, who never left the kitchen, I seemed to be the only other staff. I soon came to the conclusion that 'said lady' had a screw loose. Talking very fast she would give me my instructions, which would go something like this. "First of all I want you to clean up and change Mrs — she has messed the bed again, then get Mr — and Mr — up and dressed, and make their beds, and when you have done that get Mrs — up and dressed and take her out to the lounge." The last two sentences would be delivered as she was walking off down the corridor so I always had to follow her to get the message. Mrs — had indeed messed her bed, she was doubly incontinent, but she was a sweet wee lady with all her faculties about her. I laughed and joked with her as I washed her and was about to roll a clean sheet under her when 'said lady' appeared again. "Don't use my good sheets, go and get the old ones from the bottom shelf."

When I came back she was still there. I held a sheet up; it had patch over patch over patch, and on the corners of the patches where the material was turned under, and there were big bumps.

"These bumps could give her bedsores," I exclaimed.

"Well just use them," she said. "I am not having her foul my good sheets." This as she whirled out of the room.

I did use them, making sure that none of the bumps were touching my patient, but my smile disguised the fact that I was almost shaking with rage. I had barely finished tucking the little lady in when 'said lady' appeared again, not ten minutes after giving me all her instructions.

"Have you finished all those jobs?"

I was gobsmacked – I have always been known to work very fast. I didn't say a word, just stared at her open-mouthed and came to the conclusion that she was stark raving mad.

Being expected to do a pile of work in a fraction of the time it was possible to do it in happened every day, and every day I witnessed patient neglect. This woman was getting paid to keep these people and she was going to do it at the least cost to herself. In two weeks I'd had enough and left.

My next job was also in a nursing home. I was employed over the phone to arrive at 8 am the next morning, a Sunday. The place was on the other side of town, quite a bus ride away. I told Frank I didn't have the fare and he handed me a £10 note saying, "Don't lose the change; that's the last money we have."

Arriving on time I hung my shoulder bag on the peg in the change room and pulled on my smock. This place, also owned by a lady almost as crazy as the last one, was a whole new kettle of fish. All the inmates were mental patients of one kind or another, and once again I was the only staff member, apart from the cook and the lady proprietor. I had never dealt with mental patients before so was way out of my comfort zone. It seemed that the patients did most of the work, which was fine as occupational therapy but was probably highly illegal. I was run off my feet all day. When I left to go home, I changed and collected my bag from the peg only to find that all my money had been stolen. I had no way of knowing if it was taken by one of the patients or the overnight nurse who'd come from an agency. The boss gave me slightly more than I needed for my bus fare home, but not enough to cover a day's pay. We were skint until one of us got paid. The next day, and all the week after, I borrowed Frank's bike to ride all the way to work.

One lady patient, who did most of the work, told me she'd been Suzie, the lady friend of man who was the famous spy in the Sydney Harbour. Of course, being naïve, I believed her until I was told that it was all in her mind, just one of her delusions. And she seemed so sane to me. The standard of care here was also a disgrace. Having just come from training where everything had to be just so, and finding so many things wrong, made me very stressed. One thing about the place was that rooms had been tacked on in every place possible. It was an old house with the L-shaped laundry and woodshed tacked on the back, which had then been converted to three rooms for three men. I had been there a week when I was handed a dinner tray and asked to take it out to Mr Tate.

"Mr Who?" I asked.

It turned out that Mr Tate lived in a room that had been stuck on the sidewall of the house out of sight from the street. I hadn't even known he was there. He was bed-ridden and I wondered who had been looking after him.

Two days later, when I had not even had to time to stop and eat lunch, the boss lady, lounging in a chair ordered me to go and do this, this and this. It was the last straw. I went back to the change room, grabbed my things, silently left the house and, collecting my bike, rode home.

"You left without your pay?" asked Frank.

"Yes, and I would love to have seen her face when she found I had gone. Perhaps it will teach her to have a bit more respect for her staff." I never did go back for my pay, it just wasn't worth it.

My next job was also at an old people's home, owned by a decent, middle-aged lady called Mrs Stuart. I was on the 2-till-10 pm shift and she would help me with the evening meal which was just as well as one Alzheimer's lady spat her food out as fast as I spooned it in. She would stay to help me to settle the ladies for the night and then retire about

6.30 to her adjoining flat. After that I was entirely on my own. I found the first night a bit spooky as I crept around this strange place with a torch. Mrs Stuart had made it clear that she was always on call for an emergency, but this night she had gone out for dinner. About 8.30 pm a lady called for a bedpan and I found that she had P.V. bleeding. Elderly ladies are not supposed to have vaginal bleeding, so after tucking her in again I hurried back to the office to look at her notes with the intention of ringing her doctor. No doctor was recorded, nor could I find any doctor listed. Who looked after all the inmates?

10 pm arrived at last and with it a bright Aussie girl about my age. I was so glad to see her and hear her say that the bleeding was an ongoing thing and the doctor had decided not to do anything because of her age. She gave me a rundown on all the inhabitants, with all their foibles, likes, dislikes and characters. After that night I was at ease and never had to call Mrs Stuart from her well-earned rest.

The pay at Mrs Stuart's was slightly better than the previous two homes but still not good, and going home alone so late at night was scary. After a few weeks I saw an advertisement for nurses at a Government job, live-in, all meals, and much better wages. I desperately wanted to get away from our awful digs where I now lived alone most of the week, Frank working away somewhere. I applied and was asked to start A.S.A.P. I gave Mrs Stuart and our ghastly landlady a week's notice and moved back to a Nurses' Home.

The hospital was an old infectious diseases hospital, now converted to an old people's and invalid's home. The Nurses' Home was old and comfortable, but the dark varnished wood panelling on the bottom six feet of the walls made the place gloomy. The wards, having been originally built for infectious diseases, were spaced well apart and reached by long covered walkways. I was assigned to a ward of elderly, mostly bedridden men, with one younger man, in his forties, who was dying from muscular dystrophy. What a blessing he was. The only thing he could still move was his head, but despite this he was full of fun, the only bright spark in our day, and we all liked to spend time with him. He was a truly nice guy. Other than that it was sponging old men in their beds or carrying urinal bottles to them when they had a hard-on. One day I was disgusted and told the patient to stick his thing in himself and practically threw the bottle at him. I moaned to an older, hard case nurse and she told me she soon fixed that.

"Carry a swab of cotton wool in your pocket with meths on it, one dab with that and it soon goes down."

"What happens when the meths evaporates?" I asked. She assured me it still worked. Alas, I never got to try it because within six weeks I was on the move again.

There was one nurse in the home I have never forgotten. She would have been in her late twenties or early thirties and her name was Bobby Burns, a red-haired tear-away and granddaughter to the famous Robby Burns. She was not afraid to let anyone know that she lived with her boyfriend when he came in from where he worked at the Woomera rocket range. Now we may all have had sex with our boyfriends but there was no way you would tell anyone: we thought she was very daring. She used to tell me about the escapades of her famous grandfather and called him a drunken old soak. I told her we had a statue of him in the Octagon at the centre of my home town, Dunedin. She also told me another story, which left me thinking forevermore. It seems she had at one time been living in London and had developed cancer of the uterus. It was diagnosed so late that doctors wouldn't operate and gave her three months to live. Now London is a lonely place when you are living on your own, so, as I myself have done many times, she took to walking around the streets in the evening. One night she came upon a spiritualist church where a gathering was in progress. DO COME IN AND JOIN US the board outside said, so she did. When it became time for the lady spiritualist to call up the sick, she said something like this:

"There is someone amongst us here tonight who is very ill. She has been told she has not long to live. Won't you please come forward and let us heal you."

Now Bobby was an absolute heathen and didn't believe all that muck, as she called it, but she was ready to try anything. She went forward and several people laid their hands on her.

"I could feel the current from their hands going through me," she said. "It was an amazing experience, and eventually I could do it myself." She went back many times and when she returned to the hospital three months later, the doctors were stunned and announced her completely cured.

Frank was working back in town again and had found a nice furnished flat for us. One bedroom, a lounge, and a small kitchen, but if I lived out I had to give up my job.

I found a new one at R. M. Williams, telling them I was good at sewing. The famous firm made clothes for country people, even the cowboy boots and beautiful coloured satin shirts for country and western singers, all embroidered and spangled. I was put to work sewing denim shirts, which was fine until I got to the cuff where I had to get the needle through five or six layers of material. I made a real stuff up and was always unpicking. I soon learned the machinists trick of hammering the thick bits to soften them and rubbing candle grease on to make it slide through easier. I thought for sure I'd be sacked but after a month I was still there, the lovely forewoman very patient. One day I put the needle right threw my finger, and they all laughed and cheered. Now you are a machinist, they said. They were, however, a sensitive lot as I was to find out one morning.

Adelaide has the River Torrens running through it. In the gardens it was wide and slow-moving, very pretty, and we often used to row there. Imagine my shock when looking out the bus window on the way to work I saw a big stretch of filthy black mud, with a small creek running through the middle.

"Who pulled the plug out of the river?" I asked and was met with a stony silence. Frank got the same reaction at his work. It seems they didn't like anyone to know that the lovely *river* was just a little creek after all. We found out that once a year the weir downstream was opened so all the junk, like prams and bikes that had been thrown in, could be removed.

One day Frank asked me when I'd had my last period. Strangely enough I had never thought about it, we worked it out that it must have been over two months past. I wondered what was wrong – how could I be so naïve? A few days later I visited a gynaecologist.

I was in shock when I walked out to meet Frank who was waiting in the park over the road. I didn't think, *Oh my God, I am having a baby, what am I going to do? What will my parents say?* I just sort of floated across the road and blurted out: "He says I'm pregnant," and he said, "Oh well, I suppose we'd better get married."

I suppose I should be grateful for that, but I had never thought of marrying this man. I certainly didn't love him … he was, well, just a travelling companion.

Frank had assured me that he had never made any of his girlfriends pregnant. "I never slept with a girl I couldn't take home to my mother, and I never left a girl until she had a period and I knew she was safe."

I had always wanted him to use a condom, but he refused, saying that it was like taking a bath with your socks on, and anyway he didn't think he could have children as no one he'd ever been with had fallen pregnant. This, of course, was a downright lie because he told me much later that Margaret, the Jewish girl he'd lived with for four years in Wellington, had had three abortions without his knowledge – my first lesson in just how devious and lying men can be when they want to have sex with you.

Give him his due, he kept his word and got a licence for us to be married at the registry office, but once again he demanded secrecy. Not the first time I had met with this weird trait of his to keep everything secret. I couldn't ask anyone at work to be witness for me because they thought I was already married, and he didn't want to let on to any of his workmates.

I bought a maternity suit to get married in, but it didn't look like one. In 1956 you tried to hide your ever-growing belly. My suit had a flowing jacket and a skirt that you could let out at both sides as the baby grew. The lady clerk at the registry office gave me a filthy look, and as I was not showing I ran my hands over my flat stomach.

Out on the street, we waited for someone to come past and eventually we found two ladies who consented to be witnesses to our marriage. We had no cake, no fancy dinner, no photos, just took ourselves off to the picture theatre. And that was our wedding day.

Still at R. M. Williams, I eventually told them I was pregnant. Within two weeks I was given notice – I couldn't understand it, I'd been doing so well. Strangely, it wasn't until I began writing my story that I realised my dismissal was because I was pregnant. Women had so few rights in the Fifties.

Frank had wanted the baby to be born in England and we'd been saving frantically to pay for a berth on a ship. When he arrived home that night I tearfully told him I'd been sacked, the only time in my life. He took it well and said not to worry.

I had one more job in Adelaide before the baby was born and it was the worst ever. I got a job in a slave shop factory where they made rubber gloves. A long row of machinists sewed frantically all day. We had a radio that played music all day, but when the news came on we had silence. Nothing must happen to distract us. The reason for the machinists was that the inside of the rubber gloves were made of cheesecloth; these were then fitted over hand-shaped things and dipped in a rubber solution. We had to sew up one side, up and down between the fingers and down the other side. The tricky bit was the four-cornered gusset that fitted between the thumb and forefinger. Given that our seams were just half a centimetre wide this made for a very tricky job and the most likely place to get a hole. Unfortunately the checker stood just behind me. She would go down the row collecting our work and fit each piece over a 'hand' to check for holes. She would then collect up any with small holes in and hand them out to be repaired. I, being right behind her seemed to get the lion's share, and they told me I wasn't fast enough. I should have been sewing fourteen dozen pairs every day. I hated the place.

As luck would have it my step-mother gave me an out. She told me in a letter that they'd found large lump in her abdomen and she was to go to surgery. I did my very best acting and said tearfully I had to fly home to be there and was allowed to leave without notice and with wages intact. It turned out that the lump was a large haemorrhoid in her colon.

Frank applied, and got a job on Kangaroo Island, situated off the South Australian coast. Off we went, travelling by plane to the only town, Kingscote.

Kangaroo Island remains in my memory as one of the best phases of my life with Frank. His boss was a Mr Bulstrode who ran a welding shop, and he provided us with a small cottage away up on a hill above Kingscote. It was a palace compared with what we'd previously had and was situated, isolated and alone, on about two acres of land just over the hill from the sea. We had an iron wood stove with a big pile of mallee roots outside to feed it, and a *washing* machine that I'd never seen before or since. It comprised of a round barrel tub with an iron bar across the top that had a handle on the end; from the middle hung a round, conical contraption with open-topped tubes in. The idea was to lift the handle up and down, sucking and squeezing until all the dirt was out. It was surprisingly effective and later in England I was to see the small brass *possers* that worked on the same principle.

The toilet, or "dunny", dry of course, was situated about fifteen yards down the hill from the back door. A large grey spider, about two inches across, lived up in the top left corner near the roof. Last thing at night, before going to bed I would visit the loo, always demanding that Frank stood on the back steps as the island was full of black poisonous snakes. It was not unheard of for snakes to hide in the box that housed the lavatory tin, so I had a ritual I carried out each night. After opening the door I first shone my torch on the spider, having assured myself he, or she, was still in the web, I then shone the torch all around the tin to see if any snakes hid there. After all, getting bitten on the backside by a poisonous snake was not high my list of priorities. Having at last found that all was in order I would sit down to have a pee.

One night I had just sat down when I heard a hissing noise. I flew out the door with my knickers around my ankles screaming, "There's a snake in there," only to see Frank laughing his head off. It was he who had made the hissing noise.

"Don't you ever do that again, you bloody idiot," I screamed. "I might have had a nasty fall."

We had been in the house a few weeks when a tabby cat appeared at the door. She was not in good condition and my heart went out to her. I have never been a great lover of cats but this cat needed help. She had a hole in the retina of her eye and had a dirty and bedraggled coat. I couldn't turn her away so started to feed her. In view of her condition, I wouldn't let her inside: she may have had fleas, but after a few weeks she blossomed and became the most endearing cat I have ever had. What a character! She loved to play games. As the months went by the fields around us turned into a picture for Monet. Our two acres flowered with thousands of wild gladiolas, all purple in colour, and our little well-worn track went across the top corner. I would set out to go to town, and the cat – we never did give her a name – would race ahead of me down the tiny path. I was always aware there may be snakes basking near the path and was constantly vigilant until I reached the road. Suddenly, out onto my feet the cat would erupt, and then rush off down the path, having given me a dreadful fright.

"Stupid bloody cat, just wait till I get a hold of you," I would scream, but I couldn't help laughing at her crazy playfulness.

The only entertainment on the island was the picture theatre, and we usually went once a week. The cat would follow us down the path even though we tried to shoo her back. About halfway to town, she would disappear into a drainage pipe beside the road where she would wait until we were on our way home, where, to our utter astonishment, she would come pouncing out onto our feet and accompany us home.

Walking on the jetty one day I met an old man fishing who'd caught a lot of small fat fish – *tommy roughs* he called them. He taught me how to fillet fish and gut them, and sent me home with some for tea.

Kangaroo Island wasn't the place it is now, (2011), now it is a tourist resort, but in 1956 the locals wanted none of the *foreigners* who invaded their territory. They had allowed someone to open a coffee lounge in the main street, which was fine as they could use that, and there were other industries that had gained a foothold, but the minute they tried to expand, LOOK OUT.

It was the same with Mr Bulstrode. When we arrived he had a big backlog of welding to do for the farmers. Most of his work was the building up of tractor tracks, and there were piles waiting to be done. Frank soon found that Mr Bullstrode couldn't see to weld straight, an essential when you are doing tractor or bulldozer tracks. He and his wife explained how territorial the locals were. Mrs Bullstrode had even joined their strange (feathery leg, as we liked to call it) religion in an effort to get their patronage. She was a naïve little person. Once when we joined them for a cuppa she went off on tangents about her life in a W.A.F.S. It seemed to be the only exciting thing she'd done in her life.

As the weeks went by Frank made a big dent in the backlog of welding work, but strangely enough no new work was coming in unless it was small urgent jobs, then we heard that some farmers had sent their tracks back to Adelaide on the ferry.

One night when I joined Frank in the pub we met a Scot called Jim who told us he had bought a building block in Kingscote two years earlier but the locals had stopped him building on it. He now had shares in a big turkey farm way out in the sticks near the coast. "Would you like to come out for the weekend?"

"What will your wife say?" I asked.

"She will be delighted to have some company. Poor girl, she hardly ever gets away from the place. If they know that nobody is there they come and shoot the place up."

So it was agreed. We made a quick visit home to throw in a change of clothes and off we went, me at the wheel, for I was the only sober one. For a very inexperienced driver it was quite an adventure. The gravel road twisted up hills and down into valleys, through scrub and open fields until at last he said, "Here is where we leave the road."

The grass track ran two miles across the neighbour's fields, and what a shock. Wallabies – hundreds of them – leaped and darted away from the car lights. I felt sure I would run one over but Jim just laughed, and of course they were far too smart for that.

Jim and Norah's house was a big, long Nissan hut. It had a kitchen of sorts and a double bed at both ends screened off with curtains. I felt sorry for Norah; she obviously led a very lonely life. Being unable to drive and marooned so far from civilization, and with Jim a heavy drinker, she must have spent many a night on her own in that God-forsaken place. However she seemed resigned to her situation and welcomed us with goodwill.

After a cup of tea and a long talk, we finally fell into bed.

I was up early and off to explore, and was amazed as about a thousand birds followed me along the fence. *Gobble gobble gobble*, they said, *where is our breakfast?* I loved it, every time I said "gobble gobble gobble" they answered the same and made me laugh. Jim came to give them their food and we went back into the Nissan hut for the big breakfast Norah had prepared. She and I had a chat while I helped with the chores and the men were working elsewhere. I think she was happy to have another female to talk to.

Later in the day Jim, Frank and I went for a walk across the property and came at last to the cliffs overlooking the sea. There was a little ledge at the top so I sat down and swung my feet over to rest while we admired the view. When I looked down, not ten inches from my feet was a black snake, its head and a bit more sticking out of a crack in the rocks. I didn't dare to move.

"There's a snake at my feet," I said quietly, slowly moving my arm upwards to be pulled away.

"Just stay still," said Jim. He picked up a stick and banged it on the rock in front of the snake and it disappeared back out of sight. He then told us that snakes are much more afraid of us than we are of them and that they will never attack you unless you threaten them. Another lesson learned: I have never been afraid of snakes since.

The next day we said goodbye to Norah, and Jim drove us back home – we never saw them again, just two more ships that passed in the night.

There was just one thing I hated about Kangaroo Island, the doctor! He was a real sadist: he used to beat his poor wife up, and I saw her myself with black eyes and split lips. Before I knew this I went for a check-up and he did an internal examination. I feel sure he was deliberately vicious as he yanked his fingers upwards and I almost screamed with pain. I never went there again and dreaded the thought that he would deliver the baby.

One day we were invited by a friend to party away out at a farm. When we got there all the men were downing beer like there was no tomorrow and were feeding beer to an eight-month-old baby boy sitting on the tailboard of a Ute. It's a well-known fact that babies love beer and this little fellow was swilling it in one end and it was pouring out the other. He sat in a wet nappy with pee running out and dripping from the tailboard onto the ground. They all thought this very funny. That poor little boy was probably an alcoholic before he was five years old.

The farmhouse was above the beach and that afternoon they'd bogged a good four-wheel drive in the sand on the beach, so, they took the tractor out to pull it out and bogged that as well. There they were, both car and tractor with just the tops showing above the waves and they didn't seem to give a damn. After a while I ventured into the farmhouse, and there, to my horror was the doctor, more than a little inebriated. I couldn't help wondering what would happen if he was drunk when I went into labour.

We had to wait until the friend who drove us there was ready to go home, and he wasn't going anywhere, so Frank and I took a walk along the beach. It was beautiful in the half-dark, but suddenly a huge cacophony of sound erupted from the rocks behind us. I took to my heels and ran, with Frank following me. When we stopped for breath we wondered what could have made such a noise, certainly it was nothing we'd ever heard before. They all laughed when we returned to the house: it was the penguins, they said, letting us know we were invading their domain.

When all the jobs at Frank's work ran out, and with no more work coming in, Mr Bestrode reluctantly gave Frank notice. He was really sad to see us go, but showed us a letter, which said, "I am giving you this job, Joe, but want you to do it yourself, not that guy you have employed." Sad, when you think that Frank, whatever his faults, was a very, very good welder.

So it was that we left our little house on the island and returned to Adelaide, this time on the ferry. I was eight months pregnant.

The first thing we had to do was find accommodation and we were immediately lucky. We answered an advertisement for a room and kitchen. The people renting were a Mr and Mrs Phillips, who rented the house themselves but were allowed to sublet the back bit.

"I'm pregnant," I blurted out when we went to inspect the place.

She laughed, "Yes, we can see that."

And so they, and their fox terrier dog, Jimmy, welcomed us into their home, although our piece was shut off from theirs. I enjoyed our time there; they were a lovely couple. Mr Phillips grew vegies and tomatoes in the garden outside our door; I couldn't get over how the tomatoes ripened – green one day, red the next. He kept us supplied all the time we were there.

The first thing I had to do was register with the public maternity hospital. At that time they were into a natural childbirth binge, and clinics were held each week to tell you how to breathe and relax during labour, so you didn't need anaesthetics or pain killers. I was booked in to attend my first visit a fortnight later at the end of December. A young doctor had examined me with a Sister accompanying him. He measured my pelvic bones with the knuckles of first and second fingers. "Great pelvis, hasn't she, Sister," he said. That gave me a giggle, how could you look at a fanny and say that it is wonderful?

One Sunday Frank and I went to visit our old stamping ground at Glenelg beach. On the way home on the tram I said: "Look who is sitting up in front of us." It was Wally, the Buick owner from Leigh Creek. Frank started rolling up tram tickets and flicking them at him. When he saw us, there was much laughter and a lot of catching up to do. He told us that my nurse aid friend in Leigh Creek had divorced her awful husband and married the fair-haired Italian that had been run over with the truck. I thought they were well suited and hoped they made a go of it.

Wally came to visit us at our digs a few times and told Frank how he had broken into a store and taken a transistor radio, and how he had walked along the street with it playing right past a policeman who wished him goodnight. I was horrified. He didn't seem the type to steal and I wondered what his parents in Sweden would feel if they knew what he was doing. His father was a ships' captain.

Christmas 1956 arrived and with it came Wally bearing gifts. He presented me with a very unusual cameo brooch of three dancing ladies. I'd never seen another like it before (nor have I since) and I thought it was a strange thing to give a young woman. Two weeks later we were sitting up in bed reading the morning paper and there it was! Wally had been arrested for breaking into the home of a new Australian lady and stealing many things. Suddenly I knew where that cameo brooch had come from.

Frank left the room and returned with a small ivory and wood filigree chest. I was to see the same thing later in South Africa. Wally, he told me, had bought it all to give to me for Christmas but, "I thought you might get suspicious if he gave you the lot."

I was sick with worry. Here I was within weeks of giving birth and my idiot husband had allowed stolen goods to come into the house. If the police knew Wally had come here, we could have the house searched and be implicated. I demanded that he get rid of it all at once, but where to? It couldn't go into the rubbish bin we shared with the Phillips. That night Frank wrapped it tightly in newspaper and hid it in the base of a thick ivy creeper that grew up one of the veranda poles in the back yard. We thought it was safe, but we hadn't counted on Jimmy being in the equation. One morning I was sitting on the sunny veranda talking to Mr Phillips as he tended his garden when Jimmy started taking too much interest in the bottom of the creeper. He was down on his tummy scratching furiously to get to the hidden loot. My blood ran cold. No way could I allow him to drag it out for all to see.

Thinking quickly I scooped him up saying, "What are you up to now, you little tinker, you are always digging." I carried him to the end of the yard and played fetch with him until I hoped he had lost interest in the creeper. I didn't dare to go inside for the rest of the day, even after Mr Phillips and Jimmy had gone into the house. When Frank came home I told him he had to shift it, which he did after dark. I don't know what he did with it after that, what I do know is that I still have most of it today and have forever felt guilty.

January 19th, 1957. I awoke at 5 am. I'd had a 'show', the thick mucus glob you pass before birth, and I knew the day had come. During the morning while the pains slowly grew worse Frank sat very quietly at the table trying to mend a disembowelled radio. At midday, after a particularly sharp pain I snapped at him to get me to the hospital, and Mr Phillips drove me in.

The place was chaotic – they had already had seventeen births that day and there wasn't a bed for me. I was sat in a chair outside two labour rooms and Frank took his leave.

Beside me was a linen bag on a frame almost full of bloody linen and the staff scurried about. I was sick with nerves as I thought about the dreadful births I'd seen at the maternity hospital. Eventually a bed was found for me in a two-bed room; I was examined and left alone with a cup of tea, but not for long. They wheeled in a bed with a Geek woman aboard. Her piercing screams threatened to lift the roof. I vomited up my cup of tea. Half an hour later she was shot off to give birth. Next they wheeled in a Dutch woman. I had heard her yelling from along the hallway but not what she had been saying. She was way out of control; someone told me she'd been carrying on for four days and had started pushing before the baby was ready, now here she was in the next bed shouting obscenities.

"I don't want this bloody baby, kill it, kill it." Oooooo then an ear-splitting scream. "Get a knife and cut it out." Oooooo "You don't know what you are doing to me ... why don't you help me?" All this at the top of her voice; by now I was literally shaking and vomited up another cup of tea. The nurses couldn't have been more wonderful, they kept bringing me tea and commiserating with me. Finally a nurse came in and said, "Sorry darling I'll take her out."

She gave the woman a slap on the bottom and said, "You have got to stop this, you have upset everyone in the ward."

At last, I had a bit of quiet, the back pains were getting worse; every time one came I yanked up my knees and held tight to the bed head. Alas, they rushed in another screamer. "Sorry love, this one won't be long, she's a rush job." Sure enough as soon as they had finished prepping her she was gone.

I was alone for about an hour when they wheeled in a nice down-to-earth Australian. "You yell as much as you like," she said. "You won't upset me."

I gritted my teeth. "I'm damned if I am going to scream."

Between pains we chatted; the doctor came to examine her and I heard her say she'd had a baby before she was married. Her just being there and chatting helped to settle me down. At 7 pm after one last awful pain my waters burst. I was exhausted and fell into a deep sleep.

Later I vaguely remembered them coming to check on me several times, then a nurse said, "Theatre quick, she's ready."

I was no sooner on the birthing table than I started to bear down, and after a few good pushes the doctor put his fists at the top of my bump and pushed the baby out. It was 8.50 pm, and it was a boy. There was nothing wrong with his lungs, he protested his arrival loudly. Soon I was cleaned up and they said my husband was there to see me. Frank came in wearing a white smock with a big bloodstain on the front. I was a bit shocked and hoped it was my blood and not someone else's.

"You look better than I thought you would," he said.

"It's a boy."

"Yes, they told me. I think that must have been him passing me in the trolley as I was coming in. He was screaming the roof off."

I asked him what he'd done all day and he said he'd been to the races. *Well, that would be about right.*

They put me in a downstairs room where about nine other ladies were asleep. I found out in the morning that the upstairs, where Mums usually went with their newborns, was full and I had been put in a room where pregnant woman having pre-natal problems were housed. They all had different problems – high blood pressure, babies trying to abort or turned the wrong way. I spoke to the pretty girl at the front of me on the other side and she said that her baby was dead inside. I felt awful.

Two days later, just when I'd become acquainted with all my companions I was shifted again to a room across the hall. This also had Mums with problems, but none had a dead baby. Carol, the woman beside me, was upset. They'd just told her that they thought she had her dates wrong and the baby wasn't due for another month. Her husband would come in every afternoon and sit on her bed. The second day she said to me, "I think I have got a show, don't tell anyone, promise." Of course I didn't and later that afternoon she went into labour and was whisked away to give birth to a 14 pound baby boy. Considering I could just manage 7 pound 12 ounces with mine, this was one big baby.

Her bed space was quickly filled and that afternoon Carol's husband, who obviously hadn't been informed about his son, arrived as usual. The lady in Carol's bed was reading the paper and he leaned over to give – what he thought was his wife – a kiss before leaping off the bed. We all took delight in telling him the news before he went off to find her. The next day I was moved again; I finally made it upstairs. By this time I was a nervous wreck, four shifts in as many days and getting new people every time had left me shattered. To make it worse the woman beside me was horrible: she was like a fat blonde baby doll – cheap, nasty, and plastered with makeup. She moaned constantly about her baby, pulling faces and whining when it suckled because it was hurting her: it was the last straw and, when they told me three days later I could go home, I couldn't have been happier.

We named the baby Steven Ward, the Ward for Frank's best friend in the U.K. I worried that our little treasure would disturb the Phillips, but on the whole, he was good and didn't often cry.

I went for my check-up two weeks later; I was still bleeding, and shouldn't have been so they sent me home with ergot tablets. Ergot works by clamping down the muscles of the uterus, unfortunately it also clamps the muscles of the inside of the thighs; the pain is indescribable.

One night we were sitting on the bed, the only place apart from the kitchen table we could sit. Frank was reading the paper and I had finished breastfeeding and wanted to change Steven's nappy. I tried to get off the bed but the pain was too extreme so I asked Frank if he would get one for me. He ignored me, so I asked again.

"Get it yourself," he said.

My anger roiled – he'd been quite strange and distant since we'd come home. I expect it alarmed him that he now had a responsibility after many years of being completely irresponsible. He had always said "I hate sickly women," because his mother had always pretended to be sick to get attention, so I was never allowed to feel unwell. I rounded on him. "Why is it you will never do anything for me? You make me sick."

I didn't see it coming but suddenly he backhanded me across the face and in doing so caught Steven a tremendous blow to the head with his elbow.

Baby screamed and screamed. I was so afraid the blow had caused damage to his ten-day old brain. Frank went on reading the paper as if it had never happened. I never forgave him for that and never will.

Frank was keen to get back to England and had already made some inquiries. The *S.S. Skaubryn* was leaving soon with fares as low as £120. Frank decided we should take it. One of the things that attracted me to the trip was all the calls we would make along the way. We would leave from Melbourne, call at Brisbane – the only city in Australia I hadn't seen – on to Colombo in Ceylon (which is now Sri Lanka) – then Aden, Port Said, and on to Tilbury Docks in London.

Alas, it wasn't to be. Egypt laid claim to the Suez Canal and England, taking exception to this, started dropping bombs. The shipping company sent a letter to say we would go via the Cape of

Good Hope: our only stops would be Cape Town and Tenerife in the Canary Islands. It was a bitter blow.

And sSo it was, with Steven just nineteen days old, we set out. We travelled to Melbourne to board her, then set off to cross the rough Indian Ocean travelling far south, where it was supposed to be less rough.

The *Skaubryn* was launched on October 7th, 1950, not a big ship as ships go, her tonnage just 9,786. She was registered in Oslo and her home port was Bremerhaven. Built mainly for the emigrant trade she had also been chartered by the French and British Government to carry troops. Her officers were Norwegian, the crew German and the cuisine Italian.

Rumour aboard had it that the ship had a "hoodoo" and as things turned out I believe it had.

It was also said that the ship pitched and rolled so badly because it had had a million-dollar refit with most of the weight being put on the top decks. This I don't believe.

Our cheap fares were in the dormitories away below deck: I was in the very nose of the ship where it narrowed to a point and Frank was in the stern. These two places held the last of the soldiers' bunks. We pitched and rolled for seventeen days until we reached Cape Town. One stormy night the ship pitched so badly the propeller kept coming out of the water and the whole ship juddered. I feared we would nose dive to the bottom of the ocean. I became very seasick and vomited until only bile came up and my milk began to dry up. I implored Frank to go for the doctor. The ship had a very good hospital and well trained German staff. The doctor and nurse visited me and gave me suppositories, at least in that end they couldn't be vomited up. Within a day I was up on my feet, and ready to wash that pile of nappies.

There were about 264 passengers aboard, as opposed to the 1,205 souls it carried on the way out. They must have been packed in like sardines. We found an old menu from the trip out to Australia and despite the happy reports from immigrants posted on the internet, the cuisine they got was far inferior to ours. We were horrified when we saw it.

Up on deck, I became friendly with a girl called Margaret; I told her about the awful conditions close to the bilges and she said she had two spare beds in her cabin and why didn't I just move in. I was delighted, and for about ten days I slept well. Somehow the purser found out I was in the cabin and he approached me. Later I realised that if I had offered him a bribe I may have been able to stay there, but I didn't and was banished again back to my berth away below. A few days later Margaret asked me if I had seen her pawa Kiwi broach set in silver. I told her honestly that I hadn't. Imagine my horror when a few weeks later when we were in England Frank produced the broach. I wanted to die of shame. I found it hard to believe he could do something so despicable when the girl had been so generous to offer a bed to me and my baby. I always hoped I would meet her again so I could return it. It is still in my possession.

Life aboard was just as usual: shipboard romances, deck games, swims in the pool, sunbathing if the sun came out, and dances at night. We had a ship's concert – I sang *Stormy Weather* (how apt) and did a hula. The sixteen officers aboard socialised with the passengers every night and we used to wonder just who was on watch.

Sometimes I went on deck in the late evening and just watched over the side. As the ship cut the waves they became alive with phosphorescence that sparkled and glowed, and flying fish flew before the wake before dropping out of sight again.

The ship broke down several times on the way to Cape Town and we floundered around for an hour or three. It was said they closed down the engine when the doctor had to operate and there were some appendectomies among the young travellers.

The day before we reached Cape Town a letter was sent around saying that would arrive about 6 pm the following day and as the ship was running so late we would have just six hours ashore. The passengers rebelled. Having been deprived of our promised trip we were now to lose our one day ashore as promised. Someone organised a petition, saying unless we had some hours ashore the next day we would not come back to the ship. It was presented to the Captain who said he would cable Onslow. We were granted our request: we could stay until midday the following day.

Our arrival at the harbour was weird, our ship listing badly to starboard. Someone from a boat yelled, "What's the matter with your ship?" and the tannoy asked us not to all crowd to one side of the ship. It seems that in their efforts to get away they had already emptied the water tanks. Eventually, we were tied up and safe without tipping over.

The nurse made a bottle for Steven and looked after him while I went ashore; it was strange trying to walk on terra firma again.

The night was overcast, wet and windy, and Table Mountain had its table cloth on (as the saying goes) so it couldn't be seen. We had a walk around, visited a bar or two and talked to the friendly locals before Frank delivered me back at the ship and went off again by himself. Steven must have decided that Mum's milk was better than the bottle; he brought some of it back up before settling down until his 2 am feed.

The next morning after he'd been fed, washed, and settled to sleep, I dressed myself and raced up the stairs and out onto the deck and stood amazed. The table cloth of clouds had gone and there was Table Mountain. A wondrous sight, it towered majestically above the ship and I stood in awe for some minutes before running down to breakfast. Not wanting to miss a moment we hurried ashore, this time with baby.

The first thing I noticed was the horrible thing they called Apartheid, the racial segregation enforced by the regime of the day. It appalled me. Did these arrogant white people really think they were better than people with darker skins? There were buses for blacks and buses for whites, counters for blacks and counters for whites in the post office. Fuming, I deliberately went to the black counter to post my letters; the black girl served me politely with a happy smile. The white folks glared at me, and I longed for them to say something so I could tell them what I thought of them, but nobody did.

We wanted to go up on the cable to the top of the mount but it wasn't running so we just explored. We bought a huge bunch of black grapes from an elderly black man with a lovely smiling face, he must have known we were tourists as we chatted and shared a joke. All too soon we were back aboard and on our way.

Our trip up the coast was trouble-free, no break downs, a much calmer sea and very hot. We crossed the equator with the usual pomp and ceremony; some passengers and crew dressed as Neptune grabbed unsuspecting passengers and threw them into the pool. Because I couldn't swim I was terrified I'd be thrown in so I took Steven from his carrycot and held him, knowing I could watch the fun unmolested. Dye and buckets of water were thrown until almost everyone on deck was wet. The menu at dinner that night said:

<u>Saturday 16th March 1957</u>
<u>Equator Dinner</u>

Mocturtle Eggs a La Triton
Walrus Soup
Shark-skin fillet a La Amphitrite.
Roasted Albatross in Cod Oil.
Vegetables and Potatoes from Poseidon's Garden
Seagrass Salad - Jelly Fish Dressing
Icecream Neptunus
Seadrinks of the Mermaids.

I haven't a clue what we ate!

Our next stop was at Teneriffe in the Canary Islands. There were market stalls on the wharf to greet us but we didn't have money to buy. The place was pretty and tropical, we *did* the town and visited a local market where mostly wrinkled elderly ladies dressed all in black sold fruit and vegetables. Frank caused a furore because he was carrying the baby; it seems that no man in Teneriffe would ever carry a baby, and all the old girls pointed and laughed uproariously, showing toothless mouths and missing teeth. We got out of there – fast.

The Bay of Biscay is known for its rough weather, but compared with the southern ocean it was a pussy cat. Soon we were passing the southern coast of England, travelling close to shore and our passengers lined the rails.

"Look how green it is," many of them remarked, and truly it was a delight to see such green fields.

Our chain of things to go wrong had not deserted us; it was announced that as there was a wharfies strike at Tilbury Docks, the *Queen Mary* and *Queen Elizabeth* (two of the world's largest ships) were taking up all the space there so we would be disembarking at Plymouth on the southern coast. This was a blow for us as money was really short.

At Plymouth Harbour, there was no space available against the wharf so we anchored out in the middle of the harbor and pontoons were sent out to bring us ashore to the customs sheds.

I was nervous: Frank had bought many packets of duty-free cigarettes aboard ship as gifts for family and friends. I was very much against it but he insisted they wouldn't check a baby's carrycot, and hid them all under Steven's mattress. He was right, they didn't. I breathed a sigh of relief. Wharf workers came to carry cases and earn a tip, Frank gave our man a half-crown, (2 shillings and 6 pence). I thought it rather extravagant. We had arrived with just £35, the stupidest thing we could ever have done.

Saying goodbye to the *Skaubryn* wasn't the last time we were to hear of it. We had been in the U.K. about a year when the paper headlines shouted:

Blazing Ship Sinks
1,100 rescued
Amsterdam, Tuesday morning.

The British ship "City of Sydney" early today picked up the 1,100 passengers and crew of about 300 from the Norwegian migrant ship Skaubryn. (9,786 tons) which sank after catching fire in the Arabian Sea. She was bound for Australia.

News of the rescue was flashed by the 7,003-ton City of Sydney's radio and picked by Scheveningen Radio in Holland. The City of Sydney left Colombo on March 26th and is bound for Britain.

The Skaubryn had 736 migrants among her passengers, most were Germans and Scandinavians. But she called at Dover on March 16th to pick up 12 Britains. Later she took 150 more migrants on board from Malta.

NO RADIO CONTACT.

The ship caught fire about halfway between Aden and India. Her owners said in Oslo that they had no radio contact with her but had been told of the blaze by their agents in Rotterdam.

Captain O.R. Reinertsen, spokesman for the owners, said all efforts to contact the Skaubryn had failed. Her radio must have been put out of action since no signals had been received by Bergen Radio.

The Scaubryn had been fitted with a powerful transmitter which was normally capable of sending signals from as far as Fremantle, Australia, for reception in Norway.

Many of the migrants who had boarded the Skaubryn were refugees. Officials of the Inter-Governmental Committee for European Migration said in Bonn that they included some women and children.

Altered.

The first ship reported to be going to the rescue was the London motor Vessel Silver Lake (8,098 tons), two days out of Aden and bound for Madras.

She reported her position as 170 miles from the burning ship and altered course. But she did not expect to reach her until 6 am today.

In London Major Willie Baraclough, joint-managing Director of the Silver Lake, said that he had heard nothing about the mercy dash.

The Admiralty said; The Skaubryn's position could be anywhere in a vast area. If any of our vessels are near they will help.

The passengers later transferred to the *S.S. Roma* and were taken back to Aden. They had been lucky; just one elderly man was lost, dying of a heart attack.

We never could understand how the whole ship had become engulfed in flames, especially when it became known that the fire had started in the engine room. When we were aboard I many times had to descend through three heavy steel fire doors (always open) to get to the hot washing and drying room where I washed nappies. How had the fire not been contained? And how many times had we remarked that none of the officers seemed to be on duty?

I was to learn more about the ship later. I was in the Littlehampton library when I chanced on a book called *Voyage of Despair*. I opened it and read the first line. It said, 'It all began on the *S.S. Skaubryn*'. I took it home and read the dreadful story of two French Foreign Legion soldiers, one a Norwegian, the other from Liverpool in England, who, on their way to Vietnam on the *Skaubryn* had bribed the crew to throw a life raft to them after they jumped overboard. They were somewhere off Colombo and thought they would drift ashore. Unfortunately it all went badly wrong and they were blown away out into the middle of the Indian Ocean away from the usual shipping lanes. Eric, the English lad, eventually died and his friend told of how he had promised not to throw his body overboard. He kept his word even though a shoal of sharks eventually surrounded and followed the raft. When the sharks became impatient and began to ram the raft, trying to upset it by nudging from underneath, he finally broke his promise. Two days later, the sharks came back for him.

After three months he was picked up and taken to Singapore, the nearest port.

His story finally convinced me that the *S.S. Skaubryn* had indeed been an unlucky ship, with a Hoo-Doo on it.

England 1957 - 1961

Frank was quite pleased that we had arrived in Plymouth as he had been stationed there during the war. He had been out on the moors guarding a munitions dump on one of the nights when Plymouth received a massive bomb attack which had lit up the sky.

It was in Plymouth that he first realised that his strong Yorkshire accent could not be understood, and people at a dance had mocked him. I still believe that was the start of his gross inferiority complex. His personality would never let him believe that he wasn't as good as anyone else, and he was forever bitter and aggressive.

Anyway, here we were in Plymouth. We got a B-and-B (*bed-and-breakfast*) for the night and the next day we set out to explore. The town had taken a severe beating during the war, the bomb scars still visible. There were gaps where houses had taken a direct hit and shrapnel holes on the buildings. Later in the day we boarded the Cornish Express train to London. English trains had a corridor going along the side of the carriage with small rooms off it that had seats either side. We shared with two nice Australian lads and a nice middle-aged lady, obviously well-heeled, who had been on our ship. As we climbed away from Plymouth we looked down a long row of buildings and lots of chimneys.

"What on earth is that?" I asked and was told they were houses all joined together. I was aghast. *Did people really live like that?* I had never seen houses joined together before. The lady and I began talking about shoes as I had admired hers. I said, lifting my foot, "These are pigskin."

And she replied, "Well, they are imitation pigskin." I am sure she didn't mean to be hurtful but the remark cut deeply. One of my stepmother's sayings was: "you can always tell a person by their shoes." All my life I had had good shoes, and if it hadn't been for my stupid husband throwing away my good ones when my feet were swollen with the intense heat, I would still have had them. I felt angry and ashamed. I had been forced to buy these cheap flats because of lack of funds. I wore those shoes until the soles wore through. Frank said, "Put some cardboard in them, that's what we used to do."

In London, we got a B-and-B close to Kings Cross Station where we had arrived and from where the train north would leave. The landlady was nice but the place was awful, our room had water-stained wallpaper and ancient furniture. But it was cheap – little did I know that life with Frank would always be cheap and nasty.

We did the town for two days, anything that was free: horse guard's parade, the changing of the guards at Buckingham Palace, and feeding the pigeons in Trafalgar Square. I took some photos to send home, and we walked and walked. I loved London and always will; it's the kind of place that calls you back again and again.

Billie, Steven and Frank at Trafalgar Square

I badly needed a new coat. Frank said it would be cheaper to buy up North but for once I dug in my heels and got a fashionable looking one, cheap by Australian standards, in Oxford Street.

Frank's parents lived in Batley, Yorkshire, in what was called the heavy woollen district, and in 1957 all the mills were still running. His father was a coal miner.

Frank hadn't told them he was coming. Indeed he had not written to them for years; said he wanted it to be a surprise.

We arrived at Batley Station in the dark about 7 pm; walked down the hill, across Bradford Road then up another hill to their house in Brearley Fold. I had no idea what a *fold* was but it turned out to be a large patch of dirty long grass. One side had a row of untidy small sheds used as garages, the other side had a row of houses shaped like an upside-down L, the smaller bit of the L along the top. Frank's parents lived in the very corner of the bend. I was nervous not knowing what to expect. What I didn't expect was the biggest cultural shock of my life.

Frank, carrying Steven, knocked on the door and it was opened by his mother. She didn't know who it was at first and then screamed and grabbed him. He had to tell her be careful because he was carrying the baby.

The door opened into a small foyer. A sitting room, never used, was on the left, a narrow dark and steep staircase went upwards and a living-room-cum-everything was on the right. Frank was dragged in there and I followed sheepishly. It was then I had a good look at his mother: buxom, pepper and salt black hair, *and no teeth!* Well she did have two, her two bottom eye teeth, both dark brown. Worse still, I could have been in China – I couldn't understand a word she said, and she could barely understand me. She kept saying, "What's she saying, Frank? What's she saying?"

I was shocked to the core. For starters, no one, but no one, walked around without teeth in New Zealand or Australia, not even the poorest of the poor; least of all with two dark brown fangs. And at least we all spoke the same language.

There was pandemonium, everyone rushing hither and thither. It turned out that Frank's brother Stan, and wife Jean lived next door but one and someone rushed to get them. I was introduced around. His father was a nice old man with a nice smile, I think he had some teeth, and Jean and Stan were lovely.

I started looking around. The 'everything' room had a good coal fire burning. Very old and grubby rag mats made mostly from dark trousers covered part of the worn brown linoleum on the floor; the ceiling had been wallpapered between the beams. A square ceramic kitchen sink and wooden draining board was fitted in the corner with the biggest mugs I had ever seen hanging on hooks above it (they turned out to be pint pots). A small twin tub washing machine sat underneath the only window. An elderly sideboard was on the wall opposite the fireplace while a large table with six chairs and two worn-out armchairs made up rest of the furniture. There was a door in the far corner that went down to the cellar. I found out later that this was never used because it was so damp, the house being built slap-bang against the hill behind it with no damp course.

The only bed we could have was on an open landing at the top of the stairs between the two bedrooms (his parents slept apart) and Frank talked them into bringing the bed down into the unused front room.

I was in for another surprise: about nine o'clock they set the table, laying out cutlery, plates, salt, pepper, sauce and lashings of buttered bread and someone was dispatched to the "chippie" to get supper. This was a nightly ritual that I would never get accustomed to. It amazed me that they could eat fish, chips, scallops (made from potato slices dipped in batter) and other fried things every night and not put on weight. I couldn't eat a thing and I am sure they thought I was weird.

At last, it was time to go to bed. I dressed in my nightgown and dressing gown and breastfed Steven before putting him down to sleep. Taking my toothbrush and sponge bag I went in search of the bathroom. Frank told me I had to use the kitchen sink, and I almost froze on the spot. At home you wouldn't even dare wash your hands at the sink, now here I was being told to clean my teeth and wash in front of everyone, in the place they just washed up the dishes. My mind went back to the biology lab when we had inspected the cultures taken from our mouths, skin, and dusty corners. I was petrified that Steven would pick up germs. I began wondering if they had a lavatory; but yes, go out the door into the fold, turn right along the front of the house, into the narrow path and along to the second one from the end.

"We share it with the neighbours ... just bang on the door to see if anyone is in." *Please God, let the ground open up and swallow me.*

When Frank at last said goodnight to his mother and came to the front room he was laughing. "Mum said 'She's posh' and she wanted to know where you were going in that dressing gown?" he said.

"Why didn't you tell me there wasn't a bathroom?" I hissed. "And it's damned embarrassing going to that toilet. I could hear someone blowing off in the one next door, and was frightened to make a sound."

"Oh, you'll get used to it. I am, and I was brought up here."

"Well I wasn't, and I hate it."

The next few days were a steep learning curve for me; first I had to understand the language. The baby was a *bairn*, I understood that one, the word *barn*-meant going, not the thing we had kept hay in. *Lakeing* was playing, *Ista* was are you, *Art* was out, *Ta-neat* was tonight. So, *ista barn art ta-neat*, was: Are you going out tonight? in spoken language shorthand. What's more, they dropped their H's, which caused me lots of confusion.

Over the valley from Batley was a village hanging on top of a cliff. I thought it was wonderful – to me, it looked like a long craggy castle. Frank said it was Anging Eaton and it was many months before I learned it was Hanging Heaton It was the same with Ecmondwight where we would go to the weekend market – that turned out to Heckmondwight.

My brother-in-law Stan was a well-known cricketer, in the summer, and he played Rugby League during winter – he had cauliflower ears to prove it – and was always being asked, "Ista lakeing ta day Stan?"

Frank's homecoming after twelve years had caused quite a stir and the house always seemed full of people.

For several days I kept putting my foot in it by saying, "I don't know what you mean," or "I don't understand." And everyone would turn and look at me. I made the decision I would say nothing and just listen, sooner or later I told myself I would work out what a word meant. There was one particular word that had me stumped and that was **Coil oil.** For days I tried to work it out without luck. One day when Jean and Stan were in, Stan went out to fill the coal bucket for his mother. Ethel from next door came in and said, "Werst your Stan?" and someone answered, "Art in coil oil."

"Oh," I exclaimed, "you mean the coal-hole." And they all turned around and stared at me. I could have bitten my tongue out.

It soon became obvious that my lack of accent attracted attention. As soon as I spoke people seemed to assume I was Lady Muck, and with our severe poverty it was sometimes embarrassing. One day, with only a few pence in my pocket with which to buy dinner, I started to wheel the stolen pram into a butcher's shop. There were five young housewives all chatting with the butcher. As soon as I said "Excuse me" to the girl in the doorway they all turned to look and the butcher stopped serving his first customer and, smiling broadly, rushed over to ask what I would like. He probably thought he would get a big order. I wanted the ground to open up and swallow me.

I blurted out: "Can I have two sausages please?" Oh, the humiliation, but when I think of it now I can laugh.

I decided to try to tone down my way of speaking and deliberately learned to speak with more of a Yorkshire accent. Soon I met a young wife who'd come from further south; she and I became friends. She told me that she too had had the same problem and had also learned to change the way she spoke so as to blend in better. Mixing with her I soon adapted.

We had arrived in the U.K. with very few clothes for Steven. In Australia in the 1950's, it was usual to keep babies in nightdresses until they were big enough to wear rompers. There was no such thing as small babywear, unlike the wonderful little clothes of today. Most people made their own clothes. All I had was the shawl I'd bought at Teneriffe, about six night dresses made on Kangaroo Island with the Karitane nurse pattern, two dozen nappies, and some little singlets. Jean soon put that right. She still had two-year-old Janet's baby clothes, and, having no intention of adding to the family she was pleased to pass them on. I couldn't believe my luck! There were little woollen suits with leggings, tops, and hats to match and all sorts of fancy things. It was like winning lotto, and didn't he look grand. I couldn't thank her enough.

One of the things I soon found out was that everyone just walked in and out of each other's houses without knocking. This could be particularly embarrassing if I happened to be standing in my underwear washing at the sink – I found it very disconcerting and didn't wash properly all the time we were there. Ethel from next door might come charging in to grab a cooking pan and yell upstairs "I am just borrowing a pot, Mrs. Naylor," before flitting out again.

I don't want to give the impression that the house was filthy … given the circumstances, it wasn't too bad. However between the sink and the gas stove there was a small patch of four-inch square, white tiles and they were loose and oozing black filth. One day when I was alone in the room I lifted all the tiles, scraped all the black muck into the sink, swilled everything down and replaced them. I shuddered to think how many trillion germs I had flushed away.

Frank had had an elder brother who had died of peritonitis out in the fields where he worked. He'd had an inflamed appendix and been misdiagnosed by a lady doctor. He'd left behind a wife, Alice, and three children. They came to visit and Alice had no teeth either. There was also a younger brother, Keith, who was married to a little blonde go-getter called Beryl. At last I had met someone from the family who intended, and did, rise above their very working-class roots.

Keith had been doing his National Service in the Army and was serving in Africa when he was brought back to the U.K on compassionate grounds because of his parents fighting and his mother's histrionic behaviour.

Keith had been born fourteen years after Stan; and within days of me meeting her, Mrs Naylor (who had no qualms about washing her dirty linen in public) had told me how angry she was to find herself pregnant again, and how she had said there was to be no more sex. If I wasn't embarrassed enough about these revelations, she went on to tell me how their father would come banging on her bedroom door demanding to be let in. I was literally struck dumb.

It wasn't long before I found out just how extreme her behaviour was. One evening a row blew up out of nothing. Mr Naylor started bellowing at her and she screamed back. The row erupted at the front door into the fold before Stan rushed over and took his father into his own house to separate them. Mrs Naylor followed shouting out all his faults for all the neighbours to hear. Never in my life had I seen such degrading behavior. I had followed them out and stood open-mouthed. When she decided to go back into the now empty house, she made sure I knew just how sick she was and how no one cared as she passed. Not knowing what to do I waited a moment then followed. She had thrown herself on the side of our bed on her back, eyes shut, and pretending to be unconscious. I stood quietly at the door and watched. She must have sensed me there as I had made no noise. Suddenly she gave a great moan, threw her arm dramatically into the air and dropped it down the side of the bed. If she thought I was going to come and make a fuss of her she thought wrong; I just thought, "What a drama queen," turned on my heel and went outside again. There was no doubt this was a very dysfunctional family and I began to see why Frank hated sickly women, as he put it – he had seen so much of his mother's pretense.

It took me a while to get used to the filthy air around Batley. The factories belched out black ashes, and everything was dirty. One day I washed Steven's nappies and left them out all night as they were too wet to bring in. The next day when I bought them in they had dirty black streaks all over them.

"My God, they are filthy!" I exclaimed.

"Don't you know not to leave the washing out at night?" snarled his mother – she liked to bring me down.

I saw red and retaliated. "Where I come from we could leave the washing out for a month and it wouldn't get dirty."

Frank had a good friend, Ronny Ward, the one Steven was named after. He and Ronny had decided to emigrate together until Ronnie decided he could not leave his girlfriend Mary. They were now married and they welcomed us into their home. It was obvious to me they were much more refined than the Naylor family; in fact I had much to thank them for over the next few months. Ronnie tried to find us a home to rent, but all he could get was a house that needed a lot of repairs. It was in a row of scruffy terraces and I doubt it had been changed since it was built maybe a hundred years or so before. It had holes in the floor and the cooking facilities were over an open fire. I tried to convince Frank that we could fix it up but he wouldn't have a bar of it. England had lost so many homes during the war that a rental was very hard to find. People were angry that many investors had put their money into reconstructing Germany instead of building new homes in the country that had won the war.

We tried for a job cleaning a church in the street just behind Brearley Fold. The accommodation that went with the job was quaint to say the least. It was three small rooms, stacked one on top of the other up the corner of the church's back wall. Frank was sure he would get it; he seemed to think he was the conquering hero and had a right to it. When the churchwardens thought differently and gave it to a local couple, he was very angry.

Frank was most amused that his mother's best friend was now a woman who his mother had once looked down on, and certainly she was a bit rough. But the hilarious part was that these two old girls had been on bus trips around Europe taking in many countries. I couldn't help laughing when I thought about the shock the staff of the posh hotels must have had in seeing these two toothless old ladies in their worn-out clothes. It was, however, the grandchild of his mother's friend who found us a flat. He and his wife had a job managing a house that had been divided into flats, one up and one down. It was at the top of the lane that his parents' house backed onto and had at one time been an upmarket home. We rented the top flat for £3 a week. It wasn't the cleanest of places: the carpet desperately needed cleaning, but at least we had a bathroom and inside toilet.

One day Frank came home with a nice little black pram for Steven. It fitted the bill perfectly as the top was detachable and could be used as a carry cot – he had chosen well. When I asked him how he had paid for it he told me it was on hire purchase, but "don't worry I gave him a fictitious address … we won't have to pay for it." I wanted to die. He wouldn't tell me which shop he'd got it from so I was frightened to go downtown with it in case somebody recognised it.

We ran out of money, so Frank went job hunting. Being a welder he didn't have to look far, but to his fury, the pay was just £7/1 shilling a week. After paying the rent we had just £4 to live on. It wasn't easy.

One day I saw a notice in a little jewellers shop window saying they would buy gold and jewellery, and next day I took in the gold 21st pin that my lovely Leigh Creek Nursing Sister had given me and got enough money to buy some groceries. A couple of weeks later Frank gave me his gold and onyx ring to sell. When I started to sell some of the stolen stuff given to me by his thieving friend Wally, the young jeweller asked where I was getting all this stuff. Being a good actress I explained it had been left to me by an aunt who had died just before I left Australia. He seemed happy with the explanation, but I didn't dare take anything more in.

Being very poor had one advantage: I soon learned how to cook in the cheapest possible way. I had also learned from Frank's mother. She would take a tin of corned beef, empty it into a big pie dish with lots of onions and sliced potatoes to make a tasty dish. I soon learned to buy the cheapest cuts of meat, scrag ends of mutton (the bony bits around the neck), sheep's head stew, (a whole head, skinned by the butcher and stewed with onions and carrots and served with mashed potatoes), and pigs head brawn, the meat cleaned from the bone, chopped and pressed with gelatine. I still love it today. I never told my father that I had resorted to eating sheep's heads – I think he would have had a heart attack. There were many things still not available in England, rationing had just finished. When one day I asked for raisins at the local grocery shop they didn't know what I was talking about.

Beryl and Keith were our saviours in those early days. They loved to go cycling on the weekends and invited us to join them. They helped us buy secondhand bikes and do them up; they found a little sidecar to clamp onto Frank's bike so Steven could come as well. What wonderful days we had, biking miles out into the country. Keith would laugh at me when I couldn't ride uphill and grab my bike underneath the seat and push me up to the top. I soon got as fit as he was and didn't need his help. Cycling was very popular: there were many cycling clubs, and many village cafe's had special big rooms for cyclists where we could sit on forms at long tables and get pint pots of strong tea. What a way to see the country, and what a country it was, so pretty and picturesque. Our bikes were fitted with water bottles on the handlebars and toe clips on the pedals to fasten your feet tight. Some days during that summer we would travel over a hundred miles and arrive home elated but weary.

England instilled in me a great love of historic buildings and architecture. My home town of Dunedin in New Zealand was just over 100 years old, and we had some beautiful buildings from that period, but nothing to compete with the ancient castles and stately homes of Britain. Many of these were open to the public but we could look at them only from the outside as we didn't have the entry money. This always grieved me. How I would have loved to explore these monuments to history.

One day we went to the ancient city of York. What a wondrous place it was, surrounded by a city wall and we could walk along inside it. On some of the old streets, the upper story of the houses almost met above the street – I loved it. Of course the town had long since grown outside the walls and you had to pass out one of the city gates. On one gate a sign said, "On this gate the head of (I forget who) was displayed on a spike to look out over the city." Or words to that effect. How glad I was to live in more modern times.

Frank was by this time in another job. It was a few miles out of town and he biked there and back. The wages were £12, a big improvement.

Beryl and Keith had a little one-up-one-down house in a very old district. On washing day all the ladies hung their washing lines across the cobblestone street so it was blocked to traffic. Their toilet was a little way down the street.

"Go under the arch and turn right into a row of toilets, ours is the third last in the row, and for goodness sake don't go into the next one, it's filthy."

I didn't ask what they did if they had to get up in the night.

Despite the fact that the house was tiny they had made it into a little palace. The room on street level had a massive black Yorkshire stove that went high up the wall. It was like nothing I'd ever seen before, the sort of thing that should be saved for posterity in a museum. Beryl had stove blacked it until it shone. They had wallpapered the room in the latest red patterned paper and it was beautiful. The bedroom upstairs had received the same care and Keith had cleaned out the cellar, painted it white and turned it into a workshop and storage room. It seemed to me that landlords there had it easy – you took the place as it was and paid for all the improvements yourself.

At our flat things were not good. Not only were we having trouble paying the rent but it was very upsetting to live above the pair downstairs. The juvenile teenage creep down there would come home every night and beat his wife up. She would be screaming, "Don't hit me, don't hit me." How I longed to go down with a baseball bat and show him what it's like to be on the receiving end. Then I would get angry with myself because I didn't have the guts to do anything. They left after a month or two and we were told we could move down as the rent was 5 shillings cheaper.

Frank had gone to New Zealand in 1947 as a £10 Pom and was initially sent to Christchurch in the South Island as a welder where he was supposed to stay for two years. However, when he heard from his mate that the wages were much higher in the North Island he upped sticks and left. He told me proudly it had taken him seven years in approved employments for the authorities to say his dues had been paid. The more I learned about Frank, the more I realised he'd been bucking authority all his life.

The lovely summer was coming to an end, and Frank was itching to get away. He said wages were so much better down south and that is where we should be.

So we packed up Father's new straw hat, the wicket and the—

No, we didn't actually: once more we thinned down everything and gave stuff away until what we had left could be packed into four Panniers, two for each bike. The mattress in Steven's little sidecar was replaced with a sleeping bag and two blankets. We said our goodbyes and headed south.

Little did I realise this, our sixth move, would be just one of many over the next twenty-one years.

From Batley we went to Wakefield, Doncaster, Newark-on-Trent, Grantham and Stamford where we stopped a while to sight-see. Stamford, a beautiful little town, was called Stamford Bridge by some because of the ancient bridge across the Welland River. At that time the main road, (the A1) went right through the middle of town causing a big traffic snarl on the narrow street. But despite the traffic, its oldness enthralled me.

Dunedin in New Zealand was just 107 years old in 1955; we had no historic buildings, so England instilled in me a great love of architecture and old buildings and Stamford was magic.

Later, a bypass was built around Stamford, and later again the motorways, M1 and M2, took much of the traffic.

We continued south on the A1 but it was dreadful. Frank led the way with me behind. Huge lorries, their exhausts belching diesel out beside us, went past with an endless brum-brum-brum. On seeing the sign for Peterborough coming up I yelled to Frank.

"We have to get off this road."

He agreed and we turned left onto a side road and stayed on smaller roads all the way to the coast, bypassing London, to Southend-on-Sea.

Most nights we camped out in woods or other quiet spots; luckily the weather stayed fine.

After leaving the heavy woollen district, the countryside had brightened. We travelled through lovely villages and leafy hedge-lined lanes; it was all so different and beautiful.

We followed the coast around to Graves End (what an awful name) on to Maidstone and down to Hastings on the coast. I loved Hasting with its quaint two-storey fishing huts, and boats pulled up onto the gravel beach. From there we travelled up the coast to Deal where we slept in the dunes by the sea. One night we slept in a dry ditch, me in the sleeping bag with baby and Frank wrapped up in blankets. Unfortunately during the night it started to rain and even though we were under overhanging May trees the rain soon dripped through and we were soaked. The morning came at last and we went back into town to a dry-cleaners, explained that we had got wet while camping and could we get our bag and blankets dried. The man said, "of course, come back in the afternoon." I suggested to Frank that he should perhaps start looking for a job but he was disinclined to do so. When we returned to pick up our things from the cleaners the man refused to take any money and my faith was restored in human nature. From Deal we headed inland again to Canterbury, another ancient town where I took photos at Canterbury Cathedral.

Soon we were in London looking for digs and work. We didn't know that at that time there were over 2,000 families doing just that. Everywhere we applied for a place to rent they took one look at the baby and said no. So day followed day as we rode aimlessly around on our bikes at all times of the day and night.

London is a fascinating place in the wee small hours: I saw a blonde lady leaning out the window of a second storey flat in a very elite area, and built a story around her. Was she, I thought, a high-class prostitute? A merry widow perhaps, with pots of money? Or maybe just a clever business lady with a little boutique in Convent Garden? The possibilities were enormous; so I rode and daydreamed.

In another suburb, we found a homeless man sitting on a wall beside the footpath outside a nice terraced house. He was asleep sitting up, his hands and nose blue with cold. I stopped and stood not three feet from him but he didn't wake up. It was so sad; I wanted to help him somehow, but Frank said to mind my own business and he was probably right. We left him sitting there and rode on.

Soon the early morning milkmen in their little electric vans would start to appear. Early morning deliveries were being made, and so the city slowly returned to life.

One day we were riding down a street where the traffic was moving and stopping, moving and stopping; I got fed up of taking my toe out of the toe clip so, leaving my feet on the pedals, I leaned on a small van and rode forward when it moved. I got away with it twice but the third time I was looking around when he moved forward and I learned the truth of *Pride Comes Before a Fall.* There, right in front of Broadcasting House, I fell flat onto the middle of the street, toes still tied tightly into toe clips. It took me a while to extricate myself while horns honked and some cheered, and didn't I feel a fool.

Most nights we slept in city parks, and every night we were awoken by the police who told us it was an offence to sleep in parks. Frank explained that we were on a cycling tour and just passing through so they said, 'okay, but don't be here tomorrow'. Next night we would move to another park. One night we stayed in a big railway station where you were not allowed to stay unless you had a train ticket for the early morning.

Sitting in one of London's big stations in the late evening was a true lesson in human behaviour. They seem to collect all the weirdos, exhibitionists, down and outs, and harmless people whose minds have been broken by the big city. I could write a chapter about the ones I encountered but will tell of just one. It was one evening just as the usual flotsam started to arrive. As usual we'd gone in to wash, use the toilets, and wash and feed the baby – I was still breastfeeding. When that was done we would sit in the rows of chairs until chuck out time. A buxom Cockney lady arrived, took a seat and with a silly smile started, in a very large voice, to tell everyone what she thought of the establishment, naming names and saying the most outrageous things. She was quite funny and could have been a comedian except that she would have been sued. Not only did she defame politicians but she targeted people around her, none of whom dared answer back. She knew she had people sniggering behind their hands and loved every minute of it.

Unfortunately, she got onto the touchy subject of black immigration – England was at the time being flooded with Jamaicans, who I personally found very likable people, and Pakistanis, who did nothing to endear themselves to the English. Unfortunately, after some extremely defamatory and prejudiced remarks, who should walk past her but a tall Jamaican man.

"There's one," she shouted, pointing her finger. "There's one of the bastards come to take our jobs and houses."

The man didn't bat an eyelid, just kept walking, and staring straight ahead, but I am sure his face turned darker under that shiny black skin.

I have often wondered how long it was before someone clouted that lady as I feel sure this was her daily routine.

That night because it was wet we came back to the station when it deserted. Frank sat out while I and baby slept in the sleeping bag on a long seat in the ladies room. It wasn't easy to sleep as the seat was hard and the lights were on. Sometime during the night, I heard the two Bobbies on the beat talking to Frank.

"My wife and baby are sleeping in the ladies room," I heard him say. They came to check me out. Steven was sleeping on his back, little arms on his chest; I decided it would be best if I was sound asleep also. I heard them come in talking softly; slowed my breathing right down while they whispered above me.

"Best leave them; baby looks well cared for."

Another night we were in St James Park when a police officer with a neb cap and an Alsatian dog came to talk to us. He was a really nice man and told us to go back to sleep and he would keep an eye on us. I can't imagine why a man of that rank would be doing a night shift, but he came again to awake us at 5 am.

"Time to hit road, folks. Did you sleep well?"

One day we saw jobs advertised for staff at Lyons Corner cafes. We parked our bikes with Steven asleep in his sidecar and went upstairs for an interview. I was given the job but she said to come back when we had accommodation. On the top landing sat a big food trolley packed with cakes and goodies for the shop below. Frank grabbed two squashy cream cakes packed in little cardboard trays and stuffed them in his pocket. I was out of there fast.

When we got back to the street it couldn't have been worse. There stood two policemen, an angry, well-dressed older woman, and a small crowd of onlookers, all looking at a screaming, red-faced child in a sidecar. They had folded the hood back so he could be seen. I tried to explain that I had been looking for a job and the baby had been fast asleep when we left him. We were told not to do it again, and I said I had not wanted to wake baby but apologized – anything to get away from there before someone found the cakes missing. I felt like telling the well-dressed lady she should mind her own business but given the circumstances I thought better of it.

Things were getting grim; we were running out of money. We told the Bobbie who spoke to us in the park that we couldn't work because we couldn't find a flat, and he suggested we go to the welfare and gave us the address.

I stupidly thought they would get us accommodation but it wasn't to be. There were several people waiting to see the welfare officer and we got talking. One talkative girl in her early twenties said she'd been in the hostels before and said we would be woken up at 6 am, made to scrub floors, the food wasn't fit to eat and many more dreadful things until in the end she had me quite frightened. She was called in for an interview and while there two really nice couples arrived. It seems they had been sent to London from Birmingham to work, but something had gone wrong with accommodation arrangements and now they had very little money left and nowhere to stay. I said I didn't know what to expect and repeated what the other girl had said.

"That's it then," said one of the women jumping up, "We are getting out of here." And they all got up and left.

The other girl returned to the waiting room and soon after a long-suffering husband put his head in the door.

"Come on, Doreen, it's time to go home."

She gave him a big smile, got up and left. Everything she had said was a pack of lies, and she was well known to the welfare people. She was just another of the weird people to be found in big cities. Of course, I then felt guilty for repeating what she'd said to the other people who had left.

Frank had already been taken to a hostel for homeless men so I saw the welfare officer on my own. I was to go to a hostel for women and children for the night and he would see us both together the next day.

The home seemed okay. I was shown to a room with three beds and given a cot for Steven. They told me to leave him in the cot and come to the dining room where I would be given something to eat, but I found the cot was soaked with urine, so wet it went right through the mattress, even the blankets were soaked. I took him downstairs with me where an attendant glared at me.

"You don't bring babies to the dining room. Weren't you told to leave him in the cot."

I snapped. "That cot," I snarled, "is soaked through with urine. I most certainly will **not** put my baby in there."

The change was electric. She hadn't heard me speak before and my attitude alone must have signalled that I wasn't the usual kind of person they accommodated. Suddenly she was all sweetness and light, apologising profusely and rushing off to get clean bedding while I sat and ate with baby on my knee.

After Steven had settled to sleep I had a visit from another lady who said she had to swab my anus to see if I was carrying typhoid. I said 'No way,' but was assured that if it wasn't done I would have to leave immediately as we would not be allowed to stay. There was nothing for it but to give in. It was the most humiliating thing that has ever happened to me.

The next morning I met Frank again at the welfare office; we were asked where we came from and told we would be given rail tickets back to Batley. Frank asked about money to take our bikes and we were told we would have to sell them.

Back on the street, Frank said there was no way he was going to sell the bikes and he went down to the station and got a refund on the tickets and we set out to travel north.

After one day we were out of London and heading for Lincolnshire. We heard there was potato picking available and told to ask for a Mr So-and-So. Soon we saw the fields being picked and something Frank said made the man in charge think that we had spoken to the boss so he took us on. It was hard work; my back was aching so I resorted to hands and knees and was soon caked with mud. We worked for two days until the field was finished and everyone was paid off. All the others were paid less than us, because when Frank said, "We were told such and such a price," the foreman said, "Well if Mr S? told you that I had better pay it." It was all a total misunderstanding, but as it was slave labour anyway, who were we to enlighten him.

So off we went again with our ill-gotten gains and soon stopped at a country bakery to get bread. We chose a loaf and Frank handed over a £5 note. When the man went to get change Frank quickly pocketed two cakes from the shelves, and once more my heart was in my mouth.

"What did you do that for?" I screamed when we were far away not to be heard. "Why do you always have to steal? Don't you realise he just has to get in his car and follow us and we will be in trouble?"

"Well, in that case, we will just have to stop and eat them," he replied with a big grin. "I gave him that note so he would have to go and get change – quite clever I thought."

What could I do? He really thought he was clever.

The next afternoon we stopped at a country railway station to use the toilets and wash. The place was deserted but the rooms were open. To my delight the ladies room had very large hand basins with hot and cold running water, I couldn't believe my luck and decided to give Steven a much-needed bath. He was delighted and splashed happily while I washed him all over. I hadn't taken clean clothes in to dress him again, so I carried him out wrapped in a towel, and Frank blew a fuse.

He wanted to know what I was doing carrying him out with wet hair. Did I want to give him a cold? etc.etc. So I lost my temper and answered back – I thought that was a bit rich coming from someone who for the most time thought only of himself, and if it wasn't for his irresponsibility we wouldn't be in this situation anyway. And so it went on: I gave as good as I got. This was the very first real row we'd ever had as I was finally daring to answer back.

We were travelling north through the low lying Lincolnshire Wolds; there didn't seem to any target destination, we just rode on into the night. Soon a pea-souper fog descended all around us making it difficult to see a yard in front, never mind the side of the road. We didn't see a soul (but in 1957 very few people had cars). It was really spooky. Frank had been sniping with his clever Yorkshire tongue ever since we'd left the railway station, and I finally shouted back at him. He rode up beside me and gave me huge push sideways. Had I not by then been a very good cyclist I would surely have fallen off, but the brass lid of our little camping kettle fell clattering to the ground.

"Now look what you've done," I shouted, and stopped to find it.

Now Frank had a battery lamp on his bike but my bike had a dynamo on the front wheel, so when I stopped the lamp went out. Putting the bike down I fossicked around on my hands for a few minutes without locating it; then, realising he had gone on, I gave up and tried to catch him up. But I never did. Sure that he was still ahead of me I increased my speed, riding as fast as I dared in the fog. Nothing, he was nowhere to be found. I must have ridden for a good half an hour feeling very vulnerable being alone out there in the dark. Then suddenly there was a light ahead. It was a petrol station, well lit up but closed. I had arrived in Louth. Surely he will be waiting there under the light, I told myself, but no, the place was deserted. I was now becoming seriously worried. I rode on through Louth and into the countryside again. Another long time passed and then another dim light, this time on the left and just off the road. A country police station light shone through the gloom.

I had already decided the best thing to do was to ride back to Batley, but I didn't have a clue where to turn off. All I had in my panniers was dirty clothes, mostly nappies; Frank had the maps, the clean clothes, all the money and the small amount of food we had. I decided to ask at the police station where I had to turn left for Batley.

The middle-aged policeman and his wife were more than a little surprised to find a slip of a girl with a long ponytail on their doorstep at 10.30 at night. They quickly asked me in and listened to my tale. The lovely wife made me a welcome cup of tea and a sandwich – it was so nice to be in out of the cold.

"I can put out a bulletin to let everyone know you are here safe," the policeman said. I told him no; as I didn't want it getting into the papers. He said that, as I was over twenty-one, he had to abide by my decision. He told me I would come to Grimsby and there the road turned off to Scunthorpe and then on to Batley. They asked what I was going to do if I went on and I said I would find a haystack somewhere and sleep until morning. He said if anyone found me in their haystack to tell them to ring him and he would vouch for me. I thought that was nice but longed for them to ask me to stay the night but it didn't look as if they were going to offer.

As I was taking my reluctant leave the wife said she thought I had better stay the night – I told her I would be fine. How I kicked myself as my bike ate up mile after mile. Just one car passed going south; it slowed but didn't stop; I had tucked my hair into my woollen hat and kept my head down hoping I looked like a boy. At last I saw a haystack just off the road on the right, and the gate to the field was open. I wheeled my bike around the back, away from the road. A large amount of straw was piled up at the base of the stack and I lay down and covered myself with a generous pile. I remember having a little cry, thinking, *well that's probably my marriage over* and I wasn't sure whether it worried me or not. It must have been about 2 am and the silence was complete.

The weirdest noises woke me in the morning. I was still lying on my back just as I had started, I obviously hadn't moved as the straw was still heaped over me. The noise came again – it seemed to be only feet away. Very, very slowly I moved my hand up until it was above my eyes, then, extending a finger I gently poked a small hole in the straw. And there they were, a beautiful sight to start the day: pheasants, at least six colourful cock birds feasting on the dropped grain, the nearest so close I could have reached out and touched it. I stayed still awhile and watched but, mindful that I had many miles yet to travel, I eventually stirred and my companions took off with a noisy clatter.

It was then I got an enormous shock. No more than 50 yards away were the first houses of Grimsby, the biggest borough in the U.K.

I was soon on the road. I couldn't wash or eat, all I had to do was spend a penny.

The terraced houses of Grimsby went on for what seem like miles until finally I came to the turnoff to Scunthorpe, turned left and was on the way 'home'. My way took me past a big industrial place with cars and people milling around at start of work so I decided it must have been nearly 8 am. Mr Policeman had told me it was about 80 miles from Scunthorpe to Batley so I figured I should be there in about two hours.

Soon I was out in the countryside again and there wasn't a soul in sight, but I was even more wary about being alone now that it was daylight. A truck passed me and stopped, a man stepped out of cab and looked back at me. Now all animals have a fight or flight response built-in – that sudden rush of adrenaline – and mine kicked in swiftly. Here was danger. In a flash my legs were flying; I sped up and swerved passed him as he yelled, "The police are looking for you."

The man got back into his cab and drove past me yelling again, "I'm telling you."

When my heartbeat was back to normal I realised that Frank must have gone to the police and decided I had better pop into a police station and tell them I was okay.

The small town of Thorne was a few miles out of my way, but I knew it was the nearest so I diverted off course and found the police station. What a waste of time! The guy there wasn't the slightest bit interested. I asked him if he would let the other police station know that I was okay and on my way to Batley, but he told me I was now in another county and it was nothing to do with him. I thought it was a strange way for the police force to work but there wasn't much I could do. Many years later it was this incredible lack of communication that was to lead to the unnecessary deaths of several women when the man they dubbed the Yorkshire Ripper was spreading fear throughout Yorkshire. It was revealed when he was at last caught that had the police conferred with their counterparts over the border, he would have been arrested much sooner.

Leaving Thorne I headed for Wakefield. Now in Britain at that time they had trucks we used to call the honey carts. These trucks with big tanks aboard would suck up sewage, from holding tanks I presume, and the smell was definitely not of honey.

I must have been going about thirty miles an hour through the suburbs when I saw one parked ahead of me on the left. I also saw a black cat step off the pavement a few yard further on, on the right. At the speed I was going I knew I could swing out past the truck and back in before the cat reached my side of the road. It wasn't to be. The wretched animal looked right, saw a car coming and spurted across the road, right under my front wheel. My little racing bike had tyre rims that were just touched together for lightness instead of being welded and the front rim buckled almost in half; the bike stopped dead, bucked like a well-trained rodeo horse and hurtled me over the handlebars to skid up the rough edge of the road.

I lay for a few seconds while I decided if anything was broken, then a lady coming home with her shopping helped me up. I had a nasty graze up my left forearm, a bleeding elbow and skin off my chin. Apart from all that I had the shakes.

My Good Samaritan took me into her house just two doors away and washed down my wounds.

"What you need is a nice cup of tea," she said.

Oh, the English, a cup of tea is a panacea for all things ... but she was right, I hadn't had anything to eat or drink since early the night before. When I told her my story she insisted on making me baked beans on toast for which I was very grateful. She told me there was a small welding business just up the street and they may be able to help me. I thanked her, said my goodbyes and, carrying the front of my bike, I made it to the welding business.

The place was run by two brothers, two big burly Yorkshire men and they were lovely. I told them I had no money on me but I would send some back when I got 'home', and they said, "E lass, thars not to bother."

One set about straightening my rim by putting his knee against it and pulling. He eventually got it so the wheel would at least go round without binding, even if it acted like a drunken sailor, but I could ride it, although very slowly. They sent me on my way with smiles and a wave telling me to take care and not use the front brake. They were two generous kind-hearted men; I can't thank the people of Thorne enough.

I rode on for hours and it got quite hot. Eventually, I reached the outskirts of Batley.

Now one way out of Batley has a very steep hill and it was from that direction I arrived. I started down then, realising I was going too fast for the state of the bike and forgetting not to touch the front brake, I applied both brakes. The front-wheel stopped dead and once again I was hurtled over the handlebars into the gutter. I had a few more grazes and bruises but once again I was mainly unhurt. I picked myself up and walked the rest of the way down the hill.

I pushed the bike up to Brearly Fold and came in the back way, unsure what reception I would get from his mother as I made my way to the house in the corner. A good looking man was just leaving. He smiled and said, "You wouldn't happen to be Billie, would you? I said I was, and he said, "I am so-and-so from the News of the World."

I couldn't believe it! In less than twenty-four hours the story was out. Oh, how naive can we be when we are just twenty-two years old?

I answered his questions telling him I had lost my husband while cycling through a thick fog and had to explain why I was battered, bruised, and the bike was a mess. He asked if the photographer could take my photo and I stupidly agreed. I had this habit of putting a spare nappy pin on the left shoulder of my clothes and had quite forgotten it was there.

Next morning, to my utter horror, there I was, nappy pin and all, on the front page of the NEWS OF THE WORLD, the headline screaming.

IN A DEEP DEEP FOG HE LOST HIS WIFE

I soon found out just how many people read the NEWS OF THE WORLD, and they thought it was a great joke, but I felt a fool. Still, I suppose that not many people can boast that they have been on the front page of the NEWS OF THE WORLD.

Frank's mother wanted to know where her son was but of course, I couldn't tell her.

I asked her if I could stay until Frank got back, expecting him back the same, or next day, and she told me she now had a boarder so there was nowhere for me to sleep. I asked if I could sleep on the mat in front of the fire and it was agreed.

I thought they would never go to bed that night. I was exhausted, but no one was going to put themselves out for me. I thought of my own home and country hospitality; there was a giant chasm between the two.

At last, they retired for the night, and I curled up on the old smelly mat and was soon fast asleep. Frank had told me that they had helped to make the mats when they were kids, everyone sitting around the frame that was placed on the table to hook the pieces of scrap material through. That made them at least twenty-five years old. But when you are ship-wrecked it is any port in a storm.

I was woken next morning by Frank's father getting ready for work at the mine, and within an hour there were six reporters waiting around the door. Even getting to the lavatory meant I had to run the gauntlet, it was very embarrassing. To make matters worse Frank didn't show up that day, or even the next. Our story had been relegated to the second page but was kept alive by his non-appearance. Needless to say the story had been picked up by all the other papers, so all the reporters stood outside waiting to pounce. The story in the NEWS OF THE WORLD went back through the pages, now speculating what had happened to my missing husband. About the sixth day, a Sunday, I managed to slip away when no one was outside and go to Keith and Beryl's place for peace and quiet and some decent company. Beryl walked back with me about 4 pm. We met Alice and the children just leaving the Fold.

"I wouldn't go in there if I was you. He's back and it is a madhouse."

She was right. There were all the reporters clambering for a story: Where had he been? What had he been doing? How was the baby? On and on. Some of the papers the next day almost insinuated that he'd been off with another woman. All I wanted was to hug my baby and see if he was alright.

When bedtime came – we both slept on the mat – and everyone had gone to bed I finally got the truth … well, I hoped it was the truth. He told me that when he went to the police station they thought he may have killed me and they had set out to find me with the tracker dogs, but there was no trace. Somehow, God only knows how because I could never have done it, he had led them back to the spot where I had stopped and they had actually found the kettle lid. He'd been kept at the police station until they heard I'd been seen on the road home and let him go. A police lady had looked after, and played with Steven. He said he'd then called at Scunthorpe to look up an old friend and had stayed there for a day or two before leaving for home. At Wakefield he'd been picked up by the police for shoplifting at Boots the Chemist, where he'd stolen a child's dummy. "But," he said proudly, "they didn't find it all – I had this in my fob pocket."

He emptied from his fob pocket a cheap and nasty ring and several other small bits that he'd been able to pilfer. He told me he had to appear in the court at Wakefield on a certain date, about two weeks later.

I was absolutely livid: if the papers got a hold of this, the story of his missing days would be broadcast to all and sundry. The next day all the papers related that my missing husband had returned and that was the story dead. They never did get wind of the shoplifting charge, thank goodness, even though it was published in the local paper. When we appeared at the court, and after he was fined, he said to the policeman: "This is the country's fault."

And the policeman replied, "No, Frank, this is your fault."

This was the first, but not the last time, I was to learn that Frank was never at fault, no matter how wrong he was – it was always someone else.

Frank"s family took the shoplifting charge much better than I did: they knew the Frank of old.

After returning from Rhodesia, (now Zimbabwe) where he had spent the most of the second World War, Frank and a Jewish friend, whose father had a big warehouse full of bolts of material, stole several bolts and were selling them on the black market. The local police were well aware what he was doing and told him they would not arrest him but he was to get out of town. They did not want to see his brother Stan embarrassed as he was well respected in football and cricketing circles. So Frank had set out on the train for London, and was arrested as soon as he stepped off the train. He had spent a week in gaol, before being fined. The stolen bolts of material were confiscated, and he was fined and sent back to Batley.

We'd been staying at his parents about two weeks and the atmosphere was growing tense. I helped with the housework wherever I could and one day I used our meagre funds to buy sausages and made a sausage casserole like Mum made at home. I expected his mother to criticise but surprisingly she really enjoyed the meal. One morning Frank and his mother were having a huge row when suddenly she grabbed a knife and went for him.

"Oh, well," said Frank, jumping out of the way, "if you are going to start using knives we will just have to leave."

Frank decided we should go to Manchester. We sold the bikes and Steven's sidecar and set off. I can't remember where we stayed that night but the next day Frank came back and told me he'd been talking to a conductor on a bus and he had said to ring Aunty Lil. She was a lady who kept a house full of bed-sitting rooms and the conductor had said it was a great place to stay. We rang the number and were told to come right out as she had a room empty. The place was in Fog Lane, Didsbury in Stockport. It was said by some that Aunty Lil had married Uncle Alan for his money. He was a tall, white-haired, distinguished-looking gentleman in his seventies who had been a music teacher. She was a short, slightly chubby blonde in her fifties. Our room was on the first floor looking out onto the street. It was fully furnished, with a baby Belling stove to cook on and a sink to wash the dishes, a double bed, wardrobe, and drawers. We shared a bathroom down the hall with the occupants of a few other rooms. Everyone in the house was nice and I was happy there.

Frank set out to look for work, and soon had a welding job; however, he wasn't in the Boilermakers' Union and that was now a closed shop. He'd been in the union many years before when he did two years of his apprenticeship before running off to join the air force at the age of sixteen. He was told if he wanted back into the union he had to pay the back fees of £25, a huge amount of money in those days and quite out of the question for us. After two weeks the boss called him in, he was pleased with Frank's work he said, but he had to give him his cards. The others had threatened to go out on strike if he didn't.

So started a never-ending search for work. We ran out of money and had to go for welfare and very reluctantly were given National Assistance. We had to front up once a week to get money to live on, but, after two weeks when we went in to sign on, they said they would not pay out anymore because they didn't think he had been looking for work. When Frank told me I was furious. I knew he'd been looking. I lost my temper, stormed in and said to the girl he had so been looking and how was I to feed the baby? I told her that just the day before he had used almost the last of our money to bus out to Southport to apply for work. I'm not sure whether it was the nice London coat or the 'posh' accent but the startled lady changed her mind and handed over the usual amount promptly. It was obvious that he wasn't going to get a welding job and other work was scarce so I started to look for work myself. A cleaner's job was advertised so I applied and got it.

My new employers were another Jewish family called Rose. She was a petite blonde who had been a nurse and he was a senior surgeon at a Manchester hospital.

My job was to clean their big house twice a week and the wages were good. Mrs Rose asked me if I knew how to 'turn out a room' and of course, I didn't have a clue what she meant. The idea was that I was to vacuum the rooms then wash and clean the windows and wash all the white woodwork, skirtings, door, and window surrounds. I very soon saw the reason why: the filthy smoke-ridden air seeped in and everything was blackened. I did one group of rooms one day and another group the second day.

All the woodwork in the house was white after it had been cleaned. There was a big white staircase carpeted in purple, and the master bedroom carpet was bright red. Both showed every speck of dirt, but I worked willingly and enjoyed it.

The housekeeper, Hazel, ex-army, and her husband lived in the top floor flat, and we got on well. Mrs Rose usually cooked lunch for us all which we ate together in the big kitchen. I said to Mrs Rose once that I always loved cleaning the huge mirror at the front door because it made me feel like a million dollars. She replied that it was a rose-tinted mirror and she had put it in especially.

"When I go out in the evening I do a twirl in front of it before going out the door and I leave full of confidence."

I have never seen another mirror like it.

Christmas came and still Frank didn't have a job. My two days were just paying our expenses but nothing more. Mrs Rose knew our situation and said to me, "Billie, I thought that under the circumstances the best thing I could give you was a chicken," and she handed to me a very large one. I couldn't have been more grateful. She also gave me a beautiful little coat for Steven that had been one of her children's – it was a creamy colour, pure wool and he looked like a little lord.

I walked to and fro from work, it being only about three blocks away, but when the fog came down and captured all the smoke from winter fires it was a nightmare. One morning when I left for work it was so thick I was frightened. I stepped off the pavement and car lights appeared about a meter away. I yelled with fright and leaped back. Somehow I made it to work and back again but my throat was painful and raw. A few days later I had an appalling attack of sinusitis, my head ached so badly I thought it would explode.

In England, you had to be registered with a doctor to be on the National Health. Of course I was not, but a kindly old doctor saw me and prescribed some pills to unblock my sinuses and I was right again.

Rabbit meat was very cheap so I often stewed it for dinner. One night Steven was sitting in his high chair and he put out his hand to get something. I went to hand him a leg bone with a bit of meat on it, then, thinking there may be some bone fragment on it I brought it back to my mouth to take a bit more meat off it. Unfortunately, I hit the dead tooth I had right in my top front teeth and it snapped off. I could have died. No way was I going to walk around with this glaring gap in my face, but all the dentists were booked up for many weeks ahead. Eventually I got an appointment with a very elderly dentist; he must have been in his late sixties or early seventies, and so started my second tooth disaster.

I told him right at the beginning that my teeth were hard to extract, but like all dentists, he poo-pooed the idea. It wasn't an easy extraction as it was just a root and hard to get hold of, so first he cut away the bone around it, then, having exposed the root, he pulled and pulled and pulled. After some time I must have gone very white because all of a sudden my chair was being tipped upside down and the dentist and his nurse were running around like flies with their wings cut off. The root came out eventually, he said to me.

"Never in 50 years of practice have I had a tooth like that."

Needless to say, my mouth was a mess again, and now I had to find someone to make a plate to fill the gap. I hunted around and soon found someone who would do it promptly – I had my first partial plate.

Aunty Lil had a part-time job demonstrating things in shops. While we were there a job came up away in another city and she took it. She asked me to look after Uncle Alan while she was away because he was sick. I did, even though I found it quite awkward, he was after all our landlord. One day when he was vomiting he farted loudly and I was so embarrassed, not for me but for him. I was angry that Lil was selfish enough to go away and leave him. Another day I was in our room when I heard him screaming: "Billie! Billie!"

I screamed down the stairs only to find he was shouting: "Lilly." I wondered if he knew, as we all did, that she was having it off with the young lawyer who lived in the attic room.

We were having a hard time paying the rent so, when Aunty Lil suggested that we swap rooms with them as the one on the ground floor was cheaper, we agreed. The only thing was that whoever was in that room had to look after the boiler in the cellar. I told Frank that it was his job as all he had to do was look after Steven.

A few weeks later Aunty Lil said that if we cleaned out the cellar we could have a week free from rent.

"Just use anything you find, or keep anything you find useful."

The cellar hadn't been cleaned in years. It was coated with dust. On shelves, we found old pots of jam and tins of food from the war years – seems our Aunty Lil had been engaging in a bit of black market. The jars of jam were still edible, preserved no doubt by the sugar, but most of the tins we had to throw out. The New Zealand butter was rancid, but the tins of American margarine were still edible. I have since learned that margarine is one molecule away from plastic and has now been banned in some European countries. Not surprising ... if it doesn't rot, don't eat it.

We had been at Fog Lane for almost three months and Frank was getting restless and wanted to move on. He decided, I don't know why, that we should go to Southampton, but, he warned me I was not to tell anyone we were leaving. I couldn't see why. It wasn't as though we were doing a midnight flit and running away without paying the rent. But, I was still dancing to his tune so I said nothing, even though it hurt me to do so. I gave my notice in at the Roses and …

We packed up Father's new straw hat, the wickets and the cricket bat.

Early one morning when it was barely light, we left quietly. We hadn't made it to the gate when the window of our old room opened and Aunty Lil popped her head out.

"Billie," she called, "if things don't work out promise me you'll come back."

I turned. "Thank you, Aunty Lil, I will." But of course I never did.

I remember nothing of the trip south or the first night in Southampton, but we saw an advertisement for a caravan to rent. Frank rang up and got it. It was some miles out of town at a place called Cheriton, a picturesque country village complete with thatched cottages and white ducks on the pond. The fourteen-foot long van was owned by a doctor's wife whose husband had immigrated to Australia. It was parked behind the Flower Pots Inn. There were so many people desperate for homes in England that living in caravans had become a way of life. Most of the country public houses had the quota of vans allowed by the council in their grounds, the Flower Pots had six so we had some neighbours. They were allowed to take casuals for two weeks at a time but then they had to move on.

How Frank thought he was going to get a job living out there I don't know. I was just grateful to have a roof over my head. Needless to say, there was no work to be had so Frank decided he would go to London. Being a welder he could easily have gained work in Southampton, so why in far off London I didn't know. But by then I had given up trying to work out how his mind worked.

The Flower Pots Inn was owned by a Mr and Mrs Wheeler – very nice people, and she was a writer. I never saw her without a cigarette in her lips, the smoke of which gave her a ginger moe. For some reason, she took a liking to me and we became friends. I used to think she found me interesting because I was something different and she could get ideas for her stories. I eventually had a letter from Frank with £1 in it. When Mrs Wheeler asked me where he was staying I told her Rowton House and did she know of it. She told me it was a doss house; as indeed it was. When Frank came home after many weeks he regaled me of old men coughing and spitting on the floor and all the glories of living with down and outs.

Eventually, things got really bad. I was living on 8 shillings a week child allowance. I could buy a small soup block for very little; all I had to do was add water, so for many days Steven and I had that for lunch. One day when I went down to the village shop to buy my soup block I was waiting to be served when I looked down and saw a whole £1 note at my feet. I picked it up and when it was my turn to be served I handed it over. Afterward, I asked myself why … why did I have to be so damned honest? That money would have bought us a week's supply of food.

Eventually, we had almost nothing to eat and I was forced to push the pram several miles into the nearest town to ask for National Assistance. They reluctantly gave me a few shillings to tide me over and sent a man out to review the situation. They allocated me a small amount to live on. I had to walk all the way in to get it, but at last I could buy something different to eat. Steven was just one year old and it almost brought me to tears when I saw his little face light up at something new on his plate.

It was winter and the van was very cold. Sometimes I didn't have enough money to buy kerosene for the heater so I had to dress us in heaps of clothes and take Steven into bed with me at night to keep him warm. Mrs Wheeler must have known I was doing it tough because sometimes when I went in to buy milk she would say,

"Stop here and have a cuppa with me." And she would produce tea and homemade cakes for us both. One night she asked me to come in and have dinner with them; I couldn't have been more grateful. On top of that, she lent me books from her library so I always had something to read.

One morning we awoke to find six inches of snow. During the morning I left the van to talk to some of the other residents, telling Steven to stay in the van. Someone said "Look!" and I turned to see him crawling towards me through the snow; he must have decided that doing that was too cold because suddenly he struggled to his feet and tottered towards us. We all clapped: he had taken his first steps and from then on he walked everywhere.

The next part of our journey is somewhat hazy. Perhaps it was all so stressful that I have blocked it out, but I remember we asked the van's owner if we could take the van up to Crawley (I think) in Surrey. She was delighted; it was her home town, she said, where she had a house. I don't know who towed us or how we got there, but we parked for two weeks behind the Cambridge Hotel when the ground was covered with snow. In that time we found a site for the caravan in an orchard on a farm near Horsham. It was a lovely place, so peaceful, and up above Gatwick airport. The farm was owned by Mr Ayling and "Mrs Ayling" as I called her, but I found out later they were not married and that she had been his housekeeper. I did think it rather odd that she was so much older than him.

Frank seemed to get work here and there. We acquired a tandem bike with a sidecar and had many trips away during that summer; and Frank used it to bike to work, without the sidecar of course.

Frank arrived home one day with a dog, and I wasn't best pleased. He insisted on calling her Pommie. She was beautiful, a tiny black and tan thing with a bloated stomach. Had he known the first thing about dogs he would never have bought her as within days she had very serious diarrhoea and was very ill. We had to use our meagre funds to take her to a vet. He told us she had a serious dog infection that she had picked up at the pet shop.

"Never, never," he said, "buy a dog from a pet shop. They will almost always be infected, and they fill them up with bread to camouflage the symptoms." He gave her an injection and told us to bring her back for another in a week's time. The effect was instantaneous, she was well again, and being short of money we didn't take her back.

Needless to say when we had her we couldn't go off riding at the weekends, but of course Frank hadn't thought of that. Pommie was just the first of the many dogs he was to bring home in the years to come, no thought of how I was going to feed them, or what we would do with them if we moved on, which we always did.

Poor wee Pommie ... within two weeks she had bad diarrhoea again. I had to put her outside in a box at night as she was making such a mess on the floor. The next morning she was seriously ill. When a dog is dying they cross their front legs – she was crossing hers. I tried to get some fluids into her but it was too late. I sat with her on my knee, wrapped warmly in a blanket, crying my eyes out until she passed away, and for weeks afterward. I will not have a dog now, I have cried over so many in the past.

The next weekend we took off again on our tandem to see the country again.

Another creature Frank bought home while we lived there was a young bird that had fallen out of its nest; he'd found it while riding home on his bike. I never could decide whether it was a raven, a rook, or a crow, but I liked to think it was a raven. It very quickly became part of the family and would sit up in the corner of the van and poo down on the pillows. When it got a bit older it would spend the day outside, but it never went far.

Frank had several jobs in the summer we spent on the farm; once when he was out of work I heard of a farmhouse where they needed a cleaner so I went to introduce myself and was taken on. The bush telegraph was working well: no sooner had I started when two more households asked if I would also clean for them and I said "yes please". The first job didn't last more than a month; it had been very, very grubby and took weeks to catch up, but when a sister and her husband moved in to share the big house the farmer's wife declared that the newcomer could do the cleaning. My two other jobs lasted somewhat longer.

The second job was at a chicken farm owned by the McGregors

and what lovely people they were. On my first morning, I had a big shock. In the corner, sitting on the floor, was Mr McGregor – he had no legs. His bottom half was encased in a thick leather bag gathered at the waist, not unlike an old fashioned money bag. I didn't know where to look. In all the months I worked there his disability was never mentioned, but I did find out that he'd been a pilot who'd been shot down during the war. His disability didn't stop him from working hard; he walked on his hands swinging himself forward quite fast. They had a teenage son who worked with them looking after the chook sheds.

The job was easy. Mrs McGregor seemed to clean the house for the cleaner, it was always immaculate. The other job was at the Crombie's. He was also an injured war pilot who'd had extensive plastic surgery on his burnt face. They had taken hair from his chest to replace his eyebrows and made a brilliant job of it. The Crombie's house was an ancient, half-timbered home with big grounds. It wasn't easy to clean as the old rough-cut woodwork and leadlight windows were a haven for small spiders. There was a massive walk-in fireplace and low-beamed ceilings, with strange nooks and crannies especially on the above floor.

The summer was coming to an end and so was our stay at the farm. We received a letter from the doctor's wife to say she wanted to sell the van as she was moving to Australia to join her husband, and could we afford to buy it? Of course, we couldn't – it was a bitter blow to me. Frank had by now taken a snitcher to the poor lady for no obvious reason, but that was not unusual. He looked at a motor caravan to buy but we couldn't buy that either. It was Mrs Crombie who came to the rescue. She told me she didn't want to lose her cleaner, and if we didn't mind we could move into the loft above the garage. It was a Godsend. There was a double bed up there and a small bed for Steven, a gas camping stove and a sink to wash the dishes. We did, however, have to put up with the smell of last year's apples stored there on a rack of straw, but they were soon cleared out. A steep set of iron steps lead up from the back, which were a hazard for Steven to fall down which he eventually did, cutting his lip and bruising his face.

I said goodbye to the Aylings at the farm and asked them if they would look after my lovely black bird because they had a big empty aviary. They said they would, but when I went back a few weeks later I found him running free. As I walked along the drive beside the orchard, now covered with knee-high grass, a long silver snake quietly slipped away from my path, right in front of where the van had been. That was the only snake I ever saw in England.

I caught my lovely bird and took him back to the Crombie's; he stayed inside at night and outside close to the door during the day for about a week, but he'd had a touch of freedom and it was time to go. I remember the morning well.

I was standing at the top of the steps when he called me from a tree ten yards away; I spoke to him and he moved away a bit further and called again, away a bit further and called again. Each time he called I answered, and each time he moved a bit further away. Suddenly I realised he was saying "Goodbye, I am leaving now." He called several times more from the woods behind until at last, I could no longer hear him. I was never to see him again. I was sad; but also happy that he'd gone back to where he belonged, and I fervently hope he found, and fitted in, with some of his kind.

Life at the Crombie's could sometimes be fun. Friends of the Crombie's from Nice, in France, asked if their daughter could come as an o-pare to learn English, her name was Helene (pronounced Helain) and she duly moved in. What a character that girl was. She taught me French, now mostly forgotten, and I taught her English. She obviously came from a wealthy family – her father was a banker – but to her, we were all equals. The Crombies had two sons, the youngest about Helene's age and they quickly became sparring partners. One day, after Nigel had been baiting her, I heard them having this furious debate in her limited English. Obviously wanting to say something really insulting to him, she came rushing to find me.

"What do you call someone who cannot have children?"

"Er, well, impotent I suppose."

She rushed off and I heard her shouting at him. "You are

impotent!"

While Helene was with us there was never a dull moment; she would come to dry the dishes and demand to know what the tea towel was called, or this or that, and I would ask what it was called in French.

Out in the garden were some fruit trees, and near the house were some big pear trees dropping their crop onto the ground. England had a lot of European wasps, horrible things that invaded cake shops to eat holes in icing or attach to anything sweet. They also ate holes in fruit. The problem was that the outside hole may be small but there may be a large hole inside that could hide several wasps.

Helene had a big red Sloppy Joe ski jersey that her mother had knitted her. It had the motive of her ski club on the shoulder, and elastic through the bottom band; she would wear it with just a bra. underneath. One day when we were on our own she went out to collect the pears and bring them in to stew. She started picking them up and stuffing them up her jersey. Then, I heard her screaming.

"Beelie! Beelie!" and I went rushing out. The angry wasps had come out of the pears and were buzzing around inside her jersey stinging her badly. She was jumping around like frogs legs on a skillet. I yanked up the back of her jersey.

"Stand still, you idiot!" I yelled as I tried to brush about six furious insects away from her back. She had about eight very painful stings and I was worried she may go into shock. I took her inside and put something on the bites to ease the pain. I told her to take a basket next time. Poor Helene, I once said to her if there is anyone in the house who is going to be stung it will be you, and she was the only one who was. Sometimes wasps that seemed to be a bit drunk would get into the house; one got on to the sofa and Helene sat on it and was stung on her bum. Another time she stood on one on the carpet and got her foot stung, but still she persisted in running around in bare feet.

Alas the country life soon bored her and after about six weeks she decided to move to friends in London; the house wasn't the same without her.

Most weekends when it was fine we would set out on our tandem with Steven in the sidecar and bike for miles through the beautiful countryside. The boys were shocked when we arrived back one day and I told them we had been to Brighton and back. We were really fit, and of course Frank used the tandem to bike to work.

One day there was an enormous hail storm just about the time he would be biking home. I stood at the top of the stairs and watched in awe as hailstones the size of hen eggs crashed down. Never had I seen anything like it. It was soon gone and Frank got home saying he had taken shelter in a shop at Crawley down the hill.

Our birth control methods had gone to pot. The aforementioned cap took so long to install that all passion had gone before I returned from the bathroom; I had made it quite clear there were to be no more children while we lived like we did with no thought to the future. Our only control was for Frank to pull out at the last moment, but one night he didn't and I soon found out that I was pregnant again and not at all pleased.

Frank had been making noises for weeks about riding the tandem with sidecar attached, over the continent, to get back to Australia. He was forever running the place down when he was there, now he was telling everyone what a hell hole England was. I was very sceptical about the idea and now, of course, it was out of the question. Now he wanted to move on, the sooner the better. Truth to tell he had used up all the places he could work at within a reasonable distance.

So it was that in early winter we packed up everything to leave. We had a big bonfire down the back of the garden to burn things we didn't want or couldn't carry. There was one thing about Frank; he always kept his tin of old photos and his little keepsakes, unfortunately he didn't give me the same privilege.

Many years before, Auntie Frances (step-mum's sister) had given me a small new testament that I cherished not because I was religious in any shape or form but for the fact that it was a beautiful thing. It had bright blue leather binding and exquisite pictures; it may also have been of some value, so you can imagine my horror when I saw it burning on the fire. I screamed and snatched it out but it was too badly burned to rescue. I sat on the grass and cried and when he arrived with another armful I flew into a monumental rage. I was so angry I think I could have killed him. Of course whenever he was challenged he would say, "Aw now, come on, Bill, you didn't really need it and you don't believe in that stuff."

But that was hardly the point. I wish now that I had gone to find his treasures and burnt them to let him see how it felt. I have never forgiven him that day; it was just another nail in his coffin. The other thing I left behind that day was the teddy bear Dad had bought for me the day we went into the orphanage. He was a bit battered; his coat was thin and his paws had been mended several times, but when he was tipped over he still groaned loudly. Strangely enough old teddy bears became quite valuable in later years, but it was his sentimental value that meant most to me.

When I was in Australia and I had announced to Mum and Dad that I was married Mum packed up all my things and sent them over. I wished many times that she had kept them for me, but then she wasn't to know that we would be shifting from pillar to post like gypsies every few months. I left poor teddy sitting up on the bench, said a sad goodbye and have regretted it ever since.

Another thing she had sent which Frank burnt that day was a small pamphlet about the orphanage. It contained photographs of some of the children. There was a one of our little family, absolutely irreplaceable, and that saddened me the most.

Finally, we had put all we owned in our pannier bags and Steven's sidecar and were on our way. I have the idea that we put the bike on the train to Lewes and cycled from there, but I could be wrong. Anyway we ended up in Littlehampton renting a seaside caravan. These big caravan sites were full during the summer but now in winter we were the only ones in the whole place. When the caretaker came to empty the money we had put in to get electricity he gave most of it back saying that it was cranked up for the holidaymakers.

I really liked Littlehampton. Our caravan site was on Rope Walk which I thought was a very good name as it went along the riverside where lots of houseboats moored. These homes on water fascinated me; they were of every shape and size: old barges, a small battleship, even a beautiful old wooden yacht. How I would have loved to have seen inside some of them. It was very cold in the van as the wind swept in from the sea; some days Steven and I would walk along the beach doing some beachcombing just for something to do. All sorts of strange things can be found on a winter beach. I picked up a pair of trousers for Frank which he wore for work once I got the sand out of them.

After a month or so we answered an advertisement for a flat to rent for the winter. It was just £2 a week as opposed to £14 a week during the summer.

It was in a terraced house which was on the end of a row and owned by a nice couple called Stewart. Mr Stewart had converted the place into two flats and ours was the top one but we shared the one side door with the couple downstairs. Our stairs led straight up from the doorway and the floor was covered in a hard-wearing, soft-backed kind of vinyl, in red. We had a kitchen, a lounge in the middle and a big bedroom with two double beds. It was the best place we'd had and I felt right at home.

The biggest problem was our neighbours. The floor hadn't been sound-proofed for the people downstairs. No sooner had we moved in than the woman screamed, "Shut up that bloody noise," every time Steven ran across the floor. How I was supposed to stop a toddler from running around I didn't know, not unless I tied him to a chair and I wasn't about to do that. I was forever hushing him, but within weeks I was just about a nervous wreck. Her husband, who seemed a reasonable person, spoke to me one evening saying his wife was fed up with the noise. I told him we were not noisy people and that I tried to keep noise to a minimum but with a nineteen-month-old it was a bit hard. I also pointed out that we had put up with their noise without complaint and that their radio woke us every morning at 5 am. He said he was sorry, that he hadn't realised, and I noticed the radio, although we could still hear it, was a bit quieter from then on.

The daily abuse carried on however and one day she screamed that she was going to complain to the landlord. That got me really upset.

I decided to get in first and went to see Mrs Stewart, a really nice person who told me not to get upset and just take no notice of her. She indicated that she herself found the woman a bit weird. From that day on I felt better but I still whispered while on the stairs. One day Steven and I came home from shopping, the milk bottles were at the door and it had been raining so they were wet. I started to pick them up but Steven grabbed one.

"Me take," he said.

"Alright, but be careful not to drop it," I whispered.

He started up the stairs ahead of me so pleased to be helping, and then horrors! He dropped the bottle with a bang.

"Shut up that bloody noise!" screamed the voice from behind the door. That did it! I had never answered her back but this time I finally exploded.

"Shut your bloody mouth, you stupid neurotic cow! I've had an absolute guts full of you!" She must have got the shock of her life, and never once did she yell at me again. I was sorry I hadn't retaliated sooner.

The other gripe she had was that I was not sharing the scrubbing of the doorstep with her. Christ, just how pathetic can you get! She was obviously very working class. I felt like telling her that I came from a two thousand acre (a slight exaggeration) sheep station in New Zealand and we had more to do than get up at 5 am like she did to scrub the doorstep. Instead I told her quietly that I would be only too pleased to do it if she felt it necessary but, "If you think I am going to get up at 5 o'clock to do it you are very much mistaken."

They were a strange couple; both in their 30's and had not long been married. One day I met her in the back garden when I was hanging out the washing and I concluded she was one of the ugliest women I'd ever met. She stopped to talk; more to pick my brains than anything else I suspect. Her lanky straight hair was cut straight around the bottom to chin level. I watched in fascination as a piece of hair attached itself to her dripping nose and a drop slowly ran down its length and dropped off. So mesmerized was I, I couldn't concentrate on what she was saying. They left soon after that, but a few months later we met in a grocery shop and she greeted me like a long lost friend. I looked at her as though she'd gone mad and gave her a brief nod.

If I was big with my first child I was even bigger with my second. This one was carrying low, unlike Steven who was carried high. I felt, and hoped, it would be a girl. I eventually got so big I was embarrassed to go out. One day I took the sheets down to the laundry to get washed and a group of schoolboys looked at me and got the giggles. Try as I did, there was no way to cover that huge bump.

In England, they were very keen on home delivery, which, after the fiasco of Steven's birth pleased me no end. The midwife's name was Kath; she came to see me a few times before I was due. I had met and became friendly with a lovely refined and retired couple who had a nice home at the end of the street. The lady, whose name I forget, offered to look after Steven when the time came so that was a weight off my mind. Frank, who'd had a few jobs since we moved into the flat, was working on night shift and I had his work's phone number to call if things started to happen.

On the 2nd of May 1957, I went into labour at 4.30 am. Not wanting to sound the alarm too soon I waited an hour before waking Steven to tell him the baby was on its way. Knowing how quickly Steven had arrived after I started bearing down I didn't want to leave it too late to get to the phone thus having to deliver the baby on my own. Donning my long dressing gown and dressing Steven in his, we set off, hand in hand, to walk to the phone box at the end of the next block. It was 5.30 am and the streets were empty except for a man in a butcher's apron walking toward us on the opposite footpath. He didn't notice us until we were almost abreast. When he did he got such a shock he stopped dead and demanded:

"Where do you think you're going?"

I ignored him, and the poor man, noticing the bump, looked away and hurried on. I thought it was quite funny. Phoning the factory I asked that a message be given to Frank to come home as soon as he could, that he would know why. To Kath I said I was fine, she didn't need to come for hours, but later I may not be able to get to the phone. But she didn't take my advice. Half an hour later she arrived at the flat, with Frank close on her heels. My pains continued for a few hours but then stopped. Kath left to attend to her charges saying she would be back soon. I started walking the floor, up and down, up and down the passage until the pains started again.

Now as it happened, I had decided to have the baby on the day of the soccer cup final at Wembley. Frank said he had waited years to watch a soccer final and the baby had to arrive in the middle of it. By 1.30 pm I was in bed; the pains were getting worse. My midwife and husband were rushing in to see me, then rushing out again to watch the match on the lounge TV. How I silently cursed that match. Eventually Kath said, "Oh, you are getting bad, aren't you? I will give you some Trilene," and she slapped the mask on my face for a few whiffs. Then I was bearing down. Kath told Frank to hold my leg and give me something to push against.

"It's got black hair," he said, and a couple of pushes later, there she was, a beautiful little girl.

Kim, as I insisted she be called, (after Kim Novak the movie star, and also because it was a name that no one could shorten,) was a lovely wee thing. Like a lot of newborns, her skin was slightly jaundiced which added to her beauty.

In the lounge there was a strange big chair that opened up to a single bed; Kath suggested I be moved in there as it was warmer beside the gas fire. When I was settled and baby was tucked up asleep in the cot beside me Frank went to bring Steven home. My little boy arrived back with his nice lady carer; ran straight in, tapped me on the stomach and pointed to the cot.

"Baby gone, baby in there," he said.

The next day all was well. Baby Kim was feeding properly and I had no worries. Alas, the next day Steven had one of the severest cases of gastroenteritis I have ever seen. The poor wee lad was vomiting one end and passing almost pure white diarrhoea at the other – it couldn't have happened at a worse time. When Kath arrived to check on me and baby she said she would have to notify the district nurses as she couldn't take the chance of infecting other babies. So until I was passed out of the system as needing no more help an elderly district nurse came in to tend to us.

The day after Kim had been born I got up to find Frank doing a pathetic job of hand washing the very smelly sheets. I told him to get out of the way and set to washing everything, and getting him to hang them out. Thus I had just one day lying in.

Within a few days, Steven was well again.

The Stewarts had given us the date that the first of their summer bookings were to begin. We were to vacate a few days prior to that. We had no idea where we were going. But Frank had decided on a caravan.

One day he arrived home with a car; someone else was driving as he didn't know how to. It was an amazing car – twenty-five years old with just 9,000 miles on the clock. Seems it had been up on blocks for the past few years after its owner died. It was called an Austen Ascot, the first-ever automatic car; 18 horsepower, but it took about 16 horse to drive the motor. Later in documentaries we noted that it had been the same type of car that was driven for Prime Minister Chamberlain at the outbreak of the Second World War. It had a walnut dashboard, soft brown leather seats, carpets on the floor covered with interesting mats in the back. The back was huge; chrome and leather dickie seats pulled up from the floor, and beautiful wooden tables pulled down from the backs of the front seats. Elaborate hand holds hung down from the roof. The tyres were perfect, and the wheels were covered with aluminium disks. It was a joy to behold. If I could say anything about Frank it was this, he certainly had an eye for an unusual car.

Frank asked Kath if she would teach him to drive. She would, and they spent many an hour over the next few weeks driving around one of the old wartime airfields.

Many years later I was to wonder if Frank and Kath had an affair. Frank had this strange compulsion to look up all his old mistresses, and after I had finally left him for good and he had tracked me down, he told me he had been back to Littlehampton and looked Kath up. How he found her after twenty years I don't know — I didn't even know her surname, but he was very good at finding people.

After getting the car the next thing was to buy a caravan. He found and bought a fourteen-foot Bluebird, and we were ready to go. The fact that Frank didn't have a driver's licence was no bother to him; a few years later he got an Irish workmate who was going back home on holiday to buy him one in Ireland where no driving test was necessary. So Frank became Frances.

We found a site for the van behind the pub at Yapton, a village not far inland. Our caravan life had begun. We were told we could stay just two weeks as a casual as they already had their quota, but we stayed a month or so more. I already knew the lady in the van next door by sight, having seen her with her bright orange dyed hair while shopping in Littlehampton — it looked very strange on a lady who must have been well into her sixties. She lived in the van with her 'brother', or so she said. For a while she was friendly, that is, until I met Karen, a very nice girl my own age who lived in another van and we became friends. Karen's husband was doing his National Service in the Guards in London. They had started taking National Service lads because they couldn't get enough tall men who wanted to join the service. He would come home every few weeks walking ram-rod straight as he walked into the park. They had two little girls who were always spotless. My red-haired neighbour became quite nasty, but then she didn't have a good word to say about anyone in the park.

Frank arrived home one day with a nice two-piece suit for me which he said he'd got in a sale. When I asked how he could afford to pay for such a nice thing he laughed and told me he had changed the price tags. As always I was mortified. "The girl at the counter said, you have got a good bargain there," he said.

I had my photo taken wearing it, holding Kim in her shawl with

Steven in his Sunday best beside me. I sent it home and Mum wrote to say how nice we all looked.

About a month after Kim was born a lot of my hair fell out when I washed it. I freaked out – it was a matted mess. I barely knew the girls in the big vans behind us but I knew they were service wives and a cut above the average. I threw myself on Pauline's mercy. She sat me down in her van and spent a long time teasing out all the loose hair, ending with quite a pile. She told me the same had happened to her and the Trilene gas was the cause.

A very nasty incident was to happen while we were at Yapton. We had an old man in his eighties who used to come in an electric van to sell us bread. He would stand at my door and chat, all the time his right hand would be giggling in his pocket; not one ever to think badly about anyone I just thought he had Parkinson's disease and felt sorry for him. Now over in the corner of the park was a woman who had about six children, most of them girls and a bit wild; it came to light that he had been encouraging the older ones to ride with him down the lane where he had stopped and interfered with them. It was reported in the papers that he'd been arrested and was out on bail, case pending. The park was abuzz with talk and I was outraged. I got all the ladies together telling them he will just be fined and lose his job and that we should teach the filthy old so-and-so a lesson that he wouldn't forget. We planned to waylay him as he drove down the lane on leaving the park. We blocked the road and told him to get out and we closely surrounded him; he was terrified. The ladies played their part beautifully – not one swear word was spoken – no one raised their voice – but our spoken words left him in no doubt that we considered him the worst kind of filth. I told him if I thought he had touched my son I would slit his throat there and then. Before letting him go we told him that if we ever saw him on the site again he may find himself getting lynched. We never saw him again.

A few weeks later his case was reported in the papers. I can't remember what his punishment was, but I am sure that what we did punished him more than the courts could. The person I felt most sorry for was his wife – how did she cope with the shame?

At last, it was time to go. The hotel refused to accept our site rent saying they would soon be in trouble if we didn't leave. There was nothing for it but to hitch up, say our goodbyes and leave. We had no idea where to go.

So there we were: Frank with no driving experience, no driving license, an unregistered car, a caravan with no number plate (assuming it needed one) driving through the country aimlessly. My nerves were in shreds. Going through one village, the caravan door flew open and crashed with a loud bang into a high stone wall. Like most drivers who learn to drive late in life, Frank was never to become a good driver.

I think it was later the next day that we came to a big woodland and decided this was as good as any place to park. I don't know where we were but there was a town nearby where Frank thought he might get work. There was already one caravan parked in the woods so we drove well in and parked. The next day the man from the caravan, who seemed very pleased with himself, came to say he had told the owner we were there and he had been told to tell us to move on. Well, at least we had got a much-needed sleep. We hitched up and tried to drive out, but got hopelessly stuck in the mud; so unhitched the van and got the car out then tied a rope to the van and hauled it through the mud. This took most of the morning, and then we were on the road again.

In the next town Frank picked up a paper – he was almost never without a newspaper – photo's going back years almost always showed him with a paper as if it was a prop. There was an advertisement for a labourer at a foundry offering a caravan site with the job. He got it and soon we were back in Hampshire. The foundry was some distance from town, in a hollow below a busy road. The site held five vans. The job was something to do with making iron grids to cover the street drains; he came back each night with his clothes and body completely black. He hated the job and moaned continually. After a few weeks he developed a very bad attack of sinusitis caused by all the filth he breathed in and had to see the doctor. When he was well he told the boss he wasn't coming back and, leaving me there, set off on his own.

It was winter; bitterly cold and frosty. Sometimes we woke to a touch of snow. Most days were overcast and a heavy mist hung over the site. It was hard to keep the children occupied in the tiny van and darkness fell about 3.30 in the afternoon. When the sun shines, the pineal gland gives off endorphins that make us feel good, but with the early darkness and nothing to do, I fell into a deep pit of despair.

One of our neighbours was a man who had also worked at the foundry, but he claimed to have hurt his back there and was allowed to stay on at the site. He and his wife would cook nice meals using the cheapest cuts and a lot of know-how and one night they invited me and the children to dinner. It was to them that I ran one night when I got a dreadful fright. To keep Kim from under my feet when I was cooking I would put her on the seat beside the table and use another seat cushion to fence her in.

I had been shopping and bought some fresh bread so I broke a piece off and gave it to her to eat. Some minutes later I turned around and saw her choking. Snatching her up, I upended her and slapped on her back but nothing came up. She started to turn blue.

Screaming, I rushed next door with her; they met me outside, and just as we met my poor baby brought up a large glob of bread. I think I shook for ages. Never again did I give them soft fresh bread.

Having no way to get mail I hadn't heard from Frank, so had no idea where he was.

One day, just before dark there was a hard-knocking on the van door. It was the foundry owner and he was ropable.

"When are you going to get this van off my property?" he screamed.

I explained that I didn't know where my husband was but expected he would be back soon and have somewhere for us to go.

"I'll give you three days. If you are not gone by then I will tow you out and leave you on the side of the highway."

"Well, that's fine, if that's what you want to do," I answered. "After all it will be you who will get into trouble with the police."

After more shouting, he stormed off and I saw no more of him.

At last, Frank made it back, saying he had a job at Marlow and we would leave the next day.

After travelling for many hours, evening saw us pull in to what looked like a small old quarry at the edge of a fairly busy road where we stayed for a few days. Needless to say, it didn't last long; Frank went to work each day at Marlow, a nice little town on the Thames. I washed nappies and clothes and hung them out on a line tied to a tree. The weather had improved. I walked with the children to a farm to buy fresh milk.

Then the police arrived. They said that people going past in buses had complained about our being there. I explained why we had to leave the park behind the Yapton Hotel, and that we couldn't find another place. They could see that I wasn't the usual run of the mill hippy or a gypsy that people had such a down on; after all the children were well cared for and we were all clean and decently dressed. The policemen said they knew how hard it was to get somewhere but we couldn't stay there.

"Go to Mashe's place at little Marlow. He has vans there and may be able to take you in. Say that we sent you."

When Frank arrived home after work, we hitched up and went to find the farm.

Mashes turned out to be *Mash of Convent Garden*. They had a big market garden and their produce went to Convent Garden to supply London. For once we had fallen on our feet. There was the approved number of vans adjacent to the front drive, but hidden away behind the big old manor house were three other vans. We were allowed to join them. No sooner had we settled in than Frank arrived with another dog.

Once more I wrote to Mum and Dad to tell them of yet another change of address. Mum wrote back promptly to say she had posted a Christmas parcel to us at Yapton. I hadn't told them about the sojourn at the foundry, but I rang the hotel and they told that yes it was there. Frank said I had better go and retrieve it so Steven and I set out one morning to catch the train.

When the folks from the vans went shopping in Marlow we didn't walk away out to the road but took a short cut along a path at the edge of the fields. It was wet and the path was muddy, so I wore my little white gumboots, a new fashion at the time for country wear, and Steven wore his coloured ones. I can't remember the trip, but we made it, picked up our heavy parcel and headed home. We returned to a London train station in the late afternoon and went to the cafeteria to get something to eat. The place was full, but a good-looking businessman sat alone at a table so I asked if he minded if we sat there. He said "not at all". When Steven bend the straw he had for his milkshake, I, still a country bumpkin, told him he wasn't allowed to have another one. The man got up to leave but was soon back bearing another two straws. I was surprised and thanked him.

Our parcel held a large Christmas cake and some small gifts. I received something every year. Once I had to go to a bank in London to get £20, a lot of money in those days.

One van at the new place was occupied by a nice couple in their 30s, they had painted their van door a bright red because she said it was a welcome home after being at work all day. Another was occupied by a single man; and the other by a gypsy man and his wife, both small in stature, and they had three children who were very small for their age. I'm sure their nutrition was terrible.

The father worked for the estate. He was a very clever decorator and did all the odd jobs around the big house. He had painted their van with clever designs that made the interior look like wood panelling. Unfortunately, his wife, a chain smoker, had left cigarettes burning everywhere and completely destroyed the effect. I was soon to find out that she was a borrower. It was: "Could I have a cup of sugar?" or "Could you spare some tea?" (tea bags hadn't been invented then) or "Have you got some flour I can have?" I wouldn't have minded if she had returned what she had borrowed but she never did. This made me angry as her husband was on a weekly wage, while my husband might be out of work for weeks as he flitted between jobs. We had to go to the shops in Marlow; I felt that if I could get all the things I needed to last the week, why couldn't she?

During the Second World War, the Mashes' farm had been worked by German prisoners-of-war. There were several long barrack rooms that had held the trustees; each one had an ablution room at the end. These sheds had now been turned into pig sheds for breeding porkers, all managed by an ex-prisoner-of-war who, being so happy with his wartime treatment, had come back to stay. He was a true Aryan, tall and fair-haired with a very German face. I was lucky to be shown through the pig sheds and see how everything worked.

Just outside the place that held our vans was a pig-yard, sleeping sheds at the back and a concrete yard in the front. Unfortunately our water tap was just at the corner of the yard where the pigs came to pee, regardless of whether you happened to be filling your water container at the time. If I decided to go on filling I would get splashed with pee so it was much wiser to back off and wait.

Having observed the habits of pigs at close quarters I have never again been comfortable about calling someone a pig – pigs are truly the cleanest animals around. They would go to one corner to pee and the other corner to poo, as far from their beds as possible.

Another downside to our site was the approach: a big heap of litter from the sheds had been dumped beside the inroad and it stunk to high heaven and oozed across our access. Steven fell in this once – he had on a pair of new overalls which I had to throw away after several washes had not taken the stench out.

The gypsy kids could be a bit wild due to lack of discipline; and once, when my kids and hers had a disagreement, the oldest girl picked up a fair-sized rock and threw it. Steven got a nasty cut just above his eyebrow. I hit the roof and told her she should tell her kids not to throw rocks as they could maim someone for life. Instead of admonishing her child she defended them, so after that the air was blue.

One of the good things about living at Mashes' farm was that I could earn extra money by working at picking. While there we picked a huge supply of runner beans, unfortunately after a few weeks there was a glut of beans on the market and a large truck full was driven away to be dumped. When there was no picking I acquired an evening job at a factory a few miles away. When Frank arrived home at night I took the tandem and rode off to work – a tandem, being built for two is quite heavy, but once you get up some speed its weight carries it along at quite a pace. I would have a giggle as I shot past men, also on bikes, on their way to work at the same place. They must have thought I was a real Smart Alec. My job entailed using a template to drill holes in the glove boxes and dashboards for cars. It was interesting to see how they were made, and what went into the sloppy mix before being poured into a mould and heat pressed into shape.

While living at Mashes farm Frank decided it was time to go home for a visit. He hadn't written or communicated with his family for two years and once again it had to be a secret. We set off in the car. When we reached Yorkshire Frank donned a chauffer's hat and said I should sit in the back seat with the children to make it look as though I was the Lady-of-the-Manor. Quite used now to his silly little games, I did and it was quite funny to see all the heads in bus queues turn and watch as we went by. Back in Brearley Fold, we were welcomed by all and sundry, the car marvelled at and admired. Keith, who now had a car, suggested we all go for a day at the beach. With seven in our car and the rest in Keith's we set out with Keith in the lead. Unfortunately, on the way through the countryside he drove through a stop sign and Frank followed. A police car pulled us over. I was scared silly; no rego, no licence, I dreaded to think what it was going to cost or what trouble would follow. Strangely they both got off with a warning. As we'd been stopped beside a wide grassy verge it was decided we would picnic there before driving on. But the constant fear had taken its toll; I didn't feel like eating and after sitting silently for a while I wandered further up the road and sat to compose myself. When Jean sensed something was wrong and came to talk to me I burst into tears and howled. It all came out, the unregistered car, no licence, the way we never had money because he wouldn't stay in a job, the lot. I had never told anyone and somehow it was a release.

Jean just said, "I am not surprised, Billie. He is never going to change you know."

We got back to Mashes farm several days later, thankfully with no more incidences.

A few weeks later Frank's mother wrote to say she was coming to stay. It was arranged that I would take a day off from picking to go and meet her. I left the children with my friend Helen, and after several bus changes arrived to meet her train on time.

We were walking out of the station when who should come walking down the road grinning like a Cheshire cat, but Frank. He was supposed to be working many miles north but had irresponsibly taken the day off. I was angry. I had used up several pounds of my hard-earned wages, but at least I got home for free in the car.

His mother had never stayed in the country before and found it very strange. There was a very large pond quite near to the vans that held lots of ugly pike; it also had its complement of water birds that, to her, made funny noises.

The first night we played a card game, Sevens, around the table with another couple, with Frank blatantly cheating so she could win.

When morning came we had a histrionic exhibition from her about how she couldn't sleep (not true because I'd been up in the night to Kim and she had been fast asleep) and how much she had been frightened by all the weird noises, and – "Ooo, I couldn't stay here because I was frightened to death."

I told her laughingly that the noise was just the hooting of a lovely barn owl; but no ... Frank was to take her back to the station so she could get home that day.

I was really pissed off. After all the trouble I'd gone to to welcome her, buying food in, cooking, and going to meet her, and what's more she was so heavy the heels of her shoes had ground deep marks into my polished floor. It was all too much. We said goodbye and Frank drove her away. I was never to see her again.

Frank was forever going on about driving overland back to N.Z. so when he saw a motor van advertised for sale or exchange he couldn't resist the temptation. I didn't like the man who came to inspect our van one bit; he climbed up and inspected the roof and complained about it. When we replaced the oilcloth on the roof we should have put it out in the sun first, to let it stretch; this we didn't do and parts had sunk slightly between the timbers. It was still, of course, waterproof. Then he faulted this and that; it was all a lot of rubbish, just a ploy to get some money out of us. He informed us he would trade us for the motor van if we gave him £50.

Next, we had to go and inspect his van. His wife was a lovely lady, nicely dressed, tall and well-spoken. Somehow she just didn't seem to fit with him. They had a lovely house in a good suburb; somehow I felt it belonged to her. When she insisted we stay for lunch her husband snorted, not at all pleased, but she ignored him and sat us down to a large plate of delicious sandwiches and a pot of tea. I felt it was a bit odd, him being grumpy and eager to get rid of us, and her so gentle and kind. It didn't take much working out later: she obviously knew the little shyster was about to swindle us and was trying to soften the blow.

We went for a trial run, but hadn't got half a mile before he snapped, "That will do, turn and go back."

We did. Frank handed over the £50, the man said he would come later that evening to pick up our van and we set off back in our new 'home'.

Everything went fine until we came to the first hill and the engine started pouring out thick white smoke. The van had been a Commer ambulance before it was converted and had the flat nose, the engine being between the two front seats. Very quickly the cab filled with so much smoke we couldn't see out the windscreen. It was terrifying: Frank couldn't see to drive or pull over. My mind has blotted out how we got back.

Another shock awaited us: the caravan was gone, all our belongings stacked in a heap where it had stood. Another lesson learned.

Eventually, it was time to say goodbye to friends again – my friends, that is – Frank never made any. He had got a job in Hemel Hempstead. His new boss had told him about a friend of his who would put a caravan on their land in exchange for a baby sitter once a week. We went to see Eve and Tony Bysouth and were approved.

I have no idea how we got the clapped-out van, and the car over from Marlow but we did. This was to be our last move in England.

Hemel Hempstead was a new town, most of the houses being built after the war to house all the displaced people from London. It had all been tacked on to the original small town and was very hilly. To get to town we had to either go down Feldon Lane or go the shorter route down the little track that led to the back of Box Moor train station, through the station and then a good walk to town.

The Bysouths lived in Eve's parents' house up on Box moor, above Hemel Hempstead, and Tony was building their own house lower down on a piece of the parents' garden that had been given to them as a wedding present. Eve's parents worked for the United Nations supervising the packing of dates in Iran or Iraq. Her brother also worked for the United Nations in Sarawak.

Eve, a school teacher, was about my height with thick henna-tinted hair cut into a shoulder-length page boy. Tony worked as a carpenter at the American Air Force base and drove a three-wheeled car. They eventually became good friends. They had two children, one of each, who spoke with that high-class English accent. They didn't have a TV so went to the pictures every Thursday night while I babysat, and had a very welcomed bath.

Frank rigged up a plywood shed at the back of the van where I did the washing and put it through the Acme, hand-turned wringer. It also sheltered our dog Missie who was one of the best dogs we ever had. Missie was often mistaken for Alsatian; she was the same colour but smaller – maybe she was an Alsatian cross. Certainly, she was a good guard dog.

I was only able to do the small washing by hand, all the rest I had to lump away to the laundromat. To get there I had to go to the bottom of the hill and catch a bus up another steep hill. I never had the money to use the dryer so had to cart a heavy wet load back. Getting back up the hill with it and two small children was no small feat.

Over the months Tony's and Eve's house began to take shape. Tony, who could work only in the evenings and at the weekends, laid beautiful granite floors with under-floor heating. It was to have all the latest mod cons. I was able to see the progress as I had to go to the tap at the back of the new house to get a bucket of water each day.

We had not been there many months when Eve came to get me one evening saying their son Gwain was not well and would I take a look at him. A week earlier he'd received a small cut to his leg. When I examined him he had a red line travelling up his leg. I took them aside and told them that he had Septicaemia, blood poisoning, and he needed hospitalisation. They took my advice and the doctor told them that if it had been left much longer it could have killed him. They told me they knew now their children were in safe hands.

Tony and Eve didn't entertain much but one day we were invited to 'tea'. Tea in New Zealand means a cooked meal but we found that tea in England meant bread and jam or scones with a cup of tea. Many years later I had to laugh when I invited an English couple to tea in New Zealand and they told me they had filled up before they arrived.

Needless to say, the job Frank came to Hemel Hempstead for hadn't lasted long – they never did – and after a time he started running out of options and couldn't get a job anywhere. I don't expect it ever occurred to him that nobody wanted to employ someone with his work record. I rarely knew where he was or when he would be home: it was a guessing game. One payday he came home at 6.30 the next morning; said he'd been playing poker and lost his wages and had to stay until he won some money back.

Another time he got a job in London and travelled in on the train, having worked out there was rarely anyone on duty at the Box Moor station so would board the train without a ticket both ways. At night he left by the station's back gate to climb the hill to home.

Mum wrote to say that the Robinsons, their friends from Eldorado sheep station, were coming to England and would we meet them and show them around London. We walked them around all over the place and when it came time to leave for home we had missed a train. Mr

Robinson insisted that he pay for a taxi to take us home and they would come with us. I freaked out. Dear God, if they had seen us living in a truck we would never have heard the end of it. I told them we were miles out and it would cost him a fortune but that didn't seem to bother him. Eventually, he gave up trying and we caught the next train.

Very occasionally we would go to London ourselves, maybe to the market at Petticoat Lane or Elephant and Castle, not to buy but just to look. As I rarely got out I would become so engrossed in this new world that would forget where home was. When it became to go home I would ask, "Where's home?" This happened to me several times and I found it very frightening. It was always a tremendous relief when I eventually remembered – Frank took a delight in never telling me.

We relied mostly on jumble sales to buy clothes for ourselves and the children. Beaconsfield, the home of film studios was not far away; it was a rich area and the sales there, mostly run by the churches, were good and cheap. I would buy old knitted jumpers, some a bit matted, and unwind all the wool to knit up again as jumpers for the children. They got some really nice ones this way. I also bought coats and large skirts and cut out little jackets with dolman sleeves for them. Some matching wide elastic for the wrists and waistband and a zip up the front completed the job. I had bought a tiny sewing machine from a mail-order catalogue that did chain stitch; this meant that the ends of the seams had to be sealed because if the thread was pulled the entire seam would unravel. Not ideal but it did a far quicker job than hand sewing.

Winter came, one of the worst in years. One day as the children and I sat in the van it started to snow, great fat flakes softly floating down. We sat at the window enthralled, the rough garden soon turning into a wonderland. The small pine trees and shrubs hung with soft white … it was beautiful. When the snow stopped I wrapped the children warmly, put their gumboots on and we went out to play in the first snow they had seen. Sadly it thawed two days later and the sludge started to run down the hill. That night there was a hard frost and the sludge turned into sheet ice. With Kim in her pushchair we set out to buy groceries. While walking down Feldon Lane rather than the steep track to the station, Steven and I slipped, slithered and giggled all the way down. Getting back was another matter. In the van, with the kerosene heater going, the frost melted on the roof and froze the door shut. Never have I seen another winter like that one.

Our little Missie got cold. She'd never been allowed inside the van, there was barely room for us, but when she got sick I had no option. Poor wee girl, it had affected her nervous system, her bottom jaw juddered nonstop. She looked up at me with her pleading brown eyes and it broke my heart. I dressed her in one of my woollen polo necks, pulling it over her head and putting her front legs into the sleeves. It made a nice warm coat. I scratched together what money I had and together with the children we took her down to the vet.

As I had guessed she had a form of distemper; he gave her an injection telling me to bring her back next week. This time I made no mistakes even though it took me many weeks to pay for her treatment. She stayed inside until she was well and it was a bit warmer. She was very loyal to me and the children. One day Frank and I had a row when she was off her chain. When he grabbed a hold of me she leaped into the van, sunk her teeth into his leg then leaped out again. Dear girl, she had come to my defense even though she knew she was not allowed to come into the van.

At the laundromat, I met a woman who looked after children while their mothers worked, and realised I too could work and have a steady income if I could find someone to look after the children.

I got the first job I applied for, at John Dickinson's, a factory that made envelopes, mostly brown ones for the Government departments. I found a lady who would look after the children for £2 a week and started work. The discipline was strict; we had to clock on – more than one minute late we lost fifteen minutes pay. At night we clocked off again. I was supposed to get three months training but within two weeks they put me on a machine of my own. I didn't think anything of it at the time but realised later that it set the rest of the girls against me.

At first, I would eat my lunch with them at the end of the room, but, realising I was a miss-fit I later sat alone at my machine reading a book. This too got up their noses. I disliked their dirty talk about where the fitter had had his finger the night before or some other unsavoury subject.

I was suddenly sent to Coventry. No one would talk to me; not that it worried me in the slightest, but when they started to sabotage my machine things got serious. We were on piece work, but when the machine was shut down we went on to just 1 shilling and 8 pence an hour. That could lose you a lot of wages. It was up to the operator to keep the machine running and to do this we developed some rather dangerous habits. The rollers would sometimes get small lumps of hard glue on them, which would leave small indentations in the paper. We were supposed to stop the machine and wash the roller, but it was much quicker to check if the boss was looking, take the long knife and resting your hands on the machine, gently slope the knife down until it touched the roller and removed the glue. Of course if the knife was to slip, your hand could be grabbed by the machine and destroyed before the cut-off switch was activated.

I began to wonder why the paper jammed up every time I left it to get a bucket of water or run to the loo and was soon to find out.

One day I left the machine running when I went to get a clean bucket of water. Something made me turn around when I was halfway to the tap. I watched the girl in the machine next to me turn around on her seat and, with a piece of wire in her hand, reach out and just touch one of the papers flying out of the holder. The paper twisted and seconds later the machine cut out but not before a lot of paper had wedged tightly in the machine. This meant at least fifteen minutes downtime. That was the last straw. I got the water then charged into the boss's office and burst into tears. A darling man, he sat me down and I poured out my sad story. He was furious and said anyone caught sabotaging a machine would be sacked on the spot, (we were desperately behind all our orders) and from now on they would watch carefully.

"Billie," he said, "don't you realise why they resent you? You are far better than them. Beside you they are just rabble. Look, any time you want to talk to someone, you shut off your machine and come and talk to us," – meaning himself and the assistant manager.

This made me laugh. I went back to work and pulled out the paper jam. From then on I had no more trouble; the assistant manager walked the floor every half hour looking at each girl searchingly. I had never seen so many guilty faces avoiding his look. With no more stoppages my wages skyrocketed.

It was while I worked there that I had an accident at home. One weekend after washing all the nappies I asked Frank if he would turn the wringer for me. I held the corner to the wringer.

"Right," he said, giving the handle a violent turn downwards.

"You've got my thumb," I screamed. I jerked my hand back and left my long thumb nail stuck in the wringer, it having been pulled out by the roots.

The pain was excruciating. The doctor bound it up and I went back to work on Monday. The nail took months to grow back.

I was beginning to be very unhappy about the way our children were being looked after when I was at work. When I went to pick them up they were filthy; both had dirty faces and hands. I asked the woman if she would please wash them before I came, that I was not happy about taking them on the bus in that state, and she did.

One day Frank left saying he was going to try for a job at the car factory at Dagenham, and that night he didn't come home. He didn't come home for another fourteen nights. I was beside myself with worry. Every evening after work I sat and looked towards the road gate to see if he would return. I rang the car factory; they said they didn't have a Frank Naylor working there and had never heard of him. Was he in hospital? Was he dead? Something stopped me from going to the police. I didn't mention his disappearance to a soul, but it had been noticed by Tony and Eve.

One night when I went over for water Tony said, "Billie, where is Frank?"

I had to tell him I didn't know.

One evening, after giving the children their dinner and settling them to sleep I sat as usual with my eyes glued to the gate, and there he was. I raced out, he greeted me with a smile as though he'd done nothing wrong. I was so relieved to see him I forgot to be angry. Where had he been? Why hadn't he sent a letter?

He told me he'd got a job with a crew in the midlands painting a gasometer, (toshing they called it). A gasometer is one of those huge round things that rose above the ground in layers, the more gas it held the higher it went. He hadn't let me know because he didn't want the Bysouths to know our business. Of course, it didn't matter that I would be sick with worry, that thought would never occur to him. This maniacal desire for secrecy, again.

On Sunday evening he was away again. A week later an ambulance pulled into the drive and Frank alighted, on crutches and with a cast on the back of one leg. Somehow he had smooth-talked the hospital into getting him to the train in an ambulance, and have an ambulance meet him at the other end to deliver him home.

My boss had let me leave my job with just two days' notice that week. Poor wee Kim would start crying every time I dropped the children off in the morning. It broke my heart as I knew something was very wrong but she couldn't tell me what. Her bottom was red and inflamed and Steven told me that she stayed strapped in her pram outside all day, every day. That poor little girl! I wanted to kill the fat lazy bitch who got paid to look after her. To my everlasting shame I was too timid to say much, although she knew I wasn't happy. Now here was Frank home on crutches and once again we had no income. He had slipped off the top of the gasometer and landed feet first on the next walkway down.

"I could have broken my back if I had landed on the rails," he said.

I fleetingly thought: *you could have fallen all the way down and broken your neck, at least then I would know where I stood.*

His leg, which was black right up to the knee, had just a backcast on it because of the extreme swelling; he had broken his heel bone which takes a long time to heel. Later, he had to go the local hospital to get a proper plaster and would be off work for months.

Thoroughly demoralised yet again I wrote to Mum and Dad saying, "My world has just come down around my ears again. Frank has fallen off a gasometer and broken his heel bone. He is going to be out of work for months."

A letter came back by return mail saying: "Dad wants you back here in New Zealand and will pay your fares."

I couldn't have been more delighted. The letter went on to say that we could have the house that stood on Colin's farm which adjoined the station. We had, of course, to travel by ship but, because of New Zealand's high immigrant intake at the time, all the second class berths were booked for months ahead. That didn't stop Dad. He promptly booked us First Class. Good grief, he knew not what he'd done. There was I with no evening clothes, five secondhand dresses, a few pairs of mostly secondhand shoes, the children's clothes were minimal, but at least Frank had a good suit.

We were to leave in a month's time and had to set about selling everything we could to get some money. We would have liked to take the car with us as it would be valuable at home, but it couldn't be booked on a ship for months and we were quoted a ludicrous amount for someone to store it and deliver it to the ship. Frank sold it for just £35 a week before we left – it was the one thing we had of value, I could have cried. The van we sold to a young guy for £30; it hadn't been started for eighteen months but a mechanic friend got it going. When we tried to drive it out onto a rise it wouldn't budge an inch so we had to tow it out.

The lad and his father came the morning we left to pick it up and luckily our taxi arrived when they were trying to start it. I didn't feel too guilty about the engine, after all, he knew it had been parked up for eighteen months and with motor repairs, he had a bargain.

Frank had insisted that I tell the Bysouths that we were going back to Australia, another uncomfortable lie.

Our ship was the New Zealand shipping company's *Rangititi* on her last voyage before being sold as scrap to Japan. We boarded at Tilbury Docks and sailed in the evening. I made my way alone out onto the deck as we neared the end of the estuary; the land was black and the sky orange from a just set sun. As we reached the open sea and land faded away I said goodbye to England, glad to be going home, but still a little sad. I told myself I would never see it again. *How wrong I was.*

Truly, the only reason we were not suited for First Class was our lack of good clothes, but I found that most of the 127 passengers were no better than we were even though they had more money. About six of them stuck together, spoke with snooty accents and seemed to think they were better than everyone else. One was a certain Wing Commander B--- who, even though the war was long over, insisted on being address as Wing Commander. Most of his fellow passengers found him laughable.

The ship was old and far inferior to the *S.S. Skaubryn*, but the crew did their best to keep up appearances. I nearly died when the steward asked me on the first night if he could run my bath. No thank you! I soon found out there was a knot-hole between the men's bathroom and one of our cubicles and an eye was watching me in the shower. How I wish I had slapped a soapy face cloth at that eye. I just got out of there as fast as I could.

On the whole, the trip was good: the officers were scattered around the tables in first class; I had as my companion the very good-looking First Refrigeration Engineer, James Beaton. Our table always had lots of lively talk. In First Class, the children had their own dining room where they ate all their meals. The Chief Steward was gay and would often come in and entertain the children by wildly tap dancing around the tables. Sometimes he would sing for them, and the children thought he was great. When it was the adults turn to go for meals the children were left in the nursery in the charge of the nurse there. She would also look after them during the day when we wanted a break. It was on the ship home that I first noticed that Steven would become quite naughty whenever his home life was unstable. One day he went missing from the nursery and it took us two hours to find him. I was sick with worry as there were big gaps in the rails on each side of the steel bollards that held the ropes that tied up the ship when in port. A child could easily have fallen through. My young man got a very serious telling off that day.

There was no air-conditioning aboard and the cabins were putridly hot all the way through the tropics. Frank took to sleeping on deck but I had to stay with the children. About three nights after we left London the steward came around to tell everyone, "I have to notify everyone that we are dressing for dinner tonight."

This happened at least once a week. All I could do was don my best summer dress and wear my lovely Rains shoes. Rains were the shoemakers to the Queen, horrendously expensive. I had picked them up at a street market in London. They were high heeled, white, and seemed to be made of linen – they looked spectacular. Unfortunately they were a half a size too small but what the heck? I may not have had great dresses but I was willing to bet that no one else had a pair of Rains shoes.

Our first port of call was the beautiful Island of Madeira; they call it *the floating garden* and the description couldn't be more apt for the place was dripping with flowers. Steep terraces climbed up from the harbour, arched stone bridges crossed stone-lined drainage canals that ran across the hillside, and lizards basked idly in the sun. We climbed up all the steps to Reid's Hotel at the top of the hill and took photos of our ship below. I marvelled at the incredible azure blue of the ocean and vowed to come back one day. Sadly it will never happen.

Another few thousand miles across the Atlantic took us to the Dutch island of Curacao where we travelled by bus into Willemstad, the capital. Curacao is known for its oil refineries and the liqueur which is named after the island. The place was parched and dry but the old Spanish forts and the quarantine station were worth a visit.

The next day saw us negotiate the Panama Canal – lunch was served on deck so we would not miss the sights. That night saw us through the last of the locks and into Balboa at the end of the canal with another very short time ashore.

Our next stop was off the rocky shores of Pitcairn Island where the locals, descendants of Bounty mutineers, came out in their longboats to sell their wares while stores from the ship were offloaded and taken ashore. The islanders didn't wear shoes and we were shocked at the state of their feet. It was good to meet them and talk about their history.

The next stop, Wellington. Home at last.

New Zealand Again

The ship docked on a lovely day. We dressed the children up in their best clothes. Kim had a lovely little bought dress but Steven had to wear his long trousers as all his jumble sale shorts had fallen to pieces on the way over and it had been very embarrassing as there had been no clothes to buy in the ship's shop. With all his tearing around he was very hard on clothes.

Ready at last we joined the passengers lining the rail, and there they were, Mum and Malcolm waving in front of the big crowd awaiting our arrival.

I don't remember much about getting back to Otago; we were on the railway station at Wellington, perhaps waiting for a train to the ferry and Frank disappeared for a while. He told me later that he'd gone to phone his old live-in lover Margaret. She was the first of his exes to be looked up again.

When the train started with a bang, the way they did in those days, I laughed. "Oh, we are back in New Zealand." Why was it that in England the trains sneaked away so you hardly knew they were moving – here you were almost knocked off your feet.

The road down to Deepdale Station – changed from *Steephill* by Mum – turned off from the main north-south road at the top of Kilmog, a steep hill north of Dunedin. The homestead was in a deep valley, the main road high above it. Dad was pleased to see me. I told him we would pay him back our fares … did I really think then that things were going to change?

This was the first time I had seen the old homestead and land, but it was so good to be out in the country again with the clean air and sunshine. A large dead tree stump, white with age, stood at the gate to the garden. There was a big horned head of a wild ram, (one that Malcolm had shot) sitting on the top it. Nearby was another small cottage that had been shifted from another part of the farm to house the shearers when they came; and near that a large shearing shed. I came to know and dearly love the place over the coming months; it was one of the most tranquil places on earth.

We were to stay the first night at the homestead before having our gear taken up to Pollock's, our new home up the hill. It was called Pollock's after the people who had previously owned it – there was also a *Paddy Cains*, another farm next door owned by Colin. In the early settler's days, all this area had been in forty-acre blocks, in the days when a living could be made on that acreage. Gradually neighbours had taken over blocks adjoining. Dad's larger place had seven adjoining blocks added to it and Colin had two next door, making the overall acreage quite large. The paddocks backed onto steep bushland and the Silver Peaks, with no fences dividing them.

After dinner that evening, when we were all settled in the lounge, Mum produced the one thing I was so pleased she hadn't sent over to me, my top hat – another of Dad's trades, I think, from many years before. It was made of lovely smooth black seal skin and had its own box shaped like the hat, with a lid on it. I still have it today as I write. Seeing the hat was enough to set Frank off – he had this ghastly habit of behaving like a clown whenever he got into unfamiliar company.

Many years later I realised this was his way of trying to cover up his gross inferiority complex. So there he was with the hat on, holding the silver-topped walking stick that had belonged to Grandma, dancing and singing his way around the room like an idiot. My parents and Malcolm watched in amazement while I tried to laugh when all I wanted was the ground to swallow me up.

Next morning we loaded our tin trunk and suitcases onto the farm trailer and Colin drove us up to our new home. Frank wore the top hat, insisting he be photographed as he was the Lord of the Manor.

The house was hidden from the road behind a row of old Macrocarpa trees, a large old two-storeyed barn, an ancient orchard, and a hen house enclosed behind. The house was on a small knoll halfway down from the top of the hill. The back and far side were enclosed in a Holly hedge, and a large cherry plum tree graced the lawn. The house, a bungalow, was lovely, by far the best home I'd had since leaving home. It had two bedrooms and another in the closed-in end of the front veranda. There was a good-sized lounge, a large kitchen-diner, with a green and yellow enamel wood stove for cooking and heating the water. A scullery with cupboards and a sink was off the kitchen.

Even though it was Colin's house, it was Dad who had redecorated it all the way through. He had painted the scullery grey and the ceiling red; One day he said, "I shouldn't have painted it that colour."

"Oh no, I like it," I replied, and I did.

He had taken some care in redoing the sink bench, neatly covering it with thick, grey linoleum with pink flecks; it looked great and was very serviceable. There was no such thing as formica in those days. The sink benches were usually just scrubbed timber.

Mum had bought a house load of furniture so the place was completely furnished. I feel now I wasn't nearly grateful enough for what they had done.

The deal was we were to pay no rent but Colin would like us to paint the outside. He left the colour to us. We chose to paint it white with a dark grey roof and window surrounds with bright red window sills. A few months later it looked a picture.

One of the first things we had to do was to get Steven off to the little school at Merton – he was a very bright boy who was well overdue for school. An older girl who also caught the school bus at the top of our drive said she would look after him. I took a photo before he left for his first day.

The next thing was for Frank to find a job. Dad took us into Dunedin to go around all the places that would use welders. After several visits he stopped at another place and, as Frank got out of the car, he said to him, "And take that chewing gum out of your mouth."

He did, but still there was no job going. Nobody seemed to want a welder. What Dad didn't realise was that, unlike him, Frank didn't smoke; he chewed gum instead and had the most beautiful teeth. As I've already said, chewing gum was a disgrace in our family and probably because of that, I didn't like it either.

The only option left for work was Cherry Farm. This was the mental hospital a few miles north at Waikouaiti, a small country town. Cherry Farm was built to replace the ancient asylum near the beach at Seacliff and was over the hill from our home. Cherry Farm wasn't one big building, but a big group of villas, always in need of staff. They employed psychiatric nurses, trainee nurses as well as a lot of untrained attendants. In this group were a number of social misfits, people who liked to lord it over other people. Here they could get away with cruelty to insane or senile people who didn't know how to hit back. Frank, who had never been nursing, soon felt uncomfortable about some of the things he saw and brought his complaints home to me. He was particularly upset about an old man who wanted to go home to his wife. When he asked one of the other attendants about him he was told: "The stupid old bastard hasn't got a wife. She died years ago."

When the old man got cold at night, (and the villas could be very cold at night) they told Frank he wasn't to give him another blanket because the old bugger wet his bed. Frank, to his credit, came home very upset and asked me if we could have him at our place. I understood his worries because hadn't I myself gone through the same horrors when at first confronted with real life. But it wouldn't do, I told him. We couldn't have the old man at our place no matter how much he would like to. I told him that in time he would get used to it, and all he could do was do the best he could to help the inmates.

Step-mum had a letter from the authorities to say that her Uncle Magnas had been taken into care in Dunedin – they must have had some fun tracing his relatives. It seems that he and his 'housekeeper', who he'd been living with for many years, had not drawn their pensions for months and someone had gone to check on them and found the place a mess. They were notifying Mum and her cousins, who lived in the North Island, so they could take control. Mum hadn't seen her uncle for thirty-five years – he was her father's brother, her father having died of tuberculosis when Mum was about twenty. After the funeral Uncle Magnus, for many years the maths master at Otago Boys High School, had completely abandoned his sister-in-law and two children. Uncle Magnus was placed in an old people's home but kept walking out – he walked in on Mum and her cousin when they were trying to clear out his house and clean it. At that time, and for many years later, there were no homes for people with dementia, the only place for them was Cherry Farm, a hospital for the insane.

So it was after he had 'escaped' many times, he was sent to Cherry Farm. Fate had put him in Frank's villa and they got on fine. Mum brought him home to the farm a couple of times for dinner before taking him back; he didn't seem demented to me, more perhaps very forgetful. I even had a conversation with him.

When it came time to take him home the second time he demanded to know why he couldn't stay at the farm. Mum was horrified – in no way was she qualified to look after him. As she said to me, "You know after he came to the funeral he just abandoned us, he could have helped when we desperately short of money but he didn't. Mum had to sell our place at (and she named the street) because we couldn't pay the mortgage. I don't feel I owe him anything.'

As Ye Sow, So Shall Ye Reap?

The staff at the villa suggested it would be better not to take him out again as it would just unsettle him. So there he stayed. All was well until a few weeks later when it was Frank's day off. A Dutch guy, not known for his kindness to patients, took his place; and when Uncle Magnus asked a question he replied: "You're in a mental hospital, you stupid old fool."

Uncle Magnus went berserk. Before they could restrain him he had put his fist through a glass window in an attempt to escape, badly cutting his hand. After that, he just gave up. He died three weeks later, a sad end to a selfish old man.

One day Frank arrived home with a dog; I could have killed him. How could he be so stupid as to bring an untrained mutt to a sheep station? Never once in the twenty-one years I stayed with Frank did he ever ask my opinion; he just did what he wanted, when he wanted. The dogs wouldn't have mattered so much if he'd taken responsibility for them, walked or trained them, but he didn't. He just dumped them on me. That dog (I can't even remember what the children called him) was the only one I have ever disliked. He was medium-sized, with long scraggly black hair that hung over his eyes, and totally disobedient no matter how hard I tried to train him. Malcolm threatened to shoot him if he got amongst the sheep and one day he got out of the yard and did exactly that.

As luck would have it, the family, who could see from below what was going on up the hill, were all away for the day. No amount of calling and yelling would stop the wretched dog from chasing the hoggets around and around the hill. With the help of Steven we eventually caught him, but not before he had chased two sheep over a cliff. Absolutely frantic now, in fear of alienating my parents further; Steven and I set out with a rope to rescue them. My lovely little son was so good ... I set him well back from the drop and had him hold the end of the rope. I explained that I would climb down, tie my end of the rope to the sheep and when I shouted he was to pull as hard as he could. The bank was very steep but had broom bushes growing out from the side that I hoped would hold me. I reached the first sheep about fifteen feet down, tied the rope around it and with Steven pulling and me pushing we eventually got it over the top. The second one was even further down, struggling in mid-air on a broom bush that at any moment could give way and drop the sheep another twenty feet. I slithered down to it but had difficulty reaching the rope around it while I held on to another bush. Somehow I managed, and the pushing and pulling, me slipping and yelping with fright, started again. At last, after what seemed like a lifetime, we got it to the top. Had they been big sheep or had a long fleece there was no way we could have done it. I was exhausted and covered with nasty scratches and clay. When Frank came home that night and I told him what his stupid dog had done he thought it was funny. He didn't give a damn.

Another of that dog's tricks was to swing on the sheets on the clothesline. We had a revolving Hills Hoist at the top of the garden bank. I went out to find Fido having a great time. He caught hold of a sheet at the top of the hill, raced around until his feet left the ground and swung all the way around; he was having great fun, around and around, but my sheets had big teeth mark holes.

We were not alone in the house: we shared it with a swarm of bees. They entered the outside wall through the gaps at the end of the weatherboards. For some time we all lived in peace but one day they must have decided they were too crowded and a big swarm left the hive. They settled in the cherry plum tree in a big heap and that night we picked them up and put them into a hastily built 'hive' hoping to keep them,(which shows you what we knew about bees). The next day they left. For some strange reason the ones that were left became aggressive, and when I went around to my vegetable garden I would be attacked and stung. I put up with it for a while, but one day I was up the top of the ladder on the other side of the house painting the guttering when two bees came over the roof and stung me. That night my arm swelled up in an allergic reaction. I phoned the chemist at Waikouaiti and he said it had got into my bloodstream and he would put some antihistamine pills on the bus that day. The bus delivered all sorts of things to the mailboxes for the farms. For me, the poisoning was the last straw and I complained to Dad. He came up with a big spray gun and sprayed them as they went into the wall. There was a dreadful buzzing in the corner of our bedroom wall all that night and I felt sorry for them and guilty. If they had left me alone we could have lived in peace.

Frank was forever doing things to embarrass me and annoy my family – he just didn't think. He decided to put handrails up the path which could be quite slippery in the frost. I was away for the day when he went to the barn and helped himself to the steel pipes and wooden uprights that had once been the milking stalls.

"Did you ask? No, of course, you didn't. This is Colin's place … you can't just demolish things without asking, Frank." But it was like water off a duck's back.

When Dad came up he said, "Well he's made a good job of it but, Gwennie, he should have asked."

"I know Dad, I know."

Our next addition to the family was a bantam rooster Frank bought from the auction, goodness knows why. It turned out to be the most vicious little brute who attacked everyone that went into the outer yard. When roosters attack they jump into the air and, bending their legs, hammer their sharp spikes into their victim with lightning speed. One day he attacked Kim and put several deep spike holes in her upper legs. That was it! I went out and grabbed him, took him inside and hacked about a quarter-inch off his spikes so they could no longer do any damage. It didn't stop him flying at people though.

We had lots of ideas when we first went to live at the farm. We even designed an eight-sided house to build, but that came to nothing. We thought we may start a business keeping hens in deep litter. Dad wanted to know what we knew about hens – not a lot, but we had studied books, I told him. He scoffed at the idea – he seemed to be against almost every idea we had.

We found a house to buy over the hill at Seacliffe; it was only $2,000 because it was on railway land. It was a big federation bungalow. In the back yard, being used as a washhouse, was a little mud-brick house, the first home to be built in Seacliff in the days of the early settlers. We were keen to get our own home but Dad put the kybosh on that as well. He seemed to think that the railway might reclaim the land at any time and we would be left out of pocket. He was so wrong – the house still stands today, 50 years later.

We did get some hens though, one dozen day-old chicks from Lincoln College which at night we put under a broody hen (loaned to us by friends). The next morning, there she was strutting around as pleased as punch with her new family. Our chicks were Barred Rocks and they grew into the most beautiful black and white striped chooks.

I can't say that I was always happy in the station cottage. When we first moved in I found the isolation a bit daunting. Furthermore, step-mother was forever interfering with the children. Steven was over five years old and I had never had help with the children in all those years. Now here she was telling me what and what not to do with them. It made me angry.

Steven was at last at the little country school at Merton and Kim was alone during the day. She played quite happily out in the outside yard dressed in little overalls to keep her warm. Mum wanted to know why I kept her in trousers when she should have been in dresses. Angry, but afraid to answer back, I complied. A small spring had popped up behind the house and the water ran down the side of the knoll the cottage sat on making the yard outside the gate muddy. Kim loved to play there spooning the mud into heaps. Soon she had chapped knees.

"Look at her knees," said Mum. "They are all chapped."

"Well you told me not to put her in trousers," I snapped.

She had no answer to that.

The other thing she did was to ring me every night, (we were on a party-line,) and demand to know what I was giving the children for tea. One night I said I thought I would just give them cold meat and vegetables, and she replied that they'd had cold meat the night before and didn't I think they should have something else. I was really upset – it got to the point when I heard the phone ring I dreaded answering it. Of all the bloody nerve, I thought, I was the one who had passed my exams in nutrition, had been training for six months in a children's ward, had worked privately as a children's nurse, and here she was telling *me* what to do.

I became quite depressed. One day I told Dad that she was always interfering and he must have had word with her because things became a little better.

I should perhaps explain party-lines: all our farming days we were on party telephone lines. One single phone wire connected so many homes. If you wished to talk to the next-door neighbour you rang his code which was based on Morse code. Our number at East Taieri when I was young was 106D so our ring was long short long. If we wanted to ring someone not on our line we would turn the phone handle in one long ring and the person in the telephone exchange would answer. Anyone on the same line could 'listen in' and some people got a bad name for doing it. We had one such at Merton – I will call her Mrs McDougal. She lived in a farm above us, and 'listening in' seemed to be an obsession. If I was chatting to a friend and heard children in the background we would both know who else was on the line. Dad caught her out beautifully one night when he was talking to Tommy Dodds on another farm above us when he said, "Are you there Mrs McDougal?"

Taken by surprise she answered. "Yes."

"Well you bloody well shouldn't be," Dad shouted.

Towards the end of our stay on the farm, I had a nasty health scare. I contracted a bug that was going around causing people to lose their balance. My doctor from Waikouaiti came out to see me, and told me some folk were so bad they couldn't lift their heads off their pillows. He said it was caused by a high level of fluid in the inner ear and could be treated with diuretics. He also prescribed sulpha drugs to cure the infection and had them sent down on the bus.

We had a friend at the time who lived in Invercargill; he called to see us late one afternoon on his way north and stayed to dinner. He was very tired and went to sleep in the armchair beside the fire. Frank wound up the alarm clock and set it off beside his ear. Of course, he got the expected reaction and we were all laughing. It was then that I realised the muscles on one side of my face relaxed while the other side stayed up in a smile. It was very frightening: I thought I was having a stroke.

Having never taken sulphur drugs before, and knowing that it was possible to get a reaction from them, I assumed they were the cause.

Our friend went on his way and we went to bed, where my muscles started to make involuntary movements – eyelids twitching – my legs jerking and jumping – an arm flew in the air from under the bedclothes. I felt as if my heart was stopping and starting and knew instinctively I was facing death: it was very frightening. Eventually I got to sleep and when Kim cried out in the early hours I slipped out of bed to go to her and dropped straight to the floor. My legs wouldn't hold me. We phoned the doctor as soon as possible and he came down to see me. Meantime, thinking the culprit was the sulphur drugs, I took just the morning diuretic pill. Had I stopped to think hard, I could have worked out myself that it was the diuretic. Flushing copious fluids out of my body had depleted my muscles of calcium salts, the very thing they work on.

And that was my doctor's diagnosis and he took the pills back to the chemist. But the damage was done. I was incredibly weak and run down, and it took a good six months before I was right again. Always after that, I have been very wary of losing too much sweat. As soon as I get a dull ache in my calf muscles I reach for a teaspoon of salt in a big glass of water.

This couldn't have happened at a worse time. Frank had left Cherry Farm having worn out his welcome yet again, and had applied for, and got, a job down in Southland with accommodation. He left two days after I became sick, leaving me alone with the children. I didn't want to leave; I felt secure there, but at one time I said something to Mum and she said, "You can't stay there forever you know."

There was so much I loved about the place; the security I'd never had, the beauty, the peacefulness, the fields full of mushrooms in mushroom season, small pink ones, and large horse mushrooms sometimes as big as a dinner plate. Dad asked me once why I hadn't picked them and sold them at the gate, and I said he hadn't told me I could.

There was the big cherry plum tree in the garden, the apple, and apricot trees at an old home-site down the valley, and going out with Malcolm to shoot wild sheep that crept from the bush in the evening.

Then there was the strangest phenomenon that I loved to watch. One day I was standing at the front of the house and saw a large white cloud come over the hill from the sea; it floated slowly down the hill in front of me to settle in the valley below, blocking it from view. The next morning it gathered itself together and rose up, up the hill in front of my house and over the hill to the sea. The next afternoon as the temperature dropped about 3.30 pm it happened all over again. I used to wonder if the valley below, where the main homestead stood, was lower than sea level, and what brought about this strange happening.

About a week after he left Frank rang to say he and the boss were coming to shift us down to Balfour the next day. I rang Dad to say I was leaving and he came to see me.

"Why are you leaving?"

I explained that Frank had a house with his job. "And anyway," I said, "Mum said we couldn't stay here forever."

Poor Dad … he really didn't want me to go.

"She had no right to say that," he said.

The truck arrived the next day. I hadn't had time to pack, nor did I have any boxes to do so. His boss grew annoyed; Dad had said I could have all the furniture but we took just the beds and the table and chairs. We had the hens to catch – luckily we still had crates for them – but we left behind Frank's nasty little rooster to fend for himself.

I said a silent, sad farewell to the station and we were on the way – leaving there was just another big mistake in my life. Little did I know it was going to be the same old story: shifting, shifting and shifting.

The new house at Balfour was a big wooden house on a quarter acre, the big back lawn had turned to long coarse grass, and a row of macrocarpa trees (once a hedge) sheltered the place from the southerly wind. There was no place for our hens but with plenty of timber and sheet iron lying about Frank set to and soon had a very good hen house established.

Steven was enrolled in his new school and took it in his stride.

We didn't have enough furniture so I bought a chest of drawers and a few bits and pieces from the secondhand shop at Gore. These I stripped and did up. A few stacked apple boxes with cloths over made bedside tables

We had farm paddocks on both sides, the nearest neighbours hundreds of yards away. Balfour was a Catholic town, as someone said, "if you didn't wear a green tie your face wouldn't fit." Oh, the few busybodies in the district were nice enough to start with. They came around to see who and what we were and then didn't want to know us. I was highly amused: one day down in the village I saw my next-door neighbour duck into a shop so she wouldn't have to speak to me.

We spent the cold and frosty winter there. A few things of note happened. One of my lovely hens got crop bound from eating the long hard grass. To save her from certain death I had to operate and remove the blockage. I had no anaesthetic so used a block of ice to try and deaden the pain; I plucked a few feathers over her crop and cut through the outer skin, then pulling the skin aside so that both cuts were not above one another I cut through the thick meat of the crop and pulled out all the long grass. I stitched her up with a double strand of ordinary black cotton and kept her in a cage with just water until the next day. A week later she was laying eggs again.

The other incident involved a possum. We hadn't been in the house long before we realised we had a boarder above the kitchen; its occasional scratching caused its leg to knock on the ceiling. Out at the back door, we had the usual L-shaped structure, bathroom and toilet, washhouse (laundry) and coal and woodshed. The wash house had had the usual copper boiler but this had been removed (probably stolen) – they were not just valuable for the copper, but the fashion was to polish up the blackened outside and use them in the house as a large indoor plant pot. The removal of the boiler chimney left a hole in the roof for the possum to come and go. We heard it leave one evening and went out with the torch – there it was making its way along the rafters to the exit. We could have put up with it living in the ceiling but for its antics on every frosty night. Possums love to slide down frosty roofs, and our boarder was no exception. It would return from feeding about 1 am but before going to its nest it would climb to the apex of the iron roof. Asleep below, we would awake to a loud screeeech then a thump as it slid down the roof and landed with a bang on the veranda roof. Then it was pitter-patter, pitter-patter, up to the top again, then screeeech, bang. This could go on for half an hour or more before he, or she, got bored with the game and went to bed. After many nights of this we became a little annoyed and Frank decided to set a trap. Gin traps are now outlawed, as they should be because of their cruelty, but at that time they were being used. We set the trap outside the exit and tied it down with binder twine. In the morning the trap was gone. I felt really guilty that it had got away dragging the trap and hoped that someone would find it quickly and put it out of its misery. But at least we had no more disturbed sleep. Possums had been introduced from Australia, goodness knows why, because the effects had been devastating. Here was a prime example of why an animal from one country should never be taken to another. Opossums (as they are called in New Zealand) are wreaking havoc on the native forests by eating out the new young shoot of all the trees, while in Australia they are a protected species.

I should have expected it: within a few months, Frank found fault with his welding job and applied for a job on the rabbit board at Pukerau a few miles north on the main road. There was a house to go with it. He got the job, so once more we were on the road again.

The house was just off the main north-south road and was almost new. Our predecessor had taken away all the flooring so we bought very cheap vinyl for the kitchen floor. There was a nice hen house for the chooks and while there our little bantam hatched out a new batch of Barred Rocks for us. I also lost one of the layers; she was unwell for weeks before she died and when I did an autopsy on her I found a huge almost white liver. I wondered if it was a form of poultry hepatitis and if any of the other hens would catch it but they never did.

The garden was a mess so I set about weeding. I planted seeds by the path to the front door, but a very late snow put paid to those. Steven, poor lad, went to another new school at Pukerau, his third in less than two years.

Frank's job consisted of going out around the various farms with the gun dogs shooting any rabbits or hares the dogs may put up. I went out with him one day and thought what a lovely, carefree job he had. Sometimes he and the boss went out night shooting with a spotlight on the roof of the ute. They not only got rabbits but lots of possums.

I thought Frank was happy with the job; the wages were not great but we had a free house after all. As for me I liked Pukerau and would have been quite happy to stay there forever.

One evening I was invited to a get-together at someone's house. I put on my nice green woollen frock and did my long hair up in a chignon. It seemed to surprise them that I was really quite respectable and they asked me to join the country women's institute. I declined gracefully, sensing that for Frank the winds of discontent were already blowing.

One night a Maori lady came to ask if she could have some of the sow thistles from the overrun garden (before I had cleared it). She said it was called *puha* and they cooked it with meat; we were invited to a party. This was my first meeting with New Zealand's lovely carefree Maori people. It turned out they were a shearing gang and had just finished a big shearing job. That night I learned to cook Puha and still cook it today whenever I can find it as it is one of the most nutritional weeds – along with nettles – that you can eat.

Each morning a tall brown-haired girl with a strange ethereal look about her came down the hill and turned past the house; she wore her immaculate school uniform and was on the way to catch the school bus. I wondered who she was. Little did I know that many years later I would meet her again and, as I write 54 years later, she is still my friend.

While in Pukerau I got a job cleaning the local hall just around the corner from our house – all I really had to do was sweep it out and clean up the kitchen. The floor was very dirty, covered with beer stain and built-up dirt; I decided to wash it, but several hours and many buckets of water later it looked worse than ever. So much for trying to be perfect! I also got a job as a cleaner out on one of the farms. My employer was a little bottle blonde by the name of Dolly. She didn't really need a cleaner but seriously needed a friend and took to me straight away, not that she was my type at all. She told me a lot about herself plus the fact that her husband became very violent when he'd been drinking. I didn't like him at all but was smart enough not to show it. To me, he was just a big country bumpkin oaf.

Sadly Frank tired of his job on the rabbit board after about three months and all my hard work in the house and garden yet again was for nothing. He applied for, and got, a job over at Deep Cove on the west coast where they were building the end of the tailrace tunnel which would take water from Lake Manapori, through the underground power station built into the tunnel and out into the sea at Deep Cove. The old N.Z. *S.S Wanganella* had been sailed into the fiord and moored in Deep Cove to accommodate the workers at that end. The wages for a welder were huge. At last, I thought, we would save enough for a deposit on a house.

We moved to a house on a farm out of Mataura; I think the area was called Otakarama. The place had once had a magnificent garden; there was a big orchard with apple and pear trees, a hen shed with a big hen run enclosed with wire netting. Either side of the gate to the run the netting was smothered with climbing roses better than anything I had ever seen or have seen since. They both had small flowers, one white, the other pink – absolutely beautiful. Rock gardens, now infested with weeds, ran around the base of the house walls. There was lawn on one side and a big shrubbery on the other. Inside we had three bedrooms, a lounge, big kitchen with a green enamelled wood stove to cook on, a bathroom and toilet. Being a wooden house it groaned horribly at night as it settled down on its piles after a warm day. I would be lying in bed trying to sleep when a huge creak would come from the passageway. Given my insane fear of the dark, I would convince myself that someone was there and reach for the shotgun by my bed. I must have roamed the house with the gun at some time every night.

I asked the farmer if he would mow the lawn for me which he did and I did what I could to tidy the garden. It was summer, our lovely hens were happy in their new home; the bantams had another small house to roost in and during the day they had the run of the garden. Our scatty black mutt was chained to his kennel by the garden gate and had to be walked every day; the last thing I wanted was him chasing sheep again. As I had been left with the car and didn't have a licence I took my driving test and passed.

At last the school holidays came to an end. I enrolled Steven at the Otakarama School, taking him to meet the school bus at the top of the hill each morning and collecting him again in the afternoon. The children had played happily for weeks so poor wee Kim missed her brother badly when she was left on her own. Several times during the day she would come into the house to ask: "Steedy come home now?"

"No darling, not yet. We will go and get him soon."

Frank's wages were being paid into a bank account for which I had a cheque book; I decided to buy her a doll's pram. We found a grey steel one in Mataura which she happily tucked her dolls into and pushed them around the yard.

One day I had some bags of coal delivered from town and the driver, who I was very wary of, took a shine to our unusual hens and asked if he could buy them. I told him if I ever did decide to sell them I would want ... and I named some crazy price each for them. To my amazement, he said he would pay that. To get rid of him I said I would give it some thought and let him know.

At 11 o'clock at night about two weeks later there was a loud knocking at the door. I woke with a start, petrified. Who could it be? The dog hadn't barked.

The knocking came again. I slid out of bed and, reaching for the shotgun, made my way to the door.

"Who is it?"

"It's (he gave his name) ... I've come for the hens."

"How dare you come here at this hour, and I haven't said I would sell them."

I knew full well that it wasn't the hens he'd come for – he knew I was here on my own and thought he might get lucky.

He made some lame excuse about thinking I may have changed my mind.

"I've got a double-barrel shotgun in my hand," I told him. "If you don't leave right away I will open the door and shoot you."

I heard him walking away and as he passed the kennel the dog flew out and barked at him. *That's right*, I thought, *you silly mutt, let the man in and then come to my defense after you hear my angry voice.*

The next morning I phoned his work and spoke to the boss's wife. She agreed with me it was a damn stupid thing he'd done and promised to see he was spoken to and forbidden to come near the place again.

Dolly from the farm rang me one day. Could she come out to visit? Of course I said yes, and she duly arrived. She also took a shine to the hens and wanted to know if we would swap them and the bantams for a piglet. I wasn't keen to see the bantams go – they were so tame – but knowing in my heart that sooner or later we would have to leave and there may nowhere for the hens at the next place, I reluctantly agreed.

A week later I arrived home to find them all gone and a small pig in the run. I felt quite sad.

Frank came home after he'd been away about a month. I saw him come down the hill and climb the fence onto the road outside the orchard and went out to meet him.

He seemed quite happy with his job which was good news to me, and he left after a few days to go back.

Alas, a few weeks later, on a very wet and stormy night the phone rang about 8 pm. "I'm at the Mossman Pub. Come and get me," he commanded. My dreams of a deposit on a house flew out the window; I wanted to weep.

I aroused the children from their beds, donned coats over their pyjamas and wrapped them in blankets in the back seat of the car. I had never driven at night; the heavy rain and blustery wind did nothing for my confidence. I was very, very nervous.

It is approximately 100 miles to Mossman. I must have been three-quarters of the way there and on a long straight piece of road when a car approaching seemed to have its lights on full beam. I flicked my lights to remind them to dim them, but they must have been already dimmed although faultily aligned. The driver, instead of flashing them to let me know, put them on full beam and left them there. With the windscreen wipers barely able to cope with the heavy rain and the narrow road I was petrified I would have an accident.

Arriving at the pub I found my husband having a great time and not wanting to leave, then all the way home I was regaled about the bastards he'd had to work with and how the management told him he couldn't leave so he had just walked out, all the way over the pass in the bush. Having reached a road, he hitched a ride on a tourist bus to Mossman. A few days later the police arrived to see if he'd made it home and hadn't become lost in the bush.

He stayed at home for the next few weeks until we no longer had any money in the bank, then went off to find another job, one he could ride his bike to. That too didn't last long and he decided we would have to move into Mataura because he needed the car. The landlord came to visit me; he was all smiles saying he had just rented the other farmhouse just along the road and we would have neighbours. He was less than happy when I told him we were leaving.

The pig was now a few months old and he had to go. I was appalled at how he had ruined the hen runs by rooting underneath the wire netting and leaving big holes, but even though we couldn't keep him caged he didn't run away, just made himself at home in the garden. One evening Frank caught him by the back legs and shot him. We put him in the bath and shaved off the bristles. Not having a freezer we had to fill our small fridge. My sister Lorna and husband Jack came down from the Taieri for dinner and took some meat home.

Our next home was in Mataura and Steven shifted to his fifth school in two years. A local lad had married an Australian lady some years older than himself and they were going to Australia to live, but keeping their house in case they wanted to return. It was a nice enough place, the garden enclosed by a thick hedge but the house was very damp. Soon I developed rheumatics in my shoulder and was in awful pain. I also developed a bad chest infection.

Kim had also developed an infection while we were living at Otakarama; her temperature would go up to 104 degrees. It was now winter and very cold so I was reluctant to take her out. When I asked her where it was sore she would tap with her fist behind her right ear.

After sleeping most of the day wrapped up on the couch her temperature would go down. The next day after dropping Steven off at the school bus I set off for town to see the doctor. This happened three times in a matter of weeks. I told him I thought there was something wrong with her ear, but each time he would look and say. "There's nothing wrong with her ear." This cost 5 shillings a visit, no small sum in those days.

We didn't usually go Friday night shopping; but as the shops were shut all weekend in those days and we were now both working during the day, Friday night it had to be. With the children wrapped warmly, we set off. Kim was in a grizzly mood and as the evening wore on she became quite distraught. In desperation we took her to a chemist who poured a pink syrup for her, but when he asked her to drink it she lashed out and knocked it out of his hand. This was so unlike our lovely daughter I became alarmed. It is easy to be wise afterward but I now know we should have taken her straight to the emergency department at the hospital. Instead we took her home and into bed with us.

Eventually, she stopped crying and slept. When I woke in the morning she was sound asleep but the mess on her pillow told the story. The poor wee girl had otitis media, an infection of the middle ear. Her eardrum had burst and spewed pus six inches across the pillow. I called the doctor who came out after surgery.

"Oh," he said, "she has otitis media. You will have to take her to the hospital."

This was handy for me as I was working at the hospital. I had asked the lovely Matron if I could get a nursing job but she said there wasn't a vacancy. She was however desperate for someone who could sew; would I work in the sewing room? I was only too pleased to do so and enjoyed the job for the time I was there.

Each lunch hour I went to see Kim; she'd been given a huge dose of antibiotics. After two days I noticed she'd come out in a rash, which the junior nurse said was probably the soap but I didn't agree and reported it to the Sister. It transpired it had been caused by the medication and after the rash subsided she got patches of dermatitis in the crease of her elbows, knees and one in her hair. These were to plague her until she was well into her teens.

I changed our doctor to an excellent older one in Gore who told me that of course, the other doctor should have seen the inflammation in Kim's ear.

So it was, that when the erring doctor sent his bill for 31 shillings for a home visit, I shot off a reply saying I had no intention of paying it. He had, I wrote, caused my daughter appalling pain by his failure to diagnose her infection even after several visits. If he still insisted I should pay I intended to report him to the medical council for malpractice. We heard no more about it and a few weeks later said doctor admitted himself voluntarily to Cherry Farm Mental Hospital to get himself dried out. He was an alcoholic.

Before all this happened we had planned a trip to Invercargill to see a show called *Paris by Night*; the company travelled with twelve tons of gear and costumes and was by all accounts not to be missed.

Not wanting to leave the dog in the house while I took Kim to hospital I shut him in a big wire cage that surrounded and covered in the currant bushes in the back yard. When we got home he'd gone. The only way out was a foot wide gap at the top of the door and somehow he'd managed to climb up and escape. We searched until dark without success, then someone came to tell us he'd been run over about two miles away; he'd been taken to the vet but had died.

So it was with sad thoughts we drove down to see the show; little Kim in hospital and the dog dead. What a day!

The three of us watched the show from away up in the gods, we were the only ones there – the cheap seats were all Frank was prepared to pay for, but the show was great, what we could see of it.

Frank had two jobs in the three months we stayed at Mataura, first as a welder then on the chain at the freezing works where thousands of sheep were slaughtered and frozen to be shipped overseas.

One day he went off to Invercargill and returned with a kombi van. We should, he said, go to the North Island where the wages were better.

So we packed up Father's new straw hat
The wickets and the cricket bat
A trouser press, a brush and comb
A writing case and a gramophone.

Well, we couldn't take the gramophone – we had bought a good old oak one at an auction along with several leather-bound record-holders filled with mostly classical LPs but they all had to go. How true the proverb that a rolling stone gathers no moss.

All the local kids, some from rough families, came to watch us pack the van with what we had left. I came out with a little treasure I had bought in Panama, a small stuffed alligator, and tucked it into a corner. Later I found it missing so one of them had helped themselves to it.

At last, we were away, and we made it to my beloved Saddle Hill which we had to climb to get to Dunedin before breaking down. It was obvious that the head gasket had gone – once more Frank had been conned into a van that needed repairs. For someone who always said you couldn't trust anyone he never seemed to learn.

The van coughed and spluttered and made it to the top at last. From Lookout Point, we coasted down and found a garage. They said it would take the rest of the day to fix and to return at 5 pm to pick it up, which we did. I thought we would be paying cash for the job and was aghast when I heard Frank ask them to send the bill to our old address in Mataura. We would be back in three weeks, he assured them and would pay the account then. I knew then that the account would never be paid and the thought horrified me.

It was dark when we passed the road going down to Deepdale station, and we'd already found another fault in the van – when the lights were dipped they went out altogether.

On reaching Waikouaiti, where we put up in the caravan park for the night, I phoned Mum and Dad and told them we were off to the North Island. Whatever must they have thought?

The trip to the top of the South Island was unremarkable and two days later we lined up in a queue to drive aboard the inter-island ferry and travel to Wellington. Instead of taking the main route up the centre of the North Island, and the desert road below Mounts Ruapehu and Nauruhoe we headed to the right and up the East coast to Masterton, where I believe Grandfather Donaldson is buried, then on to Hastings and Napier. A day later we headed inland again to Lake Taupo, a huge inland sea. Frank wanted to look up an old girlfriend at Tauranga. Years before he had boarded there with her parents and he'd told me he had seduced their fourteen-year daughter. He'd told me the story of how he'd climbed out of his window at night and into hers. I had no wish to meet the girl but had no choice in the matter, so off to Rotorua we went and on to Tauranga. Frank had phoned ahead and the parents were expecting us. Obviously they had no idea about what had been going on for months under their roof.

All afternoon I felt dreadful. Not only was I scruffy because my clothes had seen better days but I had discovered a long black hair on my chin and had no tweezers to pull it out with. I tugged and tugged with my fingernails but it wouldn't budge. Frank was quite impervious to my discomfort. We were welcomed with open arms and eventually the girl arrived with her husband; I found her quite brash and self-confident, but then I was still a meek and mild little person, completely under my husband's thumb. I was so relieved when we were on our way again and heading for Auckland. Once there we just drove straight through, Frank still not looking for a job. We headed North again to Whangarei and beyond, to the beautiful Bay of Islands then back to the west coast and down to Dargaville then south again to Wellsford where a job for a welder was advertised with a house attached. We were almost out of money so Frank applied and got the job.

At last, a roof over our heads! Steven had been quite naughty on occasions as he always was when he was insecure. One night when we camped he was told not to go out on the mudflats, which was exactly what he did. He came back and climbed into the van with a thick layer of black mud clinging to his shoes. When Frank yelled at him he climbed up into the back on top of all the bedding and when Frank dragged him down a large bottle of stew I had preserved for the trip got knocked down and smashed. I am not sure what upset me the most, Steven's naughtiness or the loss of a meal.

Our new house was an old schoolhouse, a solid kauri bungalow with a veranda along the front. It sat with a few acres of land around it a few miles south of Wellsford where Frank was to work. There was no sign of the school, it had probably been sold and carted off on a truck to be someone's farm shed, but there were big heaps of cut down Macrocarpa trees. Steven went off to his sixth new school at Wellsford, being collected each morning by the school bus.

Our neighbours just up the road were the Cox family. They had a small farm and a sawmill where Mr Cox cut timber for the local farmers. He was also a champion woodcutter and competed in wood chopping competitions at the agricultural shows. I soon found out what good people they were: they came with vegetables and other goodies to welcome us. Mrs Cox had a massive garden in a paddock behind the house where she grew enough food to last the year, preserving what couldn't be eaten straight away. They had a cow, a young jersey cross that of course needed milking twice a day. Mr Cox hated the chore so, when he found out I came from a dairy farm, he asked me if I would like to take on the job of milking. As we were already getting several pints of milk a day for free I could hardly say no. It was some years since I'd milked a cow, by hand or otherwise, but I soon settled in to doing the job, singing softly to the cow until she got used to me. In return we got a bucket full of creamy milk each day – we'd never had it so good.

Of course, when we moved in we had no furniture so Frank took to going down to Auckland to the auctions, coming back with all manner of weird and wonderful things he'd bought for a song.

On the 5th November, the boss decided we were to have a bonfire night complete with fireworks and food. All the employees were to come with their wives and children and the big heap of dead trees were to provide the fire. After the fireworks had been lit and the fire was dying down all the men collected on the veranda and all the women gathered in the kitchen. How I hated that dreadful New Zealand habit.

I went out and rounded them all up and told them they had to come in and mingle. They did and everyone had a fun night. The next day the boss thanked me, saying it was the best party they'd ever been to.

There are two things I remember about our stay there. One day there was the worst thunderstorm I'd ever experienced, huge claps of thunder so close overhead literally shook the house on its foundations and the rain came down as though being poured from a giant bucket. In no time the water was flooding down the hill past the house several inches deep. Everything that wasn't fastened down was washed with it, to be caught up in the fence above the road. What a mess.

Another day I was putting the washing out. The grass was quite long and green underneath the clothesline. I moved my foot and the most appalling scream came from beneath it. I have always been a jumpy person, easily startled by loud noises, and that scream, so human-like, had my heart beating wildly. I knelt down quietly and carefully parted the grass and found a green frog: I had broken its leg. I wanted to cry and would have given anything not to have done that. I picked it up gently. Having no money and no car, all I could think of was putting it out of its misery, which I did. That little frog has haunted my thoughts ever since.

I loved it at Wellsford. The children were settled, I had great friends next door, there was a wage coming in … what more could one ask for?

But it wasn't to last: the usual three months had elapsed and Frank once more had itchy feet. He announced we were going to Auckland. So once more we packed up our meagre belongings and set off.

We found a brand new flat at a suburb called Roseneath, (I think) and oh! how I hated that place. Of all the homes I have had it was the only place I could never make into a home. It had a long lounge with floor to ceiling windows that looked out onto a right of way. The place was on high foundations so the floor was about eye level to anyone walking past and *it had no curtains!* The only place with any privacy was a bedroom, one at each end, where the windows were high on the wall. It was living in a goldfish bowl, especially at night. It is only now as I write that I realise the owners must have been breaking the law: I am sure that New Zealand law stated that homes being rented had to have cooking and washing facilities, and curtains. But there we were, each day people passing to get to the homes behind looking in to see us and our pathetic pieces of old furniture.

Kim was now five years old and school-age so she started at Roseneath Primary with Steven, which was not far away. I have no idea where Frank worked, but I got a job at the Shepherds Wools factory within walking distance of home. I loved it. First I was put in with a row of girls unwinding the wool which came in skeins. We loaded the skein onto a thing like a bike wheel and set it turning and the wool unwound loosely into a bin. These bins went to feed the big machine behind us that wound the wool into balls. I'd been working there just two weeks when once again I was promoted.

The foreman said to me, "I have been watching you. You are very quick with your hands; I would like you to join Daphne on the wool winding machine."

And so it was. Daphne was a Pom and quite dismissive of me at first, but after one day when I had learned the ropes, she found I was just as quick, if not quicker than her. She had to quickly change her tune and we got on well.

The machine had twenty bins of wool behind it and twenty cloth-covered sticks pointing upwards. We took the end of the wool and wrapped it around the stick, stomped our foot on the bar below and the stick ballooned out and spun around quickly until a ball was wound around it, the balloon went down and then we slipped a paper label over each one before flipping them all into a trough above. The paper label was flicked with a thumb to open it and the manoeuvre took less than a second. We were allowed three knots to a ball, so we always ended up with several small quarter balls we couldn't use. We were allowed to take these home, within reason, so I ended up with a bag full of useful bits with which to knit Fair Isle which I loved doing, and the children had several free striped jerseys in the years to come.

Needless to say within three months we were on the move again.

Frank had got a job as a welder for the shutdown at Christmas in the big paper mill in Kawerau in the Bay of Plenty. Every year at Christmas the paper mill and the wood chip mill shut down for a few weeks at Christmas, that was when they brought tradesmen in to do all the repairs.

Kawerau is a mill town and all the houses are owned by the mills, so we had to seek accommodation elsewhere. Lake Rotoma, just over the hill, had long served as a dormitory place for Kawerau workers and it was here we found a holiday home to let for the winter. The place had two bedrooms, a big lounge, toilet and hand basin but no bathroom. It was just above the road that followed the lake around and was on Maori land. The lack of a bath didn't bother us too much – just down the road between Lakes Rotuehu and Lake Rotoma we had the Soda Springs, boiling water bubbling up from the ground mixing with cold water spilling from Lake Rotoma making it a great place to soak once or twice a week.

A vacant block separated us from *The El Toreador*, a coffee lounge and a motel complex which also had a big swimming pool plus the local Post Office and telephone exchange. They also hosted wedding receptions there; although these were only a few each year. As I had to collect my mail there I soon became friends with the owners, Bonny and Leon Stack.

Frank's job at Kawerau lasted about a month until the mills opened again for work. He could have worked there permanently but he said he wasn't going to tie himself down in a factory. He did get another job there for a sub-contractor but of course, that didn't last. It was moving on time again, or so he thought.

The children had settled well into the Rotoma School; they had two good teachers, a married couple who were strictly no-nonsense. I put my foot down.

"I am not, absolutely not, moving away from here," I told him. "Steven has been to seven schools and you are not moving him again. You can go where you like, work where you like, but we are staying here." And stay we did, for the next eight years.

It was getting near the time when the owners would want their holiday home, (or *bach*, as New Zealanders call them) back for the summer months. I said I wanted a home of our own so we started to look around. There was quite a small modern place with asbestos walls on the hill above the little shop further around the lake, but it didn't see the sun until the afternoon and would have been freezing in winter. The owners were desperate to sell and offered to hold the mortgage for us at more pounds a week than I knew we could pay. I said no. Besides, the place was on Maori land and there would also be a yearly lease to pay for that.

It was at this time that Steven went down with mumps. He wasn't too bad but I caught the germs and I was. My face swelled up until I looked like a giant budda. One morning I got up, opened the big glass door at the front and sat in the sun in my dressing gown, looking down at the lake. Who should turn up but the elderly couple with the house to sell. They took one look at me and tried not to laugh then started to brow-beat me about buying the house. I felt dreadful and wanted to scream "Go away!" but I couldn't have opened my mouth to do so. Eventually they left, not to be seen again.

Previously the Rotoma Timber Company had held the lease of all the land around the lake for twenty years and had coursed the bush for mature trees. During that time they had allowed people to put baches up at any place around the lake they chose. Thus some nice places and some not so nice places had been built. After the timber company's lease had expired the Maori Affairs had sent surveyors in to allocate land to each bach. So it came about that one line went right through one place because the baches had been built too close and friends of mine had been left with their house on one block and their garage and garden on another. They had to pay the lease on two blocks for the rest of their lives. I wasn't too keen on buying on leasehold land.

There was one block of freehold land in Rotoma. Just as one emerged from the bush coming from the direction of Rotorua and met the arm of the lake, an unsealed road went off to the right, passed the garage and grocery shop at the bottom and continued up the hill. This area had been free-holded from the Maoris to Cobb and Co. coaches many years before. It had been the changing station for horses that pulled the coaches from Whakatane to Rotorua. There were several real houses in the street, a few baches, but mostly the building land was bare. It just happened that I saw a For Sale sign right at the top of the street. The place belonged to a retired school teacher and his wife who lived in Rotorua. I rang the number given and arranged to meet him at the house where we had a long talk. He agreed to hold the mortgage for us for a £50 deposit and £6 a week. I didn't know where I was going to get the deposit from but eventually I managed to find it and we all met at a solicitor's office to sign the agreement. At last a home of our own; it wasn't the lovely new place we had dreamed of, just an old dump really, but it was ours, a roof over our heads that no one could take away, or so I thought.

A man called Mr Offord had owned five building sections and built three houses on them, one of which was the one we'd bought. There was a little road going up between us and the big blue wooden house he was living in at the time to the three sections behind us. A bare block was on our other side then, at the point of the hill, he had built another strange long place. I think he had made all three places up as he went along, or when he could scrounge something to build with. Our back door opened into a small L-shaped kitchen with an old black wood stove directly in front of the door. Around the corner the kitchen led into a laundry and the bathroom and toilet beyond. The lounge was in the middle of the house and had glass doors opening on a big deck that had old steel pipes making the safety rails around it. From here we had a wonderful view of the arm of the lake. On still days the dark water reflected the tall native bush on the other side.

We had been in the house just a few weeks when Frank arrived home with a lovely young bitch that looked like a purebred Pointer. She had a golden tan coat with a white blaze on her chest and four white feet. All the white had brown under spots so she was a really beautiful dog. Frank said he'd found her wandering along the desert road. I didn't bother to ask what he was doing away down there. I said that someone must be looking for her and sure enough an advert appeared in the paper describing her perfectly but calling her a Setter. I said we should reply to it but Frank insisted she was a Pointer not a Setter and refused to do so. So Gyp became a member of the family and another mouth to feed.

Thanks to Gyp I met the best friend I have ever had. New Zealand has a problem with hydatid disease; water like cysts that can affect the liver, lungs, or brain. The eggs go from the sheep to the dog and on to humans. All dogs have to be dosed every six months at places set aside for dosing strips. They have something squirted down their throats which gives them violent diarrhoea within minutes from which a sample is taken. Any dogs carrying the disease has to be treated. The dogs hate it and start trembling before they even get to the gate. It was outside the gate that I met Maud. There she was, twenty-two stone and there was I, just seven stone three pounds, and we immediately knew we were soul mates, a friendship that lasted until she died twenty years later.

Maud and her husband Ernie were very good to me over the next few years. Whenever they did alterations to their house they would give me the cast-offs, bits of built-in furniture, firewood and lots of things found their way home. In return, I spent hours helping in her garden and other ways. If I hadn't had Maud as a safety valve to talk to I would probably have had a breakdown. Later, when her Mum had a stroke and became bedridden, I cycled there each day, a nine-mile trip, to give her Mum a bed bath. They paid me for about eight months until it was time for me to go back to work at the *El Toreador* where I worked each summer. Maud said I should go as they couldn't afford to pay me as much as my summer wage.

Her Mum was admitted to hospital. Maud said she wanted me to know that the doctor had asked who had been looking after her, her back he said was in an incredible condition considering she'd been lying on it for so long.

I had started work at the *El Toreador* about a year after we moved into our house, the pay was £6 a week, enough to pay the mortgage but nothing left to buy food. Bonny and Leon had started a new way of eating, a smorgasbord, every Sunday. Word soon got around and the place was packed with people helping themselves to plates of food from the long tables. The work was frantic, clearing plates, refilling dishes, sweeping up after greedy people who filled their plate too full so it overflowed onto the floor, and washing dishes.

One evening, after a frantic day Leon said we all deserved a whiskey and it wasn't until I was riding home and almost fell from my bike that I realised I hadn't eaten since breakfast. When I laughingly told them the next day they were horrified and after that would say, "Billie, will you stop now and have something to eat, and I mean now!"

I had learned to man the telephones, clean the motels, and sort the mail at the little post office so one winter when they both went away together for a week I was left in charge. It was very quiet on winter days, just the odd traveller in for a cuppa. Also during the winter we did all the baking and stacking all kinds of cakes away in boxes in the big chest freezer. Come summer we just had to fill the plates for the display cabinet and let them thaw out.

One day while we were busy baking I had a lovely surprise: some people came in to morning tea and I recognised our Dr Trotter from Oamaru Hospital. He didn't remember me naturally, but we talked for a while. He told me that our nice Sister Scott had died of cancer, that when I was there she had already had a breast removed, something that none of us knew. Maybe that was why she was so nice.

After a year or two, Leon decided to use the vacant section next door to their place to grow vegetables and what a wonderful job he made. After that he just had to go out and get fresh vegies for us to prepare each day.

I hardly know what to write about Frank in the eight traumatic years we lived at Rotoma. Most of the time we wouldn't know where he was, whether he was working, or when he would send some money. Sometimes we would expect him home and he might arrive a week later. As the years went by he would often come home the worst for drink and be violent and aggressive.

When we first moved into our house he came home with a washing machine and a lawnmower. I was really pleased until the bills came in after he had gone and I found he had bought them on hire purchase. There was never enough money to pay the full instalment on either of them. I remember after we changed to decimal currency sending off a letter saying I would give them what I could and sent $2 to each of them, knowing that as long as I paid whatever I could they could not be repossessed. It took me years to pay them off. There were periods during the winter when I wasn't working so we had no income at all – I was always sick with worry. He may be away for a month, then a $20 note would arrive; we needed that every week just to survive.

My sister Lorna was a Godsend; she was a good seamstress and would send all her girls out-grown clothes to me, they being both older than Kim. Thus Kim was always reasonably dressed. With Steven, I struggled. I could knit jerseys and make him a few clothes but it was hard.

As for me, Frank would sometimes arrive home and say, "Look, I bought you this," and hand over a blouse. I never knew whether it was stolen, or from where it had come. We always had plenty of toilet paper as he rarely left the public toilet without bringing the toilet paper with him. Unfortunately it was usually the little boxes of shiny squares that were horrible to use. He always carried a newspaper with him and would drop a pair of socks into the fold and to get a newspaper from the honesty box he would tap a coin on the top to make it sound as though money was being dropped in, pick up a paper and walk away. I lived in constant fear of his being caught and shaming us all.

After a few years of him turning up with clothes for me, I asked why he couldn't just give me the money to buy my own clothes and give me the pleasure of shopping. He looked at me as though I'd gone mad and told me I was ungrateful. Unfortunately, he never bought me knickers or bras, so eventually they were almost rags.

Christmas was always a struggle. There was only one year that he was in work at that time, it always being 'last on first off' with the employers.

It must have been before I worked for Bonny and Leon because we were flat broke. The children were looking forward to getting presents as they do, and we had nothing. Frank said when his mother and father were hard up they got an orange and a new penny in their stockings and that's what our kids would have to get. I will never forget the look of their faces that Christmas morning – an orange and a shiny shilling. I wanted to cry.

One morning, at about 9.30, Frank set off from the house to look for work. At 3 pm I was preparing dinner at the kitchen sink when he arrived back, the top of the van completely smashed in. When I raced out to meet him he said he'd been heading north out of Rotorua about lunchtime when a logging truck had come round the corner towards him. He'd swerved to avoid it and the van had rolled. Someone had helped put the van right side up and he had come home. I asked him where he'd been until lunchtime and he said he'd stopped at the pub for a drink. Of course it wasn't his fault, it never was, he would do the most blatant things wrong but it was always someone else's fault. Luckily he hadn't been stopped by the police and been done for drunk driving. For me it was just another cross to bear; we already owed $150 for having the engine fixed just weeks before, and needless to say we had no insurance.

A week or two later he set out again and I didn't hear from him for about three weeks when some money arrived. Later, a letter arrived from money lenders and I found out he had borrowed $100 against the van, they wanted the first instalment. I was absolutely shattered, not just about the $100 but he had borrowed it at huge 25% interest. His stupidity knew no bounds!

With no work and no money again Frank applied for, and got, a job as a welder at Matata over on the coast behind Lake Rotoma. There was a house going with the job but I intended to stay put. However, a few weeks later he hitch-hiked a ride home at the weekend and told me the van had been repossessed by the people he borrowed the money from. We now had no means of transport. The children and I moved to Matata.

The wooden house was a fairly modern one, the only drawback was that it backed on to a railway line. It was winter and on frosty nights when the train came through each night at 2.30 am with its heavy load of logs, the wheels would slip on the small incline behind the house. The noise was unbelievable. A slow *chuff, chuff, chuff,* and then lots of loud chuffs in quick succession; we could almost hear the driver say, "Whoops, let's start again." And again we would hear *chuff, chuff, chuff* and again the wheels would lose their grip. This might happen several times before the train reached level ground and went on its way.

Most of the inhabitants of Matata were Maori but our neighbour was Pakeha (white).

One day I was doing Kim's hair getting her ready for a children's party when I discovered she had lice. I freaked out and rushed next door.

"Don't you inspect their hair every week?" asked my neighbour.

"Why would I do that? I have never in my life or theirs seen lice."

"Well," she said, "you have to when the kids go to this school."

She produced a bottle and told me to douse her hair in it; it did kill the lice but two weeks later she was crawling with their babies. I sent an irate letter to the school and the teacher found that the little boy she sat next to had them so she sent him home.

We met a young couple while there: he'd been in jail for stealing cars and she was a rather cheap little blonde I will call Sue. She would call for me in the morning and we would ride our bikes down to the few shops. I found it embarrassing the way she hailed and spoke to all the men we passed. She seemed to know them all. I started going early or fibbing and saying I had been, rather than be seen with her. Knowing these two was to have repercussions for us later …

While at Matata we saw a purebred black and tan pointer dog that a part Maori guy used when duck shooting; Frank decided that we should let him be mated to Gyp. So it was when she came on heat the dog paid us a visit. The agreement was the dog owner was to get his pick of the pups. The Matata job lasted no longer than any of the others and soon we were home again. Frank left again to get work.

Living at Rotoma we really needed a car; we were twenty-five miles from Rotorua and nine miles from the supermarkets in Kawerau. Somehow Frank found $100 as part payment for a small car from a local man. He assured us it would get a warrant of fitness. All cars in New Zealand have to go to Government testing sites every six months to be tested for roadworthiness. This can be quite a trauma when you have an old car and no money. As it happened the new car didn't pass the test and we had to find more money to fix it. A few weeks later, when Frank was away and I hadn't seen any money for weeks, the previous owner came to see me demanding the other $50 we owed him. Sick to death of the constant worry, I exploded.

"You said it would get a warrant of fitness," I yelled. "We had to spend more than that to get it fixed."

He was so shocked at seeing this crazy spitfire screaming at him that he backed off and we never heard another word from him.

Sometime later I told Frank the car brakes were bad and needed looking at but he declared there was nothing wrong with them; he hated being told there was something wrong; he would have made a good ostrich.

One day I set off to Kawerau to get some groceries. I climbed away from the lake to the top of the hill and braked as the car built up speed downhill. NOTHING! Frantically I pumped the pedal until I got a reaction. *Right, I told myself, you will just have to pump the brake pedal and use the hand brake until you get down to the flat.*

Now the road to the Kawerau turn off was steep, with many hairpin bends and big drops down into the valley below on one side. Everything went well until I rounded another hairpin and saw in front of me two cars behind a slow-moving logging truck carrying huge logs to the mill. There was no time to brake or even grab the hand brake. The car in front of me was one of those big old square jobs, and there was nowhere to go but between it and the bank. My car hit the bank with a crash and bounced up onto a small ledge about a yard off the ground then bounced down again onto the road again about three feet behind the other car. As I hit the bank I had glanced right and seen an elderly man driving, with probably his wife in the passenger seat. In the back seat sat two elderly ladies, and not one of them seemed to notice my car right beside them.

My car had come to a standstill, nose into the bank, and all I could do was sit there and giggle. The truck and both cars drove off down the hill completely oblivious of the near-miss. Eventually, having given them time to get well ahead, I backed out of the bank and made my way in second gear and using the hand brake I parked at last outside the supermarket. Suddenly I was shaking so badly I couldn't get out of the car. Delayed shock had set in with the vengeance.

After I had pulled myself together and finished the shopping I took the car to a friend of ours who owned a small business. He found the brake fluid reservoir was empty and filled it for me and bled the brakes, charging me nothing so I could make my safe way home. How true the saying "A friend in need is a friend indeed".

That incident was to change my life. I finally realised that my husband could not be trusted, and from that day, until the day many years later when I left him if anything needed doing, I either did it myself or got it done. I became a jack of all trades and master of most.

A bailiff arrived at the house one day while I was alone. The people who Frank had borrowed the money from had been to court and got an order for anything of ours of value to be seized to pay the debt. They had taken the van to the VW place where we owed money for the engine repairs so didn't get their money back. I showed the bailiff through the house and explained my predicament. He said he didn't want to cause me any more trouble; he would tell them we didn't have anything worth seizing and he had enough old cars already in his yard that he couldn't sell so he would not take the car. So that was one debt written off.

Another time Frank set off to look for work and it was a month before I heard from him again. It was winter so I wasn't working and had no income. I decided to sell our six barred rock hens as I no longer had feed for them. The parents of one of Steven's school friends arrived to buy them but instead of handing over the $8.00 I so desperately needed they asked if I would accept a boy's bike for Steven in exchange. Too proud to tell them of my desperate situation I had no option to agree, but when they had gone I sat down and cried.

Also during that month, Gyp gave birth to her puppies. I went out one morning and there they were in her kennel. I was mortified. Quickly I shifted her into the now empty hen house and ran with any old blankets, water, and food I could find. But I had nowhere enough to feed her with and she took to escaping (I never found out how) and going to look for roadkill on the road below. I had read an old book about breeding Pointers where it said that if a golden dog was mated to a black and white one the result was a mixture of black and white pups and white with black spots; so it was, we had three black with white chests and two white with black spots. These two grew into beautiful long-haired Setters while the others stayed short hair. This proved to me yet again that Gyp was the Setter the people had advertised for.

One morning after the children had gone to school I set out on foot for the *El Toreador* to see if there was any mail, intending then to catch the bus to Kawerau, draw the 35 shillings I had in the bank and buy what groceries I could. I arrived in the kitchen where Bonny and Leon were having a late breakfast.

"There's a letter for you," said Leon and ran down to the post office below to get it. He handed me an Air letter. I took one look and died inside!

"Oh thanks," I said, trying hard to show no emotion.

The letter was from Frank, and it had an Australian stamp! I spent a few minutes more chatting then went down to the road to wait for the bus. Minutes later Leon came charging down. "Billie," he demanded, "did that letter come from Frank?"

"Yes, Leon."

"What the bloody hell is he doing in Australia?"

"I don't know, Leon."

"How are you managing? Do you need some money?"

"No, Leon, look, I will be fine. I have 35 shillings in the bank. I am going to draw it and buy some food."

"35 shillings!" he exploded' "You can't live on 35 shillings!"

Then the bus arrived and I climbed aboard. That afternoon their daughter Cheryl arrived with a big box of corn flakes, bread, butter and lots more. There was also a big leg of slightly fridge-burnt mutton for me to feed Gyp with. I was so grateful.

Bonny arrived the next day to say she was taking me to the social welfare in Rotorua; "This," she said, "has been going on long enough."

She went in first to see the lady and goodness knows what she said to them because when I left I had money to pay the weekly mortgage and enough over to pay for food.

It was wonderful, a weekly secure income. I wrote to Frank at the Sydney G.P.O. saying he had better stay there as I now had a settled income and I was sick of his behaviour. Unfortunately, it wasn't to be.

About a month later I was sitting watching television after the children had gone to bed; it was late and there was a tap on the front window. It was Frank – he'd been out there watching me. Reluctantly I let him in. Of course, it wasn't his fault that we'd been left without money. Hadn't he gone to the income tax department before he left and extracted a promise that his $70 tax rebate would be sent the next week? I did his tax returns every year as he wasn't capable of doing it, and every year he got back every penny of tax he had paid because he hadn't earned enough for a couple and two children to live on. His 'going to the tax department' was probably a downright lie because I knew he didn't seem to have the ability to look ahead at the consequences of his actions. But after a few Sherries from the bottle he brought home, and a couple of hours of his wheedling charm, I agreed to take him back. And the whole rotten mess started again.

A few days after this he came home complaining of severe pain in his upper back. He hadn't got off scot-free from rolling the van and it had now come back to haunt him. This was the beginning of his being at home for the next nine months. I drove him into the doctors who sent him to a private Physiotherapist thus running up the first big bill. After three visits we returned again to the doctor.

"What did he say?" I asked.

"He just said keep going to the Physio."

I was appalled. It didn't matter to Frank that he was running up a bill we would be hounded for, but it mattered to me. The bill was already worth five week's mortgage, off which nothing was being paid. I sprang to my feet and charged into the startled doctor's office and blurted out, "You have sent him to the Physio again! We can't pay the bill he has run up already, and we have no income … nothing."

The doctor had the good grace to look embarrassed and said he was sorry, and of course, he would give Frank a referral to the public hospital in Rotorua.

Sue from Matata came to our rescue: she arrived one day with an Albanian who she'd been working for at a takeaway shop in Kawerau, she and her husband having moved there. The boss's name was Sam and he had several alarming tin teeth in his smile. Sue was leaving the job, he explained and had recommended me as a replacement. I grabbed the chance with both hands. The wages were really good and the job was full-on cooking hamburgers and easy meals. A jukebox in the corner spewed out raucous music all day long until we had heard the latest popular song so many times we felt like smashing the record.

With a steady income, I was able to pay off some bills and catch up a little on the mortgage.

I had been there about two months when one day, just as I was about to go home, Frank arrived at my workplace. He wanted me to come to the pub where he'd been drinking with Mr Offord (who we always called Old Offord,) our next-door neighbour. I told him I was very tired and wanted to go home but he insisted. It turned out they had been drinking for hours and I could see by his demeanour that when we left Frank would do his Dr Jeckle and Mr. Hyde act – his behaviour could change in seconds from Mr Funny-ha-ha to a vicious nasty person.

Now Frank had always had trouble with constipation. Once he went for two weeks without a bowel motion, and the smells he made in the house, not only then but at all times, were unbelievable. The kids used to say "Ah Dad!" and he would say, "That is a message from port belly to port arsehole to say it is sending down a load of shit."

"You are disgusting," I would shout, as the kids and I hurriedly evacuated the room. So there he was that afternoon, sitting at a table with Old Offord dropping these appalling smells. Old Offord said "Oh for God's sake, Frank," but Frank thought it was hugely funny. Even people sitting several tables away were beginning to glare. I wanted the ground to swallow me up.

I decided I had to get away. "I'm going to the loo," I said, jumping up and grabbing my bag. I stayed a very short time then came out and headed for the door. Unfortunately it was a long way from the toilets to the door – I was almost there when I was grabbed roughly from behind.

"Where the hell do you think you are going?"

"I'm going home, Frank. The children are on their own and they will be wanting their dinner."

"Give me the car keys." He snatched my bag and took them out. I headed towards a shop and he demanded to know where I was going, giving me a flying shove. Two woman looking out the window of their shop looked startled but didn't come to my rescue.

"We need bread," I said.

"I'll get it," and, pushing me ahead, we went into the bread shop.

"Please, Frank, will you let me drive?" I asked. But no … he declared he would drive and so we set off. The road from Kawerau up to the main road is a steady incline with a small drop on either side. I was so afraid and twice had to grab the wheel to keep us on the road we were weaving so badly. Eventually we arrived at the top where there was a big pull in. He stopped the car, grabbed me by the shoulders and viciously bashed my head against the top of the door again and again then said, "I'm going for a pee," and he got out taking the car keys with him.

The trim around the door was like a springy stainless steel strip which had long since lost its covering. I felt the cut skin above my eyebrow. I had to get away! Another car pulled in but stopped about twenty feet away; Frank thankfully had stepped behind a bush.

I opened the door and ran. There were two big advertising hoardings, so I ducked behind the nearest one then slid quietly into the bush. I saw him go back to the car and, finding me gone, he began to look around, but then the other car drove away, so he stopped looking and drove after the car. He told me later that he thought I had got a lift with them.

The sky had clouded over and darkness had fallen. I waited awhile, frightened he would come back, then set out to walk the seven miles home. I hadn't got far before the sky opened up and the rain came down in bucket loads. Huge claps of thunder crashed overhead and rumbled and echoed away down into the valley while streaks of lightning hit the ground far too close for comfort. Soon water rushed down the hill four inches deep and my jandals (flip flops in New Zealand, thongs in Australia), which I lived in summer and winter, began slipping off my feet. I took them off and walked barefoot on the rough tarmac.

As I trudged determinedly upwards my biggest fear was being seen by people in a car. Out there alone I was a sitting duck to be raped. Luckily I saw just two. When I saw the lights of the first one I had little time to hide so just dived headfirst into the bush. Unfortunately someone had been cutting Manuka stakes and the stumps put several deep grazes on my cheek thus adding to my misery. On some of the elbow bends there were half-bridges hanging out over the valley and when I saw the next lights coming two bends away I was on one of them. I freaked – there was nowhere to hide, so I lay flat down, arms beneath me, head turned towards the valley and hoped I looked like a piece of log, albeit one dressed in a blue smock with a long ponytail. The lights came around the corner and swept over me, and kept on moving down the hill. I couldn't believe I hadn't been seen. As soon as the lights rounded the next bend I ran off the bridge as fast as I could. After what seemed like forever I reached the top of the hill and began the short downhill stretch to the lake. Rotoma was obviously the site of a volcano millions of year ago, but I had more to think about at the time. I could have called in at Maud's or even at Bonny's on the long walk around the lake but my pride wouldn't let me. Instead of going all the way to the shops then having to cut back up the hill I took the shortcut up through the empty land below the house. The small reservoirs of water held by the lupin leaves drenched me again and I arrived at the locked door no longer afraid but exploding with anger. I banged loudly. "Open this door now!" I screamed.

"Have you got the police with you?" he asked from within.

"Open it now or I will put this axe through it." I snatched up the axe from the chopping block at my feet. The door opened and I crashed in, axe in front of me. "Keep away from me or I will put this axe through your bloody skull." And I meant it.

He kept his distance and after a hot bath, I went to sleep with Kim in her bed.

In the morning I gasped as I saw my face in the mirror. One side was red and swollen and I had a massive black eye. Down near my chin were several deep scratches where the Manuka stumps had grazed me. I was appalled. No way could I go to work looking like that. When Frank saw me he looked shocked "Did I do that?" he asked.

Now as I put these words to paper I ask myself why I didn't get in the car and drive straight to the police station in Kawerau. A little spell in prison may have given him time to reflect.

It couldn't have come at a worse time: Lorna had let me know that the school at East Taieri was having a reunion and she wanted me to go down and stay at her place. I had never had a holiday in all the years I'd known Frank … yes, we had travelled the world and seen lots of places, but everywhere we had been I had the dreadful lack of security hanging over me. Not once had I been able to relax. Now I was earning a good wage I had decided to go; my airfare was booked for just two weeks away.

By the time I was to fly out, I still had a black mark under one eye that I had to cover with thick pancake makeup. Lorna and Jack both noticed it but nobody else made comment. I did enjoy my week away, not only meeting old friends I hadn't seen in years but being away from the day to day cares. Frank and the children met me at the airport, Kim running to me with a small bunch of flowers she had picked from somewhere. There was a strange atmosphere hanging over the car trip home, something I couldn't put my finger on. Suddenly Steven blurted out, "Oh, I keep remembering."

"Okay, what is it you are all trying to hide?"

It transpired that they'd all gone down to the lake to swim taking our dog Gyp with them; she had run back over the road then, realising she was being naughty, had rushed back straight in front of a car. The woman driver had been devastated to have run over such a beautiful dog and had rushed off to Rotorua to send a vet back. But when he arrived it was too late; Frank had picked her up, no doubt doing more damage because she had bitten him, and carried her home. I was shattered by the loss; my lovely dog who had for so long been my protector. Many a time when the children and I had been alone at the top of the hill, the houses around not being rented, she would let us know whenever someone approached. I could tell by her bark just how near the person was – the nearer they got the higher the bark. When they were really close she would be baying like the hound she was, leaving the trespasser in no doubt we had been warned.

Now she was gone. I cried the rest of the way home then went ballistic – we had just two of her pups left, Boy who was a strong male and Midge the runt of the litter and who had by far the nicest character.

"You can just get rid of these last two pups," I snarled. "And don't you ever, ever bring a dog into this house again."

What a joke! Two months later he arrived home with a purebred poodle, a little white ball of fluff who we called Peppi. I often wondered if Frank had stolen him because I couldn't see how he would have had the money to buy him.

We never knew when Frank would erupt again: he was like a semi-dormant volcano. I took a book out from the library to read about psychopaths and came to the realisation that he was indeed just that. His wit was a cry of pain, the anguish of his inferiority complex exposed an attempted act to cover up. But just how long can you go on acting the clown? Soon normal people tired of it and then he turned nasty and the double-edged barbed remarks hit home. His workmates would go silent and shun him and he would have to leave. I always knew when the time was coming, he would bring his discontent home. As soon as he got another job a few weeks of gaiety and the whole scenario would start over.

The children and I became very good at reading the situation and avoiding him. One night he didn't come home for dinner. I used to let the children stay up on Saturday night to watch a film; we heard the car arrive and no one said a word but the tension in the room was palpable. He came charging in. "Well isn't this nice and cosy?" and went to stand right in front of the TV. Steven said, "Augh, Dad, we were watching that."

"Augh, you were watching it, were you? What a shame."

And then it started. Kim shot into her bedroom and out the window, Steven rushed out the front door while I dived out the back door. He was so busy trying to catch us that we all got away. That was the night I dived down the bank into the next-door section and hid, huddled down under the tall wet lupins. He knew I was there and came with the torch. The beam went right over me and I waited to be dragged out; couldn't believe that he didn't see me. Eventually when he left and went back into the house I made my escape into the bush above the house. From there I saw the police arrive, unknown to me the children had run down to their friend's house and the parents had called them.

Another night when we escaped Kim and I walked around the lake to Bonny's; her son went back to find Steven and we all stayed there the night.

These two incidents are an example of how we lived, never knowing what the next day would bring.

Many times I thought of leaving, but with no money it was impossible. Had I swallowed my foolish pride and written to Dad he would have had me out of there fast. So I stayed and hoped that things would improve.

Apart from the job at Matata the children and I moved away another two times to keep their father in work. He got a job working in the Kaiangaroa Forest planting pine trees, so of course, he couldn't resist stealing a bundle. I don't know what he thought I was going to do with them but anyway I planted a couple at the side of the garden. I was always desperate for firewood and they grew fast. Away up the hill above I planted a few more and while up there I saw a police car arrive – they had come with a search warrant to search the house. I asked to see it and it said they were looking for tools. Sue's husband had been stealing them to sell, and as we had been seen with them a couple of weeks previously and lived out of town they surmised we may have been storing them. We were not, but underneath our bed they found Frank's tools, all of which had been stolen and which he had carefully ground the employer's stamp off and painted. They also found the big gas bottle and welding gear down in the garage under the house, also nicked, but probably because everything was coated with months of dust they said nothing.

Frank didn't stick at the tree planting very long before moving on to twenty-foot pruning. As no one is allowed to work alone he was teamed up with a student who also wanted to work there. Unfortunately, the student left after a few weeks, no doubt because of Frank's nasty tongue – it was "get someone else to work with or leave". He asked me if I would join him.

He found a farm cottage to rent in Reporoa and we moved down, the children moved to school there and we took Trixie, a pony we had been loaned, and Midge, the small black pointer who had been the runt of Gyp's litter. At the time Kaiangaroa Forest was the biggest pine forest in the world; it was huge. It had been planted during the depression years when the government took town workers out there to keep them in work. It must have been one of the smartest things a New Zealand government ever did and must have made billions of dollars in exports.

The place was laid out in blocks with pine needle paths along each side. Between us, we pruned several blocks, me with a sharp hooked saw on the end of a long aluminium pole and Frank with a small saw and ladder. One day we looked up and saw we were being watched by several men.

"Goodness," said one, "I didn't know we had a woman working in the forest."

They were the only people we would see apart from a supervisor who came each week to measure how many trees we had pruned. He and a helper would run a cord across the block at intervals and count the trees ten feet of either side of the cord.

I loved the work in the forest. I had a pair of golf shoes with spikes on the soles to grip onto the mess that lay on the forest floor. The fourteen-foot pruning had been done sometime before and the debris could be lying very thick. I used to say "if you didn't learn to swear in the forest you couldn't have survived", so frequent were the falls. It was summer – very hot and dry, and the forest was a tinder box. One group of pruners were sacked on the spot when one of them was found smoking. Luckily neither of us smoked at the time. The debris under foot became very brittle and one day I was standing on top of the mess when it broke and I dropped into a hole about fifteen feet deep. Luckily, being lined with pine needles, I had a soft landing, but it was downright spooky down there.

Highly amused, Frank yelled, "Where have you got to?"

"I'm down here."

He had to put his ladder down for me to climb out.

Some days we worked in the rain. As long as we wore wool we didn't get cold, and one day we worked with big flakes of snow coming down.

One of our blocks was beside a block of high mature trees. The undergrowth was beautiful: ferns, mosses and soft greenery had taken over, and high above the soft shush of the wind blowing through the treetops made the place quite magical. Each day when it was time for lunch I took my sandwiches in there and was reluctant to go back to work.

Unfortunately, the rot started to set in when the supervisor ran his cord through a part of our block that was sparsely wooded; Frank said he had done it deliberately, and whenever the man showed after that he would make very barbed remarks, something he was brilliant at. I tried to argue that in all fairness we did have the sparse bit so it wouldn't make much difference to our pay, but nothing would change his mind.

As it was fate took a hand …

Before the branches on the ground became so dry they would snap, they went through a springy stage. When I went to jump down from the ones I was standing on, it sprang up and caught the spikes of my shoes. I landed on my knees instead of my feet, and one knee landed on a rock. The supervisor came that day and I showed him the bruising. A week later it was so swollen I couldn't work. So ended our sojourn in the forest – they put me on compo. We packed up and went back to Rotoma. I was sent to see a specialist and then to a private hospital to have the broken bursa removed from my knee and sent home a week later on crutches. Frank took off somewhere so I was left to cope alone with the children, and eight weeks later they announced me fit for light duties. I was offered office work away over at Taupo which they knew I couldn't accept, so my lovely weekly wage was stopped.

One day Frank took the two children with him when he went into Rotorua. They were supposed to be home for tea, but tea time came and went. I started to worry. They arrived back about 9 pm and Steven rushed in saying, "Dad nearly caused a terrible accident."

When Frank came in I asked him what had happened and he said some idiots had been too afraid to pass so he did. Within half an hour the police had arrived, took him back to Rotorua and charged him with dangerous driving.

His day in court arrived and his case was the first to be heard. Unbelievably, he pleaded not guilty, so we had to sit until the end of the day while they rounded up the witnesses. The evidence was damning: the witnesses told of him stupidly overtaking a long row of cars, and then, when another car came around the bend he swerved sharp left and drove over, and broke, the tow rope attached to the first car. This of course brought the car being towed to a standstill and nearly caused a pile-up.

The judge said, "I hope your wife can drive because I am banning you from driving for six months and fining you $400."

Yet another debt for me to pay.

After that Frank got a scrub-cutting job with a young Maori guy who rented a nearby house. The job was away down the east coast at Reporoa on a sheep station. That partnership didn't last either: he came back one weekend complaining that the young fellow drove like a maniac on the winding coast road. They had been paid up to date so the Maori decided to pull out. So once again, I and the children, who were on six weeks Christmas holidays, upped sticks and went back with him to finish the job, taking with us the big old tent to sleep in.

I have nothing but praise for the Reporoa Maori. Such wonderful friendly people. Between themselves they still spoke the Maori language which I thought was wonderful, considering the earlier Pakiha teachers had strapped them for not speaking English. We hadn't been there two days before a Maori farmer from up the road came to say he would bring an old pony called Dolly around for the children to ride.

"Just put her out on the road when you leave," he said. "She will find her own way home."

When I said I would bring her back to be safe he said not to worry, she would be fine.

What a delight Dolly was. A slightly fat black pony, so quiet and tolerant, I and the children all rode her. It was a couple of miles from where we had pitched the tent near the shearing shed to where we were working. Part of it was up a dry river bed where big white stones like chunks of marble proliferated. I was enthralled.

The work was hard, but the weather was beautiful. After a hard day's work slashing, we wended our tired way back to the tent. The boss killed a sheep, giving us a whole half side to eat. How wonderful it was for me to be among country folk again.

Frank always had an insatiable need for entertainment, so every Saturday night we went into Ruatoria to the pub. One night we were playing darts with the locals when a fat policeman came in and made a beeline for me.

"How old are you, young lady?" he asked.

"I'm 35." I couldn't believe he had asked.

"I am not here for a joke."

"I'm not joking! I am 35. I have a thirteen-year-old son."

Our friend Hook (called that because he had a steel hook instead of a hand) tried to intervene but was told to mind his own business.

"I am a ratepayer," I said.

"Lots of people are ratepayers and they are not twenty-one," he replied. "I want you out now, and come into the office in the morning with your driving licence." So next day I had to drive the nine miles back into town to present my driving licence. I didn't even get an apology.

When the Ruatoria job was done we got another scrub-cutting job back home on the Maori affairs land on the other side of the lake. It was still summer and the days were very hot. All day we swung those slashers, so by the end of the day the base of my thumbs were so sore I could have cried. Years later my thumbs developed severe arthritis and turned into the palms of my hands – I still have the ugly mess today. But it had kept my husband in work and off the road while his licence was suspended. When he got it back he was once more on the road again.

If I thought for a hundred years I would never remember how many jobs Frank had had in the eight years we were in Rotoma. At one time he had a job over on the west coast at one of Mr Muldoon's THINK BIG projects. Muldoon was the current Prime Minister who had borrowed millions for several schemes. Frank came home after his first two weeks complaining about the Union's flash strikes – they would all down tools and go off to the pub for the day. This was a clever and deliberate ploy to prolong the job, but they also lost a day's pay which didn't suit Frank. Most of the union bosses were emigrants from the

U.K. and their tactics were to put many a project well over budget.

A few week later Frank came home badly beaten up. He had spent a couple of days in hospital while doctors operated to take a broken cheekbone off an optic nerve. His face was a mess and he had me take photos of it. Of course it wasn't his fault – he'd just been having a drink and playing cards … but I knew very well my husband's vicious carping tongue when he'd had a few drinks, and was well aware he had asked for it. Not that I would have dared to say so.

By 1968 he was finding it difficult to get jobs. After all, who would want to employ someone with such a bad work record. The Social Welfare people refused to pay him the dole but said they would loan him the money to go away back down to the South Island and work at West Arm on Lake Manapouri where the tailrace tunnel was still being pushed through to Doubtful Sound. I agreed with him he should go and pleaded with him to stay and give it a go until all our debts had been cleared and the mortgage paid up before we lost our home.

Three weeks after he left it was Easter. On April 10th, a huge storm came sweeping south through Cook Strait forcing the *Inter-Island Wahine* onto the rocks at the entrance to Wellington Harbour. The Cook Straits are one of the roughest waters in the world because two oceans meet there, and crossings can be bad. Fifty-one people died that day. I watched with horror on our old TV as the drama unfolded; remember standing in the garden a little later and it came to me quite clearly that Frank was on his way home. I hoped that he was on that ship, that one of the bodies was his then chastised myself for such a wicked thought.

He arrived back two days later saying that he'd missed that ferry by an hour. I asked him why he had stayed just three weeks and he replied that "He wasn't going to hang around doing nothing for three days at Easter." It took me six months to pay the fare back to the Social Welfare. Yet again he'd run up another debt for me to worry about.

I cannot move on from Rotoma with my writing before telling some of the stupid things Frank did when we lived there.

There is an old saying: "It's the thought that counts", but a little forethought before that thought is always sensible. Unfortunately, my husband didn't seem to have the capacity for that.

One day when he had been away for weeks I saw the van arriving followed by a truck. I ran out to find he had bought a pony for the children. It was a skewbald, very thin with all its ribs showing, a rough unbrushed coat, and smelly black dirt up to its first leg joints. Frank said he'd bought him from a Maori forest settlement where the pony had been contained in a sawdust bog. "He's fine … the Maori children have been riding him for months."

He didn't know the first thing about horses, it was painfully obvious to me that the pony had never been trained and to put children who had never ridden on such a beast would be lethal. Moreover, the pony, because of his harsh treatment, probably had a nasty nature. How right I was!

"Are you mad?" was my first question. "Where are we going to put him?' We had no paddock, no stable, nowhere for the pony to graze.

"We will just have to tether him somewhere," was the answer.

Once more I knew I would be left to pick up the pieces. At least the pony had a halter on so we found a rope and tethered him on the houseless section next door. Over the next week we cleared a bit of the section above us, Frank cut a few trees down and made a stall against the tall bank at the back so we had somewhere to put the pony at night. Keri from Maori affairs gave us two bales of hay for rescuing a sheepdog of his, so we installed a feeding box against the bank, so Tonto, as Steven had called him, had some feed at night. Poor wee Kim … she came one day with a bunch of grass she had pulled for him, but when she held it in to him he turned and bit her viciously, leaving her with a huge bruise across her ribs.

I wrote to Mum and Dad telling them about the pony, and Mum wrote back relaying Dad's words – the pony would turn into a rebel as soon as he got a bit of good feed into him; he would never have been broken in and I must do that straight away.

Soon a big parcel arrived, containing a saddle, bridle, and all the gear I needed to mouth the pony, along with instructions. By that time we had cleared the whole top section of lupin and tutu, so I had somewhere to train him on the flat. Tonto didn't take kindly at all to the discipline, but once I had him walking backwards with his tightly collected head it was time to start riding. Every morning before he went out to be tethered I saddled him up and rode him. He was hungry and bad-tempered but I wouldn't give in until he did as he was told. He soon learned that the longer he misbehaved the longer it would be until he got breakfast. Later, when it was time to introduce him to traffic, I rode him down the hill onto the main road. One day when I was riding him along the road through the bush between the lakes, an enormous truck laden with wood chips came towards us. I was terrified he would leap in front of it. Luckily the young driver saw my predicament and slowed right up until he passed.

Eventually, I deemed Tonto safe for Steven to ride, but Tonto had lots of tricks up his sleeve. Well aware he had a novice rider aboard he would wait until his rider was relaxed then suddenly leap sideways. Steven was eventually thrown off breaking his arm badly. The pony had to go. He was now a fine specimen but needed an experienced rider. A farmer bought him for one of his sons and months later when we went to see him he was a fine and stable pony, being ridden every day, settled and happy.

One of the things that used to upset me was the appalling deadbeats Frank used to bring home to the house. Most of them were alcoholics. There was a group from Kawerau who arrived one Sunday morning asking if we had anything to drink. Frank produced his only bottle of beer. Among the group was a young Irishman who was a communist. Patrick and I had many a talk about communism; he gave me Mao's little red book which I found fascinating. The sound of a home and a job for everyone seemed great to me. Needless to say, I eventually realised that communism couldn't work. It was a great leveller, but destroyed people's ambitions and their will to achieve. The morale of the people was so destroyed that nobody cared; countries after communism were found to be appallingly polluted and neglected.

Frank told me he had seen a photo of Patrick before he left Ireland.

"He was a young, fit cyclist, now you can see what New Zealand has done to him," he declared. According to my husband poor little New Zealand was the route of all evil.

A year or two later we heard that Patrick was going home to Ireland, working his passage aboard ship. Sadly he got just as far as Sydney Harbour where one morning his body was found floating between the ship and the wharf: he'd fallen off the gangplank coming back to the ship at night. A sad end to a wasted life.

Many people at the time were making their living selling possum skins so Frank made an appointment to sit an exam to get a cyanide licence. On the appointed day he got cold feet. "They won't give it to me because I'm a pom. You go," he said. I argued but he was adamant, so it was I who sat and received my cyanide licence, I believe the only woman in New Zealand at the time to hold one.

And so it was for the next six months after the children went off to school, I set off into the bush to lay poison or go round the baits. I would pin small pieces of white paper to a tree and squeeze a bit of cyanide onto it. Possums, being very inquisitive, would go to investigate this strange thing that smelt like banana; one sniff and their brain would explode. The meat would still be fit to eat and I would boil the carcasses up in a big iron pot in the back yard to feed to Gyp and her pups. I soon learned how to skin them and strip the tail. The most I ever got for a skin was $4.50, and I earned it, as it was an old red buck that was so tough it took me over an hour to skin.

After I had the skins off I would stretch them out and pin them on boards to dry, then they would be ready to go to the buyer. Possums have their own little smell – by the end of six months I stunk of possum fat that even a soak in the bath wouldn't eradicate.

One day, when Frank had done his usual disappearing trick and I had very little food, I decided to cook a young possum for our dinner. I stewed it with onions and carrots and served it with mashed potatoes; told the children that it was rabbit stew and they both cleaned their plates

"Mmm," said Steven as he scraped up the last of the gravy, "that was really good."

One day when going round the baits I came upon a female lying face down, but it didn't seem to be dead. I was shocked. Possums are very hard to kill and if it was just unconscious I knew I would have to kill it. I turned it over carefully with my toe and found that the movement was coming from a half-grown baby in its pouch. I was mortified, and took him home – he became a pet. In the evenings he would rush around the living room, climb up the leg of my jeans or leap from the back of the sofa onto someone's shoulder. The children loved him. Later I would take him back out to his home in the old hen house where he slept during the day.

Something was eating the new shoots out of my climbing beans at night so I went out with a torch, and there he was having a feast. Somehow he'd found a hole big enough to escape from the shed. Sadly I told the children he just had to go. We took him away over to the other side of the lake into the thick bush, placed him at the bottom of a tree trunk and he shot up the trunk and was gone. I just hoped he never met a nasty possum poisoner like me.

Bonny and Leon had a son, I hadn't thought of him as retarded until Bonny said one day that he had been a bright and clever two-year-old until one day he pushed something into a power socket and was electrocuted. The lad, who I will call Bruce, loved to tell the story about how, if you threw a dead rabbit into a pig pen the pig would eat the meat out of the skin in minutes. We heard the story ad nauseam. Bruce worked as a rouseabout for Maori affairs and always carried a gun.

One day he and Frank went off over the lake to shoot rabbits. It wasn't rabbits he brought home but two wild ducks he had shot out of season. I was furious! It was spring and the ducks may have had nests somewhere.

Sometime later Keri, Bruce's employer, kept finding dead sheep on the acres over the lake. Without telling anyone he arranged for a private detective to live in one of the lakeside holiday homes there to investigate. He soon found out that Bruce was the culprit, he had been using the sheep as target practice. The case went to court, but in deference to Bonny and Leon, Bruce's name was not mentioned in the newspapers.

One day Frank and I were walking away up in the bush; there was a slight flutter and there above us was a beautiful big native pigeon. It was the first I had ever seen and was so beautiful with its shiny white breast. Because of their declining numbers, these birds were protected. Before I could stop him he had pointed the shotgun and pulled the trigger. The beautiful bird fell at our feet. I lost it! Suddenly I was screaming and yelling abuse, with tears running down my face. I wanted to snatch the gun from his hands and kill him. But, there was no point leaving the carcass there as evidence and, as we had so little food, I snatched it up and began to rip its feathers off. He was quite shocked at my reaction. I told him if he ever again shot anything he wasn't supposed to I would go to the police and have him charged. Even now, after all these years, the thought of that beautiful dead bird upsets me.

Tonto wasn't the only pony to arrive at our place; the next one to arrive was a six month old not even trained to lead. He was a pretty pony, black with four white feet. Steven named him Sancho.

He and his father managed to get a rope on him but he dragged them both all the way down the road and into someone garden before realising he was defeated. I then had to take over and break him in. Because he was treated with love and kindness he turned out to be an absolute treasure.

Bonny had once said to me, "You should be working for yourself the way you work."

When I saw an advertisement for someone to take over a coffee lounge free of charge at the Building Display Centre in Rotorua, I jumped at the chance, applied and got it.

At last, I was growing up. I had long ago worked out that Frank had a huge personality disorder which is a polite way of saying he was a psychopath. I was now ready to stand on my own feet and break away from our poverty-stricken life. Besides, Steven had now moved on to high school and had to travel into Rotorua so it made sense to live there. Frank, with his amazing animal cunning, found an old house to rent there, on land zoned industrial. It had an orchard and about five acres of land on which to run Sancho. So we moved in with our few miserable possessions.

A Kawerau firm wanted to rent a place for one of their employees and agreed to rent our place at Rotoma. I asked that they pay the rent directly into our mortgage account which they did; and as it was much more than what we were supposed to pay we made up some of the arrears. At last, I no longer had that burden.

It soon became evident why the coffee lounge was free: hardly anyone ever came. It had a very nice setting with a display of lights from some lighting shop around two walls, some of which flickered like candles. I soon realised that the only way I was going to survive was to get some morning tea orders from factories. The first one was from a big clothing factory nearby. About 8.30 am I would visit the factory and get orders from the office staff then go round all the girls at their machines and write down their orders. Having done that I would rush back, and make up the orders ready to deliver back to the factory at 10.15. Then it was back to the coffee lounge to make up sandwiches and set out cakes ready for a few lunchtime customers.

As we had at the *El Toreador*, I made all the cakes and a favourite, apple shortcake that was served with whipped cream.

Frank had decided that now I had the coffee lounge he didn't need to work. He was more of a hindrance than a help and we had some terrible rows as he was forever messing things up. More often than not after I had delivered the factory orders he would take himself off to goodness knows where.

To bring the coffee lounge to the public's notice I put small cheap ads in the local paper. *"SHIRLEY, MEET ME AT THE BUILDING DISPLAY CENTRE COFFEE LOUNGE, 12.30 FRIDAY. BILL.* It was surprising just how effective the ads were: one lunchtime I had thirty people in. Quite a surprise.

Once a month the Lions Club, for which I had to do the catering, had a meeting at the lounge. In my effort to please I am sure I exceeded the small amount of money I was given for each person. Also, this was a late night for me; almost midnight when I got home.

Despite everything, we were barely making ends meet. When Frank returned from his nosing around one day he declared there was a restaurant standing empty opposite the train station and he thought we should try for it. I agreed.

The man who owned the lease had bought the place and financed a good cook who had been working at one of Rotorua's hotels. But, he told us, the cook was a gambler and had been helping himself to the till to finance his addiction. The place had gone bankrupt. The owner had been left with the place on his hands. He had allowed a young couple to take it over to keep it going until he could sell it, but that had ended in disaster.

It was after we moved in that the health inspector filled me in with the details. He said he'd arrived one day to inspect the premises. "There was a pile of dirty tea towels on the table. I picked up a handful and large maggots fell out. I said, 'Right, that's it, close the front door, you are banned from trading'."

He couldn't find any fault with our kitchen, my nursing had taught me all about germs, but he must have felt he needed to find something. Out in the corridor, we had a small cupboard where the sacks of potatoes were kept. He wanted the inside painted white. A bit silly I thought, but needless to say we complied.

Frank, with his obsession for secrecy, demanded that I not tell the Display Centre owners that we were leaving, and I, like a fool obliged even though I felt bad about it. Needless to say, they were shocked when I told them on the last day.

Unbelievably I was still jumping to Frank's tune.

It was a bit unfortunate that the first day we opened the restaurant was the first day of the school holidays. The town teemed with holidaymakers – talk about a baptism of fire – we were run off our feet all day. I still hadn't advertised for staff so there were just the two of us and the two children working in the kitchen where I had them putting potatoes through the chipper and washing dishes. Kim was always a good little worker, and a worrier, but my son was always pestering to get away. As a teenager he never did have a conscience. I didn't want to be too hard on them but on the other hand I didn't want them running wild. I had brought my factory orders with me so started that day, and every day, at 5 am and we closed about 10.30 at night.

The next day I put a notice in the window and an advertisement in the paper asking for staff. They soon arrived, a woman came in asking if I would give her daughter Christine a job to keep her out of mischief. I said I would, and later wished I hadn't. A lovely Maori girl called Moana came and I took her on as well – she proved to be a little gem. I then added a large very confident lady to wash the dishes and help in the kitchen. She also was a great asset.

Late night shopping was Friday night and soon we had people queuing out the door to get our takeaway hamburgers. The secret was my very special sauce, the ingredients of which I never divulged.

We were almost opposite the train station and usually got a few customers from the last train about 9 pm. Frank was really quite good with new people; he would get them all talking. Sometimes someone would come in and stop in surprise when they found tourists from around the world all talking together.

When we took the place over it was called *The Golden Sheaf*. We found a previous sign in the storage area saying *The Steak Bar*, which we hung up outside. After that we specialised in steaks with just one chicken and one fish dish, all served with salad.

All the cooking was done in front of the customer. We had a fridge display cabinet between the grill and the restaurant from where people could choose their own steak. The butcher two doors away provided us with the very best meat but his bills were huge. Frank in his wanderings found that he could buy T-bone steaks much cheaper, but slightly smaller than what the butcher was providing, at Woolworth's supermarket.

So eventually things evened out and the place was always busy even after the school holidays were finished. Later I realised that our meals were about half the price of other places in town, but then we were paying no rent. At the end of six months, I had more money in the bank than I'd ever had in my life.

Needless to say, it wasn't all plain sailing – Christine was a lazy little minx, sometimes standing for ages just looking out the window. Moana would step in and clear her tables and do her work until I put my foot down.

"You are not, repeat *not*, to do Christine's work, Moana, and I don't pay her to look out the window."

I would let them go for their hour-long lunch break one at a time, but one day Christine pleaded with me to let them both go together so I told them they could both have 1.30 to 2.30 off.

One day when they came back Christine asked me if I had any paper bags. I was too busy to wonder why and indicated a cupboard. A few days later they didn't come back at all, and by 3 pm I was getting worried. About an hour later the police arrived to tell me they'd been caught shoplifting. Apparently it wasn't Christine's first offence – no wonder her mother wanted her kept out of mischief. The wretched girl had done the shoplifting and talked Moana into taking the things home with her, knowing full well that her own mother would have found them. The police found over a thousand dollars' worth of clothes in the top of Moana's wardrobe, all collected in just one week. Given that this was in the late 60's and there were no high fashion shops in town, this was some achievement. I was really sorry for Moana's parents; they were a very nice couple of the Mormon faith. Her mother came to apologise and I said no need. I told her I would be pleased to go to court and give Moana a character reference, but it didn't come to that. The authorities knew full well who the real culprit was. Moana wanted to stay on after the holidays ended. When I told her she could stay but I would like to see her finish her schooling, her parents let her stay.

One Sunday when it was reasonably quiet, Frank took off to the pub, leaving me alone, the children being away with their friends. At midday a bus on a mystery tour pulled up with thirty-eight passengers, all wanting to be fed. I was horrified, and when I put the last meal on the table a big cheer went up. I had a few things to say to Frank when he came back that day.

I eventually started to close up at 8 pm from Monday to Thursday. One night we had some friends around to the house for the evening and Frank suggested a game of poker. I could have killed him. All four wives were against it but the men agreed, so we demanded that the stakes be kept low. After a few games, all four seemed to think they had the winning hand and not one would capitulate. The stakes went higher and higher, the heap on the table grew to alarming proportions; it was plain that someone was going to win a lot of money and three would lose far more than they could afford. Eventually one of the wives got angry saying it had gone far enough and the fairest way was to throw their cards in and share the kitty before someone got hurt. We other three agreed. A very nice guy called Jeff said that, as the ladies were not happy, perhaps that's how it should be. The kitty was shared. I served supper and everyone went home happy, or so I thought.

A couple of weeks later Frank took himself off to the pub after the lunch rush finished, saying he would be back by 4.30. He didn't come back until I was due to shut at 8, knowing that if I drove home without him he would have to walk. Luckily, as I had staff on, we had managed to cope without him. He insisted I go back to the bar with him and, knowing he was in one of his nasty moods, I agreed, to avoid a scene. I told him I would stay for one drink and no more, and that the children had been out with their friends but I had no idea where they were. When we reached the hotel who should be there but Jeff, who had agreed they should divide up the kitty. He was drinking quietly with a group of friends at the other end of bar. At the sight of him, Frank turned on his Jeckle and Hyde act storming over to have a go at him. Back and forward he went each time with another vicious jibe. I tried pleading with him to stop but he wouldn't. Suddenly Jeff snapped. He grabbed Frank's jacket in his left hand and swung him around at the same time swinging a punch with his right. The punch didn't have much weight behind it as Frank was already losing his footing. He fell backwards, tripping as he fell and hit his head on the steel footrest in front of the bar. He was out cold, a deep groove in his forehead.

I turned him to view the damage and quietly asked the barman to call the ambulance. The bar emptied like lightning, just a very apologetic Jeff and his friends remained. Frank was taken to hospital where he was to spend the next few days before being released and unable to work for another week. I asked the police to try and keep it out of the paper as I had a restaurant and they complied. A small notice appeared in the next day's paper to say that Frank Naylor had been admitted to hospital after an accident. That got all my friends ringing to see what had happened. Once more his nasty mouth had got him into trouble.

The solicitors for the building's owner advised us that the lease was up for renewal. A month later it still hadn't been signed so I asked if I could have it. They said they had to give the owner a bit more time, but two weeks later they rang and offered me the lease. I was really torn about what to do. I had found out that when the children had been down the street with their friends on Friday nights they had been shoplifting. Nothing big, just little bits of cheap rubbish, but shoplifting nevertheless. I was furious and grounded them which caused no end of whining from Steven – my son had turned into a selfish little brat who thought about nobody but himself and didn't for years to come.

The children did their homework and had dinner every night at the restaurant before going home with us at 8 pm. It was no life for them, and with no help from an irresponsible husband who I couldn't rely on I felt so helpless. Moreover, our little poodle Peppi was home all day on his own. Reluctantly, I decided that the restaurant would have to go but I would hold on until it was sold.

About a month later our dishwashing lady told us she had heard it was sold, a Maori guy had bought it and was going to turn it into a fast food outlet. Six weeks later we closed.

I didn't know what I was going to do but didn't want to be working for anyone else. We had a week or two at home at the old house. It was fun watching Peppi the poodle and Sancho the pony playing together; they were the best of pals. Peppi would chase Sancho all the way to the bottom of the paddock with Peppi barking madly behind him. Sancho would lash out with both back legs but never hit him. When they got to the bottom of the paddock they would both turn and Sancho would chase Peppi back to the house. This would go on until Peppi was puffed out and flopped at Sancho's feet. He was still a stallion of course and didn't take kindly to people he didn't know getting cheeky. I kept the religious people away by saying, "That is a pony stallion there, he doesn't like strangers. I have warned you so if you get attacked you have only yourself to blame."

Just through the hedge was a factory. One lunch hour some of the men workers came through the hedge to raid the apple trees in the overgrown garden. Sancho was always very friendly and would go to introduce himself. His closeness would frighten most people and they would try to chase him away. Not being used to this treatment he would take exception and rear up. This would really frighten them and they would make a hasty exit; then Sancho would come galloping up to the house to tell us. On that occasion, I heard him snorting and stomping at the back door and went out just in time to see the offenders disappearing through the hedge. Afraid they would get hurt I went next door to talk to the manager who said he would tell his men not to trespass.

One afternoon Steven and I got the last laugh: a very common-looking woman and her son let themselves in the gate and began to pick what I thought of as *my* blackberries. I was not pleased – what a cheek – I had intended to pick them myself to make jam. So I decided to sew a little seed of doubt. She was bending down picking with Sancho already investigating when I called out, "That is a pony stallion behind you, he doesn't like people coming into his paddock, you may get hurt."

She replied, "It's alright, I have been here before."

I went back inside knowing full well what was about to happen. About five minutes later Sancho arrived at the door to announce his displeasure. We rushed out, but there was no sign of our visitors. Then we spied them. They had jumped through the wire fence that surrounded another factory outside our gate. Between the fence and the factory wall lay years of discarded rubbish, old machinery, bits of car bodies, barbed wire, all packed tight together and impassable. There they were, climbing carefully across the top. We heard her say, "Bloody bastard horse." I got my blackberry jam.

Not long afterward we were obliged to get Sancho gelded and sell him. A couple on a farm bought him for their daughter. Later, when I went out to see if he had settled in, the lady said, "I don't know who broke him in but he is the nicest pony we've ever had. He always come running when we call."

When I said, "I did," she replied, "Well you should be very proud of yourself, but there is one thing we can't understand … he keeps chasing the sheep."

It didn't occur to me until later that Sancho must have wondered why they wouldn't play.

Steven also went out to see him; he was nowhere in sight, his new owner saying he must be over behind the hill. Steven took out his shepherd's whistle and blew it; he was the only one of us who ever mastered that thing. Over the hill at a gallop came Sancho, so please to see an old mate. The lady couldn't believe her eyes.

A fish and chip shop at Kotu, a suburb between Rotorua and Ngongataha, came on the market, and I decided to buy it. We would still have to work until 10 at night but didn't have to open until 11 am and close in the afternoon which meant I could be home for the children arriving home from school. At first all went well and we made enough to live on, but then came winter and a lot of rain. Most of our potatoes were harvested from Pukakohi, the red clay area south of Auckland. The ground turned to mud and few of the potatoes could be harvested. Prices soared. It wouldn't have been so bad had the bags held just clean potatoes, but they were caked with mud. One fish and chip shop owner got the newspaper to print a photo of the pounds of mud in each bag that we were paying top price for. Our customers complained bitterly as we had to reduce their amount of chips. There was nothing for it but one of us had to get a job.

The post office advertised for posties and I became a postie in the morning and worked in the shop at night. We were provided with a heavy pushbike, on the handlebars of which hung a very heavy leather bag. Two more leather bags hung each side of the back carrier. The new postie was always given the longest run, not because they were being spiteful but because some of the run went a way out of town where the houses were few and far between, that is, there were not so many letters. Unfortunately the long road that led to a small settlement nearly always had a nasty headwind and the bike with the front bag was not what you could call streamlined. The going was tough. Where the houses were in neat streets I had to go up and down the hill three times. Dot, the postie who showed me the run, taught me something we were not supposed to do. One group of houses were up the top of a very steep road. To get there you went up Clayton Road, the windy one, and then double-backed up the steep climb pushing your bike. Dot taught me how to leave the bike in someone's backyard and carrying the few letters to be delivered above, shinny up a steep bank on foot to the houses. This little ploy saved so much time and energy, but we were not supposed to leave our bikes unattended.

Twice on the run, our foreman would leave our overflow bags. One was left at a shop, another at an old man's house. He had two playful Siamese cats and always greeted the Postie with tales of their antics. I think the Posties visit was the highlight of his day. When we picked up our overflow bags we had to pack the mail in the right order into our leather bag.

Work started each day at 6 am. I would be up at 5.00, dress in my uniform, have breakfast and cycle to work. Two sorters would sort the mail into each run; we would pick up our mail from them and then 'run it in' in the order it would be delivered. When all the mail was sorted we would rubber band together enough to hold in your hand and pack our bags also in order. Then we would rubber band the ones for the overflow bags and be off on the road. Out on the road we would hold a bundle of mail and the handlebars in our left hand while delivering mail with the right. Sometimes if the boxes were well placed we could keep on riding while slipping in the mail as we passed.

It is well-known that for some unknown reason dogs don't like posties. We were supposed to blow our whistles when we entered a street but very few of the others did because they didn't want to alert the dogs. I did, so the first thing I had to do was make friends with all the dogs. The post office had the power to have any dog that attacked a postie destroyed, and I didn't want that. Having been bought up with dogs I wasn't afraid of them so that was a start. The small ones were the worst. One six-inch high critter up the top of Clayton Road would come screaming out and chase me around the block yapping madly. I made a game of it, which we played every day. Also in that group of houses was a place with several big dogs used for pig hunting. They belonged to a Maori family and ran free. Aware of the danger I very quickly got them on my side. Another small dog in that little cul-de-sac had no intention of making friends, he would come to meet me and bite my feet and shoe as I pedaled. It couldn't go on ... sooner or later he would draw blood. On each side of our front bag we had pieces of doweling sticking up where we attached small parcels for delivery. One day when said dog was hanging off the toe of my shoe I drew out the empty stick, bent down and gave him a sharp smack across the nose. Then I felt awful as he went howling back into his garden. After that, he stood quietly inside the gate and watched me.

The worst dog was a golden spaniel on one of the first streets. Dot had warned me about him. He would stand quietly inside the gate and watch me put mail in the box then when you moved on a few houses he would sneak up behind and fly, barking madly, at my feet, giving me the most dreadful fright. He wasn't always outside thank goodness; however, one day when it was wet and windy he gave me such a fright that I lost control of the bike and fell. I was unhurt but the mail scattered all over the wet grass and I had to sit down, sort it all and pack it again into my bag. What with that and the dreadful weather I arrived back almost an hour late and Ron the foreman wanted to know what had happened. When I told him he said that we should have reported it before. He visited the house and warned the owners to keep the dog in, after which I had no more trouble.

One morning Ron came to me ask if I'd ever had any trouble with the pig dogs. I told him no, as I had made friends with the dogs. He said that a little girl at the house had been attacked and had a badly bitten face. I told him I wasn't surprised as the children there were very cruel to the dogs, that one day the little girl had poked a stick in a dog's eye and I had reprimanded her.

Dot lived with Hini, a very pretty, part Maori girl; they both had a child out of wedlock and were lesbians, Hini a reluctant one, but when Dot offered her a home she had little choice. Dot gave her a long rein – she could flirt with as many men as she liked, but heaven help her if she slept them. And flirt she did. Men fell at her feet like flies, not knowing she was just a tease. So it was that Hini ingratiated herself into my life, leaving Dot home to babysit as always. She came to help in the fish shop and enjoyed the interaction with the customers. She also wrapped Frank around her little finger. They went to play golf together; she took him to her mother's house where they bathed naked in the hot spring bath in a shed near the house. Frank asked me if I minded if she came to live with us – we would be a nice little threesome. Appalled, I told him so in no uncertain words. The next day I accosted Hini at work, and when the forewoman asked me what it was all about, I told her – it wasn't the first time she'd attracted someone's husband I was told. I banned Hini from the shop until she could behave herself.

Sometimes on a Sunday morning we would all go riding at the stables. I always rode an old trotter who had a back leg limp so I didn't push him. Steven of course had to get a fiery mount so he could show off by riding at the gallop.

One morning just as we were leaving we had a visit from the police: we'd had a break in at the shop. When we got to the shop we couldn't believe the mess. Somehow they had managed to unscrew the bars from the small back window and climbed in. The entire floor was littered with food. Chicken had been taken from the fridge, bits of it eaten then dropped on the floor. The two big containers of semi-fried chips had been emptied onto the big centre table and decorated with a variety of things, including my red pills.

The big containers of flour now festooned the floor and walls and had also been tipped into the vats of oil that we'd just changed. Fresh fish had been trampled into the mess …

It was obviously the work of children, and unfortunately, they had found my poster powders. For making posters I kept red, yellow, orange, blue, and green powder to mix up with water; these colours now decorated our lovely white walls. What fun they'd had. What hadn't hit the walls had landed on the floor to mix into a myriad of hues. Footprints of all sizes were in the mess, the smallest of which was about five inches long. He had obviously been the lookout as the prints went back and forth to look into the street. The largest were the cops footprints which didn't impress their superior. It took us three days to clean up, getting the poster powder off the walls the hardest job but luckily it hadn't stained. Frank dismantled the wall between the front and back of the shop and made a fold-up one so it could be opened at night and allow the street lights to show through.

We had a little boy who came quite often to the shop and sadly Frank became convinced he was the one who left the small footprints and practically accused him. I had to step in and tell him to back off even though he may well have been the lad. The police thought they came from the boys' home not far away, but nothing was ever proven. Luckily we had insurance and were compensated. Of course Frank claimed for fictitious money he had in his jacket pocket.

It was while we were there that our house at Rotoma was finally paid off. The long-suffering previous owner who'd held our mortgage came to tell me that he had been as kind as he could over the interest; he charged us just an extra $80. We signed the final papers, and the house was ours at last. Soon after, the tenant whose boss had been paying the rent left his employment and we rented it again to a nice Maori girl and her Dutch partner.

Frank was getting sick of working in the shop where he wasn't needed anyway. He applied for, and got, the job of medical officer at the maximum-security prison at Paremoremo. What a joke! He didn't know the first thing about medicine but had told them he had been an attendant at Cherry Farm Mental Hospital. There was a nice house going with the job, and I was to sell the business and move up there.

The children moved up there with him and once more went to new schools. I moved out of the old house.

There was an old long couch in the back of the shop which was to be my strictly-illegal bed for the next few months. I had a suitcase of clothes and a feather eiderdown partially hidden on the bottom shelf of the long table. I had no trouble sleeping on the couch; after doing my mail run in the morning and working the shop at night I was exhausted. But one night I was woken by a bumping and pushing beneath me. Half asleep I sat up and took stock – it had to be a rat – but where had it come from? After banging furiously on the settee the bumping stopped so I lay down again. Then it started again almost immediately. Absolutely beside myself with rage I jumped up, grabbed the big broom and laid into the sofa with all my strength then, satisfied there was no more movement, I lay down and slept until the alarm went off.

Hini was once more working some nights in the shop, having asked me if she could come back and I said she could. She was a big help to me and wouldn't take any pay.

Sometimes, when I went to wash my hands at the hand basin at the back of the shop I could smell something unpleasant. Twice I called Hini over but she said I was imagining things – actually, she said something much ruder than that which I dare not repeat. I have always had a very sensitive nose that smells things before other people, like the time I told Frank to stop the car as we were leaking petrol and he didn't believe me until the car caught fire. Anyway, this faint smell went on for a few weeks until one day I let myself and my bike in the front door of the shop and found the floor alive with large maggots. To say I freaked out would be an understatement – *please don't let the health inspector arrive.*

Thinking I could hose them out the back door I lifted the big mat and there were hundreds hiding there, so I hosed and swept, hosed and swept, but just when I thought I had them all, more would crawl from under something. It was a nightmare: I had just an hour and a half until the shop opened and there was still the batter to make. Eventually I decided I had got them all, but there was still the source to find. The only thing over by the sink was the heavy electric stove; I dragged it out, and there underneath was the remains of a large rat. It must have run under there after I had belted it with the broom. I stripped off and pouring disinfectant into the basin I washed my hands and arms, then dressed in my smock. There was just enough time to make some the batter but I had to forego my dinner.

No sooner had I opened the shop door than a lady arrived to get dinner for the family. We chatted as I cooked, but as I looked down I saw another white maggot on the red terracotta tiles hurrying past my feet. Always the good actress I kept on smiling and talking and stepped sideways to stomp on it. This was to happen several times more time that night, and by closing time I was a nervous wreck.

I got up to the prison just once to see them all, only to find out Frank had allowed Steven to leave school and get a job. I was furious, but the deed was done. I was even more angry when I found out he had sold Steven the old Austen car. He'd had not thought of me alone in Rotorua without a car and having to pay delivery costs for all the shop's needs. I demanded, and got the car back, upsetting our son in the process.

Kim came down to stay with me for one weekend. I booked a motel for us. After shutting the shop on the Saturday night I took us for a treat to soak in the private spar mineral waters. Stupidly I didn't take a change of clothes and realised while dressing again, just how much my clothes stank. It was good to see my little girl after months away; my little helper.

Returning from my mail run one day, the folk from the shop next door came to tell me that a red-headed police officer from

Paremoremo Prison had come to talk to me. He asked them if my husband worked at the prison and they told him yes. He told them he would come to see me later, but he didn't show. I knew straight away that Frank was causing trouble again; he would soon be out of a job. Sure enough, he turned up with the children a few weeks later. He'd been given the sack.

We found a place to rent at Nongataha, a village near Rotorua. It had probably been someone's holiday home as it was about fifteen feet from the edge of Lake Rotorua, right at the back of a quarter acre section. There was an open-sided shed to keep two cars in. I still had the fish and chip shop but it sold soon after we moved in. Frank was not working: he decided he wanted to go back to England, so once again I went along with him. I booked the fares and paid the deposit. I wrote to my sister Lorna saying we were going, and she replied saying what on earth was I thinking?

"You know what it was like last time, and Gwen, he is not going to change."

She had sown the seed and set me thinking for which I was grateful. Why in God's name, I asked myself, was I even thinking of going back there to a life of poverty? I had already sorted all our belongings and priced them for a big garage sale, so I kept silent about my thoughts. But fate took a hand. One night Kim and I were alone. We'd had dinner and she was sitting watching TV with Peppi in her lap. Frank arrived home about 8 pm in a foul mood and had obviously been drinking. He made a nasty remark about Peppi sitting on Kim's lap, picked him up by the scruff of the neck and threw him down the front steps onto the lawn by the lake. It was time to leave! When he went into the toilet, I snatched up the keys of my car and Kim and I rushed out and drove away. We drove up to the top of the lookout over Rotorua and just sat talking and looking at the lights below. About midnight we deemed it safe to go home.

Steven was at home alone. He said after he arrived home the police had come to tell him they were keeping his father in overnight – he'd been pulled over for drunk driving and once again had refused a breath test. I said, "Great! That's it! We are going to pack and we are leaving first thing in the morning."

The kids and I don't remember much about that night. I think we grabbed a few hours' sleep and started loading the car before daybreak. We threw most of our clothes, a few sheets and blankets, some pots, pans, and dishes into the boot and the back seat of the car, and left the property. I was terrified Frank would be back before we got away.

But leaving wasn't so simple. Kim was supposed to go to a birthday party the next day and Steven wanted to collect his wages from work, tell his boss he had to leave, and why, and also say goodbye to his friends. It had already been arranged that poor wee Peppi was to go one of Kim's school friends so we left him tied up at his outdoor kennel with water and food. Once again a darling little dog had to be sacrificed because of this sick, twisted man.

Not wanting to hurt the children I told them we could delay leaving Rotorua for another day: Steven went to work and would stay that night with a friend, Kim and I headed for Rotoma and my dearest friend Maud knowing she and Ernie would look after us for the night. Maude suggested I move the car behind the shed just in case Frank came looking for us there. The next morning I went to see Bonny and Cheryl at the *El Toreador* and Bonny suggested I help Cheryl clean the motels and she would pay me. I agreed. After all, I needed all the money I could get. It was obvious that my friends were pleased that at last, I had come to my senses.

I left in time to drop Kim at the party at Rotorua; then went to the railway station car park to wait until 2 pm when I could pick her up. I had been sitting for quite some time when suddenly the passenger door was flung open and Frank slipped into the car. I was numb with fright. That man seems to have an uncanny homing device; he found me there and many times since he has found me and the children.

He demanded to know what the hell I thought I was doing. Risking a belt around the face I told him I was leaving, that I was sick of his behaviour, his never staying in a job, his violence, his refusal to settle down, the scummy dead-beats he brought to the house, in fact, I was sick of everything about him. Once again he had been pulled up for drunken driving and stupidly refused a blood test like the idiot he was. I gave it to him with both barrels. He said he hadn't been drunk, he was just testing how much petrol was in the tank.

Frank had some weird habits when he was driving: once he had driven some way with the hand brake on. After that, he developed a compulsive habit of snatching the hand brake about twice every minute all the while ranting on about something ... Sometimes I felt like screaming "*Will you stop that!*" it was so annoying. The other thing he did was drive the car until he was nearly out of petrol then, to see how much he had in the tank, he would swing the car side to side to see if the petrol gauge lever moved. If it did, he still had some petrol; if it didn't it was time to fill up. Well, this time it had attracted the attention of the police, and I couldn't have been happier.

I didn't know how I was going to get rid of him, but suddenly he said, "Well if you are going to leave you can go to hell." He got out of the car and walked away.

Kim had enjoyed her party and I collected Steven from his friends and we headed south. I had decided to go to Christchurch, it was on another island where I hoped he would never find me.

It soon became apparent that the water pump on the car was leaking and there was no way I would reach Wellington, let alone Christchurch, without getting it fixed. We made it to Reporoa where Frank Platt and his family lived. We had met and become friends when we'd been working in the forest at Kaiangaroa. Frank was an easy-going guy and very handy with cars; moreover, he had in a field beside his house about thirty old cars from which he had permission to take parts. I threw myself on his mercy saying I would pay for his work. He said he would rather have the klaxon horn that was fitted to my car. I was reluctant to let it go but agreed.

I well-remembered the time my husband had fitted it ... we were living at Rotoma and I had gone down to the store by the lake. When I came back Frank told me to look into the engine a minute. When I did he went into the car and pressed the horn. I got such a fright I sprang back and bashed my head on the bonnet, cutting my scalp. This was so typical of the stunt he would pull. Had I had a bad heart I could easily have died. The sound was something I had never, nor have ever heard since. It screamed something like HA HA OO. Frank loved to drive up to people crossing in front of him and sound the horn; everyone on the crossing would jump with fright, and someone always swore at him.

And so it was I said goodbye to the horn. Frank Platt found a pump that would fit the old Austen and we were on the road again. I have no idea where we stayed that night; I have a vague recollection of driving through Wellington and onto the inter-island ferry but have no recollection of driving off the ferry and the long trip down to Christchurch. Goodness knows where we stayed the first night in that city but I do remember looking for a flat the next day. We got one: the front part of a house just off Bealley Avenue and a walk from the city centre. Just before Christmas was not the time to be looking for a job; Kim and I went picking raspberries, which didn't pay much but we made enough to eat. On Christmas day we had baked beans on toast.

A week or two later I applied for a job as a rep. for Barnett uniforms, and got it. Inner Christchurch has a square of one-way streets around it. My territory was outside the square. They wanted me to write down every shop or factory I visited but I soon found it unpractical and told them so, saying that it took up far too much time and I visited every shop on the street anyway. I loved the job; before I left I had taken thousands of dollars in orders.

I finally got around to writing to my parents. Mum wrote back saying they had been so worried about me as they'd had a dreadfully abusive letter from Frank saying it was their fault I had left. How typical! Once again he couldn't face the fact that he was to blame, but to blame my parents was farcical.

Steven was having trouble settling down and asked if he could go back to Rotorua and see if his friend Paul would come and live with us. Like a fool I said he could go. About a week later I got a telegram to say he was on his way home with Paul. He arrived about two days later. We were sitting at the table that night eating dinner, discussing what he had done up there when he said he'd been to see his father.

"You didn't tell him where we were, did you?" I asked. He assured me that he hadn't. "Well who's that outside the door then?" I asked, because there, outside the glass door at the end of the table was Frank. There was nothing for it but to let him in. Once again he used all his charm and eventually I said he could stay. However, I made one stipulation: "You will get a job and you will stay in that job. If you leave you are gone for good."

He got a job at the American Health Studio as a masseur, and for the second time in our time together he stayed for nine months. I eventually found out how he'd got our address – Steven had told me that Frank had followed the train they were on. Frank said that when Steven had sent the telegram he, Frank, went back to say he thought Steven had got the address wrong. The girl at the counter told him the telegram had gone upstairs so he ran up there, and the lady had the telegram in her hand. She asked him what the address was so he had to read it upside down and said yes, that was right. So like his animal cunning.

I wanted Kim to go to a good girl's school so I applied to enrol her at Avonside Girls High. The headmistress said she wouldn't have her unless I could get a reference from her previous school so I wrote away and a reply came back saying that Kim was a nice girl who was no trouble at all. Avonside said they would have her. I bought a secondhand brown gym frock, new cream blouses, and all the trimmings and she started with the new term. It was there she made friends with the daughter of a millionaire builder and spent many hours at her home. At an impressionable time of her life, she saw the way that other people lived; I couldn't have been more pleased.

Before I left Rotorua I had learned the fast hula; now I wanted Kim and me to put a floor show together. I got a cleaning job at the American Health Studio and there, before the huge mirrors, we practised our dance routine. I put an advertisement in the paper asking for someone to teach me the Maori long poi, and a Maori girl replied.

She said she didn't want paying but I insisted. After I had learned the basics I practised an hour a day for three months until I had mastered the technique.

Billie with the Maori long poi

Frank said I was stupid. "Who the hell wants to see that?" he asked. But once again he was so wrong.

Meanwhile cleaning the fitness centre at night wasn't all it cracked up to be: several times we found that some filthy man had defecated in the steam room. I found it hard to envisage the kind of person who would do this, knowing that the cleaners had to clean it up. However, after we had finished work Kim and I had the large room where we could practice in front of the mirrors and make sure we made all our movements in unison.

We got a few bookings; being paid $15 a time. An old hotel away over at Granity on the west coast twenty-eight kilometres north of Westport advertised for an act to appear on Christmas Eve. I applied, explaining our act and asked for $25 which I now realise was ridiculously cheap given how far we had to travel. They replied saying "yes please".

We travelled up from Christchurch, through the Lewis Pass to Westport and up the coast. The hotel was a surprise, it belonged in another century, a two-storeyed square building coated with sheets of corrugated iron; it looked like something out of a wild west movie. The place no longer functioned as a hotel because it was so run down it wasn't allowed, but the bar was always busy. It was an old coal mining area, squeezed between the Tasman Sea and the steep, forested, cloud-shrouded mountains of the Southern Alps. We were given a warm welcome by the lady owner and shown to a large bedroom upstairs with very old wallpaper and paint; the beds, however, were clean and comfortable. The bar area where we were to perform was quite small, in fact, we would be right on top of the patrons, mostly men. That night the place was packed to the doors, standing room only, and the show went down well. Our host said with a laugh that she must have had the only full bar in the village, there being two others. She was delighted. She told us that the dining room was fully booked for Christmas dinner and would we mind if they packed us a picnic lunch so we could go off sightseeing – we said that was fine by us. The next morning we set off with our large picnic basket to see the surrounding area.

The west coast is almost all tree-clad, the trees dripping with moss and lichen from the dampness. The rain-soaked winds that drift across the Tasman drop their moisture when they hit the Alps giving the coast rains aplenty. We found our picnic basket full of delicious food:

chicken, ham, salads, bread rolls, fresh fruits, and cherries. We stopped in a scenic spot to enjoy our feast. If this was how artists were treated I was all for it. All too soon it was time to go home.

It wasn't long before I had saturated all my area and the small towns around Christchurch trying to sell uniforms. I realised this when one man told me indignantly, "You came in here two weeks ago." I decided to go to Nelson at the top of the west coast and planned to go alone taking Frank's big six-cylinder Wolseley. But he, with his insatiable need to travel, was having none of it. He took time off work, and he and Kim, who was on holiday, came with me. I found their presence really restricting; there they would be sitting in the car waiting while I might have to spend an hour or more with clients. But the Nelsonites were so pleased to see me, some said they had been waiting for ages for someone to come with uniforms. I went back to Christchurch with over a thousand dollars worth of orders. The boss couldn't believe his luck. What a great pay packet I had that week.

Meanwhile, on the home front things were not good. Steven and Paul had come home late one night with Paul holding on to a ripped off thumb. It seems they had been pushing a motorbike and Paul had put his hand down near the chain just as Steven pushed it forward cutting his thumb off at the joint. I found a dressing and bandaged it firmly to hold the wound together, then took off with them in the car to find the emergency department at the hospital. Damn Christchurch with its one way systems; I had just the vaguest idea where the hospital was and found I was driving the wrong way along a one-way street. *Please, please*, I thought, *let a police car come so I can cry for help*, but there wasn't one anywhere. Eventually I found the hospital and raced in.

"It's around the other side," they said, so I jumped back into the car and eventually found the A and E apartment. Paul lost his thumb and was in hospital for several days before coming back to our place. I eventually found out that they'd been trying to steal the bike.

Later he and Steven had a very old ute towed back to our front garden. I was furious. The last thing I wanted in the front garden was a car wreck. I found out the car yard they'd bought it from, went there and tore a strip off the owner.

"How dare you sell that heap of junk to my son!" I snarled.

"Look," he said, throwing his arms in the air, "they offered to give me $15 for it so I took it. I can see why you would be annoyed so here is the $15 back."

Needless to say, I then felt a fool for losing my temper. The ute. did, however, give the little wretches something to do and kept them out of mischief when they were not at work, and to my utter disbelief one weekend they got it going. However, I was less than impressed when they backed it out of the yard and took off out into the streets without a car licence, insurance, or drivers licences, not to mention bald tyres and who knows what else. They arrived home an hour later seemingly unscathed, to get the brunt of my fury. If I ever come back to this life again and give birth to a son I think I will drown him.

Steven had already been to court to answer for all the daft things he'd done in Rotorua; mostly traffic infringements like exceeding the speed limit in a built-up area, carrying a passenger on a motorbike, and several things more which strangely enough I had never been appraised of. All the stupid things that teenage boys do because they think they're invincible.

Paul eventually went back to Rotorua and Steven decided to go to Australia. Sadly, I have to say I was glad to see him go, it was bad enough having to put up with his father without the constant stress of wondering what dreadful thing he was going to do next.

He has written a book called, *I Tramped Through a Rhodesia War Zone* which tells it all.

I had trouble with Frank just once during our time in Christchurch. He came home one afternoon in a foul mood because he'd been drinking. He was no sooner in the door than he started being belligerent. I was immediately fearful and did my best not to provoke him but knew that at any moment I would be belted. We were in the kitchen and when he turned his back I shot out the door and went to the policeman who lived next door. Luckily he was home, but he explained that as a neighbour he couldn't afford to get involved. "Jump in the back of the car and lie down; I will throw a rug over you."

Once on the road, he radioed for help and we met another police car to which I was transferred. The new policeman drove me home and came inside. He gave Frank a real dressing down and told him that if he stepped out of line again he would be spending the night in the lock-up and would face the magistrate in the morning. I had done something that I should have done years before, and it was a long time before he lifted his hand to me again.

A few more months went by, but he was getting restless again and wanted to go back to Australia. I eventually relented but stupidly said: "When you find a place where you would like to settle, just let me know and that is what we will do."

How could I have been such an idiot? I should have known that the more we travelled the more he would want to. I did, however, make one stipulation: "I am not, repeat *not*, going to tolerate the way we have lived in the past. Kim and I will get work with our floor show as we travel so that we will never be without money."

> *So we packed up Father's new straw hat*
> *The wickets and the cricket bat*
> *A trouser press, a brush and comb*
> *Our hula skirts and a gramophone.*

Australia Again

Our first stop, of course, was Sydney. It was hot and humid and I was not impressed. Some parts were dirty and smelly and I was shocked to see a window full of T-shirts with disgusting things written on them. I couldn't imagine anyone in New Zealand wearing them never mind being able to buy them. Frank insisted we book in at the Salvation Army's People's Palace; it was in no way a palace and not to my liking, but everything about Frank was cheap and nasty. The tea was weak and the place run down. All the floors were alike so it was easy to get lost.

One afternoon we were sitting in the cafe area and drinking their revolting tea and talking about something to someone when Kim jumped up and said, "I'll go and get it."

Given that all the corridors looked alike she set off along the bottom one thinking she was going to our room. I heard a commotion and shot out to see her being manhandled by a middle-aged man. I can't remember what I said but I should have said much more; I should have threatened him with assault which was exactly what it was. I probably pointed out that all the corridors looked alike so no wonder people get confused.

He said, "This is the men's corridor and you have no idea how many girls sneak in here and have to be stopped."

Once more I had been confronted with the kind of scum employed by the Salvation Army and I was livid. All he had to say was "Excuse me, young lady, where are you going?" She would have said, "I am going to our room."

Then he could have explained that she was in the wrong corridor. Instead, he had grabbed her and tried to turn her around. She was fourteen years old and badly frightened.

Soon after that, we found a motor caravan advertised away over in Parramatta – how big was the city of Sydney. We went to see it, a Volkswagen Kombi – we liked it and bought it. We moved out of our ghastly hotel and headed for the seaside. A day later we found that one of the bearings in a back wheel was gone so had to make the long trip back to the dealership. They fixed the problem but on the way back we found they had not fastened the wheel nuts and the wheel almost fell off. One can't but wonder if it had not been done deliberately.

We went down to Botany Bay to camp by the sea. So this was Botany Bay where the first settlers arrived. I was not impressed: the sea was floating with flotsam, plastic bags and other rubbish coming in on the waves. Each day I practised the long poi, and it was here I decided I should have a finale of pois on fire. Frank said I was mad but I persisted. I shopped for bits, bought swivel joints to attach to wire that was attached to plaited wool. The balls I made from balls of canvas. This was a disaster: the swivel joints spun and put the pois out of balance, and the canvas soaked with turpentine soon burnt through and bits of burning debris flew everywhere. But I was not going to be defeated. In the months to come I experimented with many different things, even tried some old fire hose from the fire brigade that I paid for with a free performance at their club night. But that didn't last either. I eventually used fine wire fly netting stuffed with cotton wool which I still use today.

In the phone book, we found a theatre costumier who made me a costume with a high Chinese collar. He was an aged, gay man who didn't like costumes high cut at the thigh. But they were just coming into fashion. Within months I had bought an old red sparkly dress at an op. shop and made myself a much better-looking costume with the higher cut to show more leg. *If you've got it, flaunt it!* – isn't that what they say? Later again I made a black two-piece one with coloured luminous spots – quite impressive in the ultraviolet light.

We also rang a booking agent who asked us to come to his home and show him our show. He lived in one of Sydney's outer suburbs in a grubby little home. My suspicions were aroused as soon as we arrived; the door opened on security chains and a thin white face peered out. Its owner had thin black hair left long on the top so it could be combed over to hide a bald head. Having assured himself that we looked safe he took the chain off and cautiously opened the door, wide enough to put his head out and look up and down the street. It was all very strange. He ushered us in quickly and took us into a back room where we changed and did our act. He liked it.

"Let me know when you have accommodation and I'll tell you when I have something for you."

Back in the van, I told Frank. "No way. There is something very fishy about his behaviour and I don't trust him. He probably takes the money and doesn't pay the artists." It was well-known that it was hard to get work in Sydney so we decided there and then to head north.

Our first stop was at the Hawkesbury River. A caravan was already there with a disreputable man who said he was the caretaker of the place. We set about cooking a meal and after we'd eaten he asked us if we would come over for a drink. As he was already showing signs of intoxication we politely declined, which made him angry. He turned nasty, called Frank 'a bastard dirty Pom'; said we bloody well shouldn't be camping there anyway and a lot more threats and filthy language. I was sorry that Kim had to be exposed to this but it was already dark and too late to move on. We spent the night and were on the road again at first light.

The rest of our trip north was pleasant and interesting. Along the way, we found places to stop where there was a steel cooking plate and a pile of firewood ready for lighting a fire underneath. I found a strange little animal dead beside the road and thought I had found a new species. Later I learned it was a bandicoot well known in Australia.

Our first show booked was at *The Playroom* in Palm Beach on the Gold Coast – they had a Hawaiian night each Thursday. When I went in to ask they said their Hawaiian Dancers were on holiday and they would be pleased to have us. Thus we started our professional career in Australia. It was also the first time I was to try the flame pois which ended in disaster. We were working with a band called Winstern County who were also making their debut. They were decked out in white suits and the thick-soled, high heeled shoes that were the fashion of the day. They were really lovely lads.

"We've been waiting for him to leave school so we could travel," they said, pointing to the youngest member. Their music was great and they went down well. Our show was also well received but I was mortified with the end. I was about to drop the flames into a wet towel held by Frank when one came adrift. It rolled across the stage and nestled at the ankle of one of the band. He suddenly felt the heat, jumped with fright and kicked the flaming ball back across the stage where I stopped it flying into the audience with my foot. It rolled back into the middle of the stage and Frank came on to kick it into the wings.

Back up in the dressing room later, where I was still smarting from my failure, the lads arrived on their break full of enthusiasm for our act. They thought we were big professional artists. We didn't tell them we were just starting out as they were. They thought my malfunctioning gear was a huge joke and rolled up a pair of socks and starting kicking it around the room, which made us all laugh and me feel a little better. I have often wondered about them, how they got on. Did they turn to drugs and drink like so many others have. I hope not.

We travelled north again and our scrapbook tells me that we next appeared at the *Grosvenor* in Rockhampton for four nights. The band was billed *The Top Australian Show Band, Highway One*, but strangely I don't remember a thing about that booking. I didn't even drink in those days and I have never taken drugs so how I have lost four days is a mystery. I do remember Rockhampton however and its old impressive Australian buildings – we liked the town immensely.

North again, we appeared at the *Boomerang Motor Lodge* in Mackay where were billed as a 'SPECIAL EVENT'. On the way up we had to cross several wooden bridges where shallow, beautiful clear water ran. In parts, where the roadsides were bounded by dry grass, the noise of the cicadas was deafening, and occasionally swarms of locusts would take to the air as we passed. Hundreds of ugly cane toads were squashed on the highway.

Billed as Special Event

The cane toad, originally from central and south America was introduced into Australia from Hawaii in the 1930's to control the Frenchie and Grey-back beetles in the sugar cane crop. These horrible poisonous creatures have now polluted the best part of Australia's north.

Now as I write, in 2014, there is a fight to keep them out of Western Australia; but I have no doubt the toad will win, given the fact they can lay thousands of eggs at a time and have no natural predators. It is now estimated that they are now moving forward about fifty kilometres a year.

Mackay was a lovely small town. We camped just out of town where a very long wooden structure carried a sewage pipe away out through the mangroves to empty into the ocean. Kim and I walked a long way out but never reached the end. We were fascinated to see mud-hopping fish slithering about in the grey mud around the mangrove roots.

We moved into town and the caravan park for our shows on the 26th and 27th of April. One night, back at the park after our shows, I visited the toilet to find that someone had trodden on one of the beautiful bright green frogs that abounded in the place; they had then thrown the poor thing down the toilet. I was so sad that, despite the fact that its guts were hanging out, it was still very much alive. I lifted it from the toilet bowl trying not to cry, and did the kind thing, finding something to hit it on the head with to put it out of its misery.

Our next stop was at Airlie Beach where the Whitsunday Regatta was held. We appeared there on the 4th and 5th of May. During the week we took a cruise from Shute Harbour out to Hayman, Daydream and South Molle Islands. Before we left I hung over a small bridge where, in the shallow water underneath, swam tropical fish of all shapes. I could have stayed there for hours soaking it all in.

The worst thing about Airlie Beach were the midges, if that's what they were called. If you squinted your eyes you could see the tiniest white specks in the air – no one told us they could do so much damage. Soon we were covered with violently itchy bites, but they were not bites we were told, the wretched things had urinated on us it seems. Either way we were a mess and we had to go on to the cabaret floor with the awful blotches on our legs covered with makeup.

Another incident that annoyed me immensely happened on the second night: some drunken teenage male threw a lit cigarette under Kim's bare feet and she got a nasty burn. I knew who did it and should have approached management and had him thrown out. This is one of the drawbacks of working on a cabaret floor at 2 am when the audience is crowded in around you.

We headed north again up the coast to Townsville and hadn't been long on the road before we found a lovely spot, a very small lake with water lilies and abounding with small turtles. Not only were we taking in the sights but learning about the wildlife and flora as well. After taking a colour slide of the turtles I took a head and shoulders shot of Kim amongst a big display of bougainvillea flowers. When the slide was developed I was shocked to see how white her face was. The two late nights and hard work at Airlie Beach had taken its toll.

At Townsville we did the usual touristy things, climbing the hills above the town and cruising out to beautiful Green Island where I could have spent most of the day looking at the wonders of the corals and fish from the underwater observatory. We visited the Townville

Gardens, or Arboretum. Frank, who was driving, was reefing off about something as usual because some trivial thing had upset him, when Kim and I realised he hadn't seen the obstacle.

"*Speed bump!*" we yelled.

We hit the thing about thirty miles per hour and I bashed my head on the roof of the cabin resulting in a sore neck for the next few days.

It was at these gardens that we met another creature we didn't know existed. The Cassowary. It is a very large colourful bird with a bony shield above its beak and very strong legs. It was in a cage and when I drew close enough to film it, it flew at me. Not the sort of thing one would want to meet in the wild.

By now we had worked out that the north of Australia was screaming out for entertainers – no need of an agent – we just had to go in and ask to be snapped up immediately. However, we didn't try for work in Townsville, but set off for Cairns, once again camping on the coast. The water was over the road at Ingham after weeks of rain but it was shallow enough to drive through. Unfortunately, the rain had caused a lot of potholes in the road which were sometimes hard to avoid.

Lovely Cairns: 1,700 kilometres north of Brisbane, it was a sunny and vibrant little town. We grabbed a newspaper to check out the nightspots and decided to approach a licensed restaurant called *The House on the Hill* and were booked for the 11th, 17th and 18th of May.

Cairns doesn't have any beaches around the town. Like a lot of northern towns, mangrove swamps crowd the coast. However, just over the hill was a magnificent long sandy beach and it was there we camped until it was time to work.

The House on the Hill had an interesting history – it was once called *Fairview House* attached to Fairview Farm. From 1942 until 1944 it was leased by the Royal Australian Navy for £1 a month and called Z Experimental Station (ZES). Here British and Australian commandos trained for Operation Jaywick, a successful mission that resulted in several Japanese ships being blown up in Singapore Harbour. They travelled from Cairns to Singapore in an old Japanese ship thus arriving in Singapore Harbour unannounced. There was also a plaque telling of how some commandos stealthily travelled by canoes around islands further north to find if they had been occupied by the Japanese.

The establishment was a large wooden house with open verandas all round. Inside was a huge open plan area where two bands played, one on each side. The area could cope with more than one function at a time – indeed on one of the nights we were there a wedding party took up part of the venue.

Playing alongside us was Big Des Huia, supposed to a big name in New Zealand but we'd never heard of him. The bands were The Graduates, supposedly Cairns' top dance and show band, and the Langtree Trio who played dinner and old-time and jazz.

Big Des was a nice guy and not a bad singer, and both bands were great – we enjoyed working there. There was just one nasty incident that spoiled our stay: Frank had a spat with the owner, Stan. He was working on the stage getting our music ready when Stan, who was a bit of a ham and liked to get on the mike, said something to him. It must have been something like "Can't you leave that until I'm finished," and Frank answered back. The next thing we knew Frank had started our music while Stan was still talking. We were horrified. My charming husband was getting his own back without a thought of the dilemma he put us in. Our dance music was *Wipe Out* by The Beachboys which has a long loud laugh at the beginning; we would then rush on to the stage with loud screams. That and our white hula skirts behind the ultraviolet light made for a spectacular entrance. We waited a few seconds and rushed onto the stage just as Stan scurried off the other side. I expected repercussions from Stan, but nothing more was said of the incident although I was boiling with rage.

Kim and I were paid $50 for each performance which was about the average wage at the time, and we were supplied a meal afterward as we couldn't eat before the show. Some of those meals were amazing. One night we collected from the fridge big plates with half a chicken surrounded by a beautiful salad. We may have been hungry but no way could we eat half a chicken each.

Our work done at Cairns we headed south again to Townsville. Our next show was on Magnetic Island just off the coast from Townsville. Unlike most of the islands off the Queensland coast, Magnetic is not a coral island but very rocky.

Our time here is one of most pleasurable memories. We were treated like princesses by the two gay guys who ran the *Hotel Arcadia*. We were supplied with motel type accommodation – great after living in a camper van most of the time. The stage, however, was a bit of a problem; it had a quite low covering of dried palm leaves like you might expect on a Polynesian island and one of the men was worried sick that I might set them on fire. He said he had once seen an act where a girl had set herself on fire; so he stood ready with the fire extinguisher. As for me, I had to bend my knees whenever I tossed the flame pois above my head and hoped for the best. Usually we didn't go out after a show and mingle with the crowd, but on Magnetic we went out to meet the guests who were pleased to see us. I have two good photos taken on the island: one is of Kim and I sitting on the bed looking very glamorous and the other is of Kim photographing the bikini tree. They had a tree with boobs on one side and a bottom on the other – what better than to paint a bikini on it? The guys wanted us to come back the next weekend but Frank wanted to move on, so we headed inland to the heart of the country on the Flinders Highway, to Charters Towers, Hughenden, Cloncurry and then Mount Isa where copper is mined.

We stayed a couple of days and explored before pushing on to Tennant Creek on the main north road from Adelaide to Darwin. We worked one night at the hotel on the 7th of June, camping out in the bush for a day or two before the show. We had bought with us from New Zealand Frank's shotgun and the .22, so we had some target practice to while the time away. Kim and I climbed to the top of a nearby hill where rock wallabies lived, and I took a colour slide of our camp far below.

After Tennant Creek we travelled south to see Alice Springs, made famous by the book *A Town Like Alice*. The Alice is a pretty little town almost smack in the middle of Australia. Unfortunately, some Aborigines had gone on the rampage the night before we arrived because they'd been banned from the pubs, and all the way up the street hotel windows had been smashed. Groups of them sat around town drinking from bottles – it was such a sad sight. I have always felt sorry for these people. Like many indigenous people moved away from their culture they have picked up the worst habits of the white man. Foul language, petrol sniffing, and especially alcohol consumption has become a huge problem. They are a people in limbo and, with no work to fill their time, many turn to drink, and domestic violence.

The Todd River that runs through Alice Creek is lucky if it sees water once a year. Mostly it is just dry sand. Kim and I walked about one hundred yards along it and counted forty-nine large, empty half-gallon beer bottles. We were horrified.

Once a year the locals hold a *Henley-on-Todd* race, where young guns race their boats, with legs sticking out the bottom.

From Alice Springs we travelled out to see the well-known tourist spot, Stanley's Chasm, an amazing place where it seems as though a big knife has been sliced through the land leaving a deep slash. The secret is to be there at precisely midday when the sun shines directly overhead lighting up the chasm of red, ochre and cream walls. We walked quite a way up and took slides for posterity.

The road there was quite a challenge: large stones and big creek beds almost rattled the van to bits. We arrived about ten minutes past midday and already the sun was starting to pass over so narrow is the gap.

We didn't try for work in the Alice so after three days, we headed north again to drive the 1,497 kilometres to Darwin.

The Stuart Highway, which was put through during the Second World War, has some interesting features. At Barrow Creek there is a memorial for three men who were killed by Aborigines at the telegraph station in 1874. Seeing the natives coming empty-handed they presumed they had come in peace. James Stapleton, the station master, John Franks, a linesman, and Ernest Flint went out to meet them.

Sadly, it wasn't so, their visitors were dragging their spears with their toes and when within range used them to kill Stapleton and Franks. Earnest Flint died later from his wounds. Perhaps, if the white settlers had treated the Aborigines better instead of treating them as inferior beings, the resentment would not have come about. It has always dismayed me that people look down on people of a different skin colour – we are all equal under the skin.

Adelaide River is a small community about 115 kilometres from Darwin where sits a wonderful green oasis in the form of a war cemetery. In the beautifully kept green lawn there are 434 headstones, for all the people who were killed in the Japanese bombing of Darwin on the 19th of February 1942. These include the merchant seamen on the ships in the harbour at that time, secret service agents, navy men whose bodies were never found, and the civilians of Darwin and down the track who died in the bombing. A bigger memorial stands for the nine post office workers who stayed at their post during the attack and received a direct hit. But the one I liked most simply said, MOLLY MOP O MINE. She must have been someone's indigenous house girl.

Our next gig was at the *Aspa Jet Room*, a night club with meals in Darwin, booked from the 22nd until the 27th of June. Here we shared billing with yet another Maori singer, Billy Daye.

As usual, we arrived at the venue on the day we were to perform. Usually it was just a quick look to see where the dressing room was, how big the stage or cabaret floor was, and how long it took us to get into position. This day we hit a snag – the stage was a metre above the floor. The dressing room was about five metres from the side of the stage. We had to stay hidden until the music started then come out screaming and leap up onto the stage – not so easy in a hula skirt. I think we spent half the afternoon practicing; firstly without our skirts then with them on. As I was in the lead I was conjuring up horrible visions of me tripping and landing flat on my face with Kim on top of me. I wasn't sure if I should laugh or cry. However I am proud to say that neither one of us stumbled, not once in the six days we were there. Oh, to be so fit today.

It was winter: the nicest time to be in the Northern Territory. We camped down at Fanny Bay, with many other motor caravans. Here we had our first experience of water heated by solar power. The showers were always hot.

We made some great friends at the *Aspa Jet Room*. It was owned by a Greek family and we soon met all the young male relatives. The boss had a boat he would take out to catch fish for the club menu. One day the lads were supposed to go to the beach to catch baitfish, but when Alexio, the youngest one, asked if they were coming to help him they refused, saying they wanted to kick the football around the park with Frank. They seemed to treat this very handsome lad as a bit of a joke, almost as if he was a bit simple. Anyway, Kim and I agreed to go with him and had one of the most interesting experiences of our lives. It all involved a very long net which we had to drag around in a huge circle on the incoming tide, with one end anchored on the beach. As Alexio dragged it back to the shore, Kim and I had to hold the centre of the net up. It was a bit hard to hold upright with us on the outside so I said to Kim why didn't we get inside the net, which we did. Next thing we saw Alexio making frantic signs for us to get outside the net again which we did. When he had almost reached the sand again he rushed up the beach depositing an incredible variety of fish to leap about on the sand. Little pufferfish blew themselves up into important-looking balloons, long skinny garfish jerked and leaped. Alexio quickly filled his eskies (what New Zealanders call chilly bins) with small fat baitfish. We filled ours with edible fish, several scroungers coming to see what they could get. When the net was rolled and put away I asked Alexio why he'd told us not to walk inside the net.

"Poisonous sea snakes," he said. "We often get them in the net; I didn't want you to get bitten."

Frank had got a job as a welder and had invited all his workmates to a fish barbecue out at Fanny Bay where there were cooking places to light a fire under. We took some salads and bread and had a wonderful feast of cooked fish. This was the first time I encountered hermit crabs. How strange they looked, all scuttling about on the sand, inhabiting different shaped shells.

With the living so easy in Darwin we wanted to stay awhile. With nowhere else for us to work in show biz in Darwin, Kim and I looked for work. Woolworths were opening a new supermarket and advertised for workers; we were both accepted. I was to work on the checkout, and Kim was to work on the shop floor. We would walk to work in the morning, our black skirts and white blouses already soaked with perspiration when we arrived. It always shocked us when we walked into the cold of the air conditioner and returned to the outside heat at the end of the day. I learned a lot about people's habits at the checkout: Darwin's tribe of hippies ate healthy food and not much of it; overweight people came through with cakes, pies, cream, ice cream, and fatty things.

Frank's workplace was having a 'work do' out at Mica Beach one evening, so he offered the boss our floor show free. It turned out to be one of the strangest places we ever worked in – I still chuckle when I think about it. Mica Beach is a ferry ride across from Darwin. The beach below the hotel sparkled with mica in the lights as we landed – it was quite beautiful. The function was held in a big open-sided, covered area. About 10 pm, the management showed us to an empty chalet up on the hill behind, where we could change into our costumes. The narrow path that wound its way up the hill through trees and the garden was not well lit, but here and there among the shadows we spotted Aborigines already asleep in their swags. They were booked to do a corroboree the next day for a group of tourists.

Just as we had finished dressing an excited male guest arrived to see if we were okay … well, that was his excuse anyway. We told him we were fine and would be down soon but unfortunately Frank arrived just as he was leaving. He got nasty with us, as though we had encouraged him, whereas we hadn't laid eyes on the man until he arrived at the door. The time came for us to make our appearance and we gingerly picked our way down the path barefooted; we were almost at the bottom where there were no lights, when we heard, rather than saw, a large sow snuffling across the path in front of us, with goodness knows how many squealing piglets in her wake.

"Oh my god," I said, "I hope we don't stand in something nasty."

I was thinking of us screaming on to the stage with pig poo squashing out between our toes. And the fun didn't stop there – our music slowed down – went fast again – then slowed down again. Kim and I, by this time, had become very good at talking to one another without moving our mouths, all the while keeping a smile on our faces.

"What the hell's going on with the music?" I asked.

We found out later that the electricity was on direct current from the generator … yet another lesson learned.

Steven joined us in Darwin, driving in a ute with his mate Joe from Kununurra where they'd been jackaroos on a big cattle station for about a year. I hardly recognised my son when I saw him; he had grown taller and his dark eyes seemed to have shrunk into his head with so many hours spent out in the sun on horseback. Joe had a long scar on his abdomen where he'd been knifed. Later we were to find that he was a trouble-maker when drunk, which we could have done without. They stayed in Darwin until we all left together, the two vehicles travelling together.

The journey west was interesting as here and there we came upon billabongs covered with the lovely native blue water lilies: quite beautiful. One day Frank and I rattled over a cattle crossing and heard a hub cap fly off. Before we could stop to collect it we ran over a creamy white snake. The boys and Kim were travelling behind and stopped to pick it up. When they handed the hub cap to me it had the still moving snake in it. I screeched and dropped it, giving them a good laugh at my expense. It turned out the poor thing was dead. I plucked up the courage to touch it and the waves of muscles moving along its body caused it to slither through my hand. Very creepy. It was sad – the poor thing was probably a harmless grass snake that didn't deserve to die.

Another day we passed a big pond fed by a pipe gushing artesian water. We gazed in awe at the amazing birds of all sizes that wadded in the water. I had never seen most of the species, nor have I since; some were up to a meter high. Sadly we didn't have a bird book to identify them all with.

At lunchtime one day we stopped at Timber Creek which was actually quite wide and had water running in it. It was a pretty place with trees growing to the water's edge. Steve, seeing some horses on the other side, swam over and tried to catch one to ride, but the horse saw him coming and shot through. I think there may have been a bridge there at some time as a big concrete block jutted a few feet out from the bank. I drew out the camera to capture the scene so Frank climbed onto the block, stood on one leg, bend down putting the other leg up behind him and stuck his arms out sideways. I was getting heartily sick of his stupidity every time I tried to film something – I called it his 'Physyky at the fountain' trick.

We came at last to Kununurra, a lovely little place on the edge of Lake Argyle, a massive body of water formed by the damming of the Ord River. Irrigation from the dam has opened up many acres of land for farming that had previously been dry desert. We camped in a site by the lake, very picturesque with lovely weeping willows which seemed so out of place in outback Australia. Marvellous what water can do.

We had an amazing experience the first morning. I woke to the most amazing cacophony of noise and for a moment wondered where on earth I was. Then I realised it was the birds' morning chorus. Honks, squeaks, whistles, chirps, screeches, and hoots – they were all there and the noise was deafening. I wouldn't have missed it for the world.

We stayed a few days in Kununurra because Steven wanted to ride in the rodeo. His old boss from the station was the judge. We parked our van nose in to the ring to watch. Unfortunately, Steven's ride didn't last long before he was thrown, and he lost points for touching his hat. He had told his boss that his parents were there and I stupidly thought they would come over to say hello as most New Zealand farmers would have done. But then, New Zealand farmers don't think of themselves as royalty.

Soon we were on the road again towards Halls Creek. Steven and his mate decided they didn't want to wait as we worked along the way and went ahead, planning to meet us again when we got to Perth.

The road was still unsealed, and the going rough. The red bull-dust was horrible, and sometimes the van fell into a big dip in the road, so filled with dust it looked flat. A great cloud of the fine powder would fly up filling the van and nearly choking us. It seeped into everything and turned our sweaty skins bronze. In some parts, rocks showed through the road surface, one scraping the bottom of the van.

One day we passed such a wonderful sight I just had to write and tell the family about it. The place wasn't as well known in 1974 as it is now – today it is a big tourist spot and rightly so. The Bungle Bungle ranges look like huge piles of pancakes getting smaller as they go up until they round off at the top. They are reputed to be 350 million years old or thereabouts, and was originally an old river bed. The orange and black stripes are formed by the layers laid down by mud from floods and iron-bearing sand that turned to sandstone. They are part of the Purnululu National Park.

Next stop, Halls Creek, where we met some of the rudest, and up-themselves people I have ever met. The event was the Kimberley Goldfields Amateur Jockey Clubs' Presentation Ball, where we worked with a band called *The Drifters*, quite the nicest group I have met. They were older men, perhaps in their early thirties and a pleasure to talk to; which was good as the rest of the evening wasn't up to much. The show went well; crowds of young Aborigine children followed us excitedly from window to window, looking into a world from which their people were banned.

In the toilets outside the building, faeces decorated the floor and was smeared on the cubicle walls and toilet seats. It was disgusting.

I met one of the towns ladies and said to her, "Can't you teach these Aborigine children to be a bit cleaner."

She replied, "Oh well, they are all just children." She also told us there would be a march around the hall of all the females to choose the Queen (or whatever) of the Night.

I said, "Oh, my daughter might win that."

She replied laughing, "No way. The ladies from the stations take it in turns to get the prize. No town's lady has ever won it."

We stood back to watch, and sure enough, a very plain woman was chosen. What a joke!

We should have been paid on the night in cash, as artists usually are, but they were too ignorant to know that. When I asked Bert, the man who had booked us, he said he was sorry but we would have to come out to the racecourse the following morning. I was annoyed as we had hoped to start out early for Fitzroy Crossing. However, I presented myself at the racecourse at the stipulated time. They were all seated in the grandstand seemingly to have a meeting but they all appeared to be talking. Bert took me to the girl treasurer who was seated in the bottom row talking to the girl beside her. He told her I had come for our fee. She looked at me and making no comment, not even a hello, reached into her bag for the cheque book, and went on talking. A few minutes later she began writing the cheque but stopped again to go on talking.

This stopping and starting of the writing went on for some time while Bert and I stood about four feet away, completely ignored. I was fuming and Bert knew it and became embarrassed. Finally, he said, "Heather, would you finish writing that cheque please and let this lady get away."

She gave us a *Oh-are-you-still-here* look but finished writing the cheque and handed it over without a word. I still find it hard to believe anyone could be so appallingly rude.

We set off towards Fitzroy Crossing, driving on a long, very hot day in blistering temperatures. The road was unsealed and dusty. We forded the Fitzroy River on a big concrete block with water running about a foot deep over the top, and carried on until we found a place that signposted the Fitzroy Pub. Down a steep bank was a muddy creek and Frank, who was driving, was going to try to cross until Kim and I yelled at him. We parked and made our way barefoot over the creek and hence to the pub. Never in my life have I enjoyed a beer so much

… and I don't even like beer. But it was cold, which was more than I could have said for our canvas water container hanging from the bumper at the front of our van.

We met a group of workers, Aussies, English, and Irish, from the works camp down the road. They were a great group of guys working on the new bridge across the Fitzroy River. We had a great hour talking and laughing with them before setting off back to our van and them to their digs. When we reached the creek we found an elderly couple, who were on a trip around Australia; they had got their caravan stuck in the water, their four-wheel drive unable to dislodge it. The poor lady was a nervous wreck. I asked Kim to take her up onto the far bank out of harm's way and stay with her, which she did, while we all went to work. We uncoupled the van and told her husband to drive up the bank. We then coupled his winch to the caravan and told him to wind it in with us all pushing. The van came free and we kept pushing it up the bank on to the flat where we attached it to his car again. My only concern had been that the wire rope would break, come flying back, and decapitate some of us, but it went without a hitch, apart from us all having mud up to our thighs and looking a real mess They were so grateful; they couldn't believe that out there in the sticks a group of people from all over the world would materialise to help them. It was now quite dark so they said they would stay there the night.

The lads asked us to come and visit them at the camp so, after we'd cleaned ourselves up and had dinner, we did. Kim retired to her bunk and was soon fast asleep. We parked just inside the camp; Frank and I sat inside with the side door open while the workers brought camp chairs to sit outside. We were a happy group, talking and laughing about many things. It was rare for them to have visitors to talk with and they made the most of it. Their biggest gripe was the camp supervisor, and I think the cook, as he had read them the riot act for arriving back late to eat. The bitter, ferret-faced little man walked past at a distance a few times to glare at us. No one was drunk or disorderly, but he must have been jealous because he phoned the police.

One of the workers took himself off and when he came back the

Irish lad asked if he'd got everything hidden away. The man nodded.

"And the syringes?' he asked, and again the man nodded.

I was shocked but didn't show it. Someone was on drugs, certainly the man who had left looked like an addict. After talking to the supervisor the police came to see us saying it was illegal for us to be inside the camp fence. He wanted to know who we were and "Who is that?" he asked, shining his torch on Kim in her top bunk.

"That," I said in my best English, "is our daughter."

He could see we were quite respectable but told us to remove ourselves to outside the gates. The guys said they would meet us out there but we said goodbye and went back to camp by the creek beside the old couple. We spent the next morning talking with them. They had come from Port Jackson on the coast outside Sydney and had been on the road for three months.

About midday it was time for us to leave; they gave us their address and told us to come and see them if we were ever down that way. They seemed sad to see us go and once again thanked us for coming to their rescue.

Back on a tar-sealed road again we bypassed Derby and headed for Broome, 657 kilometres away. It was on this road we saw a phenomenon that we were unlikely to see ever again. We were travelling due west, on a stretch of dead straight road that reached to the horizon; it was early evening – the sun goes down early in the tropics – and there it was, dead in line with the end of the road and setting fast. Normally the western sun is blinding, but this was not. The large ball and its surrounds were aglow with colours of orange and yellow. Down, down it went, to finally drop below the horizon, and then it was dark. I see it now as I write; etched on my brain forever.

Broome was a dream, its coast lined with small red cliffs. I had Kim climb down to the first shelf so I could capture the scene on camera; she shrank back as the waves splashed up. Broome was once the centre of the pearling industry, many Asian divers losing their lives here in the dangerous occupation. We visited the cemetery, the Asian part beautifully kept, quite immaculate. Each gravestone had a bottle of water in front of it. The Muslim part was untidy, the grass unkempt, the graves marked by two thin stones standing up about three feet apart at each end. I wondered if they had been buried standing up facing Mecca. We stayed in Broome a day or two to take in the amazing scenery.

Hitting the road again we headed for Port Headland, 567 kilometres away. This was a desolate part of the road with very little to see and marked only by two roadhouses about 200 kilometres apart where we could fill up with petrol. Part of it travels near the Eighty Mile beach. One day we decided to take a side road to the beach, where we found a couple with a young family who were travelling around Australia. They'd found a sea snake washed up on the beach and, given that they are highly poisonous, it was luckily dead. However, it was a beautiful black and white creature, the only sea snake I have seen. I think it was on this stretch of road that we camped again beside the beach in a place where the road came quite close. Here I found another world wonder. The dunes were not made of sand but billions of tiny shells shaped a bit like the shell oil sign and about the size of my first fingernail. I was fascinated and I wanted to collect sacks and sacks of them to take with me.

At last, Port Headland: a grubby town where everything seemed covered with red dust. Here iron ore was loaded onto ships for export. We were amazed at how many ships awaited offshore to load the precious cargo. We didn't try for work here but set off again on the North West Coastal Highway. I believe the only town we travelled through was Roebourne, and maybe Wickham, and Karratha. Once again until we reached Carnarvon the only stops were at the roadhouses for petrol. On this road we once again had trouble with the tyres. When we set off from Sydney the van was shod with Michelin tyres suitable for the city, but definitely not for the outback. At someplace across the north, we had a terrible job getting replacement tyres which had to be ordered from some place south. Now we had a puncture. Frank changed it for the spare but could not get the punctured tyre off the rim to repair it, even though he hammered and hammered. I sat back and watched and finally said:

"Why don't you put the tyre down in front of a front wheel and drive over it?"

He did, and the tyre came away from the rim. At last, he could repair the puncture, and we were on the road again.

At that time the Americans were stationed at Exmouth. We would almost certainly have got work there but it would meaning going away north again and out to North West Cape. We bypassed the turnoff and continued on to Carnarvon. What luck! – we had arrived just in time for the Carnarvon Festival and were booked for two weekends. This was the first time we were recognised in the street and found it a bit disconcerting to be pointed and smiled at. It must be horrible to be really famous and not be able to go out without being hounded.

After Carnarvon we were on the final leg to Perth; 418 kilometres south.

Geraldton was the next decent-sized town; a pretty place on the coast where we stayed for a day.

About 200 kilometres south of there we lost the use of the clutch; something to do with a broken belt if I remember rightly. Someone stopped to help and told us we could get to Moora a short way inland if we crashed the gears, but the van had to be moving first. So there I was at the wheel with our helper and Frank pushing. I was a nervous wreck but somehow managed to get it into first gear. Frank rushed to get into the passenger seat and we were away. I crashed it into 2nd gear, then 3rd, then top. In Moora someone directed us to a house where the owners had a VW wreck and, sure enough, it had the belt we needed. We wanted to pay him for the part but he wouldn't accept any payment saying he was pleased to help. With the part fitted we were soon on the way again.

Perth at last! It had been a long few months, and time to get back to normal.

That trip from far North to Perth was by far the most beautiful stretch of country I have ever seen. It was wildflower season, and never a day passed when we didn't look in awe at the acres of wildflowers.

In the far North they were sparser but, set maybe just yards apart in the red sand with no grass or weeds between, it looked like hundreds of miles of well-cared-for garden.

Further south the land was covered with a thick growth of colour: miles of yellow, or miles of pinkish-white everlastings, or sometimes a mixture of many colours. I kept the camera clicking, it was all too good to miss.

In Perth, we rented an old house in Highgate and began to visit garage sales to buy furniture.

We went one day to a sale where an elderly couple had sold their house to downsize. We bought several things and, as we leaving, the elderly lady came down the drive carrying two big plush cushions. Apparently, she'd had a break-down and it showed. Her husband said, "She wants you to have them."

I was thrilled as they were in bright reds, greens, and yellows, featuring birds with long tails, and apparently had come from the Middle East. I thanked her profusely. Little did she know that they were to travel around the world with us and grace all my houses for many years.

Steven and Joe joined us again in Highgate. Goodness knows what they'd been up to. One night they and Frank went out drinking and on the way home they arrived at an obstacle on the footpath at the same time as a new Australian, an Italian teenager. Joe, who was a nasty drunk and obviously hadn't learned a lesson when he'd been knifed up North, pushed the lad into the street.

I was at home cooking dinner when they arrived back. Soon there was a banging at the door and there on the doorstep were about fifteen angry Italians demanding an apology. Frank and I tried to placate them but they were having none of it. When I tried to shut the door one put his foot in it and he and another man pushed their way into the hallway. I lost my temper; went into the bedroom and picking up the shotgun, checked it wasn't loaded – even though I knew it wasn't – then went out with it and told them to get out. They beat a hasty retreat and I went back to cooking dinner.

Within minutes there was the scream of sirens. We looked out and saw five police cars with flashing lights – talk about overkill! But as a detective told me later that night, "When got a call from a hysterical

Italian shouting about guns we thought that you had shot up half the street."

To make a long story short Frank was charged with having a firearm as they were illegal in Australia, and I was charged with pointing it at them. We were put in separate cells; all mine had was a bed with a grey blanket, but when I went to lie on it I found it was saturated with urine. I sat on the floor in a yoga position, back to the wall until they came to get me at 3 am. We signed papers before the elderly man who'd been called in and were then set free to walk all the way home. The next morning we appeared at court. I was fined $20 and Frank also got fined. Steven's stupid mate was not welcome in our house again.

I soon discovered what a beautiful city Perth had become. Needless to say, it had grown a lot since our last visit in the 1950s. Even today, in 2014, I believe it to be the best city in Australia. The transport system was and still is one of the best. One Sunday I wandered around and took colour slides of the wonderful mix of the old and new.

I did the van up, painting the inside and pulling out the carpet which was heavy with sand and replacing it. We sold it for a decent price and Frank bought himself another flash older car.

Kim got a job as a trainee window dresser at *Katie's* and made lots of new friends. Frank got a job over in the goldfields at Kalgoorlie. I applied for and got a job as the manageress of a sandwich bar in the centre of the city. Including myself, there were four staff and the work was full-on. I managed well, counting the till each night and delivering the takings to the head office before heading home. That being so, I was really surprised to be told a month later that my services were not required – they refused to give me an explanation. Later I was told by the staff that I had been employed as a stop-gap, that the job had been given to another woman who already ran a lunch bar but who had to give a month's notice. Their little scheme backfired however when the woman's boss offered her a pay rise to stay. They were without a manageress for several weeks.

It didn't really matter that I didn't have a daytime job; we were already working every weekend in show business. I had seen someone called Ray Sunny (who blacked his face and did Eddy Canter songs) applying for new acts; he and a pub owner had started a new agency.

We were immediately accepted.

Our first booking was at the *Charles Hotel*, considered at the time to be the top venue in Perth for entertainment. We were a support act to the well-known English comedian Jimmy Edwards. Jimmy, by then an alcoholic, came on the stage holding a bottle of Queen Anne whiskey. When the drummer (accidentally on purpose) crashed on the drums, he blew whiskey out of his mouth and spluttered, "Cor, good job those flames are not still around."

I have always had a great admiration for comedians; I think it is the hardest job in the business. He told a joke that night about a cowpat and got a good laugh, something I never get when I repeat it – the timing has got to be just right.

In the next few weeks we appeared at hotels and dance halls all over Perth, and also appeared at Perth's most southernmost suburb Rockingham, where strangely I now live, and write, thirty-nine years later.

Steven and Joe decided to join the army. When he came home on leave after passing out from basic training at Kapooka I was so proud. He was in his uniform and stood so ramrod straight and upright I could hardly believe that this wonderful handsome man was my son. Frank insisted we all go to the pub to celebrate and didn't my son attract the girls. Unfortunately he and Joe went out again another night and when he came back he proudly showed me what he'd been up to: I took one look and had hysterics. It was the weirdest feeling, that there I was, this strong, capable woman, yelling and crying all at once. I had lost all control. On his arm he'd had tattooed - BIKES, BOOZE AND BIRDS. I had been brought up to regard tattoos as cheap and degrading; I was absolutely horrified. A few years later he had it removed at the army's expense.

One of the nice girls Kim worked with wanted digs, so Annie from Queensland came to live with us. She was an artist – I still have one of her works. Frank wanted me to go to the goldfields to live, and now that Kim had sensible Annie to keep her company I felt I could go.

At first, we rented a caravan in the caravan park. I kept looking for work but jobs were scarce. One night Frank came home drunk and abusive. He was ranting at the top of his voice about something when I quietly said, "Frank, for goodness sake, keep your voice down, everyone in the park can hear you." The smack across the face came out of nowhere; it loosened an eye tooth which two days later had an abscess underneath and had to be removed. I had to buy another partial plate with another tooth on it.

The morning after he hit me I told him I was leaving, and this time for good, but as usual he came crawling. I said I would stay on the understanding that we would buy a house to get us out of the caravan park, and he agreed. I began looking for houses; saw one in Millan Street, Boulder, and it looked so awful I said no at first. Later I started thinking that, if we did it up, we could maybe make a profit. The price was just $1,200 and the deed was done.

It had two bedrooms with a porch bedroom at the front, a lounge, kitchen, and an add-on bathroom at the back. There was a big back yard, at least a quarter of an acre. Corrugated iron sheeting fenced us off from the neighbours, as well as half the back garden, the area behind the fence wild and unused. There was a drive coming in from the back alley to a large shed-cum-garage, where a lean-to housed the concrete laundry tubs. We had a big water tank, a loquat tree alongside and a pomegranate and fig tree. I had never seen a loquat tree before and loved the fruit from which I made jam. But sadly, I had my first experience with the dreaded fruit fly in the fruit of the fig. The enclosed back yard was red, hard-packed sand; rather pretty I thought, but after the rains came some plants grew in round patches. I thought they were rather pretty as well until I found out it was Bindi which produced seeds with vicious prickles. I was fast learning the ways of the outback.

Surprisingly Frank settled down very well and really enjoyed doing up the house. The kitchen had an ancient wood stove that had been painted and refused to be stripped back so I sanded it and painted the front silver and blacked the top to make it a feature. The wall was lined with flat tin which bulged here and there so I painted it white and then painted big loops on it to camouflage the bulges. We thought it looked great until someone said they looked like boobs. I could have thumped them because from then on all I could see was boobs. We bought, and Frank installed a small *calo*r gas stove and a new sink underneath the back window. We found that the floor was half red jarrah timber so we exposed it and put orange linoleum on the rest – it looked great.

We worked on the house for a year. When we took the rubbish to the tip we almost always came back with something useful, like carpet, good linoleum for the bathroom floor and all sorts of great things that folks had thrown away. I began to call it 'the rubbish exchange'. A picture house in Kalgoorlie shut down and someone bought up all the fittings. From them I bought many yards of black curtain, shiny on one side, with which I covered divans for the lounge. The little house was a picture when we'd finished.

Kim came over for a holiday and we appeared first at a hotel before going on to *Sylvester's Nite Club*. We were to appear there on two occasions, the boss saying, "I love it when you girls come – you always fill the place to capacity."

Kim at the Boulder house

A short time after we bought the house I got a job – not one I would ever imagine having. We were at the Boulder Block Hotel one night with friends and talking about me looking for a job. "Ma," our friend said, indicating the elderly lady hobbling up and down behind the bar serving, "needs a barmaid. Why don't you ask her?"

"Me? A barmaid? I've never thought about being a barmaid."

"Why don't you ask her?" he said, calling her over. And so I became the poshest barmaid the pub had ever seen; although I says so as shouldn't.

It didn't take me long to learn the ropes, and I started as I meant to go on. "You," I said, "don't buy me drinks and I don't buy you any. And if you use bad language in the bar you will not be served."

The bar was one of the old-fashioned ones: most bars had a bar on just one side, but the Boulder Block had a bar with two sides, the bar person walking along the middle. A long bar was on one side and two bars on the other side, the snug, and the back bar. The news that there was a new barmaid at the Boulder Block must have spread fast, and that "you don't have to wait to get a drink". The pub was situated just meters from the gates of the Great Boulder Mine.

Within weeks the bar was full when the shift changed in the afternoon, so much so that Ma had to advertise for another barmaid. The one we got lasted a few weeks before moving on, but by then I was fast and efficient. The bosses at the mine who wandered in every night after work sat together in the snug at one side of the bar, while all the workers filled the other side of the long bar. I got to know them all well and they told me lots of stories about the wonderful characters of the outback. There was the old lady called Dotty, who would wait until someone left to go to the toilet, then grab his beer and drink it. One guy would spit in his beer before he left to stop her. Then there was another character who would arrive at the Boulder Block in his horse and cart on payday every week. Unfortunately he was a nasty drunk, so every week when he started causing mayhem the police had to be called to cart him off to the guardhouse to sleep it off. Someone would drive the horse and cart to the police station. Eventually when the horse heard the sound of the police siren coming it would just take itself off to the police station all by itself. I believed this story as I had seen the milk cart horses in London walking on and stopping at the houses that had milk each day, without any direction from the driver.

The Boulder Block was owned by Ma and Pa – I never did learn their proper names because that is what everyone called them. Pa was in his eighties and Ma not far behind. We rarely saw Pa in the bar until he came to change the barrels in the cellar. Ma always wore a cotton print dress. She was a bit overweight and limped from arthritis and I never ever saw her without bare legs and feet. If she was upset she would go on the booze.

I will never forget the first day she did it. Into the bar she came; grabbed a bottle of sherry and poured a seven-ounce glass to the top. I watched in amazement as she drank the whole lot down in one go. She put her glass and the bottle on a shelf near the door to their living quarters and went back out. Not a word had been spoken. Before long she was back again and the same thing happened. Usually I would not see her again for the rest of the day after she had finished the bottle, but one night she came back into the bar drunk and abusive and began lashing out at her best customers, the mine bosses. I had never heard her swear before, but that night it was F—this, and F—that. I was appalled and embarrassed, it wasn't a word much used in those days. The men just sat there mute. Eventually I risked getting sacked by putting my arm around her shoulder saying, "Come on, Ma, I think it's time for you to leave now." Amazingly she complied. I led her to the door of the private quarters and ushered her through. No mention was ever made of the incident.

My shift started at 10 am and finished at 6 pm. The mornings were usually quiet so Ma and I discussed how to brighten the place up. I told her I would do the painting if she bought the paint. Needless to say, she couldn't get out fast enough to buy it after we had chosen the colours. So it was that the entire long bar was painted. I also did the small foyer that led into the snug from the street. To finish off, I painted a row of stick men walking into the bar – everybody loved them – and I was very proud of my achievement. When it was all finished Ma asked me if I would do the little storeroom that went off the back bar. The place was filthy with dirt and dust, so I told her I would do it but I wasn't going to clean it. Surprisingly she got her cleaner to clean it; I painted it pure white as it didn't have a window or skylight. What a transformation!

Ma went off to the bank once a week. One day she was away a lot longer than usual. The next day was payday, and to my utter astonishment she'd slipped me another $10.00.

"The bank manager says I'm to give you this," she said.

It was obvious to me that before I came on the scene she'd been getting ripped off big time, and that her bank balance was now improving.

As I had to work through what should have been my lunch hour Ma provided me with lunch. I never quite knew what to expect, and quite often when I got a thick meat stew it was curried. I knew then that the meat had been going off. One day she bought in fried bacon and eggs, with many little burnt bits on the plate as it had been cooked in fat that had been used before. It wasn't until I had finished eating that I discovered a large black, well-cooked blowfly. Small wonder then that I eventually got a mild case of food poisoning. I was up half the night running to the loo. I sent a message to Ma saying that I was sick and not coming in and had a long sleep in. It was late afternoon; Frank and I were sitting on the edge of the bath in the recently finished bathroom out the back, laughing about something, when around the corner of the house came Ma. She appeared suddenly at the bathroom door.

"You are not sick at all," she said, before turning and stumbling off, leaving Frank and I speechless.

I went to work next day and she sent someone else in with my lunch. She appeared at my leaving time to check the till as usual. Unfortunately, she said something about the day before and I lost my temper in front of the mine bosses. "How dare you come to my house and abuse me, saying I wasn't sick! I have had quite enough of your behaviour so I am leaving as of now!"

Fuming, I took my wages, albeit without the extra $10.00, and left.

I was without work for about a week before I heard of a barmaid's position going in Hannans Hotel in Kalgoorlie. I went to see the manager and was employed immediately.

Some of the hotels employed skimpy barmaids who wore practically nothing; Hannans was different altogether, all the bar staff were really nice respectable girls. Hannans was owned by a lady, the manager was her partner and the work, especially in the evening, was full-on. We had to work shifts. On the morning shift we cleaned the bar, and the brightly coloured brandy glasses decorating the display shelf. The evening shift was very busy, the clientele not the usual drunks, but good class citizens and every week there were dart matches, the teams filling the bar. On darts night the owner came to drink at the bar with her manager. She drank beer slowly from a small three-ounce glass and one had to watch that it was always replenished. I found the shift work very tiring along with doing the painting and working on the house as well. Going home late at night wasn't a problem and I always felt safe because, although brothels were illegal, Kalgoorlie had a whole street of them, and got away with it. They cater to this day for the men of the big mining workforce. I was never propositioned once when I lived there, thanks to the girls in the sex industry; although it is something I could never do myself.

One of the barmaids was the owner's niece; a really lovely girl. One day I moaned to her about the state of my long hair which was getting dry and bedraggled; she told me I should use conditioner, something new I hadn't heard of, and she bought me a big tube of it. The difference to my long curly hair was amazing.

After a few months at Hannans, I decided to leave because of the big workload and the shifts, and I gave in my notice. I was not unemployed for long – the bush telegraph had been busy because someone came to tell me that Ma wanted to see me. I went to see her and she asked me, "Please will you come back to work at the Boulder Block?"

I said I would. And I knew, as she knew, that I was not going to take any more of her crap!

About this time things were happening in Perth: Annie, who lived with Kim, decided she wanted to go home to Brisbane. There was no way we could leave Kim in the house on her own, so we hired a trailer and set off through the night to drive the 555 kilometres to Perth, and bring her and the furniture back to Boulder. We were stopped at Southern Cross by the police because one of the trailer lights wasn't working. He told us to get it fixed as soon as possible and let us go on. The land agent in Perth wouldn't let us have our bond back because we had not given him two weeks' notice of leaving; so we lost $150. The journey back was also done in darkness. We slunk through Southern Cross hoping the policeman who'd pulled us up previously wasn't on duty – luckily we got out of town without being seen.

It was lovely to have my darling daughter living with us again; I have a photo of her playing with our dog, who loved to leap up and try to catch the water as it came out of the garden hose. Kim needed another job and got two, doing the window dressing of clothing shops in Kalgoorlie. One of the shops was at the top of Hannan Street. Unbelievably I was to meet its owner some thirty years later after I'd returned to Australia, yet again, and began a foot care business. She was one of the elderly people whose home I went to every six weeks to care for their feet and cut toenails. It truly is a small world.

The Boulder Block didn't have any air conditioning, all I had was a fan evaporating contraption that I had to keep pouring water into; the fan blew air across the water and slightly cooled the air. However, we had a very hot summer that year, a week of over 40° Celcius, the highest day being 46. By the end of the week the heat had reached the inside of the thick grey granite blocks the hotel was built of, and it took weeks of lower temperatures for the walls to cool down. Not great working conditions to say the least. The winter, though not cold, brought lots of rain and the tail end of a cyclone that tore through town about mid-afternoon blowing tumbleweed balls ahead of it.

After much rain, a strange thing happened. One night a massive subsidence occurred not far from the hotel; the back of the gardens belonging to the houses near the Hotel disappeared into a huge hole. In some places the back fences hung precariously over the drop. I had been told by the miners that the underneath of Boulder and joining Kalgoorlie was completely honeycombed with tunnels and here was the proof. We crawled on our bellies to the edge of the pit and looked over; a very stupid thing to do now that I think of it. In several places on the side walls were the opening of tunnels. This I believe was the beginning of the huge super pit although it didn't start until 1989, and is still in operation in 2014. It is a big attraction to tourists who can stop at the lookout and look down into this massive hole. At 3.5 kilometres long, 1.5 kilometres wide and 570 feet deep it is the biggest open cut mine in Australia and one of the largest in the world.

The Boulder Block Hotel, or Tavern as it had then become, is no more. Like a lot of other things, it has been swallowed up by the pit. I have been told that it was taken down and the stones numbered so that it could be reconstructed at another place to preserve a piece of history. Sadly this has never been done.

Frank had been reasonably settled during our time there, but now with the house finished he once again got itchy feet. He still had this bee in his bonnet about travelling overland to London. It was agreed that we would go first to work in Singapore and from there drive overland. We always had separate bank accounts and my bank manager suggested I transfer money immediately while the Aussie dollar was high. I transferred $6,000 to Lloyds Bank in London, stupidly believing that it would be earning interest, only to find when we eventually got there that it wasn't.

We put the house on the market and it sold very quickly to a young couple for just slightly twice more than we'd paid for it. They also wanted to have our dog, so once again I had to say goodbye to a loyal little friend.

I had written to Steven telling him that we were going to drive overland. He was still in the army but surprised us by arriving home, driving all the way from Brisbane. He said he'd been granted a discharge. This I found out later was not true – he'd gone AWOL. I was more than a little annoyed. He got himself a job until we were ready to leave.

One of the customers at the Boulder Block was responsible for melting the gold from the mine and pouring it into brick-shaped ingots; he told us we could come to see it done. Steven and Kim came with me to watch the process. Afterward I took a photo of the two holding the ingot worth at the time $6,000. What amused us was the total lack of security, the process taking place in a shed at the back of the mine buildings with just an old wire netting door to the outside. Still, Kalgoorlie was a long way from anywhere and hard to get away from.

We spent our last two weeks in Australia in Perth where we sold the last of our cars: Steven's ute and our Mini Cooper. We were sailing to Singapore on the *SS Malaysia*, approximately 8,000 tons and riding high in the water. She was built in 1955 for the Booth Line and until 1964 had been on the Liverpool to Amazon run, going 100 miles up the Amazon river each run. We were about to spend one of the most interesting and dramatic times in our lives. From here on I will have to write from my diary.

26.2.76. We were supposed to leave today but didn't. They said it was because of a tug strike but were later told it was avoid cyclone Wally.

27.2.76 Got away today at 12.30 and headed out into a fairly rough sea; it is raining and overcast. Ship rolling and pitching; we are all feeling a little sick. Very angry because they had lost our personal luggage; not in the luggage room. Hope they get it out of the hold today.

29.2.76. In the Indian Ocean. Race meeting today. Frank bought a "horse", I was the jockey. We won, our prize was a Malaysia travel bag, plus $1 and a tiny life belt. I was a rank outsider, paying $1.40 for 10cents- Made $6.50.

2.3.76. Frank received two more life belts for winning the

men's darts and the deck quoits.

4.3.76. Singapore. WOW, what a town. We found out why we needed our typhoid and cholera injections - open drains. Everywhere smells of cooking. The Chinese and Malay markets are the most fascinating I've ever seen. Most incredible variety of food. They say that in 5 years every part of the old districts will be gone. THEY USE BAMBOO FOR SCAFFOLDING.

5.3.76. Found that here they don't use sheets on beds. (We were staying at the Railway Hotel) One on bottom and a towel like blanket on top. Jeff (1 of the ships officers who had fallen for Kim) came over and showed us around. We found our bank and deposited our bank draft. Still unable to find any decent car dealers. Starting to look around for night clubs to work at.

9.3.76. Took a cable car over to Sentoza Island; stayed for a swim, lovely beach and warm water.

10.3.76. Advertised for a van, have had lots of calls, Dormabile could be interesting

13.3.76. Bought a Kombi van today fitted out as a two-berth. (This van has already made the trip from England to Singapore, we bought it from the man who managed the school for mechanics that was funded by the Australian Government) Steve has bought the Dormabile but is not altogether satisfied with same.

Did a floor show today for a press conference and the men who inspect to see if shows are decent. I nearly died with fright; couldn't see the pois for the bright spotlight and made a mess of same. We were really surprised to be offered a contract for 10 days at $1,200 a week. Have to leave for Malaysia while the Southron Theatre restaurant applies for work permits for us. (Our visors have run out.)

17.3.76. Steve has been unable to get insurance for the van, have had to insure it in my name.

18/3/76. Supposed to be out of Singapore tonight but the Dormabile not ready for the road.

18.3.76. Malaysia. Arrived at the border without the car permits, after chasing around all day trying to get them. They say we have to take a bus over to Johore Bahru then come back over to collect the vans. Anyway we just drove over and they didn't even question our car permits; perhaps it was because our van had an expired permit on the windscreen. We have our passports stamped for two weeks. Camped the first night down the main road next to the waterworks that supply Singapore with water.

19.3.75. Had an enforced stop in a rubber plantation; Steve's petrol pump was full of filth and the carby packed up. While the men travelled in the Kombi to the nearest town to get repairs Kim and I walked amongst the rubber trees and saw how the grooves were carved in the trees for the rubber to run down into tins. There was an open shed among the trees where the rubber was run through big rollers turned by hand to make it into sheets. We had seen a man on a motorbike with a load of sheets on the pillion leave that morning. We spent the night there while the Dormabile was set to rights. The next morning we went in search of water; there was a small creek running nearby. A man who lived just on the other side of the road saw what we were doing and told us to come to his place and get fresh water from his small open tank. He had a lovely smile and could speak a little English. I asked him if he had been there when the Japanese had invaded Malaysia and he said he had. He said that they hadn't caused much trouble but had taken some vegetables from his garden.

The van fixed we drove north again up the west coast. At a little place called Banting, Steven had his cassette player fitted and a new window made to replace the broken glass one in the roof of the Dormabile. We found the villages fascinating, the shops not like anything we'd seen. Firstly they were all joined together like sheds with open fronts that were shut at night with steel mesh, pull-down doors. There was nothing, but nothing, you needed doing that couldn't be done, and be done perfectly, and we were never ripped off. A new tin window, perfectly shaped was made in no time to fill the gap. Next stop, Malaka, or Malacca as it is better known. We camped the night in the driveway of a hotel. This ancient city has such incredible architecture that I would have loved to stay longer to see, but it was not to be.

When we bought the Kombi the calor gas bottle was empty and there didn't seem to any place in Singapore that stocked it. This is the first time I saw examples of the Chinese and their 'not losing face'. I would go into a shop and ask if they sold calor gas and would get a curt "NO". Then they would just walk away or look away. If I asked if they knew where I could get some I would get the same "NO", or not be answered at all. They just didn't want to know. Personally I found it damned rude, and quite disconcerting. If you asked someone in any other part of the world they would say "why don't you try so-and-so," and do their best to help.

Anyway, we had to buy a small kerosene cooking stove which we used outside the van. In Malacca we forgot to put it away and backed over it; from then on we had to use this twisted lopsided thing.

Our next stop was at Port Dickson where we camped for the Sunday before spending Monday and Tuesday at Morib. We were near the beach house of the Sultan of Selangor. There are thirteen states in Malaysia, three have governors, the rest have sultans. We liked the Malays and Malaysia; it is a country of rubber, coconuts, palm oil, bananas, and pineapples. It is also picturesque and green.

We took a wrong turn outside Port Dickinson and saw more of the country than we intended.

<u>Back to the diary.</u>

24/3 76. Outside Port Kelang — Here we are camped in a sea of muddy clay. Had to stop quickly to put Steve's new roof window in as it was pouring with rain. Very uneasy tonight as the locals have told us the jungle starts just down the road and that armed bandits sometimes raid the village and steal bikes and anything else they can find.

25/3/76. We discovered during the night that the head man had posted two guards to watch over us – very embarrassing. (I had woken and seen two men sitting around a small fire). Asnah, who spoke English, took the day off work to come and talk to us in the morning (bringing all the women and children with her) She told us that the village had been settled 12 years before and each family was allotted 5 acres of land. She said that we were the first white (don't know why I wrote white) people to come to the village since they had been there. They all took a lively interest in my Maori skirt. I gave them an advertising poster of ours and took a photo of them all; I wrote down Asnah's address and promised to write which I did later from Singapore and sent the photos I had taken.

They took us to Asnah's house to wash the clay off our feet. We were shown through their small wooden home, clean and neat as a new pin. It was high off the ground, the floorboards of the big room above were spaced about a half-inch apart to let the air flow through. Off that room was a room with a concrete cooking block, where they cooked over a small open fire. The big room had just 1 piece of furniture, a cupboard, on which was piled their sleeping mats.

We washed our feet under the tap of a big tank, said our goodbyes and set off for Kuala Lumpur.

26/3/76. At K.L. lost Steven at the first roundabout, the traffic is a nightmare. Not an attractive city but has some fine buildings. Set off in the Kombi for Kuantan on the east coast but found the amazing Batu caves on the way. We went way underground where there are covered walks to keep you from getting smattered with bat droppings. We climbed up a very long stairway up to the temple high in the cliffs; as soon as I took out the camera Frank got up to his usual mad tricks and showed his total lack of respect. "Take a photo of me lying on the altar as a sacrifice," he said, and climbed up and laid down. I was horrified and told him to get off before he had us attacked; I expected that at any moment someone's head would pop up at the top of the steps and he would be seen, but he wouldn't budge until I had taken the photo.

An hour or so after leaving the caves we found Steven parked at a crossroads; he'd had the sense to work out that we would have to come on one the roads. I was so pleased to see him; we told him about the caves and he wanted to go back to see them so we did. We actually found some public toilets and a shower, whoopee. Later we found a place where we could get our visa's extended. That night there was the most dreadful thunderstorm.

31st. March. Hot and sunny, Kuantan on the beach.

Have been here for 4 days, a very nice beach, lots of sun but hard to sunbathe as there are too many peeping toms. Malays don't swim much, some go in fully clothed. Met a couple of Aussies, Paula and Phillip, they said the favourite sport around here is to follow Europeans around and perv on them. Things we have noticed about Malays – they are suicidal maniacs on the road, passing on double lines, blind corners and on the brow of hills. Toilet seems to be a dirty word here; we have found only 3 public toilets and all were boarded up. Most toilets are a hole in the ground with a footplate either side; we have trouble hitting the hole and so do most locals judging by the mess.

On the way over, when travelling on a very winding road through a thickly wooded area, we were passed on an elbow bend by a young Chinaman driving a grey sports car. A few miles on we came upon him standing on the road, his car upside down in a ditch among the trees with the wheels still spinning. We wound the windows down and cheered as we passed; it seemed he had met a car coming the other way.

5th. April. South of Nenasi.
Spent two nights south of Kuantan after spending 1 night at a picturesque village called Besorah North. Nice to be away from prying eyes.

6th April. Called at a lovely fishing village called Kuala Romkin and bought 4 big fish. Had the best meal we have had in weeks on the beach at Kuala Pontian; took photos of some lovely children and of us sitting on a huge tree trunk that had fallen into the surf.

When we arrived at the beach the children were dressed in their usual clothes but the girls disappeared and came back in lovely little dresses. We built a small fire and cooked our fish wrapped in tin foil on the coals. The tree mentioned in my diary must have been brought in by the tide – it was huge with all its branches intact. The waves of the incoming tide were hitting it full on so when we sat on it, our backs to the ocean, the waves crashed over us. We sat there in our bikinis screeching with laughter.

Later that day, fully clothed again, of course, we came upon a car ferry where we had to wait for hours to cross what I believe was the mouth of the wide Semberong River. There were no toilets and the stench was awful; the roadsides were so littered with filth I was horrified

11th. April. Have camped for two nights at a beach two miles south of Mersing; while there a bus load of Malay lady tourists arrived and many went into the water fully clothed. We are now 6 miles North, at a small kampong on a fabulous and beautiful beach, ideal for children or swimming as there is no surf. Tried out our first taste of water buffalo today, very tough, but at least we managed to get some vegetables and really enjoy a meal for once.

Our stay here is one of my fondest memories. Such wonderful people. Within a few days we got to know them all. Kim and I were taught how to tie our sarongs without them falling off and how to wash at the well by drawing up buckets of water and pouring it over ourselves fully clothed in our sarongs, as they did; they laughed heartily at our first attempts. Sometimes all the village ladies would bring their chairs and sit around the van to watch as I cooked a meal. The men showed Steven how to husk a coconut. One day the men arrived back from the bush with big handfuls of opaque gooey stuff which they had collected from the forest. Try as we might we never did understand what they used it for. We swam every day in the crystal clear water and kept fit.

Asha, who seemed to be the head lady, asked us to come for lunch, and we accepted. Knowing that they ate with their hands and were Muslims I reminded everyone not to touch the food with their right hand, the hand used for wiping bottoms. None of the toilets had toilet paper, just a short rubber hose attached to a water pipe. We sat on the floor at Asha's house; I cannot remember what food we had except for the dried small fish, heads and all, fried crisp in hot oil. The whole village crowded around the door to watch us eat and, although we had become used to the Asian habit of staring, it was still embarrassing.

One morning when we were sitting around the van eating breakfast a very nice elderly lady came to sell us some eggs. To me, they were obviously fresh with their shiny clean brown shells; unfortunately, Frank decided to show how smart he was and fetched a pan of water in which he placed each egg to see if it would float. I could have killed him I was so embarrassed. I tried to make up for his behaviour by being nice to the lady and slipping her a little more than what she had asked for. Little did I know that he would cause us embarrassment many times over the next few months.

15th April. Arrived back in Singapore and were too late to see the Immigration people. Seems they have refused permission for Kim to work as she is under 18. We have to see them on the 20th. And we start that night at the Southron. Moved from Hotel because we had no hot water and the stench from the toilets below was terrible. Moved to the Y.M.C.A. where we have two double rooms $13 a week. The food in the dining room is great and also cheap.

Australia house money not here yet so we are trying to get another job. Shifted from the station.

18th April. Paid a visit today to the weird and wonderful Tiger Balm Gardens. Life-sized figures in lots of different and grotesque themes and bizarre colours.

We met with the immigration on the 20th. Three nice, middle-aged gentlemen came to view our show. We were to appear topless although that was not quite correct, we had so many leis and shell beads around our necks that you couldn't see we had no bras on until we turned our backs in our routine They had been informed that I was Kim's mother and asked to speak to me; they asked if that was all we would be taking off to which I replied, "Absolutely." They complimented me on the show and gave us permission to perform. The next day we went to Immigration with a representative of the Southron to get our passports stamped 'Permission to perform at the Southron Theartre' with the dates from and to. We ended up with four such entries as our season kept being extended.

3/5/76. Had our contract extended at the Southron to 13 days and were paid $2,228. A real experience working here, everything so well organised, great lighting system and sound. Spent our day going to the zoo and to the top of the 'M', having publicity photos taken and trying to get another job. We have signed a contract for 3 shows a night in Indonesia.

Working at the Southron was one of the highlights of my life. The venue overlooking the harbour was a dream, the show well organised and every performance went without a hitch. The theatre had their band and singers, while two other acts were booked from outside. While we were there the acts changed three times so we shared a dressing room with two adagio dancers, a sword swallower and two awfully silly local comedians. The dancers were a lovely couple who we got on well with, the sword swallower was very quiet with an unhealthy pallor – he had a great act, apart from swallowing a sword – he also shoved a neon lamp down into his stomach flicking the light on and off – it was downright weird. Even worse, he swallowed three goldfish from a brandy glass then regurgitated them. One night he left them down a bit long and one little black fellow with googly eyes was quite off balance when he came back out. I looked into the glass on the dressing room bench and said, "Oh! you poor little thing. What has he done to you?"

Of course every night we had our share of stage door Johnny's … only they were not at the stage door; they hung around outside the dressing room door. When you are standing in the wings psyching yourself into flying onto the stage before a large audience everything about you is oblivious. However, one night Frank was in one of his picky moods and had a go at Kim about them. I was furious! Kim ignored them just as I did. They made no move to speak to us nor us to them, I couldn't believe that Frank could be so insensitive to upset us just before we were to perform. Kim was very upset and said she wasn't going to go on, so I had to take her aside and tell her we were being paid a lot of money and I relied on her to help me. I told her to just ignore her father as he wasn't worth worrying about. She eventually calmed down, but needless to say our show was a bit lack-lustre that night.

On our first night there we were a bit shocked to see about twenty girls in evening frocks in a partly closed-off area at the back of the venue. With them was an older woman who was in charge. We learned that these girls could be hired for the night by men who were on their own. Whether this arrangement extended beyond closing time we didn't ask. Isn't it true, you learn a little every day?

As the theatre was responsible for us we were spoilt rotten: a limousine was sent to pick us up each night and take us home again, although Frank and I sometimes walked home, me in my evening gown and high heels.

On the way back we would stop at a car park restaurant to eat as Kim and I never ate before work. I always got a delicious mutton stew from one of the stalls.

One thing we soon learned very quickly in Singapore was this: the values of the world are completely wrong. At the end of our street every day we passed a new building being built on the corner. Several ladies, who looked old but may not have been, had been contracted to lay the concrete floors. Each day we watched them mix the concrete then cart it in wheelbarrows to tip on to the floor. I asked what wages they were being paid and was appalled to find they were only getting $300 a month.

In the city, near the top of a high rise building a man and a woman were swinging in a cradle putting big slabs on to the exterior walls. The *Strait Times* did an interview with the woman and, when they asked her why she did such a dangerous job, she replied that the money was good. They were being paid $600 a month. It all seemed to be so very wrong – we were getting paid $1,200 a *week* for twenty minutes a night while they worked all day for next to nothing. It made me feel very humble.

During our stay at the Southron, the Grand Charity Dinner in aid of the Singapore Association for the Blind was held. It was organised by the Lions Club of central Singapore. What an occasion that was. I still have the pamphlet showing the photos of all the cast, with us and the Latin Show, aka the sword swallower. Everyone who was anyone was there that night including the Honourable Minister for Social Affairs. The venue was packed, and I believe this was our biggest audience ever, about 1,000 people. Many large prizes had been donated for the raffle and, with that and door tickets, a large amount of money must have been raised.

One of the nice thing about working at night is that we had the day to explore. One day Kim and I set off to go to the Jurong Bird Park. In Singapore at the time it was not uncommon to see in the street men and teenagers with shaved heads. As they all seemed to be a bit disadvantaged I thought they must come from some institution, so who should get on the bus but one of these teenagers. We were sitting in the seats by the back door that faced inwards and he sat in front of us. Suddenly he began to swing his head around and around at an alarming speed. I thought maybe he had St Vitus Dance or some such affliction. Now Kim and I were terrible gigglers; we took one look at each other and exploded. It was awful; we had no right to be laughing at the poor lad but we just couldn't stop. Eventually we managed to control ourselves and the head revolving stopped; the bus conductor came back down the aisle and tried to get him, and us, going again. I could have clouted him. I waved my hand at him, "Don't, don't."

At last, our stop arrived and we could escape, having properly shamed ourselves.

At the door of the bird park, an attendant was trying to teach a tame Mina bird to say hello to visitors. I pictured that poor bird sitting here for years saying "allo'" to everyone who walked in.

It was an interesting day. We stood for some time outside the flamingo enclosure watching them bob their heads then suddenly turn and rush madly across to the opposite side where the head bobbing started again. We tried to work out who gave the signal for them all to rush, but there didn't seem to be one. Maybe the leader just said "Go" in flamingo language.

12/5/76 back to Malaysia for two weeks then it will be back to Singapore. Getting very worried about the lack of money from the sale of the Boulder house and still not heard from New Zealand.

On that trip we met a man whose cousin guarded the crown jewels of the Maharaja of Selangor, I think it was. He arranged for us to see them. Frank had on shorts and scruffy sandals and was told it was disrespectful to come in like that. They wanted him to put trousers on. As usual he had to embarrass us by creating a scene. We were being given a great privilege, but once again he had no respect for anyone. Finally they relented and let him in, but it spoiled what would have been a great experience for us all. The display had stuffed wild animals that had been shot – tigers and other animals – there were mink coats and other furs, jewels, crowns, and a full dinner set of pure gold, I cannot remember the number of plates but it was huge.

26/5/76 Back to Singapore for two weeks. Getting very worried as we have not heard from the agent in Indonesia. Just hope to God the contract has not fallen thru.

One night the four of us popped into a local bar, one of those places where they had at least one girl who would ask any man she thinks is on his own if he would buy her a drink. She approached Frank and he said yes. We all looked at him open-mouthed. Anyway, the girl got her drink, some expensive thing but probably just fruit juice, then she came to sit beside him. After a while she asked who we all were. Steve and Kim said that Frank was their father and I said, *and I am his wife!* The look on her face was priceless. We left soon after and once out on the street Steve wanted to know what the hell he was doing buying bar flies drinks. He said, "Well I didn't know." *Unbelievable*!

Frank's behaviour was becoming more and more unpredictable. Try as I might I could not stop myself from answering back. I made up my mind that I would not write one word about him in my diary and that I achieved in spite of his appalling behaviour in the months to come.

8th June. Malaysia again. At the rest House in Johor Bahru

We have pooled our money and paid ($10,000) for one carnet for the VW. Steve was lucky to sell his Dormobile for $1,150. Have decided to leave for India on the 23rd of June. Sent a letter and a telegram to Indonesia but have had no replies; they say the Indonesian mail service is one of the worst in the world, and I have been told we will have to pay a bribe of a least $200 per person to the officials before we can get visas. No way!

Will hop back over to Singapore tomorrow to collect mail, carnet, and tinned food. We met three Germans and two brothers with a wife, who told us to take plenty of tinned meat for the Indian trip.

12Th June. Rest House Johor Bahru.

Just one day to go, then a flying visit to Singapore on Monday morning, then are off to Penang and the new territory

I have been taking stock of sicknesses to date.

Steve – very bad dysentery at Kuantan, serves him right for going to eat at the beach café instead of in the van.

Kim and Self – mild dysentery at Kuantan.

Frank – bitten by spider or most likely a scorpion on the beach at Mersing, oh my God, you would have thought he was dying. Badly bitten by mosquitoes and contracted a fever. He has absolutely refused to take the quinine tablets I hand out every morning to guard against malaria and will not tell us why. He had flu in Singapore which affected his heart and had bad chest

pains and he ached all over.
    Self – Bad hay fever.
    Kim – Skin allergy from the heat.
    Steve – bad dysentery again today.

The money from the sale of the house had finally arrived with a message to say that some papers had been lost. I didn't believe this, but at least we could stop worrying and begin our trip overland to England.

    16th June. Templer National Park. met John and Nora Keven.
    Stayed at Malacca the first night, an ancient city dating back to 12th century. We were going to stop in Kuala Lumpur last night but there is no rest house so we were sent on to Templer Park 18 miles north. This is one of the best parks we have had in all of Malaysia with a crystal clear stream and plenty of shade. John and Nora Keven arrived in their Ford motor caravan en route from the U.K. to Australia. They have given us a heap of useful information about the route ahead. Like where to stay in India – P.W.D bungalows, Inspection Bungalows, and Dak bungalows, just ask for parking.

These bungalows were put in place during the British rule of India. They were to accommodate the Government inspectors who travelled around the country. I never did find out what they inspected. These places we found out were looked after by Indian families who could speak a little English. John and Nora also gave us the name of a shop that sold English style food; we found just one, very good but very expensive. The crystal clear stream where we were parked with them was my downfall. Being brought in New Zealand where streams that run over rocks are fit to drink I did a very stupid thing. It was hot; I collected a bucket full of the water and made up some cordial of which I drank several glasses. The next morning when Kim and I went exploring we found a house about 200 yards away where all the sewerage and water from the house fed straight into the stream. I was horrified.

As I drove north the next day I said, "I really don't feel very well, I have the most awful headache." I never got headaches so I knew something was wrong. I stopped the car and Steve took over to drive the last of the 369 miles to Butterworth which is the town on the mainland opposite the island of Pulau Pinang. We crossed to Pinang and found parking at Batu Firingi on the beach. We were beside the *Golden Sands Hotel* which had a front gate leading into the showers and toilets. Unfortunately, they closed the gate at night so to use the toilets we had to walk back up to the road and down the drive to the beach. That first night I was very sick. The gate was shut before I desperately needed the toilet and Kim walked with me back to the street and down to the beach again, but long before I got there the watery faeces was running down my legs and I was leaving a trail. Luckily I had a long skirt on but it got into a mess. Kim took it back to the van and arrived back with a bath towel to cover me. The dysentery went on all night. I no longer tried to make it to the loo but just squatted down in the sand just passing water. Once a man walked by a few feet away but hurried away when he realised what I was doing. Another time I dashed out and sat too close to a tree that had green ants in it. In seconds I was smothered with them; they shot up my legs, down my neck, biting and biting. It was the last straw. I eventually beat them off and got back to bed. By 2 am it was almost over and I finally got some sleep. My family had slept all through my trauma. At 5 am I woke and stretched out my legs and instantly both legs went into violent cramp; I woke poor wee Kim and asked her to get me a glass of water with lots of salt in it. A short time after drinking it the cramp subsided.

23/6/76 Penang, Malaysia. Leaving for India today.

Arrived at the wharf today at 8 am to load the van in pouring rain. We have spent a week on the beach at Batu Tiringi in the parking lot against the Golden Sands Hotel. There we rented a shower for 50 cents each per night. Weather has been much cooler thank goodness with a lot of rain. Took us two days to complete the details for loading and get the roof rack welded. They got the van aboard at 12.30 pm after much shunting – they scratched the paintwork and bashed in the roof rack; we were all nervous wrecks by the time it landed on deck.

24/6/76 Very wet and stormy, turbulent seas – men queasy but Kim and I very sick; suspect we have not got over the attack of dysentery yet.

25/6/76 Friday Indian Sea. Weather better but cloudy.
Meals are fabulous if we can keep them down. Have found that I have lost a lot of weight; hope to gain a bit before getting to India. Have found that we are the elite of the ship after paying 4 adult fares and nearly $1000 for the van. Only about 20 people in 1st. class it is like a ghost ship up here. We were each given a nice waterproof zip bag from the Shipping Corporation of India with some writing paper and envelopes.
Got some sunbathing in P.M.

When we booked our fares we tried to book second class but were told that Europeans were not permitted to travel that way. There was one English man on board who slept down there but cheekily spent the days up in first class. His name was Ted Simon who was travelling around the world on a Triumph motorbike and later wrote the book *Jupiter's Travels*. I still have the book today but was disappointed to read very little about the crossing by ship to India. Ted told us he had insisted that he travel second class but things were a little rough downstairs. That was putting it mildly.

There was a library on board which we had to go downstairs to locate. It was divided from the men down there by a mesh wall and

Kim and I were horrified to have all these men staring at us. We grabbed some books and got out of there quickly, passing the women's bunk rooms as we went. The rooms were crowded, the bunks about four high. We were so pleased not to be travelling there. The cheapest form of travel on board was on deck; during the day they sat around on the rails or sat on the cargo holds.

26/6/76 Indian Sea. Man Overboard.

We were awakened by much activity about 6 am but went back to sleep; then Russell, a Kiwi doing an overland tour, came to tell us there was a man overboard. Seems a 12-year-old boy saw him fall but at first they didn't believe him; however they turned around and went back to find him. He was still swimming strongly and he reached a lifebuoy they threw him. With much difficulty the crew lowered a lifeboat in the heavy swell but no sooner had it pulled away than the motor packed up. We circled around and lowered another. What a fiasco; when the boat is a few feet above the water a crewman at each end strikes the hawsers with big hammers which come apart for the boat to drop into the water. However just one end came loose and the crew were almost flung into the water; the now loose iron hook swung over and hit the man still trying to free his end a terrific blow on the head. In desperation the Captain ordered the stabilisers to be put out and sure enough a large black oil slick appeared. With the hawser free at last they started the motor and set off back to pick up their elderly floating passenger. The man was hauled aboard through a side hatch wrapped in a blanket and firmly strapped to a stretcher. The boat then returned to take the other one in tow.

While we waited for the pick up we saw a large shark a few yards away just floating in the swell and watching. It was a khaki colour with white fins; Ted said it was a dangerous species.

Unfortunately, it was a Sunday when we arrived in Madras; the customs men came aboard to first-class to check us ashore. I can't remember how it had happened but I knew the van was unlocked. Even before we got to see the Customs man it had been bounced on to the wharf and had already attracted a small crowd of men looking in the windows. I was worried that we wouldn't have anything left by the time we got to it. I pushed myself forward explaining that I needed to get to the van but he wasn't going to be rushed. At last I got to dash ashore and get to the van, the audience melting away as I arrived. I think they were a little surprised to see a woman jump in, start the motor and drive to the gangway to pick up the family.

We were told that we had to leave the van in the Customs shed overnight and the paperwork would be done in the morning. This alarmed us greatly and we all tried to explain that all our possessions were in the van and were needed straight away. Eventually, they relented and rang a man who came to process us and let us get away.

We hadn't a clue where we were. Somehow we seemed to have got into a very poor part of town, the street teeming with people all around us as we crawled along. We came to a stop as a body was carried shoulder high on a stretcher past our windscreen. The deceased looked to be about twenty-three years old; only his pasty white face was showing, his body surrounded by flowers. How well India had welcomed us.

Out of the thick of humanity at last, Kim said she felt sick. We pulled into the kerb where she leaned out and vomited violently into the gutter. Somehow we found the Y.W.C.A. where we stayed the night – Russell and his motorbike were already there.

27/6/76 Hot and sweaty. Madras – India.

Our first impressions of India were of filth and squalor. The streets of Madras are obscene, littered with filth and human bodies. You have to step over the bodies of people sleeping in the street. The small horses that pull the carts are just bags of bones, but most of the oxen that pull carts are well fed. They tether these animals in the street beside their shop or house and collect their manure up by hand shaping it into pancakes and slapping it on to the wall to dry. Otherwise it is rolled into balls and left to dry in the sun. The manure is used for the cooking fires.

There seems to be few shops or consumer goods. (I realise now that we must have been in the wrong part of town.) Facilities at the Y very good for R2 each plus R3 for the van. (R11)

28/6/76 Fine cool night. Bangalore
Petrol pipe from tank burst.
Arrived here about 3 pm and stayed at the Y.M.C.A. Infantry Rd. Seems a very nice city, many more shops, and much cleaner. There are some very nice buildings. The road from Madras was fairly good, through hilly country and hilly terrain. Some very picturesque but scruffy villages at the base of the hills. Every inch of the terrain is cultivated in readiness for the monsoons. It is really very dry. Bought a gallon of Kerosene (for our cooking stove) but it is more like diesel, burns with a yellow flame and lots of black smoke. The petrol is just 72 octane and very expensive; about $1.72 Aust. or one pound English.

I cannot remember the petrol pipe bursting or what we did about it, but there is one scene of Bangalore that was etched on my brain forever. A small very thin boy sitting on the footpath holding a tiny, but beautiful, curly-haired little girl on his lap. They both had their hands out begging. I was going to give them a paper note but thought that, with so many eyes watching, it would be taken from them. I have never forgiven myself for that. However we had already come to the conclusion that we couldn't give all of India's beggars money, there was just too many of them. Mrs Gandi frowned on giving beggars money: she claimed that for every beggar you gave to, you made another, and she was probably right. Not so long before a lot of beggars in Bombay (now Mumbi) were rounded up and taken out to work somewhere. Within weeks they were all back on the streets, claiming they made more money begging that they did working.

> 29/6/76 Fine and windy.
> Chitradurga
> Car greased.
> Didn't get away until nearly midday and made it to the bungalow here where we promptly attracted a crowd. First came about six old men who sat down to watch us prepare a meal, then all the kids from the school next door jumped the fence (with their young lady teacher) and completely enclosed us. So-o-o embarrassing
> A medium-sized town under some rocky hills. Hope to get to Goa tomorrow.
> Steve changed the points – we are having ignition trouble.

This is one of my clearest memories. I couldn't believe it when all the old men arrived with their chairs to be entertained. Talk about a sideshow!

At the garage a young lad of about ten greased the car. Frank helped him, making sure all the grease nipples were found. There was one that seemed to be blocked which gave us trouble later. I can still see that little lad's smiling face. There was so much child labour in India at the time that in Bangalore I stood at the door of a small room and watched a small group of boys hand making a carpet. They were doing work that I couldn't have done.

> 30/6/76 Cooler and fine. Gotur.
> Made good time today but missed the turnoff to Goa. Should have taken a left somewhere in Dharwar but it was horribly congested so we drove on towards Poona. Stopped here to do our washing and booked a room for the night. R3. Hope to get some mail written before moving on. We took a walk down the town

and the whole village followed us. One woman rushed out to show us her little baby. He had a snotty nose which she cleaned with her fingers wiping them on her sari. The boys, as well as the girls, wear earrings, but the girls wear nose rings as well. We watched the women draw water from the well, very deep. They use nice brass urns – we hope to purchase one.

SIRUR.
1/7/76 Warm and Breezy
Visit to ancient town.

Passed through Poona today. A very old town, the streets were very narrow and an absolute maze. Took us an hour to get through and find the road to Ahmadnagar. The road took us through some green countryside, past many old villages made of stone instead of the usual mud and thatch. Found a rest home at Sirur a really ancient town with quant plumbing. In the back of the stone walls that backed on to the street were cut square holes covered with flaps of tin. These were their toilets, they flushed, (probably with a bucket) out a shoot into an open drain behind. The drain ran down the hill into a big seething cesspool we had to cross to get to our rest home.

Kim is running a temperature and is complaining of bad pains in her side. I suspect hepatitis.

In India only visitors were allowed to drink alcohol. Frank spoke to the people managing the rest house to ask where he could buy a drink. They directed him to a place inside the walls where we found it was indeed a walled village. The bar was small with just two patrons, and the drinks were on a shelf. No beer, brandy, vodka or whiskey, just a row of bottles with garish-coloured contents. There was bright red, yellow, green, and purple; I chose a shot of red and it was vile. Absolute firewater. Frank did his usual funny ha-ha act but they looked at him as though he was mad, needless to say they couldn't understand a word. We left the next morning. I was very worried about Kim but there was no doctor in the village; her temperature had gone down which was something.

2/7/76 Fine. Aurangabad
Visit to Daulatabad Fort and Ellora Caves.
Aurangabad has gigantic army barracks where the British army had been stationed for years. One of the best laid out places we have seen in India. Turned to go to the Ellora caves but found an extra bonus in the Daulatabad Ford. Frank stayed in the car while Steven, Kim and I climbed right to the top, all 600 steps. A truly magnificent feat of engineering.
The caves were impressive, mainly Buddhist. We parked behind the hotel chalets here for the night.

As I write this so many years later I find it hard to believe that I had no more to say in my diary about these two unbelievable places; I must have been so overawed by the experience that words failed me.

The Daulatabab Fort is a hill fortress that dominates the surrounding terrain as a mute witness to the Yadava Kings and their achievements. It is a city, much smaller now than it originally was inside high walls and is said to have been conquered just once when the guard on the gate was bribed to open the massive wooden gates. The gates have large steel spikes facing outwards to stop enemies using elephants to force them open.

Inside that gate are two more walls with iron gates. The outer walls measure eight kilometers. Once inside, the main street leads upward towards the China Minar tower which is sixty-four meters high. It was built in 1445 and was once covered with Persian glass tiles. A little further up we came to an eighteen-foot long cannon pointing up the valley; this left Steven open-mouthed – he couldn't imagine how they got something of that size to where it was perched on a rock. That cannon was one of several perched at strategic places. The pavilion is at the top of a 200-metre high rock which has been chipped away to form a steep cliff that rises above the inner moat filled with water. To reach it you have to climb the steps, through dark winding tunnels which have many traps to mislead invaders and small tunnels that lead out to the cliff edge to fall frighteningly to the water below. The entire fort covers 94.83 hectares; it has amazing town planning and unique water management.

The Ellora caves were another amazing experience. Three faiths meet in the temples and monasteries here, the Buddhist, the Brahmanical, and the Jain. The Buddhist shrines are the earliest dating from the 4th century AD to 9th century AD. The two amazing open-roofed monasteries carved from the solid stone hillside are two storeys high with open corridors along each side. From these stem numerous cell bedrooms with a solid rock bed.

One can only hope they had some sort of a mattress. Both of these big open spaces have amazing statues. My favourite was the massive stone elephant in the center of the Buddhist monastery, but in the Hindu monastery a stupendously carved edifice stands thirty metres high dedicated to the Hindu God Shiva.

Coming from New Zealand and Australia it made me realise just how young our countries were. How long did it take to make these amazing places when all they had were hand tools?

3/7/76

+Ajanta caves

Really enjoyed these caves. The minute carvings were perfect and the paintings have at one time been magnificent.

After leaving the caves we made our way back to the main road north and eventually found a rest home at 7 pm.

The people who looked after the rest house were very poor and had nine children; one of the eldest boys spoke English. The delightful little girl was dressed in filthy rags. They were not the scrounging types so with them watching Kim and I looked around to see what we could spare from our clothes. We put a skirt, a pair of shorts and a loaf of bread in our rubbish bag and saw them carry it into the house as we drove away.

Once again, I find it hard to believe that was all I had to say about Ajanta. If I were to write many pages I could never do justice to this amazing place. It burst into living glory again in 1819 when it was discovered in a horseshoe-shaped valley by a British soldier out hunting tigers. Noticing a strange glitter in the foliage and rubble he gathered helpers from a neighboring village and set out to explore. What they found were twenty-nine caves, some almost completely obscured by vines and earth, ranging in time from the 2nd century BC to 7th century AD. They consist mainly of twenty-four viharas (monasteries) and five chaityas (temples) most of them so hewn that a flood of natural light pours into them at some time of the day. Both the façade and the inside of these caves are decorated with amazing sculptures and on the walls frescoes. Some of the paintings were damaged while others were near perfect. Not only are there many carvings of Buddha but many of women and animals.

I bought a string of amethyst beads there which I still have today.

4/7/76 very hot.
Lost ½ of the exhaust pipe.
Had a bad case of diarrhea and vomiting at the Dak Bungalow, spent ½ the night running back and forth to the loo. Very clean and well-kept people run the place. Steve did some business and Kim swapped some stamps.

Steven had been a bit smart: in Singapore, he had bought up a few watches and calculators, things that couldn't be bought in India, and before long he had sold them all at a good profit. This was highly illegal of course and I was always worried he would be caught.

5/7/76

Stayed overnight in a Dak bungalow in the National Park; used to be the hunting lodge of a Maharaja.

In the morning we were standing outside when we heard a lot of yelping. We looked and saw a pack of about twenty wolves rushing away through the sparse trees.

6th – 7th. Extremely hot. Agra.

Arrived Agra, a better city than most; none of us are feeling well. We all have very dry mouths. Visited the Taj Mahal and felt a bit disappointed although we must admit it was a clever piece of work. Place full of filthy Indian people all begging and scraping and kissing the tomb. Parked at the back of a Tourist bungalow, a stinking place, tried to get a cup of tea and were served in filthy cups so we walked out.

Had to ferry across the Ganges with a full load of oxen and buffalo. While we waited we saw a man fetch some water from the river in a dirty tin and give it to the peanut seller. He poured it into a glass and drank it even though there was a man peeing in the river not 10 feet away and some water buffalo were swimming and pooing there. They nearly smashed our car as we drove off.

I have copied that entry just as I wrote it which goes to show how sick I must have been.

A CLEVER JOB OF WORK: this is about one of the finest pieces of artwork in the world! I can still see the tiny red roses with yellow centers set into the white marble. We joined the queue to go down the steps to the Tomb of Mumtaz Mahal. The place was packed and the progress around the tomb slow; the smell of unwashed bodies was overpowering. Some of these people had been on the road for weeks making a pilgrimage to pay their respects to the lady entombed here. I found the wailing and pawing of the tomb unbelievable – some of the women had to be dragged away.

Billie and Kim at the Taj Mahal

Outside on the street, I tried buy a small plate that was a replica of the roses. The man said yes, he would take a travellers cheque, but changed his mind when he saw someone at the door watching him. It was illegal to change money anywhere except within a Government agency. As to the mention of the Ganges, we realised later that it couldn't have been the Ganges but another wide, fast-flowing river. After inspecting my Indian map with a magnifying glass I believe it to be the Chambal River. I was driving as we approached the river and at the top of the hill was a hut with a notice saying ferry tickets were so many rupee.

When I drove down to the river I saw that the tickets were twice the price so I did a U-turn, much to the surprise of the family who wanted to know what on earth I was doing. I drove back up the hill to get a ticket. While we were waiting is when the fetching of the water happened. The herd of oxen were standing around, their urine running down into the water from where the man collected the water for the peanut seller. Steven took over the driving and drove onto the ferry, then the beasts were loaded around us, packed so tightly that an oxen was jammed up tightly against our passenger door. Her horn rested against the window – one toss of her head and it would be broken. As it was, as she breathed in and out the door panel went in and out with a click. It was quite an experience.

On the other side, the cattle were unloaded first, then it was our turn. Somehow they did something wrong and the ramp for the right front wheel gave away, and the bottom of the van was resting on the top of the ferry. Luckily the Kombi had rear-wheel drive; Steven revved the motor, released the clutch, and we flew off the ferry and landed with a bang on terra firma. I have never seen people disappear so fast; it was almost laughable.

After a brief inspection to see no damage had been done we drove on. On the top of the steep hill above was a big building belching smoke; we thought it must be a crematorium, there was an awful smell of burning flesh.

Road sign in India

7th/ 8th. Delhi Extremely hot. Tourist camp and iced water.

Arrived PM after driving on India's best road from Agra. All are weak and can't get enough to drink. Stopped at a Koshi T restaurant and got some civilised food and drink. Couldn't find the cathedral (for camping) that John and Nora told us about, but found the tourist park, only motor camp in India, another bit of window dressing for the tourists. We have an iced water fountain here- like a dream come true.

We were relieved to find a hospital just over the road so early the next day we presented ourselves at Casualty. The place was a seething mass of humanity; all the seats were taken and the people were milling around. There seemed to be no order to the way people were seen. One teenage boy appeared to be very ill with a raging temperature and was more than likely infectious. After waiting for a while Frank shocked me by losing his temper, declaring that he wasn't going to wait any longer. He charged to the front of the queue and demanded that we were seen. I was very embarrassed as many of the people were obviously sicker than we were. However, instead of being told to wait our turn, the staff took it in their stride and we were all ushered in to see the doctors. As usual my diary entry made no mention of Frank or his behavior.

8th July. Very hot. Delhi
Have suspected hepatitis.

Up most of the night with diarrhea again, makes 5 days in a row. Feeling very ill and weak. Went over the road to the hospital where they herd you through like cattle.

We have almost certainly contracted Infective hepatitis. Have been given blood tests and given medicine to help. Afternoon- went to look for food at Delhi's biggest supermarket. What a mess of a place, hardly anything to buy. No soups, tinned veg. or fruit, no flour. Got two chickens though and as our medicine is starting to take effect we enjoyed a meal, the first for about a week.

Called at the P.O. for mail but got none.

9th July. Cooler
Delhi.

Met a couple of English lads who have just driven through from U.K. (and come into the camp) They have gone off to see if the Indian Government will accept their Kombi as a gift and discharge their Carnet; if they do then we can have their exhaust, stove and air beds.

Not feeling so weak today and no diarrhea. Will have to go and forage for some more food.

The Government did except the Kombi, being hungry for any cars. We got their gas bottle (at last we could cook on our stove again), some spare tyres and the air beds. They thought it best not to remove the exhaust. We all spent a few days at the camp; they told us of a great place to eat at a hotel quite near. We went there one night and were amazed to find ourselves alone in this big empty dining room with immaculate white table clothes and all laid out to perfection. The food was good and very cheap.

One day, on the way back to the camp from town, Brian, one of the lads, found a horse that had been left to die on a piece of waste ground. He was very upset as we all were and began going twice a day with water. I wanted to help but had already been appalled at the dreadful cruelty dished out by these people to their horses. I cannot remember which city it was but I was driving and had stopped at traffic lights. On my right was a horse pulling a big cart piled high with a load. The horse was just a bag of bones – all its ribs were showing and its legs were shaking. Because it didn't move forward when told, the driver started thrashing it around the head with a whip. I was screaming livid. I leaped out of the Kombi and screamed, "Don't you dare hit that horse like that!"

My son in the passenger seat said, "Get back in the car, Mum, you are just making a fool of yourself."

The man with the whip just laughed at me! I wanted to grab the whip from his hands and give him a taste of his own medicine.

On the 14th July, both the lads and our family left the camp, they to fly to Australia and we to continue our journey. The worst was yet to come.

15/7/76 Lahore, Pakistan

Warm and fine.

Got away from Delhi late after picking up our visas for Afghanistan and getting our inoculations for Cholera again. This made us sick again for another two days. Got lost in Old Delhi twice – no landmarks. No trouble getting through the border. Lahore is much more go ahead, big hotels and more money. Hope to get an exhaust pipe for the van tomorrow.

We had gone to Old Delhi to see if any mail had arrived there for us, but there was nothing. The place was ancient, flat, and the narrow streets went every way like a gigantic slum. The lack of any building above a single storey made it hard to navigate.

When we went to get our Cholera injections there was a queue and I noticed that the needle was not changed for any of the people who were before us. I was about to protest but saw that the man changed the needle for each of us.

The difference between India and Pakistan was obvious as soon as we crossed the border: Pakistan was so much more vibrant and alive. We had no trouble finding a modern garage to fit another exhaust pipe. We camped in the grounds of a modern hotel and used the swimming pool. We were watched by three men who asked if Kim would come to shop in town and sit on a motorbike for some advertising photos. They seemed quite legitimate but I wasn't prepared to take the chance no matter how much they paid.

It was another three days before I made another entry in my diary, but in that time we had driven many miles across some of the most fascinating places on earth. From Lahore to Gujranvala, Rawalpindi, Islamabad, Peshawar, Islamabad, to Kabul. The last leg was the longest.

We had camped at a small place called Gujar Khan in Pakistan, from there we stopped at Peshawar to see the Golden Temple, over the border, through the Khyber Pass to Jalalabad and on to Kabul where we arrived about 9 pm. Frank shamed us all again at the Golden Temple by refusing to take off his sandals; he had diarrhea and needed the toilet badly. The dignified white-clad attendant wasn't taking no for an answer so he complied in the end. I hated that man a little more each day; why, oh why, did he have to trample on other people's beliefs instead of just respecting them and keeping the peace. As it was we didn't see the Temple except from over the water. Seeing there was a very long queue across the bridge to get into it, we decided to hit the road.

I drove through the Khyber Pass – what an experience! All my life I had read about this place, it seemed unbelievable to be here. There was a pull-in stopping place before descending where we had an amazing panoramic view of the road below. Soon after leaving the pass the road began to follow the Kabul River which rises in the highlands of northeastern Afghanistan. From there it flows east, passing through Kabul to finally drain into the Indus River in Pakistan. The mountains each side soon closed in; we had reached the Tan-I Garu Gorge where suddenly I seemed to be driving right into a cliff face.

"What's happened to the road?" I gasped. I soon found out, it turned into a tight left-hand elbow bend and entered a tunnel. We were in what must be one of the world's most amazing engineering feats. The road climbs 700 meters in fifteen kilometres, winding up the mountain through solid rock and around many elbow bends; sometimes there is a small open stretch. I looked over my right shoulder.

"Oh look, there's the road we just came up right below us."

Three voices shouted, "Keep your eyes on the road!"

Down on the flat again I was glad to stop and pass the driving on to Steve. We came to a toll – they wanted Afghanistan money, of which we had none. Finally, after an argument, they let us go without paying. The countryside was dry and barren; occasionally we passed a fortified farmhouse, high clay walls surrounding the clay home within. There was yet another pass before we reached Kabul.

It was dark when we reached the city centre but something didn't seem right to me. We passed a funfair place with lights and a carousel; there didn't seem to be many people there either – certainly no women. Somehow it just seemed to be so much out of keeping with the place. We learned later that President Daoud was celebrating his 3rd year of rule. We found a clay hotel, also behind a high clay wall, where we could park and use the toilets. It had been a very long day.

18/7/76 Fine, cool nights

Kabul. Afghanistan. Rest day

Seems impossible that it is just 3 days since we left Delhi. Came through from Gujar Khan (Delhi side of Rawalpindi) to here yesterday. On the road 14 hours. I drove through the Kyber Pass and Steve drove the pass to Kabul. Had a lovely sleep, air crystal clear and cool. Will stay a today to do washing and write letters.

That day Frank decided the engine oil needed changing and to my utter horror he let the oil run out straight onto the dry grass lawn. It didn't matter what we said to him, he always had some smart-arse reply.

We left town the next day to travel south the 498 kilometers to Kandahar. One has to climb a pass to get into Kabul and another pass out. This one was a slow steady climb, one where you feel the van is struggling in top gear but not right in third. Soon the engine developed a slight knock, which I discussed with Steven. We carried on for a few miles by which time the knock had become bad and I pulled over. Would we carry on or turn back?

Frank was all for going on but Steven and I overruled him. We had been warned about armed bandits on the road – to be broken down would have made us sitting ducks. Steven turned the van and headed back but soon the knock was so bad it was foolish to drive further. Eventually, a Russian jeep came past and stopped to tow us back to Kabul. The only stupid thing we did was not to negotiate a price before we set off. It was all a bit embarrassing as the jeep boiled twice on the way back. We stopped at one ford and refilled the radiator; I hadn't realised just how far I had driven, but at last we reached the outskirts of town. Then the wrangling started about how much we should pay. At last we reached an agreement. By the time we had paid up and the jeep had left we had attracted quite a crowd of men. Opposite from where we were stopped was a large open yard with open workshops all along one side.

We fix your van someone said. "Great," said Frank.

I couldn't believe his stupidity and took him aside. "Are you stark raving mad?" I hissed. "Within a day we will be stripped bare of everything." I had seen a VW sign on the road out of town, so leaving Kim with her father to guard the van Steven and I hailed a passing taxi and headed back.

As we were nearing town I said, "I saw the VW sign along here somewhere."

"V-dub," said the taxi driver, "I take you." And he did.

We paid him what he asked and gave him a tip. We were to find that many Afghans spoke a bit of English, also German, not only because of all the tourists in town but because both America and Germany had done work in the country.

We were in for a surprise at the VW place; the proprietor had been bought up in British India and spoke perfect English. Not only that but he was a perfect replica of the actor Telly Savalas who played the part of Kojak in the TV detective series. And that was what Steven called him much to the man's amusement. In no time at all our rescuer had the motor out and had towed us to the back of a hotel where many overland vans were already ensconced.

The hotel owner had married an English girl.

There was a big lounge where we could sit, rest, read or write letters. The room was furnished the local way with brightly colored mattress-like seats around the walls and lots of cushions. I loved it, it was so, so peaceful, especially as I was away from Frank and his sniping. Steven went back to see what 'Kojak' was doing and came back to say he already had the motor running on the bench.

We had no idea what the repairs would cost and it seemed we would have to be here for some time. I rang the Intercontinental Hotel and asked the manager if he wanted a floor show. He said, "yes, please." I asked for a thousand dollars but he offered $650 American dollars which was fine by me, being quite a large amount at that time. Our photographs were printed with the advertisement in the Kabul Times.

Floor show advertisement

26/7/76 Hot and dry
Kabul Entertaining at the Intercontinental Hotel.

Here we are still in Kabul after breaking down about 20 miles out on the road to Kandahar and being towed back. Have had the whole engine out, new rings and crankshaft ground down etc. Cost 6,700 Afs. (about $30 Australian) we have to run the van in for a week so we are working for a week here. Very hot with dust storms this past two days. We have a night off after doing an extra show for all the Cabinet members and Prime Minister last night. Have been parking in the hotel's car park and using the swimming pool during the day, getting very brown. Band called "The Ceylon Gems" with poor old Tom on the trumpet and the bottle. The Australian Consul came to see us one night, we didn't know him but the band pointed him out.

It was a win-win situation for us. Firstly, the repairs would have cost us over $200 in Australia, the hotel car park cost us nothing. We had been given a single room to use as we pleased and our pay far outweighed all our expenses.

When the manager asked me if we would represent the hotel and do an extra show down by the swimming pool to entertain the President and all his cabinet I was shocked as we didn't have a work permit. He assured me that no one would bother. We worked with a group of Russian artists who had come especially for the occasion. Neither Kim nor I remember much about the night; we can't remember who decided in what order the acts were to perform, but I do remember we were the support act to the star singer, an absolutely fabulous tenor.

There is a law for the rich and a law for the poor in most countries, more noticeably the Moslem ones. Did the ladies accompanying the men have the all-covering *chadderi* like the women in the street? Of course not. All the men were accompanied by elegant, bejeweled young ladies in evening dresses; I doubt very much if they were their wives.

King Zahir Shan had ruled Afghanistan for forty years but was overthrown by his cousin Daoud Khan in a bloodless coup in 1973 when Zahir Shah was in Italy getting medical treatment.

President Daoud was right to celebrate the fact that he had lasted three years. Even though the country was under Marshall Law he must have known it couldn't last. Just four years later he was shot.

I really enjoyed our time in Kabul, but it was sad to see the women so completely covered when out in the street. In fact, it was amusing to see a petite lady completely covered from head to toe with slacks and high heels sticking out of the bottom. Most of the coverings were grey silk, pleated around the head and with a fine mesh covering the eyes. Kim and I went to a shop where they were sold. I had planned to buy one as a souvenir but they were very expensive.

However, we found the men very nice. Of course, they would try to cheat you sometimes but when I caught them and waved a finger at them they would laugh and own up. Kim and I would go shopping to the market for vegies and go to the same man each day. One day after we had paid him he threw in a cauliflower for free. The fruit and vegetables were great, the meat another matter. The stalls were swarming with flies. One day while we were at the hotel I bought a piece of camel meat. Unbelievably even after cooking it in a pressure cooker twice we still couldn't get our teeth through it.

Kojak had insisted we must run the motor in before tackling the pass again; he wanted us to stay a month but we didn't want to stay that long. One day Frank, Kim and I went out into the hills to run the motor. I was surprised just how much the country was like New Zealand in many ways – for one thing, it is the only other place I have even seen a big macrocarpa tree. When we got to our destination we found big plantations of apricot trees just like central Otago.

We had lunch beside a deep rocky ravine which must run with water when the winter snows melt. It was a peaceful and beautiful spot; unfortunately, we attracted the attention of some young pre-teenage boys who started getting a bit cheeky so we packed up hastily and left.

When I look at tourist pamphlets now I wonder why we didn't go out to see the giant Buddha's carved into the cliffs but we would have had steep climbs and another pass to climb which is what we were trying to avoid.

There was an old saying about Kabul: if a child lived until it was ten years old it could have a long life – by that time they had developed an immunity to all the bugs. For many years the main water supply ran through the streets, indeed the small channel of water still ran quite swiftly when we were there. It looked clear and clean, but Kim and I saw a man washing his dishes in front of his shop and further on a man was cleaning his teeth and spitting into the water.

The Moslem religion bans homosexuality but it was rife in Kabul. How else could it be otherwise when women were banned from society – the only two women we saw in a shop were at the American Express office where we could change money.

The streets were full of young men who didn't have work. Some would approach us with something to sell. One young smiling lad was selling knitted, knee-high, fair-isle socks with soft leather soles; I wanted a pair and we haggled about the price. Frank, always the clown, offered to exchange his daughter for a pair. The boy's face lit up like a beacon.

"NO! NO!" I said. I could not believe anyone could be so stupid to say that in a Moslem country where women are almost worthless.

One thing that was sadly lacking in the town was public toilets; the back streets had turds everywhere, it was disgusting.

At last, we said goodbye to Kojak and set off. He advised us to stop every hour to let the motor cool, run with the motor cover propped up, which we did, and keep our speed down to eighty miles an hour until we'd done a few hundred miles, especially as we were so heavily loaded. Of course VW's are air-cooled but that doesn't help when the air is 40° Celsius or more.

At one place we stopped on a hill where wildflowers grew all around us. When we saw a car approaching Kim and I dived into the van to hide and the men made themselves prominent. Luckily the car passed without stopping. At Ghazni we stopped for petrol; it was my turn to pay and the man at the pump made it quite plain he didn't approve of women, not only driving but having the gall to ask for petrol. I treated him with the contempt he paid me, slowly added the cost up on the calculator – although I already knew the cost – then counting out the afs. to the last penny.

Unfortunately, we soon had a row with Frank; he was driving and started to sing which was a nice change from the sniping. I watched the speed going up and up and suggested he slowed down a bit.

Steven said, "Yes, Dad slow up, we don't want to break down out here."

Frank slammed the brakes on and the van came to a shuddering stop in a cloud of dust.

He yelled, "That does it, you can f-----g well do all the f-----g driving yourselves from now on."

And so it was that just my son and I drove all the rest of the way to the U.K. while Frank sat I the back, feet up on the shelf and against the curtains and continually handed out the insults. Snipe, snipe, snipe, while we all ignored him.

One day Steven could stand it no longer. He slammed the brakes on and pulled up, telling Frank if he didn't shut up he was going to throw him out on the road and he could find his own way back. After that he wasn't quite so bad.

4/8/76 Hot

Bojnord Iran.

Got through to Kandahar in one day after a 10 ½ hour trip. Not impressed with the town and left for Herat at 4 am. Got as far as Farrawood where it was as hot as hell and we stayed the night in a posh hotel where the Russians had resided while putting the road through. Left at 5 am and got to Herat at 11 am. Had to apply for visas for Iran and found we had to wait overnight until 12 midday to get them. Took off straight away and reached the *border 220 kms where the van was thoroughly searched – they prodded holes and poked into everything. Then over the Iranian border where they went through it all again. Stayed at Taibad the first night, 200 rials and no shower. Made it all the way here today. Down with bad diarrhea these past two days.*

The first half of the road from Kandahar to Herat was built by the Americans. It was built in concrete sections so for many miles all we heard as we passed over the joins was *bedum-bedum-bedum* which can be a little nerve-racking after a while. The second half, built by the Russians, was of bitumen, if I remember correctly, and was smoother travelling. I was driving for the first few hours and it seemed to be all slightly uphill. Ahead was a jeep carrying two girl tourists, driven by a young man who hated having a women driver pass him. His driving speed was too slow for my top gear and I had to keep changing down to third. Then I would pass him again and he would speed up, pass me then slow down again. He thought it was funny – I was not amused. This went on for ages, so we stopped and let him get ahead. Later we passed them again when they had stopped at a ford and were down cooling off in the water.

That day was the hottest day I have ever experienced in my life. The temperatures must have been in the high forties, and we began to worry about the van overheating.

We reached Farrawood about mid-afternoon and called it a day, parking at the side of the hotel in part shade. The place had once been grand; out the back, the once magnificent garden was neglected and overgrow and a large swimming pool was empty. We had the use of a bathroom and toilet just inside a nearby door but the place was filthy. There was a shower over the bath which was caked with human body grease; it was all rather sad. Down from a top storey water flowed from what might have been a faulty toilet system. By the time it hit the ground near the van it was cold so in desperation we stood under it fully clothed to try and cool down. None of us slept well that night.

At Taibad, just over the Iranian border, we met two young lads with their girlfriends. The boys' father was an American who lived in London and worked as a pilot for American Airways. We spent the evening with them talking about the way ahead for them and us; they asked us to call and see their father when we reached London and assure him they were fine.

Not long after we said our goodbyes and left the next morning we were passed on the road by a utility overloaded with passengers, some sitting on the roof of the cab. This did not surprise us as, for the past few weeks, it had been a common sight. What did surprise us however was to find about two miles on, that the utility had left the road, crashed down a bank and rolled. There were bodies strewn around, dead or alive we couldn't tell, and we were not going to stop to find out.

7/8/76 Hot and muggy.
Caspian Sea.
Arrived here two days ago and very disappointed as most of the sea is fenced off and horribly crowded. It was constitutional day and the traffic was thick. Feeling better though as we have had some regular meals. Nice bread here and cheap tomatoes. Not many green veg. Shops a lot cleaner but butchers shops not a great improvement. Cannot get dried milk so have to shop for fresh daily. Hope to leave for Teheran tomorrow.

Women here wear modern clothes but leave their faces uncovered not like the Afghanistan women and the all-enveloping chadderi that they wear.

The Caspian Sea is huge; it is impossible to see the sides or the width of it. Steven wanted to go fishing with his spear gun and knife. He donned his weight-belt and asked Kim and I to go out with him, floating on lilos, for his safety, which we did. I couldn't swim and don't like getting out of my depth. It seemed like no time before we drifted away off-shore and the sea was choppy. I was petrified. The water was full of tiny specks of what looked like some kind of vegetation, Steven eventually gave up his search for fish saying he couldn't see anything around him down below, and gratefully we headed for shore. Kim and I lay on our tummies and paddled with our arms. By the time we got back the top of our arms were badly chaffed from contact with the rough edges of the lilos.

The beach was deserted again; we had the place to ourselves. A car drove in and strangely came and parked right beside us. It turned out to be a nice couple who had come to talk to us and they both spoke perfect English. She taught English at the university and he was a chemist. I made them tea and we had a long talk. They invited us to come to their home the next day. I would loved to have gone, but given the situation with my husband, I just couldn't face socialising with him.

Just before they arrived we'd had a dreadful row with him over a very nasty remark he'd made to Kim. Instead of ignoring him as she usually did, she was hurt enough to retaliate and answered him back before taking off. He picked up a rock about the size of his fist and threw it, hitting her so hard between the shoulder blades that she almost stumbled. Both Steven and I exploded. Had he hit her on the head he may have killed her. I told him, among other things, that when we reached Teheran I was going to the British Embassy and have him flown to the U.K. He laughed and said, "Good." Steven threatened him with his spear gun; telling him this was his final warning. It was all very upsetting; we felt he was now becoming dangerous.

From the Caspian, we had to drive over another pass at 5,601 meters. I was driving as we entered the outskirts of Teheran and it didn't take me long to work out that these people were homicidal maniacs on the road. I pulled over to let Steven drive and he drove for the three days we stayed in town. There were practically no cars on the road that didn't have dents. They gave way to nobody – even pedestrian crossings were ignored. They shot out of side roads and pushed in front of you forcing you to brake sharply … it was a nightmare. Steven stopped at a pedestrian crossing one day where a crowd either side was waiting to cross. A smartly dressed elderly man with a white beard came to the driver's window and said, "Thank you very much, young man. It is nice to see that someone in this town has some manners."

The only motor camp in town was miles out on a very pot-holed road and absolutely crowded with overland buses from Germany and every type of motor home from a lot of countries. Every transport had a small label with the initials of the country of origin attached. We had SNY (I think) for Singapore and we lost count of the people who asked us what it stood for. The toilets were the dirtiest in the world – it seemed that everyone, including us, had Giardia – exploding diarrhea. I flew in one morning and had to wade in sloppy faeces on the floor; all the walls were covered even up to the ceiling – unbelievable but true. When you have to go you have to go, but at least I tried to hit the toilet. I longed to get a hosepipe and hose the place down.

Getting to the bank was a priority: our money from Singapore had still not arrived. It seemed they were not on computer.

I didn't go to the Embassy about Frank because he had said later that he wouldn't comply with anything they said.

12/8/76 Cooler nights.

Marand. Almost out of Iran.

Spent 3 days in Teheran waiting for money which didn't come. Have decided to press on. Once out of Turkey we can send our carnet back to Singapore and get our money. Don't like Iran, the men are arrogant pigs with no sense of humour, they drive like maniacs, have never seen so many accidents in my life. Saw the remains of 20 accidents today from Takestan to Marand. Have a nasty knock in the steering, very worried about it. Should cross into Turkey about midday tomorrow.

An article in the English press about the outrageous accident rate quoted there had been eighty bus accidents in one month, killing 120 people and injuring many more. The writer stated that it was high time the drivers were held accountable and needed proper training.

Smashed up vehicles appeared to be simply abandoned at the roadside; we saw a Cortina car squashed between two buses. I said it looked more like a concertina. It looked as though everyone had just got out and walked away.

17/8/76 Fine

Near Ismit - Turkey Back to civilisation.

Here we are stranded outside a petrol station waiting for petrol to be delivered. Got through the border o.k. but the trucks were banked up 10 miles each side, hell of a traffic jam there. Camped on the outskirts of Horasan first night, at a restaurant near Rafahiye next night after that village very hostile, then almost to Ismit last night. Had hoped to spend the day in Istanbul then head for the border. Food is better here; lovely bread, eggs, tomatoes, cheese, and fruit. Had a nasty experience yesterday when a drunk jumped on the front of the car. Steve slammed on the brakes and threw him off. Luckily we were in a convoy of sea-land trucks.

I believe it was at the restaurant near Rafahiye that we encountered the green man. We had originally parked in a big, what turned out to be, truck park over the road. There was a fast-flowing stream running alongside. As the evening approached more and more trucks pulled in for the night. Imagine our surprise when a man, bright shiny green all over, stepped out of a cab. Kim and I gaped as he came towards us. He only had shorts on, and his sweaty green skin glistened. He started laughing and explained in halting English that the lid had come loose and fallen off a drum carrying the powder. He had become caked in the fine powder when he tried to sweep it up. He waded into the creek and tried to wash it off without much success. Later people came from the restaurant to tell us we must move over and park beside the door which we did. I expect they were thinking of our safety.

Just after we crossed the border we came upon a small village. Kim and I went shopping for sugar and met some very nice Kurdish men with large black mustaches and great smiles. How different from the poker-faced Iranians. The shop had big bags stacked all along the walls; we couldn't see in them because we had to talk over a small counter. They couldn't speak English and we couldn't speak Turkish so no way could I get them to understand. There was much laughter as we tried French, German, miming, pretending to put sugar into tea and stirring it, all to no avail.

We waved goodbye and went on our way.

Eastern Turkey was a wild place; we drove many miles through arid high countryside where large areas of bitumen had lifted in the heat leading to giant potholes. At one place high in the hills we saw a young man taking honey from bee-hives beside the road. We stopped and asked if we could buy some and he sold us a large pint-sized jar of absolutely clear honey. Unfortunately, it had a very unusual taste and nobody but me would eat it; and that only because I hated to waste it. Other times we were driving in heavily forested areas, and it was here I caught a glimpse of a wolf in the trees beside the road.

Eventually, we caught up with three T.I.R trucks. Many of these trucks were on the road and it took us a while to work out that their T.I.R. label meant Trans-Intercontinental-Route. Steven managed to pass two of them before we came to some roadworks that went on for miles. No one was working there but for some strange reason they had piled loose earth about a meter high on the right-hand side of the road forcing all traffic to the left.

The truck in front was a long car carrier, which stopped briefly, then carried on slowly, as a car with a flat tyre had driven up on the dirt. Around the car were four men and Steven saw another one jump off the back of the truck as it pulled away. They were obviously drunk but the most alarming thing was that 303 rifles leaned against the front and back wheels. One man came to the passenger window and indicated they needed a jack and Steven said, "No, mate," and the man hammered on the door with both fists. Before we could drive on another one had jumped on the front bumper and was hanging on the gutter around the roof, his face plastered against the windscreen. Kim and I were in the front seat and a big leery grin appeared on his face.

The truck in front was a left-hand-drive and I could see he was trying to watch out for us. I told Steven to pull over so he could see what we were doing. He did, and the driver gave us room. Steven sped up then slammed the brakes on. Our unwanted passenger went flying, and Steven revved the engine and drove forward, the drunk rolling out of the way. As we passed I looked down at him – he was on the edge of a twenty-foot reasonably steep bank and had a fist-sized rock that he was about to throw at our window. Luckily he went over the edge and rolled away. Later that day we pulled to a spot above the road to eat lunch; the car carrier came past, the driver sounding his horn and laughing; he took both hands off the steering wheel and clasping them together he shook them above his head. We laughed and waved back.

We had yet another bad experience in that area: a flat battery which meant we had to jump-start the motor. Steven had pulled up on a slope above the road where we ate lunch. A well-dressed young man appeared from nowhere accompanied by four teenage boys. They demanded cigarettes, which we couldn't give them because none of us smoked, which they failed to understand and became quite angry. The clay where we'd parked was a bit boggy and the van didn't run so we asked them for a push; they must have thought they would get the cigarettes if they did, so they complied. The engine fired and as we drove off they chased us down the road shouting abuse. We were sorry not to be able to spend time in Istanbul; the traffic, although well-behaved, was chaotic and there was nowhere to park. Steven eventually had to park sideways on a steep slope outside a shop, and I was petrified the van would tip over, but it didn't. We bought some food from the shop and drove on.

19/8/76 Cool and fine.
Greece.
On our way to Thesalonica. Stayed in Alexandropolist last night and posted our carnet back to AA with mail for home etc.

Have to get our visas for Yugoslavia tomorrow. Just great to get into Greece and get good food; clothes are lovely and cheap. Camped on a delightful beach under some huge trees.

Greece was heaven after the places we'd been, now we really were back to civilisation. It was great to see beautiful buildings and real shops. Kim and I went into a fruit shop to ask directions and were greeted by a nice man who said he'd lived in Australia. We chatted for a while and he handed us a large delicious apricot each.

Our wonderful Asia overland map finished at Istanbul.

The first part of Yugoslavia over to the Adriatic coast was through mountains and tunnels and then the coast north was forever winding in and out. At some places ferries took us cross stretches of water – it was either that or drive miles inland, around the top of the fiord and back to the coast again. It was a beautiful drive but the bends were tedious. I got some fine colour slides of the coast and the sunsets.

Every inch of land appeared to have been cultivated at some time; where the land rose up from the sea, small terraces edged with stones had been made.

Steven got caught for speeding, the policeman took his passport until he paid the hefty fine.

I was still wary about the steering which knocked every time I turned the wheel. It was the same grease nipple that the little boy and Frank couldn't get grease into in India. I felt that at any minute the steering would break and we would end up in the sea. But it didn't happen.

23/8/766 Changeable
Yugoslavia
Dubrovnik

Have been here 3 days. Car deteriorating. Had to change the fan belt in Petrovac and found the pulley wheel broken, spent several hours getting the thing fixed, or trying to, before realising that we had one on the roof. Tyres still holding out but getting grim.

Spent last night and this morning in Dubrovnik, fascinating place - a walled city, perfectly preserved. Scenery is spectacular but the windy road is beginning to pall. Food good, petrol bad and smelly. Hope to be out in another two days.

We had just arrived in Petrovac when the fan belt broke. We had seen an abandoned VW Kombi up the hill; somehow we managed to find out who owned it and located him. He was a very nice young man; we pointed out the broken part and with sign language asked if we could buy the part from his vehicle. He understood us but we couldn't understand what he was trying to explain. Eventually he motioned us to follow him; he threw open the engine cover to show us NO MOTOR. Oh no!

Kim came to the rescue, saying, "Do we have one in the trunk on the roof?'

When we bought the van the seller had given us all the spare parts and sure enough, there was 'one on the roof'. What a relief. The other thing that was starting to fail was the timing; Steven had to tinker with it several times. Needless to say, the dreadful petrol didn't help.

I absolutely loved Dubrovnik – such a wonderful ancient city. The walls start at the top of the hill then, once inside, you find your way down narrow paths between the houses. The carved doors, the huge hinges, and door-knockers were all wonderful. I wished we could have stayed longer.

24/8/76 Fine

Near Venice Into Italy

Made good time today after an early start. Crossed over the border at 4.30 pm. No Formalities. Seems very civilized. We stopped for a drink at a lovely country bar-cum-café. And a very nice Aussie girl served us.

Want to spend a day in Venice tomorrow.

All I had to say about Venice was:

Venice fine for one visit, glassware superb and majestic old homes.

Truthfully Dubrovnik had spoilt Venice for us. Both cities seemed to be the same age and have the same stamp. Venice was much more crowded.

27/8/76 Cool and fine.

France

Crossed the alps from Italy to France this AM. Have got as far as Roanne past Lyon. Not an impressive city - prefer Italy. The alps were beautiful. Tried to find the highway from Lyon to Dijohn - didn't want to go by the autostrada as it cost us F22 from Chambery to Lyon. Passed through several long tunnels, probably saved us another long climb. Petrol a hell of a price – cost us F30 for 16 litres

Paree tomorrow- we hope.

In Paris we found a caravan park. We all needed a shower badly so Kim got out our French English dictionary and tried to write out the words we needed; she must have got it right because when she presented the note to the lady owner she understood at once. Wonderful, a hot shower at last. We all scrubbed and washed our hair. That night we took the train into the city; I was surprised to see so many dark-skinned people there. In those days there were no dark-skinned people in Australia except our own Aboriginals and they were not very dark. We went to Monte Mart and were a bit shocked by the prostitutes standing everywhere in garish clothes and overdone makeup.

The next day we explored the beautiful city.

At last, we were on the final leg of our journey; from Le Havre, France, to Dover, England – by ferry. Our trip had taken us just a few days over six months. What a relief to see again the White Cliffs of Dover.

England Again

We found a place to park near London. The change in Frank was astounding. Suddenly he was Mr Nice Guy, all sweetness and charm; he began crawling around me but I was not having a bar of it. I told him that, after the way he had behaved the last few months, he was finished; this time for good. As soon as we had our affairs sorted I was leaving and never wanted to see him again. He thought he could talk me around, but not this time.

Our first priority was to get to the bank and sort out our finances. I was really annoyed to find that the thousands we had sent over about eight months before had been sitting in a *holding* account, not an *interest* account. How like a bank – using our money at no cost. We drew out the money and divided it in two. I left an account open to receive the money still due from Singapore.

Frank suggested we go for a trip around the south of England to wait until the carnet money came through. Once again he had to go dragging up the past by visiting all the people we had known. We went to the Flower Pots Inn at Cheriton – they had sold out and moved away. We went to the farm above Gatwick airport and Frank went to Mrs Pope's house – she had sold long ago. I could never, never understand his obsession of racking up the past and wanted no part of it, especially with him around.

Back in London, the money from Singapore had arrived. We shared it out and all set about making our own way. Steven bought himself a Triumph motorbike and was going to stay in London. Kim and I were heading north where most of the working men's clubs were, and possible work. And Frank? Well, no one knew what he was going to do and no one cared. We had promised the brothers in Iran that we would call on their father and Steven thought he would ask if he could leave some of his gear there and if we could use their address so we didn't lose touch. He set off on his motorbike with us following.

The boys' father was at home and was so pleased to see us; he said, of course, we could send mail here and yes, Steven could leave a suitcase.

As we had paid half each, the van rightly belonged to both of us, but I told Frank he could have it and everything in it that wasn't our stage gear or clothes. We had been informed there were lockers at the Manchester station where we could leave our bags so, anxious to get away, we decided to travel on the late afternoon train. Mr Charming saw us off – he couldn't have been nicer.

We arrived at Manchester at 2.30 am. The few people who alighted soon disappeared and we were left alone on the station. The promised lockers were all locked, with the keys removed because of the fear of the IRA – who were busy doing nasty things at the time – putting bombs in them. There we were with two large square tartan cases on wheels, one big flat suitcase, and a long army kit bag with all our costumes and lights in it. It was too much to cart around in a taxi to find accommodation for the rest of the night so we decided to wait for the morning and the opening of the 'left luggage' office. About 3.30 am two policemen entered the station and wanted to know all about us. They were really nice guys; they wanted to know why we had so much luggage so we explained our trip and our stage gear. We sat chatting and laughing for over an hour; they told us about the fights with the football hooligans and I accused them of enjoying it, which they admitted to. Kim wandered off with one of them looking at the posters around the walls; my companion saw me keeping an eye on them. "She's alright," he said. "She won't come to any harm."

But I still watched, so many months of not being able to trust anyone.

Eventually, they decided they had better leave, but before they went we asked where we should or should not get accommodation and they gave us a list of suburbs.

Morning came at last and the station came to life. The 'left luggage' opened and we left our gear after filling in a form to say it contained no bombs. Kim went off to the toilet and bless her little cotton socks, she got talking to the toilet attendant. She came back with the name and phone number of a man called Brendon who may have a flat for us. We rang the number; he gave us an address – Warrick Road – and arranged to meet us at 9.30 am. The bus driver assured us he would tell us when we got to Warrick Road; he did, but little did we know there was a famous cricket ground at another Warrick Road and that is where he left us. There turned out to be no such number in that Warrick Road and after many inquiries a kind gentleman told us of the other Warrick road in Chorlton Cum Hardy several suburbs away. Now late, we took to our heels and ran; thank goodness for flat-heeled shoes. In the new woolen coats we had bought in London we arrived hot and sweaty; Brendon was still there.

The newly decorated flat was on the 3rd floor of a terraced house; the top of the stairs had not been blocked off as it should have been, so the two rooms opened straight off the top landing. The place was furnished. It had a kitchen, just a gas stove and a sink, a table and chairs and a sofa that could be slept on. The other room had a double bed and a wardrobe, the small window looking down onto the street. This room had a door – made necessary by the authorities in case of fire – going into the bedroom of the next house which Brendon also owned. The key was enclosed in a box.

The place was small, but ten times bigger than the Kombi, the rent £10 a week. I offered a month in advance. We went back to the train station, picked up our luggage and were settled by nightfall.

14/9/76 Manchester Cool.

New Flat

Moved to Manchester from London at two am. Spent the rest of the night on the station talking to two handsome bobbies. Had to wait until 7.30 to get our luggage into the left luggage. All the rest are shut because of bomb scares. Found a flat by 10.30 and moved in, it's small but cozy. Have at last come to an agreement with Frank and we have parted, he was so good and saw us off on the train. Have to start hunting for work soon.

Our first concern was to get jobs. We signed on for the dole but were never given any jobs to apply for. We registered with a theatrical agent but were never to hear a word from her.

We had been in our flat about three weeks when we heard someone banging on the door downstairs. The boys in the flats below were all out so like a fool I went down to answer it. There on the doorstep stood Frank – I felt sick, having hoped to never ever see him again. But there he was. I demanded to know how he'd got our address, but he wouldn't tell me. Weeks later I found out he'd got it from my bank in London by giving them a sob story.

He asked to come in and 'TALK" so I had no option. We did talk but I told him nothing had changed. After weeks of peace there Kim and I were all uptight and wary again. He wanted to go and see the Blackpool lights and wanted us to go with him. Blackpool is famous for its Christmas lights, which we had never seen, so we agreed, hoping when we came back he would go away. He hadn't had the timing on the van fixed so it sputtered and jerked all the way there.

The lights were wonderful ... all the trams were lit up with different themes. I stood in the rain for about an hour, which led to a nasty cold, and photographed them all. He dropped us back home and we were not to see him again for some weeks.

When he did turn up it was to tell us that he'd been in touch with an old friend of his who was now a theatrical agent; he said he may be able to get us work and had arranged for us to do a charity performance for the blind over in Scunthorpe. It was a long way to go but we drove over. Imagine our shock when we got there to find that the club didn't have the right gear to play our music. Much later I learned the trick of putting a microphone down on the floor in front of our player but at the time we had no option but to play our tape as loud as it would go:

it was a disaster.

Until she came into our dressing room we didn't know we were to be the support act to Lynne Perry who played Ivy Tilsley in Coronation Street from 1971 until 1994. She was really lovely and we shared a laugh as she struggled to put on false fingernails. In Coronation Street she took quite a serious part, but on stage she was a very funny comedian. Frank's friend, who was supposed to be there to see us, didn't turn up and told Frank that he'd been told we weren't very good. I was sure if he'd seen the act he would have known that we had a great act if our music had been okay.

There was an advertisement in the newspaper for people to work in Germany; anyone interested was to meet in a local hall on a certain night. Kim and I went along. The job was to sell waterless cookers to the American troops based there. Just Kim, myself and another girl called Mavis signed up. Mavis was one of those strange, awkward, loopy girls with absolutely no idea how to dress or present herself. She spoke often of a boyfriend she'd had and lost. I found out later that she lived in one room with boxes of things stacked right up to the ceiling, all the way around. I was aghast when I first saw it.

Anyway, we were given a few days training and had a special script we had to stick to and recite. It all sounded very false to me, not good if I expected to sell anything. If you want to sell something you really have to believe in the product which I'm afraid I didn't. Anyway, the darn things were $300 a set which seemed like a lot of money to me.

I had already bought a green mini car, and it was arranged that we were to follow the boss in my car to Germany, but first, we were to meet him on the ferry at Dover. I drove to London then down to the ferry at Dover by which time it was dark and raining hard. The lights of cars coming towards me on the dual carriageway almost blinded me – it was a nightmare – and by the time we were aboard and met up with the boss I was exhausted.

The trip over was fine and in no time we were through Customs and on the road. Following our boss's car was not easy as he really planted his foot and my wee mini had a job keeping up. In the short time I'd had the car I had learned that the petrol gauge was faulty – when it was showing almost empty it would suddenly run out of petrol and stop dead, which was rather embarrassing. So there it was, almost empty, the road mostly deserted; we were out in a country area, and it was raining. A closed petrol station appeared on my right. I pulled in and there we slept the night. Despite that the three of us were packed into that tiny car, we were all so exhausted we slept well and nobody bothered us. When the station opened at 7 am we made use of the toilets, filled the tank and soon we were in Brussels and on the way to Kaiserslautern where we arrived by early afternoon.

Our home for the next month was to be at the home of someone's grandmother who rented out rooms and made our meals. I'd been dubious about how we would find the Germans after them losing the war, but they couldn't have been nicer. Our hostess was a wonderful, homely lady and we all got on well. Our first surprise was the huge bed for Kim and I – there was a bottom sheet but no top one, a soft feather duvet the only bed covering.

3/11/76 Cold
KAISERSLAUTERN GERMANY.
Here we are in our hotel room swatting up on our script. We started knocking on doors last night at the American sector. We are to get $60 a sale, but making a sale is the problem.
Have kept our flat in Manchester – just in case.
Having trouble with the car - thought I had it fixed yesterday, but will not start again today. Oh hell.

Because we had to make sure that the man of the house was back from work we had to work at night. The Americans were mostly housed in big complexes several storeys high. The boss would deliver each of us to the separate blocks where he wanted us to work each night and pick us up at 9.30 pm. The corridors and stairwells could be a bit spooky, and I worried about Kim working on her own as rape in those places was not unheard of. Also the stair lights were on a timer. I found I had to climb the stairs quickly or the lights would go out before I reached the next floor, leaving me in the pitch blackness. Needless to say, I let it happen only once.

I met some weird people, a middle-aged lady who was obviously very lonely and would have kept me all night talking; a young couple who'd just arrived and didn't know anyone; a short, fat man who called me to come in and then flew into a temper when I did. I answered him back so he called the MPs and got me throw off the block. Although we'd been issued with IDs we hadn't been told that we were not supposed to selling door to door there. The thing that struck me most was the incredible ignorance of the average American foot soldier. In the month we were there I was not to meet one person who knew where New Zealand was, and most couldn't even place Australia. Their ignorance didn't just stop at geography: they were just appallingly uneducated.

Eric, a gay man who took each of us out with him when we first arrived, seemed to be able to make a sale every night. However, he didn't work the complexes, he worked the higher class and higher rank who rented flats and houses in the city. He would walk the streets until he found an American name on the letterbox and ring the bell to be buzzed in. Just meeting these people made one realise that they were streaks ahead of the average soldier.

During the daytime, we had time to explore. I went down into the town one bitterly cold morning to take photos. Kaiserslautern, like the rest of Germany, was unbelievably clean and beautiful. Unlike the Brits who would drive along throwing cigarette packets and fish and chip wrappers out of car windows, the Germans would do no such thing; the place was Spartan.

During the day I also worked on the car; it would start, but after running a few minutes it would cough and splutter and stop. I suspected a fuel blockage and stripped the carburetor down several times. It was unlike any carburetor I'd ever seen ... it had a bar running up the back of it and, when I pulled the choke on, a ring attached to the carburetor ran up the bar. I discovered that the bar was dirty and the choke was stuck on, so, after cleaning the bar, the car ran perfectly – except that I now needed a new gasket.

It was time to go back to Manchester. In the month we'd been there Kim was the only one who'd made a sale. She was paid her $60 American dollars. We got away by late morning, and I drove until dark, then asked Mavis if she would drive while I rested in the back seat. We soon found out what a bad driver she was, especially as she drove back through the lit up, wet streets of Luxembourg. Eventually we arrived back at the night ferry and Mavis drove aboard and parked. We reached Dover by daylight and went down to the car deck where I discovered as I began to drive off that I had no brakes.

"Didn't you notice the brakes were failing?" I asked Mavis.

"Well, I did notice they weren't too good.'

"Then why the hell didn't you say so?'" I snapped. I drove off carefully, one hand on the steering wheel, the other on the hand brake. I smilingly chatted up the Custom guys, told them we had no brakes and asked where the nearest garage was. They directed us to the top of the hill and stamped our passports with another six months' stay. The garage wanted £165 to repair the leak and refill with brake fluid. The car would be ready mid-afternoon. So there we were with a day to explore Dover.

At the bank, they wouldn't give me any money until they rang my bank in Manchester to see if I was good for it; and *I* had to pay for the call. I was flabbergasted.

Steven was working in London and sharing a flat with three other Australians. I decided to find their address and ask if we could spend the night sleeping on their floor. After driving around the district a while I eventually made it and we piled into our sleeping bags and slept well until Steven awoke us early. He made us some breakfast then I followed him on his motorbike to the start of the motorway where we said goodbye; Kim and I to travel north, he to his work.

I was soon to realise what a fool I'd been not getting a new gasket;

the car was guzzling petrol, and I had to stop at almost every petrol outlet to fill up.

Back home again Kim applied for a job as a window dresser in a shoe shop in Manchester and got it.

Unemployment was high, and although I asked around there was nothing going. Luckily I still had quite a bit of money behind me.

Just wandering around the district I began talking to Brenda who managed a secondhand furniture shop. Whenever I was down that way I dropped in to talk to her. She must have told the boss – one Malcolm McDonald – who offered me a job; the wage £30 a week (under the counter) but he wanted me to stay on the dole, something I wasn't happy to do. I loved the job except for cleaning the filthy stoves that came in. Unlike New Zealand and Australia, where owners renting houses have to supply cooking facilities and window coverings, in England renters in most cases have to supply their own stoves. Thus we had gas and electric stoves arriving frequently, most of them having never been cleaned. But I expect Malcolm got them for a song.

The shop was tiny, but there was a large forecourt between the shop and the street. Every morning we would cart wardrobes, lounge suites, you name it, out for display. Every evening we would cart what hadn't been sold back in again, sometimes struggling to get it all in the door, especially if Malcolm had added to it during the day. Most days everything had to be stacked. Malcolm also had a shop at Didsbury where the better class things were sold. Ron, his handyman off-sider, lived in the flat above the shop. Within a few months, I was to learn some things from Brenda I would rather not have learned. Firstly, she was living with the boss, having left her husband and two children. Secondly, she told me how Malcolm would go to inspect a deceased estate and give a quote to buy. Then, during the night he and Ron would take the truck around and empty the vacant building and take the ill-gotten gains away to hide in garages he rented all over town. Many months or even years later it would appear in the shops. I was horrified, but never let on that I knew. We also had a casual woman called Jean who was called in when needed. I found out that she was cheating on her husband, that the man friend had a small hideaway where they could meet once a week. He was married, but his wife was badly disabled. I was beginning to learn about the morals of the English and wasn't impressed.

One day she asked me to cover for her when she wanted to go out with said boyfriend at night; she asked me to say that she was around at my place. I said I would if asked but was not happy about being drawn into this deception. I was to meet her husband a few weeks later when they asked me to meet them at a pub for a night out. Being lonely and never going out I agreed; I found her husband very nice and easy to talk to; but thankfully her evening at my place didn't come up.

A strange thing happened while we were at work one day: a middle-aged woman with curly hair came in selling bits of lace. She said she was a Welsh gypsy. She looked at Brenda and told her some things about her life, then told me I had two children, that one was away, but don't worry he would be back soon. She mentioned something that could have applied to Frank. Then she told me I was going to get sick.

"You will get a fright and go to hospital, but don't worry you are going to be alright." She said if we crossed her palm with silver she would tell our fortunes, but she'd already been so accurate she had frightened us and we declined her offer.

We each bought a piece of lace; I wore that lace inside my bra for the next few years whenever I did a floor show. One of her prophecies came true the next week: I had a letter from Steven asking if he could come and sleep on our floor until he could get a flat of his own.

We were still looking for floor show work and I approached someone at the *Poco-a-Poco Theatre Club* and was given a booking for a week as support act to Stu Frances, Granada Land's comedian of the year. It was truly the most beautiful club we'd ever worked in. Life-sized artificial palm trees with beautiful brass fronds stood each side of the large half-round stage and on the small dance floor above the stage. The large ground floor was filled with tables and chairs and a sweeping mezzanine floor hung above with tables all around the edge, a great place to view the show from.

Poco-Poco Theatre Club

The show was not unlike the one in Singapore: the club had its own dancers, an M.C. and band. We hit it off straight away with Trevor who played the cast's music and handled the lights – he had his control room upstairs at the end of the mezzanine floor. He didn't want to keep our tapes so we had to deliver them to him each night. Kim and I, unlike other artists in the U.K who often turned up looking scruffy, always arrived in evening dress. This drew attention to us as soon as we walked in. One night I put on the Cheong Sam I'd had tailor-made in Singapore; unlike most that had splits up the side, this one had the split up the front. Walking in it was fine; that is until I had to walk upstairs when it was likely to trip me up. One night when we got to the top of the steps I tripped and hurtled forward to crash into the end of an occupied table. The look I got from the thirtyish man who almost wore his dinner was priceless; it seemed to say *OH MY GOD, THERE'S A FLY IN MY SOUP*. When we had shut the door in Trevor's room; I leaned against the wall and slid down, then we both burst into laughter. Trevor asked "What are you two girls finding so funny?" and Kim told him that I had almost landed in someone's soup.

It was a good week, except for one night when I had hurt my back at work lifting a wardrobe. I went on that night loaded with pain-killers and with a couple of vodkas under my belt. Another night all the tables around the edge of the stage were filled with elderly ladies – it must have been a night out for a ladies club. I chose that night to set fire to my hair.

Long poi performance

Strangely there was always dead quiet when I swung my flame poi's and into the silence came a scream from one dear old lady who shot out of her chair screaming "My God, she's on fire!"

Keeping up appearances

I dropped one poi which rolled to the edge of the stage near her and used that free hand to slap my hair, putting out the flames. I retrieved the poi I'd dropped saying loudly, "Let's try that again." This time things went right, both poi's in one hand, one circle in front, one circle behind my head. I felt sorry for that poor lady, she must have felt a fool. I gave her a smile and a wink as I took a bow.

9/12.76 Bloody cold
Manchester Poco-a-poco club

Have just finished a one-week booking at the most fantastic club at Stockport, second billing to Stu Frances comedian. Very tired, burning the candle at both ends has its disadvantages. Kim has full-time job as window dresser at a shoe store. I have been promoted from part-time in a second-hand shop to running my own shop at Withington village. Had a busy day.

This was the last entry in my diary.

Malcolm had taken over my new shop from his father; he'd had a girl running it for him who had left. It was an old place, much larger than the other place, and dirty. Behind the screened-off back of the shop lay lots of old bits of furniture; a big box of really awful deformed white mugs, obviously seconds from some factory that Malcolm refused to dump, and various small bits and pieces. I particularly liked a beautiful, quite large, old desk badly in need of restoration and soon managed to sell it. But before the shop could open it needed cleaning. Ron came to help and, after many buckets of water, we finally had the bare wooden floor clean. I liked Ron. We'd been going out together for a while but there was no way I would ever have become involved sexually with him as he would end up getting hurt. He had absolutely no class, would never have thought of going out to dinner or to the theater, never mind a museum or art gallery – all the things I thrived on. Ron's idea of a night out was to go to a small dark drinking club that he belonged to up some narrow stairs. The only entertainment was a jute box, a most annoying thing that wouldn't play tunes in the order they were selected.

Once the shop was cleaned, Ron and Malcolm moved some stock in. I was suspicious of one load that included a nice set of drawers full of beautifully embroidered doilies and table clothes, not the sort of thing that someone would sell, I thought. It was the middle of winter so business was quite slow. Malcolm insisted the front door was to be kept open at all times so, as there was no heating, I had to wrap up warmly.

One night when I left to drive home a thick fog had descended on the city. I had the most petrifying drive of my life. My car lights penetrated about three feet in front of the car. There was one part of the road where, at traffic lights, the road shrunk from two lanes into one on the other side; I had no idea where I was. Car lights appeared in front of me out of the gloom. Had I gone too far and passed my street? I was lost! Where was I? Suddenly, just as I had convinced myself that I must have passed my turn off and be in the next suburb, I saw the bright lights of the service station on my right. Another thirty feet and I had to turn right. Thankfully I made it across without being hit by oncoming traffic.

One day I noticed a man standing outside the shop window. He had a gadget in his hand which he pushed on every time someone passed him. I was intrigued but went about my business. After an hour he came in to explain what he'd been doing and I met the only man I have ever truly worshipped in my life.

He worked for Joe Coral, the bookie, and part of his job was to look for old shops they could take over for a betting shop, but first, they wanted to know if enough people passed the shop to make it worthwhile. His name was Derek, and yes, love is blind. He was a little taller than I, had a big gut – I expect he hadn't seen his willie for quite some time except in the mirror – and underneath his hard toupee he was completely bald. But, he had personality plus. It is said that Gemini people are the best partners for Aquarians, and so it proved to be. I sat on my high stool behind the counter, he stood in front and we talked, and talked.

Finally, he said, "Would you come out with me?"

I replied, "I thought you'd never ask."

He used to call me his touch of class, and yes, I suppose I was. He had a wife and two children, but they lived separate lives in the same house where they had separate rooms. He told me she had started having an affair with someone else just six months after their marriage, now they just went their separate ways. He had a big collection of country music in his room and his big ambition was to go to Nashville. I didn't see a lot of him as he had to travel with his job and sometimes appeared in court to argue the case for a betting shop, but we went out to nice restaurants when we did meet, and whenever he could he would pop into the shop or our flat. Derek was a manic depressive and had 'down' times.

We'd not seen Frank for six months, for which we were truly thankful – I should have known it was too good to be true. The phone rang in the shop one day – it was Brenda from the Chorlton-cum-Hardy shop.

"Oh, Billie, I am so sorry … a man came in and asked where you were and I told him. I have just realised it was probably your husband."

I was horrified. Sure enough, he arrived and refused to leave. I called the police who came and told me that even if he was violent or we were separated and he was not keeping me, there was nothing the police could do as he was still my husband. I wondered … could that possibly be true, that they could give me no protection. However the policeman told Frank that as I was working he would have to leave the shop, but before he could do so Malcolm arrived and ordered him out in no uncertain terms. Frank complied, but; he had backed his car into a spot over the road where he could watch the shop, and there he stayed until it was time for me to leave.

If there had been a way I could have exited from the back of the shop I would have taken it, but the back yard was enclosed by a high wall. Frank followed me home and forced his way inside. We had a talk: he told me he'd been on cruise to Australia and back again. How very like him – he just lived for the day. Now he needed a job and somewhere to stay. I made it clear it wouldn't be with us. I rose to put the kettle on and when my back was turned he grabbed me by the hair, pulled my head back and held a carving knife to my throat. "You realise I could cut your throat right now."

"Well go right ahead if you want to spend the rest of your life in prison. The kids in this street know who you are."

He eventually put the knife down and left. When he had gone I noticed the tea towel that had been hanging on the wall had been taken: I should have known he would steal something. Many years before he'd given me one like it, probably stolen. It was a picture of a girl in a very untidy room, bras hanging on the back of a chair, things all over the floor ... the words said: NEXT WEEK I'LL GET ORGANISED. He said it was like me but I was never that bad; nevertheless, I had found another one in England and bought it.

The next day I took time off and went to a solicitor and said, "Get me a divorce." He told me I would need to get Frank's signature; more strange and ridiculous English laws.

Kim and I arranged with Frank's brother Keith, and his wife Beryl, for us to go over to Batley in Yorkshire to stay with them for the coming holiday weekend. I had been taking color slides since leaving Australia, sending the film reels away to be processed and giving their address for them to be sent back. So far we hadn't collected them so we were looking forward to seeing them.

We drove over the Pennines and found to our dismay that Frank was already there, unexpectedly of course, and had arranged to stay in their caravan parked outside the house. That night we all went to Keith's club. Frank was very subdued, not at all like his usual show-off behavior. He stood drinking by the bar most of the night instead of sitting with us at our table. We were home by eleven and after a cuppa were ready to retire to bed. I made to go upstairs with Kim but Frank grabbed me and said I was spending the night with him in the caravan. I told him no way and he got nasty. Keith made him take his hand off me and told him to get out to his bed in the van. A tussle ensued with Keith pushing Frank out the door and locking it. I was really upset, but at least his family had seen what he was like when he'd been drinking. I apologised to Beryl and Keith and told them we would leave and drive back to Manchester rather than cause any more trouble, but they wouldn't have it. Kim and I drove back to Manchester after an early breakfast the next morning. Once more he had ruined what could have been a nice weekend. And I still hadn't been able to talk to him about a divorce.

With me going out with Derek and Kim having no one she was very lonely. We didn't fit into the pub culture of England, but I did go with her one night when she met her workmates at a pub. We were both amazed to see the girls drinking ½ pints of beer. However there was a band and I enjoyed watching Kim dance. The DJ, an up-himself type, asked her out. Derek and I were going out the same night so I waited and told him straight that I had waited to see who my daughter was going out with before leaving. He didn't ask her again, no doubt because she wouldn't have sex with him. We talked it over and decided she could go home to New Zealand. Her father, who had by now decided to sign the divorce papers, came to pick her up and take her the airport. I was alone and lonely in the flat.

I took to going out for walks in the evening. I found the local Chorlton-Cum-Hardy gardens which were beautiful and took lots of photos. Mostly I just walked around the nearby back streets looking at the lovely homes and gardens. However, one night I did a really silly thing: I walked all the way to Didsbury before turning back. I wasn't a quarter of the way back before I had appalling hip pain. I had never been able to walk far with my bad hip so what I had done was really stupid. I took to sitting on walls when there was one, or anything else where I could rest. I felt very alone and vulnerable and hoped no one took me for a prostitute. It was about 11 pm before I staggered up my stairs.

Just one week later they found another body of the Yorkshire Ripper dumped on a path beside some allotments about two hundred meters from my door.

The shop at Withington wasn't paying. Some days I took very little so Malcolm decided to close it and I returned to the shop at Chorlton-Cum-Hardy. That shop wasn't taking enough to warrant two salespeople either so after a few weeks Malcolm said he would have to put me off. He had assumed I was still on the dole. I needed another job and got one a week later as a cashier in the canteen of Kendal

Milnes department store also known as Harrods of the North or The House of Fraser on Deansgate in Manchester central city. The wages were just £30 a week, £10 of which I lost as income tax. My rent was £10, so I was left with £10 to live off. Not good. However we did get a good midday meal thrown in which saved me cooking at night. I didn't know until I got there that their old-fashioned tills didn't add up, and, as my mental arithmetic had never been that good, I was shocked. They told me I would be fine, and I was eventually; I had to look at a tray of food and count it up in my head. I quickly learned to count in tens, something I still do today.

I made many friends among the staff of the shop as well as the ones I worked with, most of whom were elderly. Frances, the other cashier, was seventy-two years old and still doing her own painting. She told me she'd been painting her kitchen ceiling the night before and I'd been horrified. She also told me she had worked for twenty-five years at a cotton mill and paid into her superannuation from her wages every week. When the firm went bankrupt they lost everyone's superannuation as well – this made me so angry. No firm should have access to their employees savings this way. I saw another old lady almost running past my till one day and said to her, "Mary, why are you running?" She answered that if she didn't get her work done she would get the sack. I told her to slow down, that if she needed to run they should put on more staff, and the boss heard me say it.

A young gay guy called Chris came to my cash register every day. We discovered he lived in the next street to me so he asked me to go out with him, no strings attached of course. I was glad to comply as visits from Derek were now few and far between. He told me he had never had a successful relationship with a man or a woman. It was great to go out with a man and not feel threatened. We went to a gay club one night, all men, apart from me. They couldn't have been nicer, and several of them came to our table and thanked me for coming; they all seemed so happy dancing together.

Chris told me that one night when he'd been walking around the neighborhood in the evening (as I did myself frequently) he'd come upon a spiritualist church with a notice saying PLEASE COME IN. He did, and the medium said he had a man who only had one leg and was blind in one eye coming through. Chris knew it could only be his father and got an encouraging message. This made me more interested in the psychic world.

Frank was back again from wherever he'd been and needed a place to stay. Chris said there was a bedsit in his complex empty and I stupidly told Frank, who moved in. Damn, he was just one street away, but I told myself it wouldn't last, and it didn't.

My flat was becoming unbearable; the two Irish boys in the middle flat shared a bathroom and toilet with us. They came back from the pub at night and peed all over the bathroom floor, and a few months after I had complained to Brendon he took the vinyl up around the toilet and replaced it. The footpaths outside our house were littered with dog droppings as the people in the street let their dogs out at night to defecate. The boys coming back from the pub around the corner would walk in it and traipse it up the carpeted stairs. Kim and I were the only ones who ever cleaned up the mess or cleaned the bathroom. Moreover they never cleaned their flat – now the place had taken on the stench of boiled cabbage. Moreover, I no longer felt safe. The top of the stairs was not blocked off, I just had two doors opening off the top landing. Only the bedroom door had an inside lock on it. When someone came to the front door asking for me the guys downstairs just let them in saying "top floor." Thus Frank, or anyone else for that matter, could walk in on me.

The crunch came one morning when I heard a stamping and banging down below. I opened the door and found the whole stairwell filled with smoke. I flew down the stairs and found their kitchen well alight. The stupid idiot had thrown a cigarette butt into the rubbish bin below the window and set it alight; that, in turn, had set fire to the curtains and the paint around the window. He had pulled the curtains down and thrown them on the floor so now the rubber backed carpet was burning in patches, giving off a terrible smell. Even worse, the old Bakelite radio was well alight and the gas coming from it was asphyxiating. I grabbed another saucepan and kept filling it from the running tap, and eventually we got it under control.

My biggest worry was that the fire may still be smoldering behind the window frames and would flare up again, and my contents were not insured. I had made inquiries but being where the flat was, the price was exorbitant. Had the place gone up in flames I would have lost everything.

With my clothes stinking to high heaven I set off to work, stopping at the telephone box to ring Brendon and ask him to check the damage a.s.a.p. before catching the bus to work.

Not long after Kim had gone home to New Zealand I arrived home from work to find two telegrams waiting for me on the hall shelf. I was numb with fear – it had to be bad news. As I climbed the stairs I said, "Please don't let it be Kim … please don't let it be Kim." I put the kettle on and made a coffee; then sat on the sofa and opened the first one.

"Gwen, Dad passed away suddenly at 10 am July 3rd. Love family."

The second one was from Kim with the same news. I was shattered. I had never been really close to my father, never been able to ask about my mother or other things I wanted to know, now it was too late.

Why, why, I asked myself through my tears, *why hadn't I tried when I had the chance.*

The next day was Sunday and I had to go to work as the staff of the store were stocktaking. I couldn't leave my seventy-two-year-old friend on the other till to cope with the lunchtime rush. I told them my father had died and please not to say anything or it would reduce me to tears. Somehow I managed to get quietly through the day.

The next day I went to an Interflora Florist and ordered flowers to be sent. I gave them a message to go with them. "For Dad from Skinny. Goodbye, and God bless."

I couldn't go home to his funeral as the Home Office had my passport. They had told me it would take two weeks to get it back if it was needed so I didn't bother to try. When I did go home many months later my step-mother told me the huge bouquet of flowers that had arrived was truly magnificent. I hadn't thought about how much £30 in English money equated to in New Zealand.

Billie's Dad's Grave

It was hard to exist on just £10 a week; I was forever having to draw out money from my savings. The *George and the Dragon* pub just behind my workplace wanted a new barmaid. I nipped around during lunch hour and got it. The wages were not great but the tips could be over £1 a night. My first job when not busy was to clean up the shelves that obviously hadn't been wiped down in months. I soon learned how to pull a pint using the big handles; there was definitely a knack to it. I got on well with the regulars who always said "have one for yourself" whereby I would take a shilling, (ten pence) and put it in my tip glass. I didn't like the landlords: they were as hard as nails and common as muck. But the great thing about nursing is this, it teaches you to fit in with almost everyone, and these two knew when they were onto good thing, so left me to get on with the job.

I was really burning the candle at both ends. They told me to help myself to something to eat but I never did. One night something went very wrong: my eyesight shrunk to a tiny circle while all around the edges was blurry. I lifted a pint over the bar but not high enough and it spilled all down my front. It was all quite frightening and I decided I would have to slow down. Someone told me much later it was the start of a migraine.

Sadly, the job finished abruptly thanks to my son and his friend. It was the boss's birthday and he'd had rather too much to drink when 'Sonny', as we sometimes called him, and his friend arrived. They sat quietly drinking until closing time and, just after last orders were called, the friend asked for another drink. Without thinking I pulled him another half-pint which of course I shouldn't have. It was sitting on the bar and the boss came along and, maybe deliberately, knocked it over. Sonny's friend hit the roof and demanded a refill. The boss then turned on me saying I shouldn't have poured it. Needless to say things got nasty – the friend didn't get a refill nor was he given a refund which I thought was a bit much. I repaid the money myself and told Sonny to take his friend and get out which they did. I cleaned up thus finishing my shift, collected my pay and told them, "Well that's that then," and walked out. When I got home I remembered I hadn't taken the money from my tip glass, and it had been full.

I would love to have been a fly on the wall in that place the next day when they found themselves without a barmaid. I bet his hard-faced wife had a few things to say about him losing (although I says so as shouldn't) one of the best barmaids they'd ever had.

My son had taken up with a married woman with two little girls. They had rented a house about two suburbs away and it was quite expensive. He asked me to come and move in with them, so I did.

Our divorce went through on the 19th of September 1977 with the decree nisi six months later. Frank was supposed to pay the expenses but I knew he never would so I paid out the £475 myself. I also didn't ask for maintenance because I knew I would never get it.

As I was no longer married to an Englishman I could no longer claim the right to stay in the country … unless, they told me, I could prove that my relatives had been born in the British Isles. To do that I had to produce my grandfather's birth certificate, his marriage certificate, my father's birth and marriage certificates, and my birth certificate. I didn't know where to start. I knew that my Scottish grandfather had gone to Australia first where he drove Cob and Co. coaches but did he get married there? It was going to cost me a fortune in search fees, so I decided not to bother. I had inquired about buying two joining cottages out in a country village but now it was just a dream.

When I came home from work one day Sonny's lady friend told me that when she was dropping the girls off at school she saw someone sitting on a motorbike watching her and thought it might have been her husband. A few days later she got a phone call from the school to say a man had charged in and grabbed the kids. It *was* her husband. He took the girls home which left just three of us in the house. A short time later my darling son asked his father to come and join us and help with the rent. I was livid. How like Sonny to think only of himself.

About a month later Frank was on the move again, back to New Zealand this time. He pleaded with me to give him a LOAN, saying he was really short of money and, like an idiot, I gave him £50 which was never returned. He pleaded with me to drive him to the railway station so eventually, I agreed. I had no intention of going into the station but he started causing a scene so I agreed. Then he demanded I go onto the platform. We stood outside until the "All Aboard" came. He demanded a kiss, to which I said, "Just get on the train, Frank."

He boarded, then threw open the window above me and, as the train pulled silently away, he leaned out and gave me a vicious slap on the face, almost knocking me off my feet. The noise turned everyone's attention. I turned around and, with head held high, I walked away. The three porters at the gate were looking at me with pity as I passed them. I never expected to see him again, but it wasn't to be.

A few months later I got a letter from Kim which said poor Grandma (my step-mother) thinks you are never going to come home – I decided it was time to leave before I was thrown out. When I told them at work I was leaving they wanted to know why so I told them what I would have to do to get the right to stay. I had never seen Frances lose her cool but now she was furious.

"How dare they?" she stormed. "They let all this riff-raff stay but someone like you has to leave."

It was a nice compliment but seeing her so hopping mad made me just want to laugh. I kept in touch with a few of them after I got home, one of them telling me that one of the bosses had said, "The place doesn't seem the same now Billie has left." I must have left my mark.

I had been up until 3 am talking to Derek when he came to say goodbye, as neither of us wanted it to end, so I slept in the back of Sonny's works van while he and his girlfriend drove me down to Heathrow airport. They waited with me until I had checked in my luggage, which was overweight, so instead of paying the extra I opened my case and gave several things to the girlfriend, including my good leather brogue shoes with the soft, but heavy, rubber soles. This was something I deeply regretted when I got home as it cost me far more to replace them than it would have had I paid for the excess baggage.

On Singapore Airlines I cried all the way to Orly Airport in France. I was so upset I didn't know we were there until we landed.

The plane had very few passengers so we had all been seated alone so we could stretch out over three seats. At Dubai, I stayed aboard while the Chinese crew cleaned around me. One of the stewards asked me if I would go out with him that night as I was stopping over. I told him no, as I had some shopping to do. In fact I had timed my trip to get back for my niece's wedding and needed a wedding present.

Singapore had a hot and steamy evening; I felt I had come home. The hotel had sent a small bus to pick up its expected guests, about twelve of them. There was something familiar about the good-looking young driver with the most beautiful white teeth in the world, but I was tired and thought no more about it. I was aware that he kept looking at me in his mirror but I was so used to be being stared at I took no notice. Suddenly he blurted out, "I know who you are … you are that dancer that appeared in the Southron Theater. My cousin was the manager." Now everyone on the bus was looking; I could have belted him. I admitted it was I, but didn't say "yes, and you were that stage door Jonny that ogled us every night.'"

It was great being back in my old stamping ground. I did the shops next day and bought my niece a beautifully embroidered table cloth with serviettes. That night I flew out on the last leg of my homeward journey, arriving mid-afternoon.

New Zealand Again

I expected Kim to be there to greet me, and she was, but who should step out from behind a column and kiss me but Frank. I was screaming livid. I couldn't believe that he would have the effrontery to do this after belting me as his train left Manchester. I was also shocked that Kim had told her father I was coming home. She was sharing a flat with an older woman and I was to spend the night there but Frank had also been asked to dinner. It was awful! I felt sick, and dinner was a disaster – we just argued all the time. The lady Kim was sharing with tried to keep the peace but I was too angry not to retaliate to his carping.

Kim, her boyfriend and I left that night on the midnight train to go down to Palmerston where I was to stay with my step-mother until I got settled. It was early morning when I saw from the train window the war memorial obelisk high on the hill above this small, pretty country town which told me we were approaching our destination. At 5 am we dragged my four-wheeled tartan bags from Singapore up Ronaldsay Street, making enough noise to waken the dead.

Home at last. After all my wandering in the past few years I couldn't believe how wonderful it was to be there. My step-mother had been up early and put water bottles in our beds and laid out towels and pretty nightgowns and towels for us. I had to admit, she had class. Everything was the best. Compared to the way we had been living, this was paradise.

I wrote a letter to Derek sending him some photos of the house and garden with the war memorial obelisk high on the hill behind. Compared with the grotty state house where he lived he must have thought we were millionaires. I received a reply.

Warrington
5th January 1978

Dear Billie,

After what has seemed to me to be an absolute eternity I received your letter this morning, and believe me it was a ray of light to brighten up the January gloom. It seems to be a long time for delivery from the 19th of December but it was in the newspapers this week that there was a backlog of some four million overseas letters and parcels in the London sorting office so perhaps this explains the lengthy delay.

I was very pleased to read that you got home safely and that Kim was at the airport to meet you, must have been a very touching moment for both you and her. I imagine the appearance of Frank dampened the meeting a little, but knowing you as I do I believe that this would be only a temporary setback.

I do hope that you use all the common sense that I know you have in dealing with him and that he doesn't become a burden to you again.

With the delay in your letter arriving I was beginning to think that you'd had second thoughts and had decided to leave me as just a memory and I had just begun to feel that I had completely lost you forever. My thoughts went back to our last night together and I felt as I drove away that I dearly wanted to come back into the house that night, but I knew that turning back would only prolong the inevitability that you were leaving. I woke up on Sunday morning thinking about you and had a very restless kind of day. At about take-off time I went outside, looked skywards and said to myself "Goodbye, Billie," and prayed that your journey would be a safe one and that someday you and I would meet again. Since you left I do really feel that part of my life is missing and that the sanity which you used to give to me is now a very long way away from me. When you were here I sometimes got the impression that you thought you were just someone that was a nice convenience (a bit on the side) for me and I did my best to convince you that this was not so. I would like to put the record straight right now and tell you that without any doubt at all you were the nicest person that's ever been my pleasure to meet. You treated me like a king in every way and just being in the same room with you was sheer joy. When I was with you not a damned thing in this whole world mattered. I sit many hours and think about hours spent with you and never is there any occasion that the thoughts are not uplifting and filled with pleasure. I have felt an emptiness inside since you left and on two occasions I have driven round to Warrick Road and just sat outside No. 18 with my thoughts. I suppose the time I was at my lowest was over the Christmas and New Year holidays when I had more time to think about where you were and what you would be doing, but since the arrival of your letter I feel very much elated. Since you have been gone I have traveled quite a lot and on Tuesday of this week I had to go to Sheffield so it came naturally to me to sit outside the pub that we visited and let my thoughts drift back to our trip. It was really beautiful with the snow on the hillside and the air cold and crisp with no city smog. I toasted your good health with my half-pint of bitter and wished both you and Kim a happy and prosperous New Year. Speaking of Kim, it seems from your letter that she is doing alright on her own and I would like you to wish her all the very best from me.

Tomorrow I am in court at West Bromwich in a fight with old enemy Ladbrokes so I will have to be on my best behavior and use my powers of persuasion.

In about two weeks' time, I have to go to Glasgow for a few days but because the weather is likely to be bad for driving I am flying up there and will hire a car on arrival. I suppose you could say I am going up in the world.

I must say, Billie, that I am very impressed with your new double-barreled name and, as I always said you were a really uppity woman, I believe it really will suit you!!

I was glad to read that you have managed to get a flat of your own but don't forget to let me have your change of address as soon as you settle in.

Well I think I have exhausted the pen so will close for now, please look after yourself and keep yourself happy. You are constantly in my thoughts and with me in spirit. I look forward to hearing from you very soon.

Yours lovingly, Derek XXXX

P.S. I found the words to an old song the other day, which really say far better than I can, my thoughts of you.

> *For all you mean to me*
> *My thanks to you.*
> *For every memory*
> *My thanks to you*
> *My thanks for everything we loved to share*
> *For all the joy you brought when you were there*
> *These foolish words of mine can never say*
> *How slow the hands of time when you're away*
> *As years go rolling by my whole life through*
> *I'll give my love and all my thanks to you.*

I wrote back to Derek giving him my new address in Dunedin. As usual, I sent it to his work address, but I never heard from him again. I wondered all sorts of things ... had he got my letter? Being a manic depressive, had he committed suicide? or had he just decided that he knew it was best that we no longer kept in touch? But suffice to say he has forever been in my thoughts.

I hadn't intended to stay in N.Z. but after a few months alone, I went to a singles' night and met John. We talked all night.

John was a nice guy, but another working-class Pom, so I should have known better. His hair was filthy and on his collar, he reeked of sweat, and he had nicotine stains on his hand; not to mention food stains on his tie, but I felt sorry for him. We began to go out together. He sold insurance for Government Life and three months previously had broken up with a woman who wanted him to move in with her after their long term relationship. She didn't have a job and lived in a government rented house but, as he told me years later, "I wasn't going to keep her."

Selling insurance was a job that suited John down to the ground; he could stay in bed all morning and go out at night to sell insurance. Unfortunately just before I met him he'd had a row with the office manager who told he would get no more leads unless he cleaned out his message box. It seems that all the reps. had boxes in which leads were put in from people who had rung in enquiring about insurance.

John was a hoarder – he never threw away a T.A.B. racing ticket – no doubt his box was full of them. I was soon to learn at home that his underwear drawer was where he kept them. Eventually it was so full of tickets I couldn't get his underpants in. He was not required to be at the office during the day as he should have been out knocking on doors. But no, he prayed on his friends, rushing off to sell insurance for the new baby, the new wife, etc. He sold insurance to me, and my two children against my wishes because I knew they could not keep up the payments. I paid for them myself for a while until I too had to give up. He played golf on Friday with his friends.

John was just a very lazy person. He lived in an old house he shared with two other men, each having their own room and sharing all the rest of the house, but after knowing him for about a month I said to him he may as well move in with me as he always seemed to be at my place. I had a small flat below a house. It had been very scruffy when I moved in but I redecorated the whole place at my expense and tidied up the garden.

As John was forever complaining about his job I encouraged him to look for another one. He eventually got a job selling superannuation for the government. But did he change his ways? Of course not, he was being paid about $250 a week to spend some time in the office and he got commission for what he sold, but he still stayed in bed late and played golf on Friday. I repeatedly told him he would get the sack but he would say he was selling super.

I had found it quite hard to get a job when I got home; the country had 10% unemployment, but after a month I got one managing a coffee lounge for a couple of university students. We were very busy; mostly I found out later because we were far too cheap. Being new to town I had no idea what other places were charging. The place was open until late at night and manned by students after my staff and I left at 5 pm. They left mess most nights, which of course was a thorn in the side of my day staff.

Andrew, who cooked all the cakes and biscuits, and Paul, who made soups and omelets, had to manage it all as well as studying. We also made sandwiches, toasted sandwiches and other things to order. Eventually, after eighteen months, they decided it was all too much and wanted to close the daytime operation. It was decided that I would take over the day times in my own name, but it didn't work out. I would come in in the morning and find that my stock had been sold by the students during the night, the dishwasher was still full of filth because they hadn't rinsed the leftovers off the plates first, and my offsider Donna and I had to do all the cleaning, including washing the windows out on the footpath.

After two weeks we decided to call it a day. I was out of work again, but not altogether as I had been doing cabaret work intermittently as well. I had promised to do my show at my friend Shona's wedding and at last, she came home from overseas and married her Italian man. I asked John to say when he introduced me that I was pleased she was getting married at last so I could now hang up my slippers. The fantastic lady organist who provided the music for the night told me I was far too good to retire and she would get me jobs when she was doing the rounds of the working men's and Returned Servicemen's clubs. I took to the floor when she had her rest time over the next few months.

It was about this time that one night I met my doctor in the supermarket.

"Billie," he said, "My nurses have been to trying to get in touch with you."

I had been in for a pap smear and they had found abnormal cells. I was rushed into hospital for a cone biopsy, and luckily, after a few frightening days, I was told the good news that all the troublesome cells had been removed. It wasn't until months later that I remembered the Welsh fortune teller's statement. "You are going to get sick, and you will get a fright but don't worry, you will be fine."

A job was advertised for a temporary telephonist at Wakari Hospital. I applied and got the job, replacing a lady who was an alcoholic and had been sent to dry out.

I had no experience but picked it up so quickly the House manager who employed me told me after two weeks that someone asked him where I worked a switchboard before. I was supposed to be there just six weeks but he kept me on for another two weeks to see if the returned lady could cope. Another vacancy became available in the Medical Records department. I applied and was given the job, my nursing training greatly helping me as I recognised and understood most of the papers. I was to stay in this job for over sixteen years.

The records department at our hospital was run by the main office down in the town at Dunedin Hospital where all the recent records were kept. We were also responsible for the admissions. At that time Wakari Hospital was on medical acutes two days a week and Surgical acutes another two days, but most of our admissions were arranged. This gave us time to send for the patients records if they had any, print all their admission sheets, prepare the wrist band and packet them up to be dispatched with said patient to the ward when they arrived. Our department was also responsible for the statistics, all comings and goings were noted, and my companion worker Mary also did the coding of all the cancer patients as we had the cancer unit at our hospital. All medical records are coded before being filed away, these disease numbers end up at the World Health Organization; this is how the number of each disease is recorded for almost every country in the world.

We also had the burns unit and children's ward at our hospital and were literally run off our feet. It was a complex and responsible job and I went home every night exhausted. The stats book could cause us all sorts of problems: if one of the wards forgot to tell us that a patient had been discharged or admitted without going through our office we would have to go back and alter all the figures. If we put a figure in a wrong column it could take days to find the mistake when we did the monthly report. In my time there we had a change of computer program six times, the last being the best. It gave us access to patient records from any other hospital they had been in anywhere in New Zealand ... where that hospital had the same system. Better still, it did the statistics for us and saved us so much time.

Two new wards, 12a and 12b, were added for geriatric assessment – to cope with the increase of elderly people. There was a large shared day room and an outpatient clinic. The wards also had a flat attached so a couple could come for a few days after the man or wife had been discharged to see if he could cope with her or she with him. Many times a woman left a widow had to be taught how to pay bills as Dad had always done this, or a man had to be taught to make his meals.

After a few years a new hospital was built down in Dunedin and most of our patients were transferred there. Most of our wards were left empty as the hospital was refurbished. Our staff were transferred with them and I was left in charge of our office. We no longer did operations and the theatres were closed off. Eventually children's ward became the Psycho. Geriatric assessment ward, the burns ward became the young disabled ward, ward four changed from the cancer ward (although we still had the cancer unit) to the dementia ward, ward five became the elderly disabled ward and so on.

Otago's mental hospital at Cherry Farm north of town was closed down and the patients were moved to our upgraded Nurses' Home that had stood empty for years. So many changes.

During my time there I attended conferences in Auckland, Picton in the Queen Charlotte Sounds, and Dallas, Texas, USA for a week. They certainly know how to do things there, but they don't know how to drink. Ask for a vodka and you will get almost a glass full.

On the home front, things were fine for a start. John had a former wife, Mary, who'd had a nervous breakdown – not surprising as he'd hardly ever been home. If he wasn't working at sea he was working as a shearer. And when he was working at home he spent a lot of his time at a football club. The poor woman must have had a dog's life. He was still paying the rent for the house she lived in and giving her a small amount to live on. He decided we could not get married until she turned 60 and could get her age pension.

We bought a house at Glenmore overlooking the Leith Valley. It wasn't a grand place but it was home, and when Mary got her pension we got married in the Chapel at the hospital. John had decided that we should keep separate bank accounts because "I'm not having you question how much money I take out." John was a compulsive gambler!!

Before we bought the house it was decided we would go halves on all the bills, but it didn't quite happen that way. He paid half the mortgage, rates, electricity, and phone bills. I paid for everything else. I set about redecorating the house and doing the garden; but when I bought the first lot of paint and said you owe me $14.40 he became annoyed and said he would give it to me next week. Of course his next week never came.

When he saw me writing down all the expenses in a book so I knew how much was being spent on the house he hit the roof saying, "You are just doing that so you can throw it up later." I was aghast and assured him I was doing no such thing and said I wouldn't bother to do it – another of my big mistakes. I went on to paint and decorate the entire house, updated the bathroom, changed most of the rotten wooden window frames to aluminum, put a beautiful new kitchen in, a tar seal floor in the garage and an automatic door on. I had a window put into the basement and built a small room down there, doing everything except the window myself. Lastly I had a glass conservatory built on the front of the house – I must have spent at least $50,000.

I also worked hard in the garden: I collected rocks from up the valley in my little van and carted them up to the garden from the street. I joined the Otago Alpine Garden Club – we had many trips to other people's gardens and, on long weekends, had trips away to the tops of mountain ranges where the wonderful alpine plants were a delight to see. On most ranges, we were allowed to collect plants and seeds so my garden soon became full of little composite plants. It was a picture in the spring. I wanted John to join me on our trips away, other member's wives and husbands came along but I always went alone while he sat at home by the phone putting his bets on.

Our marriage was definitely one-sided because I always went to watch soccer with him even though the class of soccer was appalling and bored me stiff. I also accompanied him to the races or walked around the part of the golf course with him; the whole course being too far for me with my arthritic hip.

John had decided he would do the vegetable garden and mow the lawn; but he left the lawn until it was too long and never cut the edges, (I had to do that) and the vegetable garden was always a mess.

When we were first together we both belonged to the Civil Service Club, a club for government workers, and would go there every Friday night. I would catch the hospital car down to town and walk slowly up the street to meet John in his office where I would wait for him to finish the work he should have been doing instead of playing golf. I kept telling him he would get the sack but he refused to listen. Unfortunately, the T.A.B was just a few doors from his office so he could slip over there to place bets during the day, and lose track of time. As the years went by his gambling became an obsession … like an alcoholic who "has to have a drink", John "had to put a bet on." It was terrible to watch: he just lived in another world.

We never went on holiday unless there was a race meeting at the end of it. Kim was living in Australia so sometimes we went there, but he took to going to the T.A.B. there as well and losing track of time. For the last few years I went on my own, and like a fool always brought him back a leather jacket as they were much cheaper there although I paid up to $200 for each one.

On one of my holidays to Queensland, I saw, for the first time, artificial trees made from silk leaves set into branches of Tortured Willow. They had not yet arrived in New Zealand so I decided to start a business making them at home and put an order in with the importer who agreed to supply me. When I returned home full of excitement and told John, he said, "Well, I am not going to help you!"

I made my little downstairs room into my workshop and worked there every night until late, and most weekends. At first, I made big trees but they were hard to sell as they had to be priced at hundreds of dollars because the leaves were so expensive. I would mix cement and sand and set the stems into concrete in a plant pot.

One day I used a small dish and set short pieces of willow into it; once set I added red leaves to make a bonsai tree. Thrilled with the result I rushed it upstairs to show John, and he too was impressed. I had struck the jackpot – they sold like hotcakes. Someone started a market at the Forbury Park race track undercover – it wasn't a huge success but I did sell a few. Then there were craft fairs and country fairs to go to where my trees sold well. At the Invercargill craft fair I always took more than $1,000 in the two days. It was a long way to go but worth it. John did eventually come to help me, but only because I paid him; he sold a tree to every T.A.B. betting shop in Dunedin – I gave him $20 for each one sold which of course was all my profit. More money for him to bet with.

Tortured Willow trees grew prolifically in Dunedin so I had no trouble getting good supplies. People seeing my stall would ask if I would come and prune their tree when they grew too big; I was always too happy to oblige and usually John came to help me.

It wasn't easy working at my demanding job and working at home as well so, after a few years, I advertised the business and sold it for a good price. I did, however, keep the option to work outside the district at the country fairs, which I did for another year.

John often talked about the time he had a budgie which he trained, so one year I gave him a baby bird for Christmas. He called him Fred, and he was to give us fun for seven years. He soon learned to talk and developed an amazing vocabulary. He would say: "This is the evening news with (I forget the man's name) and Angela De-Audney." And one night he blurted out, "I bloody told you!"

"You see, now you've got Fred saying it," to which John replied, "I don't say that."

"Well, where do you think he learned it?"

Sadly John was far too lenient with Fred; he had the run of the house and spent very little time in his cage. Eventually, he refused to eat any of his seed. John would let him eat toast with vegemite on it for breakfast which he shouldn't have done. Vegemite is rich in Vitamin B but it also has a lot of salt. At night Fred ate mashed potato and anything else from our plates that took his fancy. If I was late putting dinner on, an angry little bird would come shrieking into the kitchen and run his undercarriage through my hair. There was no doubt who was the boss of the house. He had his own idea about who could do what and who couldn't.

If John presented his finger Fred would step on to it but he would never do it for me. He would, however, come to sit on my crossed arms every night; then run along my upper arm and peek down the space below my elbow; I would sneak a finger up at him. He would shriek and run back towards my hand, but he could never resist coming back for another look. Eventually he would get bored with our game and go off to do something else. John had bought a small plastic boy figure when we were on holiday in Hong Kong, he liked to fool his friends by telling them to pull his shorts down whereby they would be sprayed with water. The little boy lived on top of the display cabinet and became Fred's friend. Whenever he got mad at something or felt like a good natter he would go up there and, nodding his head madly up and down, he would tell the little boy all about it.

John started taking Fred out in the car with him, then he would walk along the street with him on his shoulder and into the T.A.B. John loved to show him off and this stupid behavior had to eventually end with trouble. One Sunday we went out over the hill to collect some fine gravel from the creek for the concrete to set my trees in. John thought he would be clever and take Fred out of the car even though I told him not to. Fred, of course, not being used to this completely new and strange place with the waving trees and running water, flew off and landed high up in a willow tree. I was absolutely livid, knowing full well that birds not used to the outdoors will always fly up and be afraid to fly down. John was afraid of heights. I wasn't too fond of them myself, but it was always me who had to climb on the roof at home or climb to the top of ladders. No amount of calling could get him down so I, of course, had to climb up to get him.

Willows are not the sort of trees that one would normally climb; their branches grow straight up so how the hell I got up there I don't know. Somehow I managed to get up to a place where the branches would have been too thin to hold me and I was just about three yards from the left of a frightened little bird. I couldn't reach him and was afraid that he would take off again and go higher. I talked quietly to him; talking, talking, and reached out as far as I could without crashing earthwards. After what seemed like an age he scuttled along his branch and stepped, for the first time ever, onto my finger. Now the fun began, I had to get down the tree with one arm, all the time worrying that he may decide to take off again. I don't remember one second of the descent. I could have been killed or badly injured had I fallen, but I didn't even get a thank you!

Fred sometimes had us laughing. We were driving up the Blenheim (at the top of the South Island) to go to a race meeting of course, and on the Canterbury Plains we both started to sing. Fred, sitting on the back of the driver's seat, joined in. He stretched his neck and squawked almost not stop – I would like to say it was melodious but it wasn't.

Fred was seven when he died. There'd been times when he'd obviously been in pain. One night, when John was in hospital and I wasn't cooking dinner, I poured hot water over noodles for a quick snack. Fred decided he wanted some too and I stupidly allowed him to eat them. In no time he was all hunched up and miserable. I felt dreadful, and to this day can't eat the things.

John rang me at work one day. "Billie, he's dying."

I raced out to the car and sped home. John was holding him against his chest. I put my finger by his feet and he held on tight, then thinking I might find something I could feed to him with an eyedropper I pulled my finger away. A few minutes later he was dead. I cursed myself: Why, oh why, hadn't I let him keep holding my finger? I was shocked to find how tiny and thin he was.

I buried him in a shoebox out under the beech tree. The next morning before I left for work I said to John as he lay in bed, "You killed that little bird with malnutrition."

But John didn't want to know; he knew full well he was guilty.

When we had been married a few years John asked me if I would mind if he went in with two of his friend and bought a racehorse, a trotter. Like a fool I said he could. Unfortunately it didn't stop at one horse and at one stage they had four.

A compulsive gambler and a racehorse owner are NOT a good combination. They had one pacer, Rosie's Boy, who did almost pay his way and a trotting mare, Featherlight, who became the New Zealand champion mare over two miles. Her mother was Madam Feather. Unfortunately, Featherlight was also the name of a condom, which caused a bit of amusement. Needless to say we always had to go to every race that the horses were running in, or he did, no matter how far away they were.

Thanks to Featherlight and Rosie's Boy John had to go down several times to the parade ring to accept a trophy or just have a photo taken. He would put his nose in the air like Lord Muck and go off down the stairs. All other men would take their wives with them, but not John. He never once asked me to go with him, so our lounge walls were adorned with the pictures that I too should have been in. Stupidly, I never once criticised him for this or his gambling. It wasn't until years after I had left him that I realised what a fool I had been to let him get away with the things he did.

John didn't know the first thing about horses, whereas I had been brought up with them. When the horses were running locally it was I who walked them after a race. When he didn't have the money to pay the trainer it was I who had to find the money. We were told by his lady trainer one night that she had given the driver instructions not to push the horse hard as the horse was "Just going for a run". John put over $300 on him at the tote. I was aghast. When I reminded him that the trainer said the horse was just out "for a run" he snapped at me, "Don't tell me I can't bet on my own horse!"

He certainly didn't have any horse sense and lost over $600 that night.

For many years I went with him to the Forbury Park night time trots. John was one of those 'always late' people; he would drive there like a maniac, park the car in the members' stand, jump out and run, terrified he wouldn't get his bets on the first race. A lot of people would go as a group and enjoy the night but I was never allowed to have anyone with us. Apart from sitting together to watch each race I spent most of the night on my own. Eventually I stopped going with him and when he mentioned it, I replied, " John, you never talk to me at the races."

We went with a young trainer to the thoroughbred sales and this time they paid $6,000 for a beautiful chestnut gelding; the grandson of Sir Triston, the world's most famous racing stallion. The mere fact that he'd been gelded at six months should have alerted them to the fact he was highly strung. He was to be trained over the hill at Mosgiel, but when he eventually started racing he would never settle. One day they put a good jockey on him and he was about to run into second place but, when the jockey hit him with the whip, he lashed out with both back legs and lost all momentum. The jockey said later, "He's a bloody clown."

Almost every Sunday John liked to go to visit the horse in his paddock, taking a carrot with him. The horse would come running – he had a lovely nature but was thoroughly spoilt. This horse would have eventually come right with time and patience, but keeping racehorses in training with no returns is an expensive business. Sadly, he was sold as a hack for just a few hundred dollars.

One of John's most annoying traits was to lock his keys in the car – usually outside a T.A.B. – his head so full of his gambling that nothing else fitted. I lost count of the times the phone would ring: Please would I bring his spare car keys. Things came to a head one night when he'd gone to the night trots: Please would I bring over the keys and leave them at the Stewards room. I was annoyed as I had my old gardening clothes on and had to get into something more respectable and drive away over to the other side of town. Luckily a friend was manning the gate to the member's car park so I explained what I was doing and was let in. When John came home that night I told him that I would never again come running with his car keys so don't bother to ask. I told him it was about time he starting thinking about what he was doing. He never did ask again but admitted much later that he'd had to call the R.A.C out several times to get them to unlock the car.

With all this going on I was still looking after my step-mother. Two weeks before Dad had died he'd bought a building plot on the other side of the village where it was much easier to walk to the shops. The house and ten acres of land at the top of Ronaldsay Street was put on the market. We put a lovely home on the new block, the house built elsewhere and brought by truck to the site. She moved in.

I went out often on the weekends to put a garden in, spending money on plants I didn't really want to spend as I too was trying to get back on my feet. She had an old bath she wanted turned into a fish pond so I carted old railway sleepers to support it after I'd sunk it into a hole. My brother Colin was paid to fence the place off, but her own son never once did anything to help.

When Dad made his Will he had the money put in trust for all of us, knowing full well that, had he left it to our step-mother, our half-brother would get the lot when she died. As it was he had already had far more than any of us.

When she was eighty years old, she told me she wanted to go into the local rest home. The proprietors had always invited the local aged to Christmas dinners and visits so they had no fear of becoming permanent residents. I told her if she went in there would be no going back. But she was adamant, saying someone had been knocking on her windows at night and her coal was being stolen from the big bin at the back door. Life, alone in the house at night, must have been frightening.

The day I moved her in, I cried, feeling I had lost my home. I carted all her things into our house and she came in to help me have a garage sale to get her some money.

I had been doing her feet every six weeks so she now came to stay in our house to get them done. I liked having her stay, but being in such a stressful job I was used to getting home, pouring myself a vodka lime and water and sitting in the total silence for a while, just to get my feet back on the ground. No phones ringing; no urgent demands, just lovely quiet. When she was there, having been on her own all day, she wanted to talk.

I took her to a stage show for her birthday, and to a concert where I was doing a charity performance to make money for a wonderful school jazz band who were going to America. I don't remember ever getting a thank you. However, I did get the chance to ask her some questions.

Why on earth, I asked, did she marry a man who had four children? I knew, of course, she was in her late twenties when they'd married and had been 'left on the shelf' but her answer took me by surprise.

"Well," she said, "it was because of Alma. She had been staying with us at Glenross Street for about six months. If your father had married someone else we would have lost her."

So many things fell into place for me then: Grandma's preference for Alma, and her nastiness to me when she died.

Over the years John's gambling got so bad it eventually took over our life. I had been stupid enough to put a phone in at the side of the bed; he would wake in the morning, pick up the phone and dial the T.A.B, then say, "oa95861" and then his code. It is thirty years since I heard it and it is still etched on my brain.

The worst eventually happened – he'd been given the sack at work. Someone came down from Wellington and told him to pack up his desk and not come back. They do this, of course, to stop employees from taking a list of customers with them. Needless to say I was appalled when I came home from work the next day and John told me he had got dressed and gone into the office, only to be ordered out. He had a small amount in superannuation from which he could draw a pension but he couldn't draw an age pension as I was earning too much.

"You can pay for everything now," he told me.

I said I would, but he had to pay for the groceries once a fortnight. He then decided that I should ask if I could work just three days a week so he could get the pension. Like a fool, I agreed and life became a struggle. One morning I went to the fridge to make myself a sandwich to take for lunch, and the cupboard was bare. I charged into the bedroom.

"How much did you spend on groceries yesterday?" I demanded.

"$14, but I will get more on pension day ... Tuesday."

"Do you realise I have to pay through the nose now to eat in the canteen?" I was livid. I knew full well that he would have kept back enough money to gamble with.

The canteen at work used to be very cheap and the food excellent, but a new policy had been bought in that every ward, and every department, including mine, was given a grant and we had to keep within its boundaries. John didn't know it but no food in the house was another nail in his coffin.

A few weeks after this I had cooked breakfast and taken it out into the warm conservatory where we could eat at the table I'd bought at a garage sale and painted white. Surprisingly John and I never argued. If I wanted to discuss something with him he would just walk away so nothing was ever solved. I don't know how it started but it was something trivial to do with vegemite.

He flared up and yelled; "You're a bloody liar!"

I was shocked and quietly replied, "I may be a lot of things but I am not a liar. I've had enough, I'm leaving you."

I looked up the 'To Lets' in the morning paper and there was a warehouse flat advertised just down the road. I jumped in the car and went down to look at it. Soon I was loading my van with all the things I would need and within an hour of me saying I was leaving I was out of the house. John hadn't said another word.

The place was up some outside steps above what had been a

factory. It was just one big room with a closed-in kitchen and bathroom at one end. Two huge doors with a pulley above them outside were at the other end; unfortunately they had big gaps around them and as it was the middle of winter the place was freezing. The only heating was an electric heater in the middle of the floor. One of the first things I did was to put a chain on the entrance door so I could open it a few inches as I felt quite vulnerable with no houses nearby. John soon found out where I was and was at the door saying: "You are ruining my life, Billie Foster."

"And what do you think you have been doing to mine for years, John?"

Like a fool I eventually went back to him because I had several problems: firstly the mortgage for our house was coming out of my bank account, plus I was paying $150 a week rent. Also, I had booked a stall for the coming craft fair to sell my silk trees and all my stock was still at the house. I should have insisted that all the our money go into a joint account; that I control the payments for his horses and the household bills and he would have just $50 a week to gamble with. But, I did nothing, and life went back to what it was before.

My life-saver for many years had been my electric organ. Almost every night I would leave him to his gambling and go to the bedroom where the organ lived to play and sing. The organ had lots of 'voices' and I would experiment with combinations to see which backing suited which song. Sometimes I would play for up to two hours. One of the songs I sang was *After I've Gone*.

> *After I've gone and left you crying*
> *After I've gone there's no denying*
> *You'll feel sad, you'll feel bad*
> *You'll miss the only girl that you ever had*

One night when I went back into the lounge, he said, "I don't like the sound of that 'after I've gone bit'."

I made no reply.

John's sister came out from England for a holiday. I decided we should show her some of the country by me doing some of the big markets up north. So, with the van loaded to the top, we set off towards Christchurch. Featherlight, the champion mare, was resting in a paddock out towards Akaroa and John insisted we turn off and take his sister out to see her. He insisted it was not far so I complied; but after many, many miles I began to get angry I was the one paying for the petrol. It wasn't as though she wanted to see the bloody horse anyway. We eventually arrived and Featherlight, being the unfriendly horse she was, took off to the far side of the big field. But there was John telling his sister that Featherlight was the horse that had stayed close by. He didn't even know his own horse – talk about adding insult to injury.

When we reached Christchurch John suggested we stop for a coffee. He left us in a coffee lounge and said he wouldn't be long. We had our coffee and ordered another then waited and waited. Finally I said to Cicily that we'd better leave as we were getting dirty looks from the staff. It was close on midday and they would need the seats for the lunch crowd so we went outside and waited again. Much later I wished I had just driven away and left him; we had waited two hours. I drove north like a maniac. On one corner he said, "You are driving too fast," and I snarled back, "I wouldn't have to drive so fast if you hadn't wasted all morning."

I had to drive all the way to Blenheim before dark to find out where the market was. We arrived just on 5.30. Luckily I found the market place without trouble and we booked into a motel quite close. The next day was a success I sold $360 worth of stock. The next day we were on the way to Nelson where three months earlier I'd booked a stall for the big market there. We were approaching Canvas Town, named for all the miners' tents when the gold rush was on many years before; I was about to drive the bypass when John shouted, "Turn here!"

I started to argue but he shouted again and then suggested we stop for a coffee. I slammed the brakes on and turned. It was a quaint little town with shops that had the old V-shaped windows that came out to the footpath. But it was like a ghost town. All the shops were shut and not one living soul was to be seen, not anywhere. Cicily and I started walking down the pavement looking for a coffee shop and window shopping as we went, John had rushed down the other pavement and then we saw him rushing back. I stopped.

"He's not looking for a café at all! He's looking for a T.A.B.!" I told Cicily. Of course, there wasn't one and was he annoyed!! There wasn't a coffee shop either. Back on the road he ranted and raved.

Our next stop was at Pelorus Bridge in the Richmond Forest Park. Thinking it was just a normal motel I had booked the accommodation sometime before. Betty and I had camped there when on our cycling tour when we were nursing and I remembered it as the most beautiful and peaceful place. The rooms, which were all tenanted, were all joined together, however the toilets and showers were away through the bush. I told Cecily that if she had to go there during the night to wake me and I would come with her, which I did, really thankful that I had packed a good torch. I had a quiet chuckle when I thought of what my sister-in-law would have done had she heard an opossum make its awful hoarse sound: probably scream very loudly. My choice of accommodation did not please my husband, however. He could get no radio, and there was no telephone or television.

"You did it on purpose," he snarled; but of course I had done no such thing.

Arriving in Nelson we booked into a motel not far from the market venue, and then went out to dinner – me paying of course. The following morning I was up early but John didn't want to get out of bed, insisting we didn't have to leave so early. I should have left without him but like a fool, I waited. When we got to the market at last the number 32 spot I had paid for months before had been taken by someone else. I went to see the lady in charge of affairs and instead of telling the people to move, as I would have done, she gave me a site among the people selling unwanted things. I spent the day beside a young lad selling tomatoes and someone selling a pile of mostly junk. In desperation I put some of my trees on top of the van and made several sales by people seeing them from a distance. Instead of making far more than I did in the small market in Blenheim as I should have done, I took over a hundred dollars less. I was not pleased.

I had said to Cis. that she should go off to have a look around the town, which she did. When the market packed up at midday she had not returned. John had already gone to the T.A.B. so I packed up alone, then sat in the van to wait and wait. Suddenly she popped up on the other side from which she had left. "Ha, found you," she said. "You shifted the car."

Of course, I had done no such thing and pointed out the huge pots with trees in in front of the toilet. What she had done was to walk around in a circle. She had bought me a sandwich for which I was very grateful; then we sat and waited for John. He eventually appeared and wanted us to come back with him to the T.A.B. as his friend's son's greyhound was running in a race soon. So back we traipsed. He and Cis put money on it and won a few dollars so at last we could leave.

I was leading the way back to the van when John caught me up. "Cis tells me you haven't had any lunch."

"How would we have had any lunch?" I snapped, "I was waiting for Cis to come back and then we were waiting for you." It had now gone 3 pm.

From Nelson we continued down the west coast. Cis sat in the van looking straight ahead seeming totally uninterested of the wild scenic beauty. "Look at that river down there, Cis," I would say.

At Fox Glacier we walked up to see the ice. I had never seen a glacier and it was awe-inspiring; massive pale blue chunks of ice made from pure clean water. It was quite a hike to get there, and at one place a small creek of crystal clear water about six inches deep had to be crossed. A solid board about a foot across had been placed over it as a bridge to walk over, but Cis refused to walk it. I even offered to walk backward and hold her hands but she refused, which made me a little bit angry. Why, oh why, had I taken her on this expensive trip when she didn't appreciate it. But then I thought about the difference of my life and hers. I'd been bought up on a farm where we were not short of money; had ridden horses, driven tractors, handled livestock, worked a pack of dogs, trained as a nurse, was still a cabaret artist, had travelled all over the world. I had climbed around on the tops of mountains and had always been a daredevil.

Her father was a poor farm laborer with four children living in a rented house. She had married young to a useless womaniser who had taken off and left her with a young daughter. She had worked hard to provide a life for them both. When the daughter was thirteen Cis was on evening shifts, and the daughter was on the street picking up men for sex. The police came to take the girl into care. The girl was screaming as the police dragged her out and Cis had picked up her umbrella and hit the policewoman. She'd been given a prison sentence. After six months inside, where she had a nervous breakdown, she was released and given a council house which she had to share with a women who had a mental problem. I got this information from John and his siblings' step-mother – a lady who I liked immensely – when we went to England on a trip. Years after Cis's visit to N.Z. the lady she lived with died and Cis had the house to herself for the rest of her life. Cicely's daughter never again got in touch with her. I kept in touch with the family and Cis wrote to tell us that her granddaughter had called to see her. She was so happy.

From Fox Glacier we continued down the west coast and turned inland to Haast Pass; the change in the weather from one side of the alps to the other amazing. Wet and overcast on the west side, bright and sunny on the east.

Cis left for home a few days after we returned home. I told her to make sure John got her to the airport on time as he was never on time anywhere. He told me when I got home that she had pestered him to get her there; I hoped that she had more success than I ever did.

Life with John didn't become any easier; money he 'borrowed' to pay his horse trainers fees and other things was never paid back. We never went anywhere together, and I had stopped going to the night trots horse racing with him.

All I ever seemed to do was work. I couldn't even watch the

television in peace without the picture disappearing as he looked up the gambling odds. I bought a small secondhand TV and put it in the back bedroom where I could watch in peace. This, the Otago Alpine Club and my organ were my only entertainment.

Things went downhill badly when an organ key became faulty. I rang the only repairer in Dunedin and he arranged to come at a certain time in the morning. Unfortunately, I had to work and asked John to be there to meet him. I arrived home very tired after a busy day to find my organ had not been fixed. John's excuse had been that the man had come late. I rang the organ repairer the following morning and was told he'd been met with abuse from John because he'd been unexpectedly held up.

"I have never been spoken to so rudely," he told me, and refused to come again to do the job, so now I had no organ to play. I was furious!

"So," I said to John, "putting your bets on is more important than getting my organ fixed, is it?"

He didn't even bother to apologise.

Steven had had a rubbish skip business in Perth, Western Australia for many years, and both he and his wife had trucks on the road. He knew things were not good with me in Dunedin, so wrote to say, "We need an office manager here so why don't you come over and take the job? Free board and good wages."

I thought about it and decided yes. When I told John I was leaving, he didn't say a word; just withdrew into 'You have hurt my feelings mode'. We each engaged a solicitor and drew up an agreement; it seemed he was entitled to half my superannuation, whereas I could not have a claim on his as he was drawing it as a pension. He argued that he needed more. I said his horses were worth money but he argued they were a liability. I should have insisted that a value was put on them but I didn't. To make a long story short we sold the house for $116,000, there was an $8,000 mortgage owing on it. He got all the furniture all paid for by me. I packed just enough to get me started: a few sheets, blankets, towels, plates, etc. and left behind some things that had been my parents and some of my treasures. I ended up with just $37,000.

By borrowing back my van, which I had sold to a friend, I helped John move into a new house he had bought. But I got the last laugh — I deliberately made my travel bookings early so he would have the job of moving all the furniture and cleaning our house. His solicitor said he could do our settlement agreement for us. I knew full well that John would have to pay for it but kept my mouth shut. He complained bitterly about it later by letter. I get angry with myself now when I think about all the things I should have said ... like you are nothing more than a lazy, useless piece of working-class crap, your gambling means more to you than I do, and what's more I despise you! The trouble was, I didn't.

When the taxi arrived to take me away I went into the bedroom, took hold of his hand and put my forehead on his. He held my hand so tight, but neither one of us said a word. I cried all the way to the airport. I had on a soft, light brown leather suit that I'd had made with money from my silk trees and my tears made big dark spots all over it. I checked my luggage in and sat down. Then the strangest thing happened ...

I suddenly felt as though a thousand tons had been lifted from my shoulder. I was free!!

Epilogue

Australia again. I wish I could say that life was good for me from that time on, but sadly I still had a lot to learn. My son met me at the airport and it horrified me to see he looked like a criminal. His hair was in a ponytail, and all the way back to his house he talked about himself and all his problems. On and on. No "sorry your marriage didn't work out, Mum. Did you have a good flight? How are you feeling?" As usual it all about himself.

My son's second wife had been bought up by her father after her mother had left him with most of the children; she and Sonny were leasing a ten-acre block and the house was not inviting. He showed me to the bedroom I was to sleep in and I was appalled. No effort whatsoever had been made to welcome me, the room was full of dust, a dead air plant on a piece of wood sat on the window sill and the single bed had an old grey blanket on it and an old purple sleeping blanket opened up to cover it. I could not believe what I was seeing. However here I was and I had to make the best of it.

After unpacking my nightclothes I went out to the kitchen where my son was standing by the sink eating baked beans out of a can.

"We do for ourselves around here," he said.

Soon he was boasting about how they were growing marihuana and he showed me where they had it hidden in a barrel in the sand; he had no shame, and I thought, "What have I got myself in to?"

I should have walked out straight away, but once again I stupidly accepted the situation. About two months after my arrival they bought a nice house on a five-acre block from where we ran their rubbish skip business.

I stayed with them for about a year, running the office, cooking most of the meals and doing the housework and garden while he and his wife drove the trucks all day. It never ceased to amaze me what great things people threw out. We kept all the good things and things the family didn't want were given to me to sell at garage sales.

Letters from John kept arriving; one twenty-eight pages long was covered with tear stains; he told me all about how he had cried for eight days, how he had had to clean the house and how HE had had to pay for our settlement. Not one word, of course, to say sorry about his gambling. Many months passed before a letter arrived saying he now realised that he hadn't treated me well.

While living at my son's I met a very nice man from Auckland who liked gardening. I told myself not to become involved with another loser and this man, as much as I liked him, had no job and an old car. Then I met Kevin, a builder interested in doing up old houses which was what I wanted to do. He told me he had just sold a farm in Wanneroo so I assumed he must at least have had SOME money. We started to go out together. A few weeks later he came down to the block to stay overnight.

"We should compare finances," he said. I agreed, and he produced a small bank book – all he had to his name was $654. And he still owed thousands on his small car. I was shattered!

My superannuation was still intact in New Zealand and with the rest of my savings I had over $70,000 and my second-hand car was paid for. I should have ended it there and then but he talked me round.

Kevin boasted about being brought up in a high-class suburb of Perth; his father was an illegal bookie, but as Frank would have said: "You couldn't take him to a shit house" He didn't know how to dress, or how to mix with respectable people. He thought nothing of walking around the supermarket farting loudly; needless to say I pretended he wasn't with ME. When the "I am on my best behaviour" bit ended I soon found out what I had let myself in for. Kevin thrived on causing trouble and never a day went by when he didn't find something to cause an argument. By this time I had bought a house up in a small coastal village above Perth; but not before I had seen a solicitor and drawn up a pre-nuptial agreement to make sure that everything would remain mine. At least I was learning.

I was to find out that Kevin had a long history of abusive behaviour towards women; another mental case to add to my list. After seven month of abuse I gave him one week to get out of my house.

I worked hard doing up the house and luckily found two handyman who did the jobs that I couldn't do, which was not a lot. One of them called Tom told me he knew a man who was just right for me and did I want to meet him. Well, nothing ventured nothing gained, so I said "yes."

A few days later the doorbell rang and there he was – I met a wonderful Irish gentleman. He had been a Captain in the Indian army during the war, could speak several languages and had several university degrees. He was beautifully spoken and had the most beautiful smile. When we went out he was always well dressed. We never lived together but stayed in each other's houses for the next twenty-three years. At last I had a companion I could talk to and discuss things with. We travelled several times to places around the world. I worked hard and restored several houses and am now for the first time in my life, financially secure.

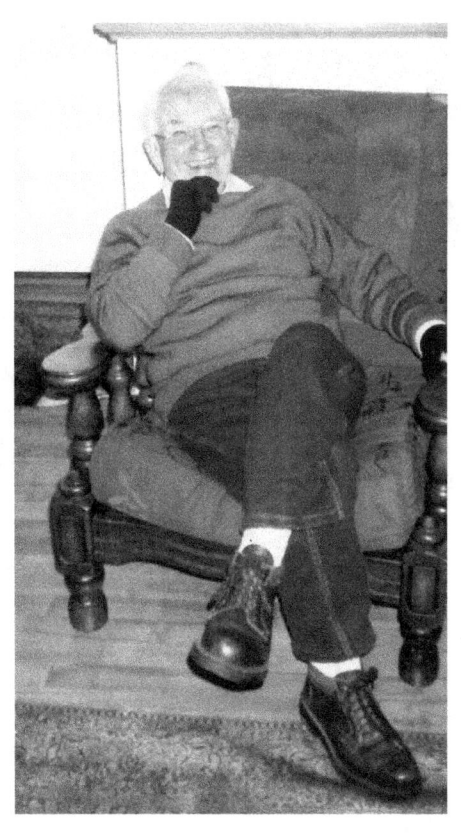

Paddy

My lovely Irish man died in April 2018 at the age of 93.

Frank and John also died that year. The police had found Frank sleeping in a bus shelter in Hull. He told them he was on his way back to Batley. We had told him he would end up in the slums of London and that is exactly where he had been for twenty-five years. Kim had visited him in his foul-smelling flat and left him her email address. She was contacted in Australia by a Social worker who told her that Frank couldn't go back home as the place had been broken into and trashed. They admitted him to a nursing home where he settled at first but then became violent so had to be shifted. He was diagnosed as being bi-polar. He died soon after at the age of 96.

Frank in later years

John spent his last days in care in Dunedin. On my last trip to New Zealand, I went to see him; he didn't know who I was. He said "Billie used to have dark hair," and "I loved Billie." He also told me his son had taken his eftpos card. I managed not to laugh and say "I wonder why?" It was good to see him looking so well, and I still didn't say a word about his gambling. He died in his 90th year.

As for Kevin, well he died many years ago of cancer of the throat. They took his larynx out and he couldn't talk. He had done some nasty things around town after I kicked him out and had no friends and after destroying so many people with his mouth I began to wonder if there was a God after all.

*****

About the Author

At eighty-four years of age, and a grandmother to three and a great grandmother to one, Billie is still performing her singing routine at charity events, and is still writing.

A professed activist, her primary interest is Women's Rights and believes 'you need to stand up and be counted.'

She still enjoys renovating but is quite comfortable living in her current home in a southern suburb of Perth, Western Australia.

www.ingramcontent.com/pod-product-compliance
Lightning Source LLC
Chambersburg PA
CBHW071114080526
44587CB00013B/1334